£9.86

The Methuen Book of
Sixties Drama

introduced by

Graham Whybrow

Roots
Arnold Wesker

Serjeant Musgrave's Dance
John Arden

Loot
Joe Orton

Early Morning
Edward Bond

The Ruling Class
Peter Barnes

Methuen Drama

Published by Methuen 2001

3 5 7 9 10 8 6 4

First published in 2001 by
Methuen Publishing Limited,
11–12 Buckingham Gate, London SW1E 6LB

Methuen Publishing Limited Reg. No. 3543167

A CIP catalogue record for this book is available from the British Library.

ISBN 0 413 76280 7

Typeset by SX Composing DTP, Rayleigh, Essex
Printed and bound in Great Britain by
Cox and Wyman Ltd, Reading, Berkshire

Contents

Introduction

The Methuen Book of Sixties Drama brings together five plays that are now contemporary classics of British theatre. The collection includes Arnold Wesker's *Roots* (1959), John Arden's *Serjeant Musgrave's Dance* (1959), Joe Orton's *Loot* (1966), Edward Bond's *Early Morning* (1968) and Peter Barnes' *The Ruling Class* (1968).

The anthology celebrates the distinctive voice and style of the playwrights: each play sets its own challenges and finds dramatic form for its material. Yet the plays also emerge from a particular cultural moment in post-war British theatre. All five playwrights were born between 1931 and 1934, so these plays are partly an artistic response to the social, cultural, economic and political questions of the 1950s and 1960s. Two plays were in fact produced in 1959 (Wesker's *Roots* and Arden's *Serjeant Musgrave's Dance*), but the reputation of the plays continued through the 1960s.

Arnold Wesker (b. 1932) established his name as a playwright with a series of remarkable plays written and produced over a five-year period: *Chicken Soup with Barley* (1958), *Roots* (1959) and *I'm Talking About Jerusalem* (1960), collectively known as the 'Wesker Trilogy', *The Kitchen* (1959) and *Chips with Everything* (1962).

Wesker's *Roots* focuses on the homecoming of young Beatie Bryant, who returns to her family of Norfolk farm workers with stories of her boyfriend Ronnie. Beatie is caught between conflicting worlds and values: the apparent inertia, subsistence and routines of rural life, and ideas about culture and politics that she has gleaned from her boyfriend in London. In breathless, paratactic style, Beatie quotes Ronnie: ' "You can't learn to live overnight. *I* don't even know,' he say, 'and half the world don't know but we got to try. Try,' he say, ''cos we're still suffering from the shock of two world wars and we don't know it. Talk,' he say, 'and look and listen and think and ask questions.' But Jesus! I don't know what questions to ask or *how* to talk' (Act 2, Scene 1).

In *Roots*, Wesker finds a metaphor and expressive form for the liminal moment of one woman on the threshold of discovering her own voice and identity. The play leaves open the question of whether liberation is personal and individualistic, or social and collective.

John Arden (b. 1930) started writing stage plays in the late 1950s, among them *All Fall Down* (1955), *The Waters of Babylon* (1957) and *Live Like Pigs* (1958). Arden is best known for *Serjeant Musgrave's Dance*, an imaginatively conceived and visualised 'unhistorical parable'. The play is set in a northern English mining town in the late nineteenth century, with striking miners in conflict with the local mayor, constable and parson. The traumatised Musgrave seems by turns a regular soldier, a recruiting officer, a deserter and a pacifist. The play pivots on Musgrave's use of violence to stop war: 'I brought it in to end it' (Act 3, Scene 2).

Serjeant Musgrave's Dance is presentational in style, using exposition, action, dialogue and song to challenge an audience to scrutinise the characters' actions and their consequences. The play abstracts from historical detail to probe ethics and contradictions at the level of fable. On its first run at the Royal Court, the play met with bafflement and hostility from theatre critics and achieved only 21 per cent at the box office; yet it later became a set text on the school syllabus. Forty years on, *Serjeant Musgrave's Dance* continues to resonate in a post-colonial world gripped by internecine wars and cultures of retributive violence within borders.

Joe Orton (b. 1933) wrote several outstanding plays before he was murdered in 1968, including *Entertaining Mr Sloane* (1964), *Loot* (1965) and the posthumously produced *What the Butler Saw* (1969).

Loot is at once parody and farce, drawing on many formal components from generic thrillers and murder mysteries. But here a dead body is shoved into a wardrobe, a coffin is stuffed with cash, and the police inspector is disguised as a man from the Water Board. Orton's genius is to sustain the dramatic logic of the play through technical virtuosity and theatrical brilliance. The play teems with references to authority (the law, church and police) and the vocabulary of precarious respectability (good citizen, decency, 'traditional positions'). At the same time, the action coruscates remorselessly to challenge, provoke and disturb an audience.

Edward Bond (b. 1934) wrote some of the outstanding plays of the 1960s, including *The Pope's Wedding* (1962), *Saved* (1965), *Early Morning* (1968) and *Narrow Road to the Deep North* (1969). Two of these plays ran into conflict with the authorities: the production of Bond's *Saved* led to the prosecution of the English Stage Company (the Royal Court Theatre), and *Early Morning* is said to be the last play to be banned by the Lord Chamberlain before theatre censorship was abolished by the Theatres Act 1968. *Early Morning* was given one performance as a Sunday night 'production-without-décor' on 31 March 1968 in club conditions (and then a matinee to an invited audience, including critics). The play was revived as a full production in 1969 as part of the Edward Bond season at the Royal Court.

Bond's uncompromising vision and oppositional spirit is seen clearly in *Early Morning*, which groups historical figures (including Queen Victoria, her Siamese twins Crown Prince George and Prince Arthur, and prime ministers Disraeli and Gladstone) with contemporary characters (such as Len and Joyce). Written in 21 scenes, the play is by turns comic, fantastical, dark and probing. Bond continues his thematic interest in violence, but the working-class milieu of *Saved* gives way here to the drastic classes of the Victorian monarchy and nineteenth-century politicians. The play memorably contains images of Prince Arthur conversing with the skeleton of his dead Siamese twin on his shoulder, and the casual cannibalism of the Victorian characters in Heaven. *Early Morning*'s structural irony and terse, declaratory verbal technique combine in a play that is fierce, iconoclastic and mordant.

Peter Barnes (b. 1931) gained his reputation as a playwright with *The Ruling Class* (1968), having worked as a prolific screenwriter and after the production of two stage plays *The Time of the Barracudas* (1963) and *Sclerosis* (1965).

The Ruling Class opens with the 13th Earl of Gurney in full evening dress giving a toast to England ('this teeming womb of privilege, this feudal state') and standing to attention to the National Anthem. It then cuts to his Lordship's bedroom, where the aristocrat prepares for his auto-erotic asphyxiation, dressed in a three-cornered hat and a white tutu ballet skirt. Gurney's ritual is disrupted when, standing on a pair of steps with a silk noose around his neck, he accidentally slips on the ladder and hangs himself. It is a characteristic Barnes moment, with its irreverence, bathos and furious pace: this scene is no more than the prologue to the play. *The Ruling Class* then focuses on the next Earl of Gurney, a Franciscan monk with the psychotic delusion that he is 'the Creator and ruler of the Universe', and his relatives who plot to create a male heir to continue the family lineage. Forty years on, the play seems infused with the spirit of 1968 as it dissolves, inverts and challenges social categories. As a playwright, Barnes' vision is combative, free-wheeling and anti-establishment.

The Methuen Book of Sixties Drama offers five plays that continue to test the limits and extend the range of modern drama. In that sense, they are contemporary classics in the theatre: plays from the past that speak to us now. We hope this anthology is both an inspiration and a spur to audiences and playwrights in the future.

Graham Whybrow, July 2001

Arnold Wesker was born in Stepney in 1932. His education came mainly from reading books and listening to BBC radio. He pursued many trades, from furniture maker to pastry cook, until 1958 when *Chicken Soup with Barley* was read by George Devine and produced at the Belgrade Theatre, Coventry. *Roots* followed in 1959, and together with *I'm Talking About Jerusalem* the three plays created an enormous impact as the 'Wesker Trilogy' at the Royal Court in 1960. His other plays include *The Kitchen* (1961), *Chips with Everything* (1962, voted 'Play of the Year'), *Their Very Own and Golden City* (1965; winner of the Italian Premio Marzotto Drama Award in 1964), *The Four Seasons* (1965), *The Friends* (1970), *The Old Ones* (1972), *The Wedding Feast* (1974), *Shylock* (1976), *Love Letters on Blue Paper* (1977), *Caritas* (1981), his six one-woman plays (1982–92), *One More Ride on the Merry-Go-Round* (1985), *Lady Othello* (1987), *When God Wanted a Son* (1997), *Break, My Heart* (1997) and *Denial* (2000). Arnold Wesker has also written for film and television and published several collections of poems, short stories, essays and lectures.

Roots

NOTE TO ACTORS AND PRODUCERS

My people are not caricatures. They are real (though fiction), and if they are portrayed as caricatures the point of all these plays will be lost. The picture I have drawn is a harsh one, yet my tone is not one of disgust – nor should it be in the presentation of the plays. I am at one with these people: it is only that I am annoyed, with them and myself.

This is a play about Norfolk people; it could be a play about any country people and the moral could certainly extend to the metropolis. But as it is about Norfolk people it is important that some attempt is made to find out how they talk. A very definite accent and intonation exists and personal experience suggests that this is not difficult to know. The following may be of great help:

When the word 'won't' is used, the 'w' is left out. It sounds the same but the 'w' is lost.

Double 'ee' is pronounced 'i' as in 'it' – so that 'been' becomes 'bin', 'seen' becomes 'sin', etc.

'Have' and 'had' become 'hev' and 'hed' as in 'head'.

'Ing' loses the 'g' so that it becomes 'in'.

'Bor' is a common handle and is a contraction of neighbour.

Instead of the word 'of' they say 'on' e.g. 'I've hed enough on it' or 'What do you think on it?'

Their 'yes' is used all the time and sounds like 'year' with a 'p' – 'yearp'.

'Blast' is also common usage and is pronounced 'blust', a short sharp sound as in 'gust'.

The cockney 'ain't' becomes 'ent' – also short and sharp.

The 't' in 'that' and 'what' is left out to give 'thaas' and 'whaas', e.g. 'Whaas matter then?'

Other idiosyncrasies are indicated in the play itself.

Introduction*

Roots and Rejection

Tony Richardson, assistant artistic director to George Devine, took me to lunch in the restaurant used by the Court's crowd – Au Père de Nico – the first time, possibly, I was taken to a 'posh' eating place of the 'artistic' kind. Tony enjoyed introducing me to this corner of Chelsea's sophisticated life. I think he thought he was corrupting me.

We talked about a future. Tony wanted to know if I was planning another play. I was, about a Norfolk farm-labourer's daughter who returns home after living in London with her Jewish boyfriend. Autobiography again. In a letter dated 30 May to Dusty, my Norfolk wife-to-be, on her twenty-second birthday, I had given more thought to it:

> In the Norfolk play . . . I'm spoken about all the time but I never appear. In the play I fail to turn up – ever, and after some terrible misery and 'there I told you so' from the family you turn round and say 'So what! I do not need him now! I'm better than I thought I was and I do not need him now!' and the triumph of the play is not my triumph but yours. The intellectual has betrayed but the ordinary girl has found her own voice, her own language. Funny that, the triumph of *Chicken Soup* is also not my triumph but my mother's. I wonder why . . .

On the 20th March 1958 Tony wrote offering a £25 option 'for your next play – the Norfolk one you outlined for me . . . a minimum amount but standard for all the plays we have commissioned . . .' Ten days later George Devine wrote to invite me to join the next Writers' Discussion Group. Giddy times.

* These notes are culled from my autobiography *As Much As I Dare* (Century, 1994).

Unlike many writers who complain they dread writing, that they must drag themselves to the desk, that it is all blood, sweat, tears and pain, it is not so for me. Or rather, yes, all those things, but as with the pleasures of sex they are part of the giddy times. I went to stay with my mother-in-law-to-be in Norfolk where I planned to begin writing. Letters from her tied cottage, called Beck Farm, to my wife-to-be describe the shaping of the play that was to become *Roots*.*

17 June
. . . It does not seem so strange me sitting here, in the front room, typing. Mother is laying the table for dinner in the kitchen and it is only twelve o'clock . . .

. . . I brought three of your paintings here for the family to see. The copy of the Van Gogh – which Joy and Ma like, the jazz band one in red, blue and white, and the two standing figures in green, red and blue. They didn't quite know what to say but I know they liked them – if only for the colours. I just asked Ma if she could live with a couple of them in the room and she say 'that would make no difference to me.' . . .

19 June
. . . Father Bicker was up most of the night helping two old sows give birth. He'll be tired today. He does work hard. The funny think was how Mother was telling how some people don't think he works so hard and she was adding how he had offered to swop places with them. And then when I was discussing this with Joy she told me how Mother don't think he work hard! Your mother is a strange woman, she talks to you as though she were making a political speech. And when she tells a story she acts all the parts with such gusto that I feel sure she would have made a good dramatic actress. I find her stories entertaining though, except when she repeats them. And how she hop from one anecdote to another . . .

* I see the letters already contain attempts to capture Norfolk dialect and rhythms.

20 June
The Norfolk play is beginning to take shape in my mind. I
can see it a little more clearly now, I think I would like to
start on the first act – perhaps I shall this afternoon when
your mother goes into Harleston to post these letters. That
would be wonderful if I managed to get the outline down
of the first act . . .

. . . This morning she [Mother] asked Gully [Poppy
Bicker] if he wanted a bath and he said yes, so she said to
him he could have one after me. 'I don't mind that' he said
to me 'as long as you don't shit in it so's it stick to me and
I can't get it off.' That's a sign I am being treated as one of
the family, isn't it? I couldn't quite make out whether
Mother Bicker was embarrassed for me or not. He doesn't
swear any more than Ann Jellicoe or Miriam or any of the
other Court people do. That is something you shall have to
get used to when we meet them – Lindsay too, they swear
like troopers. I think it is slightly affectation with them
though . . .

Roots was first entitled 'Not Only the Corn'. Thank God I
renamed it. From the start it was to be about a girl whose
boyfriend never turned up, for certain, that. And just as
certain – the shock would lead to self-discovery. But what I
was as excitedly eager to capture as much as anything was the
slow pace of pause and silence in Norfolk rural life.

Many moments would have to be concocted – like the
intimate conversations between Beatie and her sister Jenny,
and Beatie's dance to Bizet's 'L'Arlesienne Suite' at the end
of Act Two. But the stories told by Mrs Bryant would, I knew,
be those I'd heard and noted down from Mother Bicker,
while other moments would come from my relationship with
Dusty. One of her dreams became the dream in Act Two
when Beatie looks at herself in the mirror after her bath and
observes:

Isn't your nose a funny thing, and your ears. And your
arms and your legs, aren't they funny things – sticking out
of a lump –

But the denouement is concocted. The tea-party, the family's confusion, the mother's wrath and Beatie's last hosanna speech are pure invention, except for one element: I *did* write a letter to Dusty saying our relationship should end but she ignored it and replied asking me to pack and post a parcel of selected Jewish deli foods. I think that response of cheerful insouciance as much as any other aspect of her character suggested to me we could be lifelong partners.

I seem to remember *Roots* taking about three months to complete. By the end of August 1958 it must have been in the hands of Devine and Richardson. I was excited by its structure – a collection of moments juxtaposed in a way I thought added up to poetic impact. George and Tony turned it down.

I can't remember how I heard about it. I remember only the gist of what was explained: they were disappointed. Disappointed but – they had a suggestion. They felt, quite rightly, that nothing really happened in the first two acts and their suggestion was: combine the first and seconds acts into one act; make Act Three into Act Two; and write a new third act in which the London lover, Ronnie, appeared. After all, they reasoned most reasonably, everyone in the audience would by now be so keyed up and curious about this boy they would want to see him, witness his impact upon the family who had been driven mad with anticipation.

I said I would think about it, and did, though not for long nor, I suspect, seriously. I knew the value of what I'd written. These brilliant men of the theatre had missed the point. Their suggestions had shocked me they were so banal. I rejected them and prepared to face the end of my career as a playwright.

Roots was turned down while still being read by council members one of whom was Dame Peggy Ashcroft. She not only admired the play but recognised it immediately as a role for Joan Plowright. Joan read it and announced she would play the role anywhere. Bryan Bailey of the Belgrade had by now read the play and was clamouring for the rights. What did John think?* Poor John was languishing in Wormwood Scrubs (2952 Dexter) from where he wrote:

* John Dexter, director of Wesker's first five plays.

Look here, I want to direct *Roots – Home is Where You Live*. [Did I ever call it that or is it John's humour? His humour, I hope!] I don't have to read it, I know you, I know the subject. If I had a cheque book I'd reach for it. Let's go to Coventry and use our kind of actors – (Alfie [Lynch] and Patsy Byrne for instance). I have more pleasure in remembering *Chicken Soup* than in anything I have ever done in my life . . . one of those absolutely enchanted times, when time and place perfectly cohered. If Bryan wants it, try to wait for me.

Of course I waited. Some time in the middle of March, it must have been, I met John out of prison with our first car, a secondhand Hillman Minx, convertible, and took him home to Clapton Common where he was fussed over and looked after for six weeks till his spirits recovered and he began sorting out his life. Dusty was working behind the counter at Sainsburys in Mare Street, Hackney, for £3 10s a week, and I was still having to help my brother-in-law, Ralph, in his basement joinery workshop to top up our weekly earnings. John couldn't wait to read *Roots*. I have the sharpest memory of returning from work – it must have been the evening of the same day – to an excited ex-con who leapt into my arms declaring how wonderful the play was, that it didn't need changing as Tony and George had suggested, and that he knew exactly what to do with it.

He at once began assembling the elements to make *Roots* work. The Court didn't want it? Right, Bryan Bailey did – we'd go to Coventry, this time to enjoy the luxury of three weeks' rehearsal instead of two. Joan Plowright said she would do it anywhere? Splendid – we'll get her to Coventry. And there was this clever designer, a woman, tall, lean and beautiful – the daughter of the eminent writer and independent member of parliament, Sir Alan Herbert, 'Herbert' a name with ancient lineage – who had been a scene painter at the Court and had just been given her first chance by George to design Tony Richardson's production of Ionesco's *The Chairs*. Her second design project was John Dexter's production of the Yeats play *Purgatory*. They had obviously

worked well together and, like Joan Plowright, Jocelyn
Herbert was a star in the making.

This is what I remember. We took Jocelyn to Norfolk. She
wanted to see the settings on which I had based the play. John
did *not*! Joan Plowright pointed to half a page in one act and
suggested it really belonged to another. She was right. John
decided that real liver and onions had to be fried on stage. 'It
was,' he recorded, 'a practical problem of how long it needed
to cook and serve and eat it . . .' The front rows gasped at the
smell that wafted towards them as soon as the curtain went
up. The major problem was pace. John's instructions to the
cast were firm and clear: 'Don't be rushed. You'll hear
shuffling, coughing – ignore it. *Dictate* the pace, they will
accept it . . .' There may have been disagreements here and
there between us, none stick in memory. We shared, and
communicated it to the cast, a sense of being involved in
something special. It was partly to do with the outrageousness
of the play's rhythm, that long, delicate curve stretching from
a very very slow beginning across three scenes to the end of
Act Two and the exultant Bizet dance. We felt ourselves in
possession of an experience in the theatre which, if we could
pull it off, would be dynamic, unique.

What I see as plainly as yesterday is that first night – 25
May, the day after my twenty-seventh birthday, five days
before Dusty's twenty-third – John on my left, Dusty on my
right, sitting dead centre in the front row of the balcony at the
Belgrade. The opening was breath-takingly slow. Patsy
Byrne, solid, experienced, intelligent, trusting utterly in the
play and John's direction, called to her child off stage, waited,
went into her child's room, moved slowly back into the
kitchen, returned to her frying pan, and cooked. Charlie Kay
took his time coming in from work, placing his bike in the
same room, arching his back with pain. Patsy looked at him
for a long time, watching, before asking: 'Waas matter wi' you
then?' Slowly they built up the exchange that was to become
the running joke in the play about Mother Bryant saying the
pain in his back was due to indigestion.

JIMMY. Don't be daft.

JENNY. That's what I say. Blast, Mother, I say, you don't git indigestion in the back. Don't you tell me, she say, I hed it!

JIMMY. What heven't she hed.

On which line the audience laughed, as we had hoped, planned, plotted, schemed, rehearsed day after intense day! The actors had captured and held them. John's hand reached to clutch mine. 'They've done it,' he whispered. When I turned to nod and share the moment, I saw – he had tears in his eyes.

The applause, after Beatie's dance – scattily and touchingly danced by Joan in a mixture of hornpipe and impromptu nothing-steps, sending shivers down our backs – was a great whoop of joy. By the end – after Gwen Nelson's poignant defence of Mother Bryant, and Joan's amazed, triumphant discovery that she was no longer quoting someone else but using her own words – we knew we had brought it off.

The next morning disparate groups of actors, friends, and theatre staff assembled in the Belgrade's restaurant upstairs to pour over enthusiastic local reviews. The buzz of excitement flew from table to table, and as I sat with my family I could see George Devine and Bryan Bailey, their heads down and huddled, negotiating a deal to transfer our production to the Royal Court. Bryan Bailey was killed not long afterwards in a motor accident on the first of the nation's motorways – the M1 from London to Coventry, a development rendering the city an industrial base of huge value. It just cost them one of their newest sons. Bryan fell asleep at the wheel. Overworked. Over-enthusiastic.

The London reviews were even more ecstatic. Milton Shulman in the *Evening Standard* 'begged' audiences to see the play. Ken Tynan, unprecedented for a critic, came out of the theatre in a state of such euphoria that he had to telephone and congratulate me. Giddy, giddy times until –

The play opened at the Royal Court on 30 June. A month later, 30 July, it transferred to the Duke of York's on St Martin's Lane during one of the hottest summers on record. Bernard Levin writing in the *Daily Express* claimed: 'I have now seen this great, shining play three times, and it seems to have grown visibly in stature each time . . .' It didn't help. Audiences stayed away. The play had to be taken off long before anticipated. It was the first of the gods' mean sporting with me.

When the play was first published at the end of 1959, a volume on its own, by Penguin Books, I signed and placed a copy in a plastic wrapping and gave it to Mother Bicker, who by then was my mother-in-law. It remained in its wrapping for years. She left it lying around on the window-ledge for neighbours to see. I don't think she ever read it.

Arnold Wesker
Blaendigeddi
July 2000

AUTHOR'S NOTE

A play is ultimately a cooperative effort, and I would like to acknowledge my indebtedness to all the actors and actresses who eventually brought my plays alive on the stage. And in particular I cannot offer enough thanks for the understanding brought to the production by John Dexter, the director, many of whose ideas are contained in the versions as published.

NOTE TO ACTORS AND DIRECTORS OF THE *TRILOGY*

In twenty years of seeing the *Trilogy* performed I've observed one major weakness: an inability to make the characters physically – and thus intellectually – live on the stage. The emotion of a character often succeeds in coming through, but frequently there appears to be no comprehension of how the characters exchange ideas and thoughts, as though actors knew what made people weep but not what made them think; they have been made to stand still and utter 'significant' lines 'significantly', whereas debate in these plays, the cut and thrust of domestic polemic, should take place in the midst of physical action. Sarah should, for example, be cutting bread on a line like 'You can't have brotherhood without love'. The family inquest at the end of *Jerusalem* should be conducted while crates are being packed, floors swept, curtains pulled; thoughts should be thrown over shoulders, down the stairs, over the washing-line, from outside while emptying garbage. If the physical business of living does not continue then the dialogue will emerge pompously and fall with dull thuds from characters who will appear no more than cardboard cut-outs.

A.W.
July 1978

Roots was first presented at the Belgrade Theatre, Coventry, on 25 May 1959, with the following cast:

Jenny Beales	Patsy Byrne
Jimmy Beales	Charles Kay
Beatie Bryant	Joan Plowright
Stan Mann	Patrick O'Connell
Mrs Bryant	Gwen Nelson
Mr Bryant	Jack Rodney
Mr Healey	Richard Martin
Frankie Bryant	Alan Howard
Pearl Bryant	Brenda Peters

Directed by John Dexter
Designed by Jocelyn Herbert

The play transferred to the Royal Court Theatre, London, on 30 June 1959, and subsequently to the Duke of York's on 30 July 1959. At the Duke of York's the part of Mr Healey was played by Barry Wilsher.

Act One: An isolated cottage in Norfolk, the house of the Bealeses

Act Two, Scene One: Two days later at the cottage of Mr and Mrs Bryant, in the kitchen

Scene Two: The same a couple of hours later

Act Three: Two weeks later in the front room of the Bryants'

Time: 1959

Act One

A rather ramshackle house in Norfolk where there is no water laid on, nor electricity, nor gas. Everything rambles and the furniture is cheap and old. If it is untidy it is because there is a child in the house and there are few amenities, so that the mother is too overworked to take much care.

An assortment of clobber lies around: papers and washing, coats and basins, a tin wash-tub with shirts and underwear to be cleaned, Tilley lamps and Primus stoves. Washing hangs on a line in the room. It is September.

Jenny Beales *is by the sink washing up. She is singing a recent pop song. She is short, fat and friendly, and wears glasses. A child's voice is heard from the bedroom crying* 'Sweet, Mamma, sweet.'

Jenny (*good-naturedly*) Shut you up Daphne and get you to sleep now. (*Moves to get a dishcloth.*)

Child's voice Daphy wan' sweet, sweet, sweet.

Jenny (*going to cupboard to get sweet*) My word child, Father come home and find you awake he'll be after you. (*Disappears to bedroom with sweet.*) There – now sleep, gal, don't wan' you grumpy wi' me in the mornin'.

Enter **Jimmy Beales**. *Also short, chubby, blond though hardly any hair left, ruddy complexion. He is a garage mechanic. Wears blue dungarees and an army pack slung over his shoulder. He wheels his bike in and lays it by the wall. Seems to be in some sort of pain – around his back.* **Jenny** *returns.*

Waas matter wi' you then?

Jimmy I don't know gal. There's a pain in my guts and one a'tween my shoulder blades I can hardly stand up.

Jenny Sit you down then an' I'll git you your supper on the table.

Jimmy Blust gal! I can't eat yit.

Jimmy *picks up a pillow from somewhere and lies down on the sofa holding pillow to stomach.* **Jenny** *watches him a while.*

Jenny   Don't you know what 'tis yit?

Jimmy   Well, how should *I* know that 'tis.

Jenny   I told Mother about the pain and she says it's indigestion.

Jimmy   What the hell's indigestion doin' a'tween my shoulder blades then?

Jenny   She say some people get indigestion so bad it go right through their stomach to the back.

Jimmy   Don't be daft.

Jenny   That's what I say. Blust Mother, I say, you don't git indigestion in the back. Don't you tell me, she say, I hed it!

Jimmy   What hevn't she hed.

Jenny *returns to washing up while* **Jimmy** *struggles a while on the sofa.* **Jenny** *hums. No word. Then –*

Jenny   Who d'you see today?

Jimmy   Only Doctor Gallagher.

Jenny *(wheeling round)*   You see who?

Jimmy   Gallagher. His wife driv him up in the ole Armstrong.

Jenny   Well I go t'hell if that ent a rum thing.

Jimmy *(rising and going to table; pain has eased)*   What's that then?

Jenny *(moving to get him supper from oven)*   We was down at the whist drive in the village and that Judy Maitland say he were dead. 'Cos you know he've hed a cancer this last year and they don't give him no longer'n three weeks don't you?

Jimmy   Ole crows. They don' wan' nothin' less than a death to wake them up.

Jenny   No. No longer'n three weeks.

Girl's voice (*off*)   Yoo-hoo! Yoo-hoo!

Jimmy   There's your sister.

Jenny   That's her.

Girl's voice (*off*)   Yoo-hoo! Anyone home?

Jenny (*calling*)   Come you on in gal, don't you worry about yoo-hoo.

Enter **Beatie Bryant**, *an ample, blonde, healthy-faced young woman of twenty-two years. She is carrying a case.*

Jimmy   Here she is.

Jenny (*with reserve, but pleased*)   Hello, Beatrice – how are you?

Beatie (*with reserve, but pleased*)   Hello Jenny – how are you? What's that lovely smell I smell?

Jenny   Onions for supper and bread for the harvest festival.

Beatie   Watcha Jimmy Beales, how you doin' bor?

Jimmy   Not so bad gal, how's yourself?

Beatie   All right you know. When you comin' to London again for a football match?

Jimmy   O blust gal, I don' wanna go to any more o' those things. Ole father Bryant was there in the middle of that crowd and he turn around an' he say (*Imitating.*), Stop you a-pushin' there, he say, stop you a-pushin'.

Jenny   Where's Ronnie?

Beatie   He's comin' down at the end of two weeks.

Jimmy   Ent you married yit?

Beatie   No.

Jimmy   You wanna hurry then gal, a long engagement don't do the ole legs any good.

Jenny   Now shut you up Jimmy Beales and get that food down you. Every time you talk, look, you miss a mouthful! That's why you complain of pain in your shoulder blades.

Beatie   You bin hevin' pains then Jimmy?

Jimmy   Blust yes! Right a'tween my shoulder blades.

Jenny   Mother says it's indigestion.

Beatie   What the hell's indigestion doin' a'tween his shoulder blades?

Jenny   Mother reckon some people get indigestion so bad it go right through their stomach to the back.

Beatie   Don't talk daft!

Jenny   That's what I say. Blust Mother, I say, you don't git indigestion in the back. Don't you tell me, she say, I hed it!

Beatie   What hevn't she hed. How is she?

Jenny   Still the same you know. How long you staying this time?

Beatie   Two days here – two weeks at home.

Jenny   Hungry gal?

Beatie   Watcha got?

Jenny   Watcha see.

Beatie   Liver? I'll hev it!

Beatie *makes herself at home. Near by is a pile of comics. She picks one up and reads.*

Jenny   We got some ice-cream after.

Beatie (*absorbed*)   Yearp.

Jenny   Look at her. No sooner she's in than she's at them ole comics. You still read them ole things?

Jimmy   She don't change much do she?

Beatie   Funny that! Soon ever I'm home again I'm like I always was – it don' even seem I bin away. I do the same lazy things an' I talk the same. Funny that!

Jenny   What do Ronnie say to it?

Beatie   He ent never bin here, not in the three years I know him so he don't even know. But I'll tell you (*She jumps up and moves around as she talks.*) I used to read the comics he bought for his nephew and he used to get riled –

Now **Beatie** *begins to quote Ronnie, and when she does she imitates him so well in both manner and intonation that in fact as the play progresses we see a picture of him through her.*

'Christ, woman, what can they give you that you can *be* so absorbed?' So you know what I used to do? I used to get a copy of the *Manchester Guardian* and sit with that wide open – and a comic behind!

Jimmy   *Manchester Guardian*? Blimey Joe – he don' believe in hevin' much fun then?

Beatie   That's what I used to tell him. 'Fun?' he say, 'fun? Playing an instrument is fun, painting is fun, reading a book is fun, talking with friends is fun – but a comic? A comic? for a young woman of twenty-two?'

Jenny (*handing out meal and sitting down herself*)   He sound a queer bor to me. Sit you down and eat gal.

Beatie (*enthusiastically*)   He's alive though.

Jimmy   Alive? Alive you say? What's alive about someone who can't read a comic? What's alive about a person that reads books and looks at paintings and listens to classical music?

There is a silence at this, as though the question answers itself –
reluctantly.

Well, it's all right for some I suppose.

Beatie   And then he'd sneak the comic away from me and
read it his-self!

Jenny   Oh, he didn't really mind then?

Beatie   No – 'cos sometimes I read books as well. 'There's
nothing wrong with comics,' he'd cry – he stand up on a
chair when he want to preach but don't wanna sound too
dramatic.

Jimmy   Eh?

Beatie   Like this, look. (*Stands on a chair.*) 'There's nothing
wrong with comics only there's something wrong with
comics all the time. There's nothing wrong with football,
only there's something wrong with *only* football. There's
nothing wrong with rock 'n' rolling, only God preserve me
from the girl that can do nothing else!' (*She sits down and then
stands up again, remembering something else.*) Oh yes, 'and there's
nothing wrong with talking about the weather, only don't
talk to me about it!' (*Sits down.*)

Jimmy *and* **Jenny** *look at each other as though she, and no doubt
Ronnie, is a little barmy.* **Jimmy** *rises and begins to strap on boots
and gaiters ready for going out to an allotment.*

Jenny   He never really row with you then?

Beatie   We used to. There was a time when he handled
all official things for me you know. Once I was in between
jobs and I didn't think to ask for my unemployment benefit.
He told me to. But when I asked they told me I was short on
stamps and so I wasn't entitled to benefit. *I* didn't know
what to say but he did. He went up and argued for me –
he's just like his mother, she argues with everyone – and I
got it. I didn't know how to talk see, it was all foreign to me.
Think of it! An English girl born and bred and I couldn't
talk the language – except for to buy food and clothes. And

so sometimes when he were in a black mood he'd start on me. 'What can you talk of?' he'd ask. 'Go on, pick a subject. Talk. Use the language. Do you know what language is?' Well, I'd never thought before – hev you? – it's automatic to you isn't it, like walking? 'Well, language is words,' he'd say, as though he were telling me a secret. 'It's bridges, so that you can get safely from one place to another. And the more bridges you know about the more places you can see!' (*To* **Jimmy**.) And do *you* know what happens when you can see a place but you don't know where the bridge is?

Jimmy (*angrily*)   Blust gal, what the hell are you on about.

Beatie   Exactly! You see, you hev a row! Still, rows is all right. I like a row. So then he'd say: 'Bridges! bridges! bridges! Use your bridges woman. It took thousands of years to build them, use them!' And that riled me. 'Blust your bridges,' I'd say. 'Blust you and your bridges – I want a row.' Then he'd grin at me. 'You want a row?' he'd ask. 'No bridges this time? 'No bridges,' I'd say – and we'd row. Sometimes he hurt me but then, slowly, he'd build the bridge up *for* me – and then we'd make love! (*Innocently continues her meal.*)

Jenny   You'd what, did you say?

Beatie   Make love. Love in the afternoon gal. Ever had it? It's the only time *for* it. Go out or entertain in the evenings; sleep at night, study, work and chores in the mornings; but love – alert and fresh, when you got most energy – love in the afternoon.

Jimmy   I suppose you take time off from work every afternoon to do it?

Beatie   I'm talking about weekends and holidays – daft.

Jenny   Oh, Beatie, go on wi' you!

Beatie   Well, go t'hell Jenny Beales, you're blushin'. Ent you never had love in the afternoon? Ask Jimmy then.

Jenny (*rising to get sweet*)   Shut you up gal and get on wi'
your ice-cream. It's strawberry flavour. Want some more
James?

Jimmy (*taking it in the middle of lacing up boots*)   Yes please,
vanilla please. (*Eating.*) Good cream ent it? Made from the
white milk of a Jersey cow.

Beatie   This is good too – made from pink milk ent it?

Pause.

Jimmy   Yearp! (*Pause.*) Come from a pink cow!

Pause. They are all enjoying the cream.

Jenny (*eating*)   You remember Dickie Smart, Beatie?

Beatie (*eating*)   Who?

Jenny (*eating*)   We had a drink wi' him in the Storks when
you was down last.

Beatie (*eating*)   Yearp.

Jenny (*eating*)   Well, he got gored by a bull last Thursday.
His left ear was nearly off, his knee were gored, his ribs
bruised, and the ligaments of his legs torn.

Pause as they finish eating.

Beatie (*euphemistically*)   He had a rough time then!

Jenny   Yearp. (*To* **Jimmy**.) You off now?

Jimmy   Mm.

Jenny *collects dishes.*

Beatie   Still got your allotment Jimmy?

Jimmy   Yearp.

Beatie   Bit heavy-going this weather.

Jimmy   That ent too bad just yit – few more weeks an' the
old mowld'll cling.

Beatie   Watcha got this year?

Jimmy   Had spuds, carrots, cabbages, you know. Beetroot, lettuces, onions and peas. But me runners let me down this year though.

Jenny   I don't go much on them old things.

Beatie   You got a fair owle turn then?

Jimmy   Yearp.

Jimmy *starts to sharpen a reap hook.*

Beatie (*jumping up*)   I'll help you wash.

Jenny   That's all right gal.

Beatie   Where's the cloth?

Jenny   Here 'tis.

Beatie *helps collect dishes from table and proceeds to help wash up. This is a silence that needs organizing. Throughout the play there is no sign of intense living from any of the characters –* **Beatie***'s bursts are the exception. They continue in a routine rural manner. The day comes, one sleeps at night, there is always the winter, the spring, the autumn, and the summer – little amazes them. They talk in fits and starts mainly as a sort of gossip, and they talk quickly too, enacting as though for an audience what they say. Their sense of humour is keen and dry. They show no affection for each other – though this does not mean they would not be upset were one of them to die. The silences are important – as important as the way they speak, if we are to know them.*

Jenny   What about that strike in London? Waas London like wi'out the buses?

Beatie   Lovely! No noise – and the streets, you should see the streets, flowing with people – the city looks human.

Jimmy   They wanna call us Territorials out – we'd soon break the strike.

Beatie   That's a soft thing for a worker to say for his mates.

Jimmy   Soft be buggered, soft you say? What they earnin'
those busmen, what they earnin'? And what's the farm
worker's wage? Do you know it gal?

Beatie   Well, let the farm workers go on strike too then! It
don't help a farm labourer if a busman don't go on strike do
it now?

Jenny   You know they've got a rise though. Father
Bryant's go up by six and six a week as a pigman, and Frank
goes up seven 'n' six a week for driving a tractor.

Jimmy   But you watch the Hall sack some on 'em.

Jenny   Thaas true Beatie. They're such sods, honest to
God they are. Every time there's bin a rise someone gets
sacked. Without fail. You watch it – you ask father Bryant
when you get home, ask him who's bin sacked since the rise.

Beatie   One person they 'ont sack is him though. They
'ont find many men'd tend to pigs seven days a week and
stay up the hours he do.

Jenny   Bloody fool! (*Pause.*) Did Jimmy tell you he've bin
chosen for the Territorials' Jubilee in London this year?

Beatie   What's this then? What'll you do there?

Jimmy   Demonstrate and parade wi' arms and such like.

Beatie   Won't do you any good.

Jimmy   Don't you reckon? Gotta show we can defend the
country you know. Demonstrate arms and you prevent war.

Beatie (*she has finished wiping up*)   Won't demonstrate
anything bor. (*Goes to undo her case.*) Present for the house!
Have a hydrogen bomb fall on you and you'll find them
things silly in your hands. (*Searches for other parcels.*)

Jimmy   So you say gal? So you say? That'll frighten them
other buggers though.

Beatie   Frighten yourself y'mean. (*Finds parcels.*) Presents
for the kid.

Jimmy   And what do you know about this all of a sudden?

Jenny (*revealing a tablecloth*)   Thank you very much Beatie. Just what I need.

Beatie   You're not interested in defending your country Jimmy, you just enjoy playing soldiers.

Jimmy   What did I do in the last war then – *sing* in the trenches?

Beatie (*explaining – not trying to get one over on him*)   Ever heard of Chaucer, Jimmy?

Jimmy   No.

Beatie   Do you know the MP for this constituency?

Jimmy   What you drivin' at gal – don't give me no riddles.

Beatie   Do you know how the British Trade Union Movement started? And do you believe in strike action?

Jimmy   No to both those.

Beatie   What you goin' to war to defend then?

Jimmy (*he is annoyed now*)   Beatie – you bin away from us a long time now – you got a boy who's educated an' that and he's taught you a lot maybe. But don't you come pushin' ideas across at us – we're all right as we are. You can come when you like an' welcome but don't bring no discussion of politics in the house wi' you 'cos that'll only cause trouble. I'm telling you. (*He goes off.*)

Jenny   Blust gal, if you hevn't touched him on a sore spot. He live for them Territorials he do – that's half his life.

Beatie (*she is upset now*)   What's he afraid of talking for?

Jenny   He ent afraid of talking Beatie – blust he can do that, gal.

Beatie   But not talk, not really talk, not use bridges. I sit with Ronnie and his friends sometimes and I listen to them talk about things and you know I've never heard half of the words before.

Jenny   Don't he tell you what they mean?

Beatie   I get annoyed when he keep tellin' me – and he want me to ask. (*Imitates him half-heartedly now.*) 'Always ask, people love to tell you what they know, always ask and people will respect you.'

Jenny   And do you?

Beatie   No! I don't! An' you know why? Because I'm stubborn, I'm like Mother, I'm stubborn. Somehow I just can't bring myself to ask, and you know what? I go mad when I listen to them. As soon as they start to talk about things I don't know about or I can't understand I get mad. They sit there, casually talking, and suddenly they turn on you, abrupt. 'Don't you think?' they say. Like at school, pick on you and ask a question you ent ready for. Sometimes I don't say anything, sometimes I go to bed or leave the room. Like Jimmy – just like Jimmy.

Jenny   And what do Ronnie say to that then?

Beatie   He get mad too. 'Why don't you ask me woman, for God's sake why don't you ask me? Aren't I dying to tell you about things? Only ask!'

Jenny   And he's goin' to marry you?

Beatie   Why not?

Jenny   Well I'm sorry gal, you mustn't mind me saying this, but it don't seem to me like you two got much in common.

Beatie (*loudly*)   It's not true! We're in love!

Jenny   Well, you know.

Beatie (*softly*)   No, I don't know. I won't know till he come here. From the first day I went to work as waitress in the Dell Hotel and saw him working in the kitchen I fell in love

– and I thought it was easy. I thought everything was easy. I chased him for three months with compliments and presents until I finally give myself to him. He never said he love me nor I didn't care but once he'd taken me he seemed to think he was responsible for me and I told him no different. I'd *make* him love me I thought. I didn't know much about him except he was different and used to write most of the time. And then he went back to London and I followed him there. I've never moved far from home but I did for him and he felt all the time he couldn't leave me and I didn't tell him no different. And then I got to know more about him. He was interested in all the things I never even thought about. About politics and art and all that, and he tried to teach me. He's a socialist and he used to say you couldn't bring socialism to a country by making speeches, but perhaps you could pass it on to someone who was near you. So I pretended I was interested – but I didn't understand much. All the time he's trying to teach me but I can't take it Jenny. And yet, at the same time, I want to show I'm willing. I'm not used to learning. Learning was at school and that's finished with.

Jenny   Blust gal, you don't seem like you're going to be happy then. Like I said.

Beatie   But I love him.

Jenny   Then you're not right in the head then.

Beatie   I couldn't have any other life now.

Jenny   Well, I don't know and that's a fact.

Beatie (*playfully mocking her*)   Well I don't know and that's a fact! (*Suddenly.*) Come on gal, I'll teach you how to bake some pastries.

Jenny   Pastries?

Beatie   Ronnie taught me.

Jenny   Oh, you learnt that much then?

Beatie   But he don't know. I always got annoyed when he tried to teach me to cook as well – Christ! I had to know something – but it sank in all the same.

By this time it has become quite dark and **Jenny** *proceeds to light a Tilley lamp.*

Jenny   You didn't make it easy then?

Beatie   Oh don't you worry, gal, it'll be all right once we're married. Once we're married and I got babies I won't need to be interested in half the things I got to be interested in now.

Jenny   No you won't will you! Don't need no education for babies.

Beatie   Nope. Babies is babies – you just have 'em.

Jenny   Little sods!

Beatie   You gonna hev another Jenny?

Jenny   Well, course I am. What you on about? Think Jimmy don't want none of his own?

Beatie   He's a good man Jenny.

Jenny   Yearp.

Beatie   Not many men'd marry you after you had a baby.

Jenny   No.

Beatie   He didn't ask you any questions? Who was the father? Nor nothing?

Jenny   No.

Beatie   You hevn't told no one hev you Jenny?

Jenny   No, that I hevn't.

Beatie   Well, that's it gal, don't you tell me then!

By this time the methylated spirit torch has burned out and **Jenny** *has finished pumping the Tilley lamp and we are in brightness.*

Jenny (*severely*)   Now Beatie, stop it. Every time you come home you ask me that question and I hed enough. It's finished with and over. No one don't say nothing and no one know. You hear me?

Beatie   Are you in love with Jimmy?

Jenny   Love? I don't believe in any of that squit – we just got married, an' that's that.

Beatie (*suddenly looking around the room at the general chaos*) Jenny Beales, just look at this house. Look at it!

Jenny   I'm looking. What's wrong?

Beatie   Let's clean it up.

Jenny   Clean what up?

Beatie   Are you going to live in this house all your life?

Jenny   You gonna buy us another?

Beatie   Stuck out here in the wilds with only ole Stan Mann and his missus as a neighbour and sand pits all around. Every time it rain look you're stranded.

Jenny   Jimmy don't earn enough for much more 'n we got.

Beatie   But it's so untidy.

Jenny   You don' wan' me bein' like sister Susan do you? 'Cos you know how clean she is don' you – she's so bloody fussy she's gotten to polishing the brass overflow pipe what leads out from the lavatory.

Beatie   Come on gal, let's make some order anyway – I love tidying up.

Jenny   What about the pastries? Pastries? Oh my sainted aunt, the bread! (*Dashes to the oven and brings out a most beautiful-looking plaited loaf of bread. Admiring it.*) Well, no one wanna complain after that. Isn't that beautiful Beatie?

Beatie   I could eat it now.

Jenny   You hungry again?

Beatie (*making an attack upon the clothes that are lying around*)
I'm always hungry again. Ronnie say I eat more'n I need. 'If
you get fat woman I'll leave you – without even a
discussion!'

Jenny (*placing bread on large oval plate to put away*)   Well, there
ent nothin' wrong in bein' fat.

Beatie   You ent got no choice gal. (*Seeing bike.*) A bike!
What's a bike doin' in a livin' room – I'm putting it outside.

Jenny   Jimmy 'ont know where it is.

Beatie   Don't be daft, you can't miss a bike. (*Wheels it
outside and calls from there.*) Jenny! Start puttin' the clothes
away.

Jenny   Blust gal, I ent got nowhere to put them.

Beatie (*from outside*)   You got drawers – you got
cupboards.

Jenny   They're full already.

Beatie (*entering – energy sparks from her*)   Come here – let's
look. (*Looks.*) Oh, go away – you got enough room for ten
families. You just bung it all in with no order, that's why.
Here – help me.

*They drag out all manner of clothes from the cupboard and begin to fold
them up.*

How's my Frankie and Pearl?

Jenny   They're all right. You know she and Mother don't
talk to each other?

Beatie   What, again? Whose fault is it this time?

Jenny   Well, Mother she say it's Pearl's fault and Pearl she
say it's Mother.

Beatie   Well, they wanna get together quick and find whose fault 'tis 'cos I'm going to call the whole family together for tea to meet Ronnie.

Jenny   Well, Susan and Mother don't talk neither so you got a lot of peace-making to do.

Beatie   Well go t'hell, what's broken them two up?

Jenny   Susan hev never bin stuck on her mother, you know that don't you – well, it seems that Susan bought something off the club from Pearl and Pearl give it to Mother and Mother sent it to Susan through the fishmonger what live next door her in the council houses. And of course Susan were riled 'cos she didn't want her neighbours to know that she bought anything off the club. So they don't speak.

Beatie   Kids! It makes me mad.

Jenny   And you know what 'tis with Pearl don't you – it's 'cos Mother hev never thought she was good enough for her son Frankie.

Beatie   No more she wasn't neither!

Jenny   What's wrong wi' her then? I get on all right.

Beatie   Nothing's wrong wi' her, she just wasn't good enough for our Frankie, that's all.

Jenny   Who's being small-minded now?

Beatie   Always wantin' more'n he can give her.

Jenny   An' I know someone else who always wanted more'n she got.

Beatie (*sulkily*)   It's not the same thing.

Jenny   Oh yes 'tis.

Beatie   'Tent.

Jenny   'Tis my gal. (*Mimicking the child* **Beatie**.) I wan' a 'nana, a 'nana, a 'nana, a 'nana. Frankie's got my 'nana, 'nana, 'nana.

Beatie   Well, I liked bananas.

Jenny   You liked anything you could get your hands on and Mother used to give in to you 'cos you were the youngest. Me and Susan and Frankie never got nothing 'cos o' you – 'cept a clout round the ear.

Beatie   'Tent so likely. You got everything and I got nothing.

Jenny   All we got was what we pinched out the larder and then you used to go and tell tales to Mother.

Beatie   I never did.

Jenny   Oh, didn't you my gal? Many's the time I'd've willingly strangled you – with no prayers – there you are, no prayers whatsoever. Strangled you till you was dead.

Beatie   Oh go on wi' you Jenny Beales.

By now they have finished folding the clothes and have put away most of the laundry and garments that have till this moment cluttered up the room. **Beatie** *says* 'There', *stands up and looks around, finds some coats sprawled helter-skelter, and hangs them up behind the door.*

I'll buy you some coat-hangers.

Jenny   You get me a couple o' coats to hang on 'em first please.

Beatie (*looking around*)   What next. Bottles, jars, knick-knacks, saucepans, cups, papers – everything anywhere. Look at it! Come on!

Beatie *attempts to get these things either into their proper places or out of sight.*

Jenny   You hit this place like a bloody whirlwind you do, like a bloody whirlwind. Jimmy'll think he've come into the wrong house and I shan't be able to find a thing.

Beatie   Here, grab a broom. (*She is now gurgling with sort of animal noises signifying excitement. Her joy is childlike.*) How's Poppy?

Jenny   Tight as ever.

Beatie   What won't he give you now?

Jenny   'Tent nothing wi' me gal. Nothing he do don't affect me. It's Mother I'm referring to.

Beatie   Don't he still give her much money?

Jenny   Money? She hev to struggle and skint all the time – *all* the time. Well it ent never bin no different from when we was kids hev it?

Beatie   No.

Jenny   I tell you what. It wouldn't surprise me if Mother were in debt all the time, that it wouldn't. No. It wouldn't surprise me at all.

Beatie   Oh, never.

Jenny   Well, what do you say that for Beatie – do you know how much he allow her a week look?

Beatie   Six pounds?

Jenny   Six pound be buggered. Four pounds ten! An' she hev to keep house *an'* buy her own clothes out of that.

Beatie   Still, there's only two on 'em.

Jenny   You try keepin' two people in food for four pound ten. She pay seven an' six a week into Pearl's club for clothes, two and six she hev on the pools, and a shilling a week on the Labour Tote. (*Suddenly.*) Blust! I forgot to say. Pearl won the Tote last week.

Beatie   A hundred pounds?

Jenny   A hundred pounds!

Beatie   Well no one wrote me about it.

Jenny   'Cos you never wrote no one else.

Beatie   What she gonna do wi' it – buy a TV?

Jenny   TV? Blust no. You know she hevn't got electricity in that house. No, she say she's gonna get some clothes for the kids.

There is a sound now of a drunk old man approaching, and alongside of it the voice of **Jimmy***. The drunk is singing:* 'I come from Bungay Town, I calls I Bungay Johnnie.'

Well I go t'hell if that ent Stan Mann drunk again. And is that Jimmy wi' him? (*Listens.*)

Beatie   But I thought Stan Mann was paralysed.

Jenny   That don't stop him getting paralytic drunk. (*Listens again.*) That's Jimmy taking him into the house I bet. A fortune that man hev drunk away – a whole bleedin' fortune. Remember the fleet of cars he used to run and all that land he owned, and all them cattle he had and them fowl? Well, he've only got a few acres left and a few ole chickens. He drink it all away. Two strokes he've had from drinking and now he's paralysed down one side. But that don't stop him getting drunk – no it don't.

Jimmy *enters and throws his jacket on the couch, takes off his boots and gaiters, and smiles meanwhile.*

Jimmy   Silly ole bugger.

Jenny   I was just telling Beatie how he've drunk a fortune away hevn't he?

Jimmy   He wanna drink a little more often and he'll be finished for good.

Jenny   Didn't he hev all them cows and cars and land Jimmy? And didn't he drink it all away bit by bit?

Jimmy   Silly ole sod don't know when to stop.

Jenny   I wished I had half the money he drink.

Jimmy   He messed his pants.

Jenny   He what? Well where was this then?

Jimmy   By the allotment.

Jenny   Well, what did *you* do then?

Jimmy   He come up to me – 'course I knowed he were drunk the way he walk – he come up to me an' he say, ''Evenin' Jimmy Beales, thaas a fine turnover you got there.' An' I say, 'Yearp 'tis.' An' then he bend down to pick a carrot from the ground an' then he cry, 'Oops, I done it again!' An' 'course, soon ever he say 'done it again' I knowed what'd happened. So I took his trousers down an' ran the ole hose over him.

Beatie   Oh, Jimmy, you never did.

Jimmy   I did gal. I put the ole hose over him an' brought him home along the fields with an ole sack around his waist.

Beatie   He'll catch his death.

Jimmy   Never – he's as strong as an ox.

Jenny   What'd you do with his trousers and things?

Jimmy   Put it on the compost heap – good for the land!

Now **Stan Mann** *enters. He's not all that drunk. The cold water has sobered him a little. He is old – about seventy-five – and despite his slight stoop one can see he was a very strong upright man. He probably looks like everyman's idea of a farmer – except that he wears no socks or boots at this moment and he hobbles on a stick.*

Stan   Sorry about that ole son.

Jimmy   Don't you go worrying about that my manny – get you along to bed.

Jenny   Get some shoes on you too Stan, or you'll die of cold *and* booze.

Stan (*screwing up his eyes across the room*)   Is that you Jenny? Hello ole gal. How are you?

Jenny   It's you you wanna worry about now ole matey. I'm well enough.

Stan (*screwing his eyes still more*)   Who's that next to you?

Jenny   Don't you recognize her? It's our Beatie, Stan.

Stan   Is that you Beatie? Well blust gal, you gotten fatter since I seen you last. You gonna be fat as Jenny here? Come on over an' let's look at you.

Beatie (*approaching*)   Hello Stan Mann, how are you?

Stan (*looking her up and down*)   Well enough gal, well enough. You married yit?

Beatie   No.

Stan   You bin courtin' three years. Why ent you married yit?

Beatie (*slightly embarrassed*)   We ent sure yit.

Stan   You ent sure you say? What ent you sure of? You know how to do it don't you?

Jenny   Go on wi' you to bed Stan Mann.

Stan   Tell your boy he don't wanna waste too much time or I'll be hevin' yer myself for breakfast – on a plate.

Jenny   Stan Mann, I'm sendin' you to your bed – go on now, off wi' you, you can see Beatie in the mornin'.

Stan (*as he is ushered out – to* **Beatie**)   She's fat ent she? I'm not sayin' she won't do mind, but she's fat. (*As he goes out.*) All right ole sweetheart, I'm goin'. I'm just right for bed. Did you see the new bridge they're building? It's a rum ole thing isn't it . . . (*Out of sound.*)

Jenny *makes up bed on couch for* **Beatie**.

Jimmy   Well, I'm ready for bed.

Beatie   I can't bear sick men. They smell.

Jimmy   Ole Stan's all right – do anythin' for you.

Beatie   I couldn't look after one you know.

Jimmy   Case of hevin' to sometimes.

Beatie   Ronnie's father's paralysed like that. I can't touch him.

Jimmy   Who see to him then?

Beatie   His mother. She wash him, change him, feed him. Ronnie help sometimes. I couldn't though. Ronnie say, 'Christ, woman, I hope you aren't around when I'm ill.' (*Shudders.*) Ole age terrify me.

Jimmy   You sleepin' on that ole couch tonight?

Beatie   Suppose so.

Jimmy   You comfortable sleepin' on that ole thing? You wanna sleep with Jenny while you're here?

Beatie   No thanks, Jimmy. (*She is quite subdued now.*) I'm all right on there.

Jimmy   Right, then I'm off. (*Looking around.*) Where's the *Evening News* I brought in?

Jenny (*entering*)   You off to bed?

Jimmy   Yearp. Reckon I've had 'nough of this ole day. Where's my *News*?

Jenny   Where d'you put it Beatie?

Jimmy (*suddenly seeing the room*)   Blust, you movin' out?

Beatie   Here you are Jimmy Beales. (*Hands him the paper.*) It's all tidy now.

Jimmy   So I see. Won't last long though will it? 'Night. (*Goes to bed.*)

Jenny   Well I'm ready for my bed too – how about you Beatie?

Beatie   Yearp.

Jenny (*taking a candle in a stick and lighting it*)   Here, keep this with you. Your bed's made. Want a drink before you turn in?

Beatie   No thanks gal.

Jenny (*picking up Tilley lamp. Leaving*)   Right then. Sleep well gal.

Beatie   Good night Jenny. (*Pause. Loud whispers from now on.*) Hey Jenny.

Jenny   What is it?

Beatie   I'll bake you some pastries when I get to Mother's.

Jenny   Father won't let you use his electricity for me, don't talk daft.

Beatie   I'll get Mother on him. It'll be all right. Your ole ovens weren't big 'nough anyways. Good night.

Moves to door.

Jenny   Good night.

Beatie (*an afterthought*)   Hey Jenny.

Jenny (*returning*)   What now?

Beatie   Did I tell you I took up painting?

Jenny   Painting?

Beatie   Yes – on cardboard and canvases with brushes.

Jenny   What kind of painting?

Beatie   Abstract painting – designs and patterns and such like. I can't do nothing else. I sent two on 'em home. Show you when you come round – if Mother hevn't thrown them out.

Jenny   You're an artist then?

Pause. Such a thought had not occurred to her before. It pleases, even thrills, her.

Beatie   Yes. Good night.

Jenny   Good night.

Beatie *is left alone. Looks out of window. Blows out candle. We see only the faint flow of moonlight from outside and then –*

The curtain falls.

Act Two

Scene One

Two days have passed. **Beatie** *will arrive at her own home, the home of her parents. This is a tied cottage on a main road between two large villages. It is neat and ordinary inside. We can see a large kitchen – where most of the living is done – and attached to it is a large larder; also part of the front room and a piece of the garden where some washing is hanging.*

Mrs Bryant *is a short, stout woman of fifty. She spends most of the day on her own, and consequently when she has a chance to speak to anybody she says as much as she can as fast as she can. The only people she sees are the tradesmen, her husband, the family when they pop in occasionally. She speaks very loudly all the time so that her friendliest tone sounds aggressive, and she manages to dramatize the smallest piece of gossip into something significant. Each piece of gossip is a little act done with little looking at the person to whom it is addressed. At the moment she is at the door leading to the garden, looking for the cat.*

Mrs Bryant   Cossie, Cossie, Cossie, Cossie, Cossie, Cossie! Here Cossie! Food Cossie! Cossie, Cossie, Cossie! Blust you cat, where the hell are you. Oh hell on you then, I ent wastin' my time wi' you now.

She returns to the kitchen and thence the larder, from which she emerges with some potatoes. These she starts peeling. **Stan Mann** *appears round the back door. He has a handkerchief to his nose and is blowing vigorously, as vigorously as his paralysis will allow.* **Mrs Bryant** *looks up, but continues her peeling.*

Stan   Rum thing to git a cold in summer, what you say Daphne?

Mrs Bryant   What'd you have me say my manny. Sit you down bor and rest a bit. Shouldn't wear such daf' clothes.

Stan   Daf' clothes? Blust woman! I got on half a cow's hide, what you sayin'! Where's the gal?

Mrs Bryant   Beatie? She 'ent come yit. Didn't *you* see her?

Stan   Hell, I was up too early for her. She always stay the weekend wi' Jenny 'fore comin' home?

Mrs Bryant   Most times.

Stan *sneezes.*

What you doin' up this way wi' a cold like that then? Get you home to bed.

Stan   Just come this way to look at the vicarage. Stuff's comin' up for sale soon.

Mrs Bryant   You still visit them things then?

Stan   Yearp. Pass the ole time away. Pass the ole time.

Mrs Bryant   Time drag heavy then?

Stan   Yearp. Time drag heavy. She do that. Time drag so slow, I get to thinkin' it's Monday when it's still Sunday. Still, I had my day gal I say. Yearp. I had that all right.

Mrs Bryant   Yearp. You had that an' a bit more ole son. I shant grumble if I last as long as you.

Stan   Yearp. I hed my day. An' I'd do it all the same again, you know that? Do it all the same I would.

Mrs Bryant   Blust! All your drinkin' an' that?

Stan   Hell! Thaas what kep' me goin' look. Almost anyways. None o' them young 'uns'll do it, hell if they will. There ent much life in the young 'uns. Bunch o' weak-kneed ruffians. None on 'em like livin' look, none on 'em! You read in them ole papers what go on look, an' you wonder if they can see. You do! Wonder if they got eyes to look around them. Think they know where they live? 'Course they don't, they don't you know, not one. Blust! The winter go an' the spring come on after an' they don't see buds an' they don't smell no breeze an' they don't see gals, an' when

they see gals they don't know whatta do wi' 'em. They
don't!

Mrs Bryant   Oh hell, they know *that* all right.

Stan   Gimme my young days an' I'd show 'em. Public
demonstrations I'd give!

Mrs Bryant   Oh shut you up Stan Mann.

Stan   Just gimme young days again Daphne Bryant an' I'd
mount you. (*Pause.*) But they 'ont come again will they gal?

Mrs Bryant   That they 'ont. My ole days working in the
fields with them other gals, thems 'ont come again, either.

Stan   No, they 'ont that! Rum ole things the years ent
they? (*Pause.*) Them young 'uns is all right though. Long as
they don't let no one fool them, long as they think it out
theirselves. (*Sneezes and coughs.*)

Mrs Bryant (*moving to help him up*)   Now get you back
home Stan Mann. (*Good-naturedly.*) Blust, I aren't hevin' no
dead 'uns on me look. Take a rum bor, take a rum an' a
drop o' hot milk and get to bed. What's Mrs Mann thinking
of lettin' you out like this.

*She pulls the coat round the old man and pushes him off. He goes off
mumbling and she returns, also mumbling, to her peeling.*

Stan   She's a good gal, she's right 'nough, she don't think I
got it this bad. I'll pull this ole scarf round me. Hed this
scarf a long time, hed it since I started wi' me cars. *She*
bought it me. Lasted a long time. Shouldn't need it this
weather though . . . (*Exits.*)

Mrs Bryant (*mumbling same time as* **Stan**)   Go on, off you
go. Silly ole bugger, runnin' round with a cold like that.
Don't know what 'e's doin' half the time. Poor ole man.
Cossie? Cossie? That you Cossie? (*Looks through door into front
room and out of window at* **Stan**.) Poor ole man.

*After peeling for some seconds she turns the radio on, turning the dial
knob through all manner of stations and back again until she finds some*

very loud dance music which she leaves blaring on. Audible to us, but not to **Mrs Bryant**, *is the call of* 'Yoo-hoo Mother, yoo-hoo'. **Beatie** *appears round the garden and peers into the kitchen.* **Mrs Bryant** *jumps.*

Mrs Bryant   Blust, you made me jump.

Beatie (*toning radio down*)   Can't you hear it? Hello, Mother. (*Kisses her.*)

Mrs Bryant   Well, you've arrived then.

Beatie   Didn't you get my card?

Mrs Bryant   Came this morning.

Beatie   Then you knew I'd arrive.

Mrs Bryant   'Course I did.

Beatie   My things come?

Mrs Bryant   One suitcase, one parcel in brown paper –

Beatie   My paintings.

Mrs Bryant   And one other case.

Beatie   My pick-up. D'you see it?

Mrs Bryant   I hevn't touched a thing.

Beatie   Bought myself a pick-up on the HP.

Mrs Bryant   Don't you go telling that to Pearl.

Beatie   Why not?

Mrs Bryant   She'll wanna know why you didn't buy off her on the club.

Beatie   Well, hell, Mother, I weren't gonna hev an ole pick-up sent me from up north somewhere when we lived next door to a gramophone shop.

Mrs Bryant   No. Well, what bus you come on – the half-past-ten one?

Beatie   Yearp. Picked it up on the ole bridge near Jenny's.

Mrs Bryant   Well I looked for you on the half-past-nine bus and you weren't on that so I thought to myself I bet she come on the half-past-ten and you did. You see ole Stan Mann?

Beatie   Was that him just going up the road?

Mrs Bryant   Wearin' an ole brown scarf, that was him.

Beatie   I see him! Just as I were comin' off the bus. Blust! Jimmy Beales give him a real dowsin' down on his allotment 'cos he had an accident.

Mrs Bryant   What, another?

Beatie   Yearp.

Mrs Bryant   Poor ole man. Thaas what give him that cold then. He come in here sneezin' fit to knock hisself down.

Beatie   Poor ole bugger. Got any tea Ma? I'm gonna unpack.

Beatie *goes into front room with case. We see her take out frocks, which she puts on hangers, and underwear and blouses, which she puts on couch.*

Mrs Bryant   Did you see my flowers as you come in? Got some of my hollyhocks still flowering. Creeping up the wall they are – did you catch a glimpse on 'em? And my asters and geraniums? Poor ole Joe Simonds gimme those afore he died. Lovely geraniums they are.

Beatie   Yearp.

Mrs Bryant   When's Ronnie coming?

Beatie   Saturday week – an' Mother, I'm heving all the family along to meet him when he arrive so you patch your rows wi' them.

Mrs Bryant   What you on about gal? What rows wi' them?

Beatie   You know full well what rows I mean – them ones you hev wi' Pearl and Susan.

Mrs Bryant   'Tent so likely. They hev a row wi' me gal but I give 'em no heed, that I don't. (*Hears van pass on road.*) There go Sam Martin's fish van. He'll be calling along here in an hour.

Beatie (*entering with very smart dress*)   Like it Mother?

Mrs Bryant   Blust gal, that's a good 'un ent it! Where d'you buy that then?

Beatie   Swan and Edgar's.

Mrs Bryant   Did Ronnie choose it?

Beatie   Yearp.

Mrs Bryant   He've got good taste then.

Beatie   Yearp. Now listen Mother, I don't want any on you to let me down. When Ronnie come I want him to see we're proper. I'll buy you another bowl so's you don't wash up in the same one as you wash your hands in and I'll get some more tea cloths so's you 'ont use the towels. And no swearin'.

Mrs Bryant   Don't he swear then?

Beatie   He swear all right, only I don't want him to hear *you* swear.

Mrs Bryant   Hev you given it up then?

Beatie   Mother, I've never swore.

Mrs Bryant   Go to hell, listen to her!

Beatie   I never did, now! Mother, I'm *telling* you, listen to me. Ronnie's the best thing I've ever had and I've tried hard for three years to keep hold of him. I don't care what you do when he's gone but don't show me up when he's here.

Mrs Bryant   Speak to your father gal.

Beatie   Father too. I don't want Ronnie to think I come from a small-minded family. 'I can't bear mean people,' he say. 'I don't care about their education, I don't care about their past as long as their minds are large and inquisitive, as long as they're generous.'

Mrs Bryant   Who say that?

Beatie   Ronnie.

Mrs Bryant   He *talk* like that?

Beatie   Yearp.

Mrs Bryant   Sounds like a preacher.

Beatie (*standing on a chair*)   'I don't care if you call me a preacher, I've got something to say and I'm going to say it. I don't care if you don't like being told things – we've come to a time when you've got to say this is right and this is wrong. God in heaven, have we got to be wet all the time? Well, have we?' Christ, Mother, you've got them ole wasps still flying around. (*She waves her arms in the air flaying the wasps.*) September and you've still got wasps. Owee! Shoo-shoo! (*In the voice of her childhood.*) Mammy, Mammy, take them ole things away. I doesn't like them – ohh! Nasty things.

Beatie *jumps off chair and picks up a coat-hanger. Now both she and her mother move stealthily around the room 'hunting' wasps. Occasionally* **Mrs Bryant** *strikes one dead or* **Beatie** *spears one against the wall.* **Mrs Bryant** *conducts herself matter-of-fact-like but* **Beatie** *makes a fiendish game of it.*

Mrs Bryant   They're after them apples on that tree outside. Go on! Off wi' you! Outside now! There – that's got 'em out, but I bet the buggers'll be back in a jiffy look.

Beatie   Oh yes, an' I want to have a bath.

Mrs Bryant   When d'you want that then?

Beatie   This morning.

Mrs Bryant   You can't hev no bath this morning, that copper won't heat up till after lunch.

Beatie   Then I'll bake the pastries for Jenny this morning and you can put me water on now. (*She returns to sort her clothes.*)

Mrs Bryant   I'll do that now then. I'll get you the soft water from the tank.

Mrs Bryant *now proceeds to collect bucket and move back and forth between the garden out of view and the copper in the kitchen. She fills the copper with about three buckets of water and then lights the fire underneath. In between buckets she chats.*

(*Off – as she hears lorry go by.*) There go Danny Oakley to market. (*She returns with first bucket.*)

Beatie   Mother! I dreamt I died last night and heaven were at the bottom of a pond. You had to jump in and sink and you know how afeared I am of water. It was full of film stars and soldiers and there were two rooms. In one room they was playing skiffle and – and – I can't remember what were goin' on in the other. Now who was God? I can't remember. It was someone we knew, a she. (*Returns to unpacking.*)

Mrs Bryant (*entering with second bucket; automatically*)   Yearp. (*Pause.*) You hear what happened to the headache doctor's patient? You know what they say about him – if you've got a headache you're all right but if you've got something more you've had it! Well he told a woman not to worry about a lump she complained of under her breast and you know what that were? That turned out to be thrombosis! There! Thrombosis! She had that breast off. Yes, she did. Had to hev it cut off. (*Goes for next bucket.*)

Beatie (*automatically*)   Yearp. (*She appears from front room with two framed paintings. She sets them up and admires them. They are primitive designs in bold masses, rather well-balanced shapes and bright poster colours – red, black and yellow – see Dusty Wesker's work.*) Mother! Did I write and tell you I've took up painting? I started five months ago. Working in gouache. Ronnie says I'm good. Says I should carry on and maybe I can sell them for curtain designs. 'Paint girl,' he say. 'Paint! The world is full of people who don't do the things they want so you paint and give us all hope!'

Mrs Bryant *enters.*

Beatie   Like 'em?

Mrs Bryant (*looks at them a second*)   Good colours ent they. (*She is unmoved and continues to empty a third bucket while* **Beatie** *returns paintings to other room.*) Yes gal, I ent got no row wi' Pearl but I ask her to change my Labour Tote man 'cos I wanted to give the commission to Charlie Gorleston and she didn't do it. Well, if she can be like that I can be like that too. You gonna do some baking you say?

Beatie (*enters from front room putting on a pinafore and carrying a parcel*)   Right now. Here y'are Daphne Bryant, present for you. I want eggs, flour, sugar, and marg. I'm gonna bake a sponge and give it frilling. (*Goes to larder to collect things.*)

Mrs Bryant (*unpacking parcel; it is a pinafore*)   We both got one now.

Mrs Bryant *continues to peel potatoes as* **Beatie** *proceeds to separate four eggs, the yolks of which she starts whipping with sugar. She sings meanwhile a ringing folk song.*

Beatie

Oh a dialogue I'll sing you as true as me life.
Between a coal owner and a poor pitman's wife
As she was a-walking along the highway
She met a coal owner and to him did say
Derry down, down, down Derry down.

'Whip the eggs till they're light yellow,' he say.

Mrs Bryant   Who say?

Beatie   Ronnie.

Good morning Lord Firedamp the good woman said
I'll do you no harm sir so don't be afraid
If you'd been where I'd been for most of my life
You wouldn't turn pale at a poor pitman's wife
Singing down, down, down Derry down.

Mrs Bryant   What song's that?

Beatie   A coalmining song.

Mrs Bryant   I tell you what I reckon's a good song, that
'I'll wait for you in the heavens blue'. I reckon that's a lovely
song I do. Jimmy Samson he sing that.

Beatie   It's like twenty other songs, it don't mean
anything and it's sloshy and sickly.

Mrs Bryant   Yes, I reckon that's a good song that.

Beatie (*suddenly*)   Listen Mother, let me see if I can explain
something to you. Ronnie always say that's the point of
knowing people. 'It's no good having friends who scratch
each other's back,' he say. 'The excitement in knowing
people is to hand on what you know and to learn what you
don't know. Learn from me,' he say, 'I don't know much
but learn what I know.' So let me try and explain to you
what he explain to me.

Mrs Bryant (*on hearing a bus*)   There go the half-past-
eleven bus to Diss – blust that's early. (*Puts spuds in saucepan
on oven and goes to collect runner beans, which she prepares.*)

Beatie   Mother, I'm *talking* to you. Blust woman it's not
often we get together and really talk, it's nearly always me
listening to you telling who's dead. Just listen a second.

Mrs Bryant   Well go on gal, but you always take so long
to say it.

Beatie   What are the words of that song?

Mrs Bryant   I don't know all the words.

Beatie   I'll tell you. (*Recites them.*)

I'll wait for you in the heavens blue
As my arms are waiting now.
Please come to me and I'll be true
My love shall not turn sour.
I hunger, I hunger, I cannot wait longer,
My love shall not turn sour.

There! Now what do that mean?

Mrs Bryant (*surprised*)   Well, don't you know what that mean?

Beatie   I mean what do they do to you? How do the words affect you? Are you moved? Do you find them beautiful?

Mrs Bryant   Them's as good words as any.

Beatie   But do they make you feel better?

Mrs Bryant   Blust gal! That ent meant to be a laxative!

Beatie   I must be mad to talk with you.

Mrs Bryant   Besides it's the tune I like. Words never mean anything.

Beatie   All right, the tune then! What does *that* do to you? Make your belly go gooey, your heart throb, make your head spin with passion? Yes, passion, Mother, know what it is? Because you won't find passion in that third-rate song, no you won't!

Mrs Bryant   Well all right gal, so it's third-rate you say. Can you say why? What make that third-rate and them frilly bits of opera and concert first-rate? 'Sides, did I write that song? Beatie Bryant, you do go up and down in your spirits, and I don't know what's gotten into you gal, no I don't.

Beatie   I don't know either, Mother. I'm worried about Ronnie I suppose. I have that same row with him. I ask him exactly the same questions – what make a pop song third-rate. And he answer and I don't know what he talk about. Something about registers, something about commercial

world blunting our responses. 'Give yourself time woman,'
he say. 'Time! You can't learn how to live overnight. *I* don't
even know,' he say, 'and half the world don't know but we
got to try. Try,' he says, ''cos we're still suffering from the
shock of two world wars and we don't know it. Talk,' he say,
'and look and listen and think and ask questions.' But Jesus!
I don't know what questions to ask or *how* to talk. And he
gets so riled – and yet sometimes so nice. 'It's all going up in
flames,' he say, 'but I'm going to make bloody sure I save
someone from the fire.'

Mrs Bryant   Well I'm sure *I* don't know what he's on
about. Turn to your baking gal look and get you done,
Father'll be home for his lunch in an hour.

A faint sound of an ambulance is heard. **Mrs Bryant** *looks up but
says nothing.* **Beatie** *turns to whipping the eggs again and* **Mrs
Bryant** *to cleaning up the runner beans. Out of this pause* **Mrs
Bryant** *begins to sing 'I'll wait for you in the heavens blue', but on
the second line she hums the tune incorrectly.*

Beatie (*laughs*)   No, no, hell Mother, it don't go like that.
It's –

Beatie *corrects her and in helping her mother she ends by singing the
song, with some enthusiasm, to the end.*

Mrs Bryant   Thank God you come home sometimes gal
– you do bring a little life with you anyway.

Beatie   Mother, I ent never heard you express a feeling
like that.

Mrs Bryant (*she is embarrassed*)   The world don't want no
feelings gal. (*Footsteps are heard.*) Is that your father home
already?

Mr Bryant *appears at the back door and lays a bicycle against the
wall. He is a small shrivelled man wearing denims, a peaked cap,
boots, and gaiters. He appears to be in some pain.*

Beatie   Hello poppy Bryant.

Mr Bryant   Hello Beatie. You're here then.

Mrs Bryant   What are you home so early for?

Mr Bryant   The ole guts ache again. (*Sits in armchair and grimaces.*)

Mrs Bryant   Well, what is it?

Mr Bryant   Blust woman, I don't know what 'tis n'more'n you, do I?

Mrs Bryant   Go to the doctor man I keep telling you.

Beatie   What is it father Bryant?

Mrs Bryant   He got guts ache.

Beatie   But what's it from?

Mr Bryant   I've just said I don't know.

Mrs Bryant   Get you to a doctor man, don't be so soft. You don't want to be kept from work do you?

Mr Bryant   That I don't, no I don't. Hell, I just see ole Stan Mann picked up an' thaas upset me enough.

Mrs Bryant   Picked up you say?

Mr Bryant   Well, didn't you hear the ambulance?

Mrs Bryant   There! I hear it but I didn't say narthin'. Was that for Stan Mann then?

Mr Bryant   I was cycling along wi' Jack Stones and we see this here figure on the side o' the road there an' I say, thaas a rum shape in the road Jack, and he say, blust, that's ole Stan Mann from Heybrid, an' 'twere. 'Course soon ever he see what 'twere, he rushed off for 'n ambulance and I waited alongside Stan.

Beatie   But he just left here.

Mrs Bryant   I see it comin'. He come in here an' I shoved him off home. Get you to bed and take some rum an' a drop o' hot milk, I tell him.

Beatie   Is he gonna die?

Mr Bryant   Wouldn't surprise me that it wouldn't. Blust, he look done in.

Mrs Bryant   Poor ole fellah. Shame though ent it?

Mr Bryant   When d'you arrive Beatie?

Mrs Bryant   She come on the half-past-ten bus. I looked for her on the nine-thirty bus and she weren't on that, so I thought to myself I bet she come on the half-past-ten. She did.

Mr Bryant   Yearp.

Mrs Bryant   You gonna stay away all day?

Mr Bryant   No I aren't. I gotta go back 'cos one of the ole sows is piggin'. 'Spect she'll be hevin' them in a couple of hours. (*To* **Beatie**.) Got a sow had a litter o' twenty-two. (*Picks up paper to read.*)

Beatie   Twenty-two? Oh Pop, can I come see this afternoon?

Mr Bryant   Yearp.

Mrs Bryant   Thought you was hevin' a bath.

Beatie   Oh yes, I forgot. I'll come tomorrow then.

Mr Bryant   They'll be there. What you doin' gal?

Mrs Bryant   She's baking a sponge, now leave her be.

Mr Bryant   Oh, you learnt something in London then.

Beatie   Ronnie taught me.

Mr Bryant   Well where *is* Ronnie then?

Mrs Bryant   He's comin' on Saturday a week an' the family's goin' to be here to greet him.

Mr Bryant   All on 'em?

Mrs Bryant *and* **Beatie**   All on 'em!

Mr Bryant Well that'll be a rum gatherin' then.

Mrs Bryant And we've to be on our best behaviour.

Mr Bryant No cussin' and swearin'?

Mrs Bryant *and* **Beatie** No.

Mr Bryant Blust, I shan't talk then.

A young man, **Mr Healey**, *appears round the garden – he is the farmer's son, and manager of the estate* **Bryant** *works for.*

Mrs Bryant (*seeing him first*) Oh, Mr Healey, yes. Jack! It's Mr Healey.

Mr Bryant *rises and goes to the door.* **Healey** *speaks in a firm, not unkind, but business-is-business voice. There is that apologetic threat even in his politeness.*

Mr Healey You were taken ill.

Mr Bryant It's all right, sir, only guts ache, won't be long goin'. The pigs is all seen to, just waiting for the ole sow to start.

Mr Healey What time you expecting it?

Mr Bryant Oh, she 'ont come afore two this afternoon, no she 'ont be much afore that.

Mr Healey You're sure you're well Jack? I've been thinking that it's too much for you carting those pails round the yard.

Mr Bryant No, that ent too heavy , sir, 'course 'tent. You don't wanna worry, I'll be along after lunch. Just an ole guts ache that's all – seein' the doctor tonight – eat too fast probably.

Mr Healey If you're sure you're all right, then I'll put young Daniels off. You can manage without him now we've fixed the new pump in.

Mr Bryant I can manage, sir – 'course I can.

Mr Healey (*moving off outside*)   All right then, Jack, I'll be with you around two o'clock. I want to take the old one out of number three and stick her with the others in seventeen. The little ones won't need her, will they? Then we'll have them sorted out tomorrow.

Mr Bryant   That's right, sir, they *can* go on their own now, they can. I'll see to it tomorrow.

Mr Healey   Right then, Jack. Oh – you hear Stan Mann died?

Mr Bryant   He died already? But I saw him off in the ambulance no more'n half-hour ago.

Mr Healey   Died on the way to hospital. Jack Stones told me. Lived in Heybrid, didn't he?

Mr Bryant   Alongside my daughter.

Mr Healey (*calling*)   Well, good morning, Mrs Bryant.

Mrs Bryant (*calling*)   Good morning, Mr Healey.

The two men nod to each other, **Mr Healey** *goes off.* **Mr Bryant** *lingers a second.*

Mrs Bryant (*to* **Beatie**)   That was Mr Healey, the new young manager.

Beatie   I know it Mother.

Mr Bryant (*returning slowly*)   He's dead then.

Mrs Bryant   Who? Not Stan Mann!

Mr Bryant   Young Healey just tell me.

Mrs Bryant   Well I go t'hell. An' he were just here look, just here alongside o' me not more'n hour past.

Mr Bryant   Rum ent it?

Beatie (*weakly*)   Oh hell, I hate dying.

Mrs Bryant   He were a good ole bor though. Yes he was. A good ole stick. There!

Beatie   Used to ride me round on his horse, always full o'
life an' jokes. 'Tell your boy he wanna hurry up and marry
you,' he say to me, 'or I'll hev you meself on a plate.'

Mrs Bryant   He were a one for smut though.

Beatie   I was talkin' with him last night. Only last night he
was tellin' me how he caught me pinchin' some gooseberries
off his patch an' how he gimme a whole apron full and I
went into one o' his fields near by an' ate the lot. 'Blust,' he
say, 'you had the ole guts ache,' an' he laugh, sat there
laughin' away to hisself.

Mrs Bryant   I can remember that. Hell, Jenny'll miss
him – used always to pop in an' out o' theirs.

Beatie   Seem like the whole world gone suddenly dead
don' it?

Mr Bryant   Rum ent it?

Silence.

Mrs Bryant   *He's* a nice man Mr Healey is, yes he is, a
good sort, I like him.

Beatie   Don't know about being nice. Sounds to me like
he were threatening to sack Father.

Mr Bryant   That's what I say see, get a rise and they start
cutting down the men or the overtime.

Mrs Bryant   The Union magazine's come.

Mr Bryant   I don't want that ole thing.

Beatie   Why can't you do something to stop the sackings?

Mr Bryant   You can't, you can't – that's what I say, you
can't. Sharp as a pig's scream they are – you just *can't* do
nothin'.

Beatie   Mother, where's the bakin' tin?

Mr Bryant   When we gonna eat that?

Beatie   You ent! It's for Jenny Beales.

Mr Bryant   You aren't making that for Jenny are you?

Beatie   I promised her.

Mr Bryant   Not with my electricity you aren't.

Beatie   But I promised, Poppy.

Mr Bryant   That's no matters. I aren't speedin' money on electricity bills so's you can make every Tom, Dick 'n' Harry a sponge cake, that I aren't.

Mrs Bryant   Well, don't be so soft man, it won't take more'n half-hour's bakin'.

Mr Bryant   I don't care what it'll take I say. I aren't lettin' her. Jenny wants cakes, she can make 'em herself. So put that away Beatie and use it for something else.

Mrs Bryant   You wanna watch what you're sayin' of 'cos I live here too.

Mr Bryant   I know all about that but I pay the electricity bill and I says she isn't bakin'.

Beatie   But Poppy, one cake.

Mr Bryant   No I say.

Beatie   Well, Mummy, do something – how can he be so mean.

Mrs Bryant   Blust me if you ent the meanest ole sod that walks this earth. Your own daughter and you won't let her use your oven. You bloody ole hypercrite.

Mr Bryant   You pay the bills and then you call names.

Mrs Bryant   What I ever seen in you God only knows. Yes! An' he never warn me. Bloody ole hypercrite!

Mr Bryant   You pay the bills and then you call names I say.

Mrs Bryant   On four pounds ten a week? You want me
to keep you *and* pay bills? Four pound ten he give me. God
knows what he do wi' the rest. I don't know how much
he've got. I don't, no I don't. Bloody ole hypercrite.

Mr Bryant   Let's hev grub and not so much o' the lip
woman.

Beatie *begins to put the things away. She is on the verge of the tears
she will soon let fall.*

Mrs Bryant   That's how he talk to me – when he do talk.
'Cos you know he don't ever talk more'n he hev to, and
when he do say something it's either 'how much this cost' or
'lend us ouple o' bob'. He've got the money but sooner than
break into that he borrow off me. Bloody old miser. (*To*
Beatie.) What you wanna cry for gal? 'Tent worth it. Blust,
you don't wanna let an ole hypercrite like him upset you, no
you don't. I'll get my back on you my manny, see if I don't.
You won't get away with no tricks on me.

Beatie *has gone into the other room and returned with a small packet.*

Beatie (*throwing parcel in father's lap*)   Present for you.

Mrs Bryant   I'd give him presents that I would! I'd walk
out and disown him! Beatie, now stop you a-cryin' gal –
blust, he ent worth cryin' for, that he ent. Stop it I say and
we'll have lunch. Or you lost your appetite gal?

Beatie *sniffs a few tears back, pauses and –*

Beatie   No – no, that I ent. Hell, I can eat all right!

Curtain.

Scene Two

Lunch has been eaten. **Mr Bryant** *is sitting at the table rolling
himself a cigarette.* **Mrs Bryant** *is collecting the dishes and taking
them to a sink to wash up.* **Beatie** *is taking things off the table and*

putting them into the larder – jars of sauce, plates of sliced bread and cakes, butter, sugar, condiments, and a bowl of tinned fruit.

Mrs Bryant (*to* **Beatie**)   Ask him what he want for his tea.

Mr Bryant   She don't ever ask me before, what she wanna ask me now for?

Mrs Bryant   Tell him it's his stomach I'm thinking about – I don't want him complaining to me about the food I cook.

Mr Bryant   Tell her it's no matters to me – I ent got no pain now besides.

Beatie   Mother, is that water ready for my bath?

Mrs Bryant   Where you hevin' it?

Beatie   In the kitchen of course.

Mrs Bryant   Blust gal, you can't bath in this kitchen during the day, what if someone call at the door?

Beatie   Put up the curtain then, I shan't be no more'n ten minutes.

Mr Bryant   'Sides, who wants to see her in her dickey suit.

Beatie   I know men as 'ould pay to see me in my dickey suit. (*Posing her plump outline.*) Don't you think I got a nice dickey suit?

Mr Bryant *makes a dive and pinches her bottom.*

Ow! Stoppit Bryants, stoppit!

He persists.

Daddy, stop it now!

Mrs Bryant   Tell him he can go as soon as he like, I want your bath over and done with.

Beatie   Oh Mother, stop this nonsense do. If you want to tell him something tell him – not me.

Mrs Bryant   *I* don't want to speak to him, hell if I do.

Beatie   Father, get the bath in for me please. Mother, where's them curtains.

Mr Bryant *goes off to fetch a long tin bath – wide at one end, narrow at the other – while* **Mrs Bryant** *leaves washing-up to fish out some curtains which she hangs from one wall to another concealing thus a corner of the kitchen. Anything that is in the way is removed.* **Beatie** *meanwhile brings out a change of underwear, her dressing-gown, the new frock, some soap, powder, and towel. These she lays within easy reach of the curtain.*

I'm gonna wear my new dress and go across the fields to see Frankie and Pearl.

Mrs Bryant   Frankie won't be there, what you on about? He'll be gettin' the harvest in.

Beatie   You makin' anything for the harvest festival?

Mr Bryant (*entering with bath, places it behind curtain*)   Your mother don't ever do anything for the harvest festival – don't you know that by now.

Beatie   Get you to work father Bryant, I'm gonna plunge in water and I'll make a splash.

Mrs Bryant   Tell him we've got kippers for tea and if he don' want none let him say now.

Beatie   She says it's kippers for tea.

Mr Bryant   Tell her I'll eat kippers. (*Goes off, collecting bike on the way.*)

Beatie   He says he'll eat kippers. Right now, Mother, you get cold water an' I'll pour the hot.

Each now picks up a bucket. **Mrs Bryant** *goes off out to collect the cold water and* **Beatie** *plunges bucket into boiler to retrieve hot water. The bath is prepared with much childlike glee.* **Beatie** *loves her*

creature comforts and does with unabashed, almost animal, enthusiasm
that which she enjoys. When the bath is prepared, **Beatie** *slips*
behind the curtain to undress and enter.

Mrs Bryant   You hear about Jimmy Skelton? They say
he've bin arrested for accosting some man in the village.

Beatie   Jimmy Skelton what own the pub?

Mrs Bryant   That's him. I know all about Jimmy Skelton
though. He were a young boy when I were a young girl. I
always partner him at whist drives. He's been to law before
you know. Yes! An' he won the day too! Won the day he
did. I don't take notice though, him and me gets on all right.
What do Ronnie's mother do with her time?

Beatie   She've a sick husband to look after.

Mrs Bryant   She an educated woman?

Beatie   Educated? No. She's a foreigner. Nor ent Ronnie
educated either. He's an intellectual, failed all his exams.
They read and things.

Mrs Bryant   Oh, they don't do nothing then?

Beatie   Do nothing? I'll tell you what Ronnie do, he work
till all hours in a hot ole kitchen. An' he teach kids in a club
to act and jive and such. And he don't stop at weekends
either 'cos then there's political meetings and such and I get
breathless trying to keep up wi' him. OOOhh, Mother it's
hot . . .

Mrs Bryant   I'll get you some cold then.

Beatie   No – ooh – it's lovely. The water's so soft Mother.

Mrs Bryant   Yearp.

Beatie   It's so soft and smooth. I'm in.

Mrs Bryant   Don't you stay in too long gal. There go the
twenty-minutes-past-one bus.

Beatie   Oh Mother, me bath cubes. I forgot me bath cubes. In the little case by me pick-up.

Mrs Bryant *finds bath cubes and hands them to* **Beatie**.

Mrs Bryant (*continuing her work*)   I shall never forget when I furse heard on it. I was in the village and I was talking to Reggie Fowler. I say to him, there've bin a lot o' talk about Jimmy ent there? Disgustin', I say. Still, there's somebody wanna make some easy money, you'd expect that in a village wouldn't you? Yes, I say to him, a lot of talk. An' he stood there, an' he were a-lookin' at me an' a-lookin' as I were a-talkin' and then he say, missus, he say, I were one o' the victims! Well, you could've hit me over the head wi' a hammer. I was one o' the victims, he say.

Beatie   Mother, these bath cubes smell beautiful. I could stay here all day.

Mrs Bryant   Still, Jimmy's a good fellow with it all – do anything for you. I partner him at whist drives; he bin had up scores o' times though.

Beatie   Mother, what we gonna make Ronnie when he come?

Mrs Bryant   Well, what do he like?

Beatie   He like trifle and he like steak and kidney pie.

Mrs Bryant   We'll make that then. So long as he don't complain o' the guts ache. Frankie hev it too you know.

Beatie   Know why? You all eat too much. The Londoners think we live a healthy life but they don't know we stuff ourselves till our guts ache.

Mrs Bryant   But you know what's wrong wi' Jimmy Beales? It's indigestion. He eat too fast.

Beatie   What the hell's indigestion doin' a'tween his shoulder blades?

Mrs Bryant   'Cos some people get it so bad it go right through their stomach to the back.

Beatie   You don't get indigestion in the back, Mother, what you on about?

Mrs Bryant   Don't you tell me gal, I hed it!

Beatie   Owee! The soap's in me eyes – Mother, towel, the towel, quickly the towel!

Mrs Bryant *hands towel to* **Beatie**. *The washing-up is probably done by now, so* **Mrs Bryant** *sits in a chair, legs apart and arms folded, thinking what else to say.*

Mrs Bryant   You heard that Ma Buckley hev been taken to Mental Hospital in Norwich? Poor ole dear. If there's one thing I can't abide that's mental cases. They frighten me – they do. Can't face 'em. I'd sooner follow a man to a churchyard than the mental hospital. That's a terrible thing to see a person lose their reason – that 'tis. Well, I tell you what, down where I used to live, down the other side of the Hall, years ago we moved in next to an old woman. I only had Jenny and Frank then – an' this woman she were the sweetest of people. We used to talk and do errands for each other – Oh she was a sweet ole dear. And then one afternoon I was going out to get my washin' in and I saw her. She was standin' in a tub o' water up to her neck. She was! Up to her neck. An' her eyes had that glazed, wonderin' look and she stared straight at me she did. Straight at me. Well, do you know what? I was struck *dumb*. I was *struck* dumb wi' shock. What wi' her bein' so nice all this while, the sudden comin' on her like that in the tub fair upset me. It did! And people tell me afterwards that she's bin goin' in an' out o'hospital for years. Blust, that scare me. That scare me so much she nearly took me round the bend wi' her.

Beatie *appears from behind the curtain in her dressing-gown, a towel round her head.*

Beatie   There! I'm gonna hev a bath every day when I'm married.

Beatie *starts rubbing her hair with towel and fiddles with radio. She finds a programme playing Mendelssohn's Fourth Symphony, the slow movement, and stands before the mirror, listening and rubbing.*

(*Looking at her reflection.*) Isn't your nose a funny thing, and your ears. And your arms and your legs, aren't they funny things – sticking out of a lump.

Mrs Bryant (*switching off radio*)   Turn that squit off!

Beatie (*turning on her mother violently*)   Mother! I could kill you when you do that. No wonder I don't know anything about anything. I never heard nothing but dance music because you always turned off the classics. I never knowed anything about the news because you always switched off after the headlines. I never read any good books 'cos there was never any in the house.

Mrs Bryant   What's gotten into you now gal?

Beatie   God in heaven Mother, you live in the country but you got no – no – no majesty. You spend your time among green fields, you grow flowers and you breathe fresh air and you got no majesty. Your mind's cluttered up with nothing and you shut out the world. What kind of a life did you give me?

Mrs Bryant   Blust gal, I weren't no teacher.

Beatie   But you hindered. You didn't open one door for me. Even his mother cared more for me than what you did. Beatie, she say, Beatie, why don't you take up evening classes and learn something other than waitressing. Yes, she say, you won't ever regret learnin' things. But did you care what job I took up or whether I learned things? You didn't even think it was necessary.

Mrs Bryant   I fed you. I clothed you. I took you out to the sea. What more d'you want. We're only country folk you know. We ent got no big things here you know.

Beatie   Squit! Squit! It makes no difference country or town. *All* the town girls I ever worked with were just like me. It makes no difference country or town – that's squit. Do you know when I used to work at the holiday camp and I sat down with the other girls to write a letter we used to sit and discuss what we wrote about. An' we all agreed, all on us, that we started: 'Just a few lines to let you know', and then we get on to the weather and then we get stuck so we write about each other and after a page an' half of big scrawl end up: 'Hoping this finds you as well as it leaves me.' There! We couldn't say any more. Thousands of things happening at this holiday camp and we couldn't find words for them. All of us the same. Hundreds of girls and one day we're gonna be mothers, and you *still* talk to me of Jimmy Skelton and the ole woman in the tub. Do you know I've heard that story a dozen times. A dozen times. Can't you hear yourself Mother? Jesus, how can I bring Ronnie to this house.

Mrs Bryant   Blust gal, if Ronnie don't like us then he –

Beatie   Oh, he'll like you all right. He like people. He'd've loved ole Stan Mann. Ole Stan Mann would've understood everything Ronnie talk about. Blust! That man liked livin'. Besides, Ronnie says it's too late for the old 'uns to learn. But he says it's up to us young 'uns. And them of us that know hev got to teach them of us as don't know.

Mrs Bryant   I bet he hev a hard time trying to change you gal!

Beatie   He's *not* trying to change me Mother. You can't change people, he say, you can only give them some love and hope they'll take it. And he's tryin' to teach me and I'm tryin' to understand – do you see that Mother?

Mrs Bryant   I don't see what that's got to do with music though.

Beatie   Oh my God! (*Suddenly.*) I'll show you. (*Goes off to front room to collect pick-up and a record.*) Now sit you down gal and I'll show you. Don't start ironing or reading or nothing, just sit there and be prepared to learn something. (*Appears with pick-up and switches on.*) You aren't too old, just you sit and listen. That's the trouble you see, we ent ever prepared to learn anything, we close our minds the minute anything unfamiliar appear. *I* could never listen to music. I used to like some on it but then I'd lose patience, I'd go to bed in the middle of a symphony, or my mind would wander 'cos the music didn't mean anything to me so I'd go to bed or start talking. 'Sit back woman,' he'd say, 'listen to it. Let it happen to you and you'll grow as big as the music itself.'

Mrs Bryant   Blust he talk like a book.

Beatie   An' sometimes he talk as though you didn't know where the moon or the stars was. (**Beatie** *puts on record of Bizet's* L'Arlésienne *Suite.*) Now listen. This is a simple piece of music, it's not highbrow, but it's full of living. And that's what he say socialism is. 'Christ,' he say. 'Socialism isn't talking all the time, it's living, it's singing, it's dancing, it's being interested in what go on around you, it's being concerned about people and the world.' Listen Mother. (*She becomes breathless and excited.*) Listen to it. It's simple isn't it? Can you call that squit?

Mrs Bryant   I don't say it's all squit.

Beatie   You don't have to frown because it's alive.

Mrs Bryant   No, not all on it's squit.

Beatie   See the way the other tune comes in? Hear it? Two simple tunes, one after the other.

Mrs Bryant   I aren't saying it's all squit.

Beatie   And now listen, listen, it goes together, the two tunes together, they knit, they're perfect. Don't it make you want to dance? (*She begins to dance a mixture of a cossack dance and a sailor's hornpipe.*)

The music becomes fast and her spirits are young and high.

Listen to that Mother. Is it difficult? Is it squit? It's light. It make me feel light and confident and happy. God, Mother, we could all be so much more happy and alive. Wheeeee . . .

Beatie *claps her hands and dances on and her mother smiles and claps her hands and –*

The curtain falls.

Act Three

*Two weeks have passed. It is Saturday, the day Ronnie is to arrive.
One of the walls of the kitchen is now pushed aside and the front room
is revealed. It is low-ceilinged, and has dark brown wooden beams.
The furniture is not typical country-farmhouse type. There may be one
or two windsor-type straight-backed chairs, but for the rest it is cheap
utility stuff. Two armchairs, a table, a small bamboo table, wooden
chairs, a small sofa, and a swivel bookcase. There are a lot of flowers
around – in pots on the window ledge and in vases on the bamboo table
and swivel case.*

*It is three in the afternoon, the weather is cloudy – it has been raining
and is likely to start again. On the table is a spread of food (none of
this will be eaten). There are cakes and biscuits on plates and glass
stands. Bread and butter, butter in a dish, tomatoes, cheese, jars of
pickled onions, sausage rolls, dishes of tinned fruit – it is a spread!
Round the table are eight chairs.* **Beatie***'s paintings are hanging on
the wall. The room is empty because* **Beatie** *is upstairs changing and*
Mrs Bryant *is in the kitchen.* **Beatie** *– until she descends –
conducts all her conversation from upstairs.*

Beatie   Mother! What you on at now?

Mrs Bryant (*from kithcen*)   I'm just puttin' these glass
cherries on the trifle.

Beatie   Well come on look, he'll be here at four thirty.

Mrs Bryant (*from kitchen*)   Don't you fret gal, it's another
hour 'n' half yet, the postman hevn't gone by. (*Enters with an
enormous bowl of trifle.*)There! He like trifle you say?

Beatie   He love it.

Mrs Bryant   Well he need to 'cos there's plenty on it. (*To
herself, surveying the table.*) Yes, there is, there's plenty on it. (*It
starts to rain.*) Blust, listen to that weather.

Beatie   Rainin' again!

Mrs Bryant (*looking out of window*)   Raining? It's rainin' fit to drowned you. (*Sound of bus.*) There go the three-o'clock.

Beatie   Mother get you changed, come on, I want us ready in time.

Mrs Bryant   Blust you'd think it were the bloody Prince of Egypt comin'. (*Goes upstairs.*)

The stage is empty again for a few seconds. People are heard taking off their macs and exclaiming at the weather from the kitchen. Enter **Frank** *and* **Pearl Bryant**. *He is pleasant and dressed in a blue pin-striped suit, is ruddy-faced and blond-haired. An odd sort of shyness makes him treat everything as a joke. His wife is a pretty brunette, young, and ordinarily dressed in plain, flowered frock.*

Frank (*calling*)   Well, where are you all? Come on – I'm hungry.

Pearl   Shut you up bor, you only just had lunch.

Frank   Well I'm hungry again. (*Calling.*) Well, where is this article we come to see?

Beatie   He ent arrived.

Frank   Well, he want to hurry, 'cos I'm hungry.

Beatie   You're always hungry.

Frank   What do you say he is – a strong socialist?

Beatie   Yes.

Frank   And a Jew boy?

Beatie   Yes.

Frank (*to himself*)   Well, that's a queer mixture then.

Pearl (*calling*)   I hope he don't talk politics all the time.

Frank   Have you had a letter from him yet?

Pearl   Stop it Frank, you know she hevn't heard.

Frank   Well that's a rum boy friend what don't write. (*Looks at paintings, pauses before one of them and growls.*)

Pearl   Watch out or it'll bite you back.

Beatie *comes down from upstairs. She is dressed in her new frock and looks happy, healthy and radiant.*

Frank   Hail there, sister! I was then contemplating your masterpiece.

Beatie   Well don't contemplate too long 'cos you aren't hevin' it.

Frank   Blust! I'd set my ole heart on it.

Pearl   That's a nice frock Beatie.

Frank   Where's the rest of our mighty clan?

Beatie   Jenny and Jimmy should be here soon and Susie and Stan mightn't come.

Frank   What's wrong wi' them?

Beatie   Don't talk to me about it 'cos I hed enough! Susie won't talk to Mother.

Pearl   That make nearly eighteen months she hevn't spoke.

Beatie   Why ever did *you* and Mother fall out Pearl?

Frank   'Cos Mother's so bloody stubborn that's why.

Pearl   Because one day she said she wanted to change her Labour Tote man, that's why, and she asked me to do it for her. So I said all right, but it'll take a couple of weeks; and then she get riled because she said I didn't want to change it for her. And then I ask her why didn't she change him herself and she say because she was too ill to go all the way to see John Clayton to tell him, and then she say to me, why, don't you think I'm ill? And I say – I know this were tactless o' me – but I say, no Mother, you don't look ill to me. And she didn't speak to me since. I only hope she don't snub me this afternoon.

Beatie   Well, she tell me a different story.

Frank   Mother's always quarrelling.

Pearl   Well I reckon there ent much else she *can* do stuck in this ole house on her own all day. And father Bryant he don't say too much when he's home you know.

Frank   Well blust, she hevn't spoke to her own mother for three years, not since Granny Dykes took Jenny in when she had that illegitimate gal Daphne.

Beatie   Hell! What a bloody family!

Frank   A mighty clan I say.

Jimmy *and* **Jenny Beales** *now enter.*

Jenny   Hello Frankie, hello Pearl, hello Beatie.

Frank   And more of the mighty clan.

Jenny   Mighty clan you say? Mighty bloody daft you mean. Well, where is he?

Frank   The mysterious stranger has not yet come – we await.

Jenny   Well, I aren't waitin' long 'cos I'm hungry.

Pearl   That's all this family of Bryants ever do is think o' their guts.

Frank (*to* **Jimmy**)   Have you formed your association yit?

Jenny   What association is this?

Frank   What! Hevn't he told you?

Jimmy   Shut you up Frank Bryant or you'll get me hung.

Frank   Oh, a mighty association – a mighty one! I'll tell ye. One day you see we was all sittin' round in the pub – Jimmy, me, Starkie, Johnny Oats, and Bonky Dawson –

we'd hed a few drinks and Jimmy was feelin' – well, he was feelin' – you know what, the itch! He hed the itch! He started complaining about ham, ham, ham all the time. So then Bonky Dawson say, blust, he say, there must be women about who feel the same. And Starkie he say, well 'course they are, only how do you tell? And then we was all quiet a while thinkin' on it when suddenly Jimmy says, we ought to start an association of them as need a bit now and then and we all ought to wear a badge he say, and when you see a woman wearin' a badge you know she need a bit too.

Jimmy   Now that's enough Frank or I'll hit you over the skull.

Frank   Now, not content wi' just that, ole Jimmy then say, and we ought to have a password to indicate how bad off you are. So listen what he suggest. He suggest you go up to any one o' these women what's wearin' a badge and you say, how many lumps of sugar do you take in your tea? And if she say 'two' then you know she ent too badly off, but she's willin'. But if she say 'four' then you know she's in as bad a state as what you are, see?

Long pause.

Jenny   He'd hev a fit if she said she took sixteen lumps though wouldn't he?

Pause.

Pearl   Where's mother Bryant?

Beatie   Upstairs changin'.

Pearl   Where's father Bryant?

Beatie   Tendin' the pigs.

Frank   You're lucky to hev my presence you know.

Beatie   Oh?

Frank   A little more sun and I'd've bin gettin' in the harvest.

Pearl   Well, what did you think of that storm last night? All that thunder 'n' lightnin' and it didn't stop once.

Beatie   Ronnie love it you know. He sit and watch it for bloody hours.

Frank   He's a queer article then.

Jenny   He do sound a rum 'un don't he?

Beatie   Well you'll soon see.

Jimmy   Hev he got any sisters?

Beatie   One married and she live not far from here.

Pearl   She live in the country? A town girl? Whatever for?

Beatie   Her husband make furniture by hand.

Pearl   Can't he do that in London?

Beatie   Ronnie say they think London's an inhuman place.

Jimmy   So 'tis, so 'tis.

Beatie   Here come father Bryant.

Mr Bryant *enters. He is in denims and raincoat, tired, and stooped slightly.*

Frank   And this be the male head of the mighty Bryant clan!

Mr Bryant   Blust, you're all here soon then.

Beatie   Get you changed quick Father – he'll be along any minute look.

Mr Bryant   Shut you up gal, I'll go when I'm ready, I don't want you pushin' me.

Mrs Bryant *comes from upstairs. She looks neat and also wears a flowered frock.*

Frank   And this be the female head o' the mighty Bryant clan!

Mrs Bryant   Come on Bryant, get you changed – we're all ready look.

Mr Bryant   Blust, there go another one. Who is he this boy, that's what I wanna know.

Mrs Bryant   He's upset! I can see it! I can tell it in his voice. Come on Bryants, what's the matters.

Mr Bryant   There ent much up wi' me, what you on about woman. (*Makes to go.*) Now leave me be, you want me changed look.

Mrs Bryant   If there ent much up wi' you, I'll marry some other.

Frank   Healey bin at you Pop?

Beatie   The pigs dyin'?

Mrs Bryant   It's something serious or he wouldn't be so happy lookin'.

Mr Bryant   I bin put on casual labour.

Jenny   Well isn't that a sod now.

Mrs Bryant   Your guts I suppose.

Mr Bryant   I tell him it's no odds, that there's no pain. That don't matters Jack, he says, I aren't hevin' you break up completely on me. You go on casual, he say, and if you gets better you can come on to the pigs again.

Mrs Bryant   That's half pay then?

Beatie   Can't you get another job?

Frank   He've bin wi' them for eighteen years.

Beatie   But you must be able to do something else – what about cowman again?

Mr Bryant   Bill Waddington do that see. He've bin at it this last six 'n' half years.

Jenny   It's no good upsettin' yourself Beatie. It happen all the time gal.

Jimmy   Well, we told her when she was at ours didn't we.

Mrs Bryant (*to* **Mr Bryant**)   All right, get you on up, there ent nothin' we can do. We'll worry on it later. We always manage. It's gettin' late look.

Mr Bryant   Can he swim? 'Cos he bloody need to. It's rainin' fit to drowned you. (*Goes off upstairs.*)

Mrs Bryant   Well, shall we have a little cup o' tea while we're waitin'? I'll go put the kettle on. (*Goes to kitchen.*)

Everyone sits around now. **Jenny** *takes out some knitting and* **Jimmy** *picks up a paper to read. There is a silence. It is not an awkward silence, just a conversationless room.*

Pearl (*to* **Jenny**)   Who's lookin' after your Daphne?

Jenny   Ole mother Mann next door.

Pearl   Poor ole dear. How's she feelin' now?

Jenny   She took it bad. (*Nodding at* **Jimmy**.) Him too. He think he were to blame.

Pearl   Blust that weren't his fault. Don't be so daft Jimmy Beales. Don't you go fretting yourself or you'll make us all feel queer look. You done nothin' wrong bor – he weren't far off dying 'sides.

Frank   They weren't even married were they?

Jenny   No, they never were – she started lookin' after him when he had that first stroke and she just stayed.

Jimmy   Lost her job 'cos of it too.

Frank   Well, yes, she would, wouldn't she – she was a State Registered Nurse or something weren't she? (*To* **Beatie**.) Soon ever the authorities got to hear o' that they told her to pack up livin' wi' him or quit her job, see?

Jenny   Bloody daft I reckon. What difference it make whether she married him or not.

Pearl   I reckon you miss him Jenny?

Jenny   Hell yes – that I do. He were a good ole bor – always joking and buying the gal sweets. Well, do you know I cry when I heard it? I did. Blust, that fair shook me – that it did, there!

Jimmy   Who's lookin' after *your* kid then, Pearl?

Pearl   Father.

Pause.

Jimmy (*to* **Frank**)   Who do you think'll win today?

Frank   Well Norwich won't.

Jimmy   No.

Pause. **Mrs Bryant** *enters and sits down.*

Mrs Bryant   Well the kettle's on.

Pearl (*to* **Beatie**)   Hev his sister got any children?

Beatie   Two boys.

Jimmy   She wanna get on top one night then they'll hev girls.

Jenny   Oh shut you up Jimmy Beales.

Mrs Bryant   Hed another little win last night.

Jenny   When was this?

Mrs Bryant   The fireman's whist drive. Won seven 'n' six in the knockout.

Jenny   Yearp.

Frank (*reading the paper*)   I see that boy what assaulted the ole woman in London got six years.

Mrs Bryant   Blust! He need to! I'd've given him six years and a bit more. Bloody ole hooligans. Do you give me a chance to pass sentence and I'd soon clear the streets of crime, that I would. Yes, that I would.

Beatie (*springing into activity*)   All right Mother – we'll give you a chance. (*Grabs* **Jimmy***'s hat and umbrella. Places hat on mother's head and umbrella in her arms.*) There you are, you're a judge. Now sum up and pass judgement.

Mrs Bryant   I'd put him in prison for life.

Frank   You gotta sum up though. Blust, you just can't stick a man in prison and say nothing.

Mrs Bryant   Goodbye, I'd say.

Beatie   Come on Mother, speak up. Anybody can say 'go to prison', but *you* want to be a judge. Well, you show a judge's understanding. Talk! Come on Mother, talk!

Everyone leans forward eagerly to hear mother talk. She looks startled and speechless.

Mrs Bryant   Well I – I – yes I – well I – Oh, don't be so soft.

Frank   The mighty head is silent.

Beatie   Well yes, she would be wouldn't she.

Mrs Bryant   What do you mean, I would be? You don't expect me to know what they say in courts do you? I aren't no judge.

Beatie   Then why do you sit and pass judgement on people? If someone do something wrong you don't stop and think why. No discussin', no questions, just (*Snap of fingers.*) – off with his head. I mean look at Father getting less money. I don't see the family sittin' together and discussin' it. It's a problem! But which of you said it concerns you?

Mrs Bryant   Nor don't it concern them. I aren't hevin' people mix in my matters.

Beatie   But they aren't just people – they're your family for hell's sake!

Mrs Bryant   No matters, I aren't hevin' it!

Beatie   But Mother I –

Mrs Bryant   Now shut you up Beatie Bryant and leave it alone. I shall talk when I hev to and I never shall do, so there!

Beatie   You're so stubborn.

Mrs Bryant   So you keep saying.

Mr Bryant *enters, he is clean and dressed in blue pin-stripe suit.*

Mr Bryant   You brewed up yit?

Mrs Bryant *(jumping up and going to kitchen)*   Oh hell, yes – I forgot the tea look.

Mr Bryant   Well, now we're all waitin' on him.

Jenny   Don't look as if Susie's comin'.

Beatie   Stubborn cow!

Silence.

Jenny   Hev you seen Susie's television set yit?

Beatie   I seen it.

Frank   Did you know also that when they fist hed it they took it up to bed wi' them and lay in bed wi' a dish of chocolate biscuits?

Pearl   But now they don't bother – they say they've had it a year now and all the old programmes they saw in the beginning they're seein' again.

Mrs Bryant *(entering with tea)*   Brew's up!

Beatie   Oh, for Christ's sake let's stop gossiping.

Pearl   I aren't gossiping. I'm making an intelligent observation about the state of television, now then.

Mr Bryant   What's up wi' you now?

Beatie   You weren't doin' nothin' o' the sort – you was gossiping.

Pearl   Well that's a heap sight better'n quotin' all the time.

Beatie   I don't quote all the time, I just tell you what Ronnie say.

Frank   Take it easy gal – he's comin' soon – don't need to go all jumpin' an' frantic.

Beatie   Listen! Let me set you a problem.

Jimmy   Here we go.

Beatie   While we're waitin' for him I'll set you a moral problem. You know what a moral problem is? It's a problem about right and wrong. I'll get you buggers thinking if it's the last thing I do. Now listen. There are four huts –

Frank   What?

Beatie   Huts. You know – them little things you live in. Now there are two huts on one side of a stream and two huts on the other side. On one side live a girl in one hut and a wise man in the other. On the other side live Tom in one hut and Archie in the other. Also there's a ferryman what run a boat across the river. Now – listen, concentrate – the girl loves Archie but Archie don't love the girl. And Tom love the girl but the girl don't go much on Tom.

Jimmy   Poor bugger.

Beatie   One day the girl hears that Archie – who don't love her, remember – is going to America, so she decides to try once more to persuade him to take her with him. So listen what she do. She go to the ferryman and ask him to take her across. The ferryman say, I will, but you must take off all your clothes.

Mrs Bryant   Well, whatever do he wanna ask that for?

Beatie   It don't matters why – he do! Now the girl doesn't know what to do so she ask the wise man for advice, and he say, you must do what you think best.

Frank   Well that weren't much advice was it!

Beatie   No matters – he give it. So the girl thinks about it and being so in love she decides to strip.

Pearl   Oh I say!

Mr Bryant   Well, this is a rum ole story ent it?

Beatie   Shut up Father and listen. Now, er – where was I?

Mr Bryant   She was strippin'.

Beatie   Oh yes! So, the girl strips and the ferryman takes her over – he don't touch her or nothing – just takes her over and she rushes to Archie's hut to implore him to take her with him and to declare her love again. Now Archie promises to take her with him and so she sleeps with him the night. But when she wake up in the morning he've gone. She's left alone. So she go across to Tom and explain her plight and ask for help. But soon ever he knowed what she've done, he chuck her out see? So there she is. Poor little gal. Left alone with no clothes and no friends and no hope of staying alive. Now – this is the question, think about it, don't answer quick – who is the person most responsible for her plight?

Jimmy   Well, can't she get back?

Beatie   No, she can't do anything. She's finished. She've hed it! Now, who's to blame?

There is a general air of thought for a moment and **Beatie** *looks triumphant and pleased with herself.*

Mrs Bryant   Be you a-drinkin' on your tea look. Don't you worry about no naked gals. The gal won't get cold but the tea will.

Pearl   Well I say the girl's most responsible.

Beatie   Why?

Pearl   Well, she made the choice didn't she?

Frank   Yes, but the old ferryman made her take off her clothes.

Pearl   But she didn't hev to.

Frank   Blust woman, she were in love!

Beatie   Good ole Frank.

Jenny   Hell if I know.

Beatie   Jimmy?

Jimmy   Don't ask me gal – I follow decisions, I aren't makin' none.

Beatie   Father?

Mr Bryant   I don't know what you're on about.

Beatie   Mother?

Mrs Bryant   Drink you your tea gal – never you mind what I think.

This is what they're waiting for.

Pearl   Well – what do Ronnie say?

Beatie   He say the gal is responsible only for makin' the decision to strip off and go across and that she do that because she's in love. After that she's the victim of two phoney men – one who don't love her but take advantage of her and one who say he love her but don't love her enough to help her, and that the man who say he love her but don't do nothin' to help her is most responsible because he were the last one she could turn to.

Jenny   He've got it all worked out then!

Beatie (*jumping on a chair thrusting her fist into the air like Ronnie, and glorying in what is the beginning of a hysteric outburst of his quotes*) 'No one do that bad that you can't forgive them.'

Pearl   He's sure of himself then?

Beatie   'We can't be sure of everything but certain basic things we must be sure about or we'll die.'

Frank   He think everyone is gonna listen then?

Beatie   'People *must* listen. It's no good talking to the converted. *Everyone* must argue and think or they will stagnate and rot and the rot will spread.'

Jenny   Hark at that then.

Beatie (*her strange excitement growing; she has a quote for everything*)   'If wanting the best things in life means being a snob then glory hallelujah I'm a snob. But I'm not a snob Beatie, I just believe in human dignity and tolerance and cooperation and equality and –'

Jimmy (*jumping up in terror*)   He's a communist!

Beatie   'I'm a socialist!'

There is a knock on the front door.

(*Jumping down joyously as though her excited quotes have been leading to this one moment.*) He's here, he's here! (*But at the door it is the* **Postman**, *from whom she takes a letter and a parcel.*) Oh, the silly fool, the fool. Trust him to write a letter on the day he's coming. Parcel for you Mother.

Pearl   Oh, that'll be your dress from the club.

Mrs Bryant   What dress is this then? I didn't ask for no dress from the club.

Pearl   Yes you did, you did ask me, didn't she ask me Frank? Why, we were looking through the book together Mother.

Mrs Bryant   No matters what we was doin' together I aren't hevin' it.

Pearl   But Mother you distinctly –

Mrs Bryant   I aren't hevin' it so there now!

Beatie *has read the letter – the contents stun her. She cannot move. She stares around speechlessly at everyone.*

Well, what's the matter wi' you gal? Let's have a read. (*Takes letter and reads contents in a dead flat but loud voice – as though it were a proclamation.*) 'My dear Beatie. It wouldn't really work would it? My ideas about handing on a new kind of life are quite useless and romantic if I'm really honest. If I were a healthy human being it might have been all right but most of us intellectuals are pretty sick and neurotic – as you have often observed – and we couldn't build a world even if we were given the reins of government – not yet any-rate. I don't blame you for being stubborn, I don't blame you for ignoring every suggestion I ever made – I only blame myself for encouraging you to believe we could make a go of it and now two weeks of your not being here has given me the cowardly chance to think about it and decide I –'

Beatie (*snatching letter*)   Shut up!

Mrs Bryant   Oh – so we know now do we?

Mr Bryant   What's this then – ent he comin'?

Mrs Bryant   Yes, we know now.

Mr Bryant   Ent he comin' I ask?

Beatie   *No he ent comin'.*

An awful silence ensues. Everyone looks uncomfortable.

Jenny (*softly*)   Well blust gal, didn't you know this was going to happen?

Beatie *shakes her head.*

Mrs Bryant   So *we're* stubborn are we?

Jenny   Shut you up Mother, the girl's upset.

Mrs Bryant   Well I can see that, I can see that, he ent coming, I can see that, and we're here like bloody fools, I can see that.

Pearl   Well did you quarrel all that much Beatie?

Beatie (*as if discovering this for the first time*)   He always wanted me to help him but I never could. Once he tried to teach me to type but soon ever I made a mistake I'd give up. I'd give up every time! I couldn't bear making mistakes. I don't know why, but I couldn't bear making mistakes.

Mrs Bryant   Oh – so we're hearin' the other side o' the story now are we?

Beatie   He used to suggest I start to copy real objects on to my paintings instead of only abstracts and I never took heed.

Mrs Bryant   Oh, so you never took heed.

Jenny   Shut you up I say.

Beatie   He gimme a book sometimes and I never bothered to read it.

Frank (*not maliciously*)   What about all this discussion we heard of?

Beatie   I *never* discussed things. He used to beg me to discuss things but I never saw the point on it.

Pearl   And he got riled because o' that?

Beatie (*trying to understand*)   I didn't have any patience.

Mrs Bryant   Now it's coming out.

Beatie   I couldn't help him – I never knew patience. Once he looked at me with terrified eyes and said, 'We've been together for three years but you don't know who I am or what I'm trying to say – and you don't care do you?'

Mrs Bryant   And there she was tellin' me.

Beatie I never knew what he wanted – I didn't think it mattered.

Mr Bryant And there she was gettin' us to solve the moral problem and now we know she didn't even do it herself. That's a rum 'un, ent it?

Mrs Bryant The apple don't fall far from the tree – that it don't.

Beatie (*wearily*) So you're proud on it? You sit there smug and you're proud that a daughter of yours wasn't able to help her boy friend? Look at you. All of you. You can't say anything. You can't even help your own flesh and blood. Your daughter's bin ditched. It's your problem as well isn't it? I'm part of your family aren't I? Well, help me then! Give me words of comfort! Talk to me – for God's sake, someone talk to me (*She cries at last.*)

Mr Bryant Well, what do we do now?

Mrs Bryant We sit down and we eat that's what we do now.

Jenny Don't be soft Mother, we can't leave the girl crying like that.

Mrs Bryant Well, blust, 'tent my fault she's cryin'. I did what I could – I prepared all this food, I'd've treated him as my own son if he'd come but he hevn't! We got a whole family gathering specially to greet him, all on us look, but he hevn't come. So what am I supposed to do?

Beatie My God, Mother, I hate you – the only thing I ever wanted and I weren't able to keep him, I didn't know how. I hate you, I hate . . .

Mrs Bryant *slaps* **Beatie***'s face. Everyone is a little shocked at this harsh treatment.*

Mrs Bryant There! I hed enough!

Mr Bryant Well what d'you wanna do that for?

Mrs Bryant   I hed enough. All this time she've bin home
she've bin tellin' me I didn't do this and I didn't do that and
I hevn't understood half what she've said and I've hed
enough. She talk about bein' part o' the family but she've
never lived at home since she've left school look. Then she
go away from here and fill her head wi' high-class squit and
then it turn out she don't understand any on it herself. It
turn out she do just the same things she say I do. (*Into*
Beatie*'s face.*) Well, am I right gal? I'm right ent I? When
you tell me I was stubborn, what you mean was that *he* told
you *you* was stubborn – eh? When you tell me I don't
understand you mean *you* don't understand isn't it? When
you tell me I don't make no effort you mean *you* don't make
no effort. Well, what you blaming me for? Blaming me all
the time! I hevn't bin responsible for you since you left
home – you bin on your own. She think I like it, she do!
Thinks I like it being cooped up in this house all day. Well
I'm telling you my gal – I don't! There! And if I had a
chance to be away working somewhere the whole lot on
you's could go to hell – the lot on you's. All right so I am a
bloody fool – all right! So I know it! A whole two weeks I've
bin told it. Well, so then I can't help you my gal, no that I
can't, and you get used to that once and for all.

Beatie   No you can't Mother, I know you can't.

Mrs Bryant   I suppose doin' all those things for him
weren't enough. I suppose he weren't satisfied wi' goodness
only.

Beatie   Oh, what's the use.

Mrs Bryant   Well, don't you sit there an' sigh gal like you
was Lady Nevershit. I ask you something. Answer me. You
do the talking then. Go on – you say you know something
we don't so *you* do the talking. Talk – go on, talk gal.

Beatie (*despairingly*)   I can't Mother, you're right – the
apple don't fall far from the tree do it? You're right, I'm like
you. Stubborn, empty, wi' no tools for livin'. I got no roots

in nothing. I come from a family o' farm labourers yet I ent
got no roots – just like town people – just a mass o' nothin'.

Frank   Roots, gal? What do you mean, roots?

Beatie (*impatiently*)   Roots, roots, roots! Christ, Frankie,
you're in the fields all day, you should know about growing
things. Roots! The things you come from, the things that
feed you. The things that make you proud of yourself –
roots!

Mr Bryant   You got a family ent you?

Beatie   I'm not talking about family roots – I mean – the
– I mean – Look! Ever since it begun the world's bin
growin' hasn't it? Things hev happened, things have bin
discovered, people have bin thinking and improving and
inventing but what do we know about it all?

Jimmy   What is she on about?

Beatie (*various interjections*)   What do you mean, what am I
on about? I'm talking! Listen to me! I'm tellin' you that the
world's bin growing for two thousand years and we hevn't
noticed it. I'm telling you that we don't know what we are
or where we come from. I'm telling you something's cut us
off from the beginning. I'm telling you we've got no roots.
Blimey Joe! We've all got large allotments, we all grow
things around us so we should know about roots. You know
how to keep your flowers alive don't you Mother? Jimmy –
you know how to keep the roots of your veges strong and
healthy. It's not only the corn that need strong roots, you
know, it's us too. But what've we got? Go on, tell me,
what've we got? We don't know where we push up from and
we don't bother neither.

Pearl   Well, I aren't grumbling.

Beatie   You say you aren't – oh yes, you say so, but look
at you. What've you done since you come in? Hev you said
anythin'? I mean really said or done anything to show
you're alive? Alive! Blust, what do it mean? Do you know

what it mean? Any of you? Shall I tell you what Susie said when I went and saw her? She say she don't care if that ole atom bomb drop and she die – that's what she say. And you know why she say it? I'll tell you why, because if she had to care she'd have to do something about it and she find *that* too much effort. Yes she do. She can't be bothered – she's too bored with it all. That's what we all are – we're all too bored.

Mrs Bryant   Blust woman – bored you say, bored? You say Susie's bored, with a radio and television an' that? I go t'hell if she's bored!

Beatie   Oh yes, we turn on a radio or a TV set maybe, or we go to the pictures – if them's love stories or gangsters – but isn't that the easiest way out? Anything so long as we don't have to make an effort. Well, am I right? You know I'm right. Education ent only books and music – it's asking questions, all the time. There are millions of us, all over the country, and no one, not one of us, is asking questions, we're all taking the easiest way out. Everyone I ever worked with took the easiest way out. We don't fight for anything, we're so mentally lazy we might as well be dead. Blust, we are dead! And you know what Ronnie say sometimes? He say it serves us right! That's what he say – it's our own bloody fault!

Jimmy   So that's us summed up then – so we know where *we* are then!

Mrs Bryant   Well if he don't reckon we count nor nothin', then it's as well he didn't come. There! It's as well he didn't come.

Beatie   Oh, *he* thinks we count all right – living in mystic communion with nature. Living in mystic bloody communion with nature (*indeed*). But us count? Count Mother? I wonder. Do we? Do you think we really count. You don' wanna take any notice of what them ole papers say about the workers bein' all-important these days – that's all squit! 'Cos we aren't. Do you think when the really talented people in the country get to work they get to work for us? Hell if they do! Do you think they don't know we 'ont make the effort? The writers don't write thinkin' we can understand, nor the painters don't paint expecting us to be interested – that they don't, nor don't the composers give out music thinking we can appreciate it. 'Blust,' they say, 'the masses is too stupid for us to come down to them. Blust,' they say, 'if they don't make no effort why should we bother?' So you know who come along? The slop singers and the pop writers and the film makers and women's magazines and the Sunday papers and the picture-strip love stories – that's who come along, and you don't have to make no effort for them, it come easy. 'We know where the money lie,' they say, 'hell we do! The workers've got it so let's give them what they want. If they want slop songs and film idols we'll give 'em that then. If they want words of one syllable, we'll give 'em that then. If they want the third-rate, *blust!* We'll give 'em *that* then. Anything's good enough for them 'cos they don't ask for no more!' The whole stinkin' commercial world insults us and we don't care a damn. Well, Ronnie's right – it's our own bloody fault. We want the third-rate – we got it! We got it! We got it! We . . .

Suddenly **Beatie** *stops as if listening to herself. She pauses, turns with an ecstatic smile on her face –*

D'you hear that? D'you hear it? Did you listen to me? I'm talking. Jenny, Frankie, Mother – I'm not quoting no more.

Mrs Bryant (*getting up to sit at table*)   O hell, I hed enough of her – let her talk a while she'll soon get fed up.

The others join her at the table and proceed to eat and murmur.

Beatie   Listen to me someone. (*As though a vision were revealed to her.*) God in heaven, *Ronnie!* It does work, it's happening to me, I can feel it's happening, I'm beginning, on my own two feet – I'm beginning . . .

The murmur of the family sitting down to eat grows as **Beatie***'s last cry is heard. Whatever she will do they will continue to live as before. As* **Beatie** *stands alone, articulate at last –*

The curtain falls.

John Arden was born in Barnsley, Yorkshire, in 1930. While studying architecture at Cambridge and Edinburgh universities, he began to write plays, four of which were premièred at the Royal Court Theatre: *The Waters of Babylon, Live Like Pigs, Serjeant Musgrave's Dance* and *The Happy Haven*; while a fifth, *The Workhouse Donkey*, was produced at the Festival Theatre, Chichester. For a year he held an Annual Fellowship in Playwriting at Bristol University, and Bristol Old Vic produced *Ironhand*, his free adaptation of Goethe's *Goetz von Berlichingen*. *Armstrong's Last Goodnight* was first produced at the Glasgow Citizen's Theatre and later at the National Theatre. *Left-Handed Liberty* was specially commissioned by the Corporation of London to commemorate the 750th Anniversary of Magna Carta and was produced at the Mermaid Theatre. Recent revivals of Arden's plays include *Live Like Pigs* (Royal Court Theatre, London, 1993) and *Armstrong's Last Goodnight* (Edinburgh Festival, 1994). He is married to Margaretta D'Arcy, with whom he has collaborated on many plays. Arden's first novel, *Silence Among the Weapons* (1982), was short-listed for the Booker-McConnell Prize for Fiction. His other novels are: *Books of Bale* (1988), *Cogs Tyrannic* (1991), which won the PEN 'Silver Pen' Award, and *Jack Juggler and the Emporor's Whore* (1995). He also won the V. S. Pritchett Award in 1999 for his short story 'Breach of Trust'.

Serjeant Musgrave's Dance

An Un-historical Parable

Introductory Note

In 1958, during the dress-parade of *Live Like Pigs*, I was sitting at the back of the Royal Court, watching the actors in their drab costumes move about in a new set, a monochrome of various shades of grey. I thought, 'Oh, yes. That's what I asked for, that's what I've got. Gritty realism, right? a black-and-white socially conscious movie. Wouldn't it be nice to have at least one character in a bright red coat like an old-fashioned soldier?

Later on, when the play itself was shaping itself in my mind, sprung off by this incident as much as by the hideous contemporary activities of the British Army in Cyprus, I talked about it to the folk-music authority, the late A. L. Lloyd. He was at the Royal Court to sing the between-scene stanzas in *Pigs*, to tunes of his own digging-out. And thereupon he dug out, for me, a whole set of eighteenth- and nineteenth-century ballads about the old pre-Kipling redcoat soldiery. I put one of them straight into the play (Sparky's song, Act One, Scene One), and the rest into the coal-box of my working imagination – together with my father's collection of photographic postcards of his own old regiment, the East Yorkshire, taken at the end of the Victorian era in their garrison at Beverley. The album with these pictures had been one of the treats of my childhood, only to be looked at with washed hands.

This is a realistic, but not naturalistic play. Therefore the design of the scenes and costumes must be in some sense stylised. The paintings of L. S. Lowry might suggest a suitable mood. Scenery must be sparing – only those pieces of architecture, furniture, and properties actually used in the action need be present: and they should be thoroughly realistic, so that the audience sees a selection from the details of everyday life rather than a generalised impression of the whole of it. A similar rule should also govern the direction and the acting. If this is done, the obvious difficulties, caused by the mixture of verse, prose, and song in the play, will be considerably lessened.

The exact date of the play is deliberately not given. In the London production, the details of costume covered approximately the years between 1860 and 1880. For instance, the soldiers wore the scarlet tunics and spiked helmets characteristic of the later (or 'Kipling') epoch, while the Constable was dressed in tall hat and tail coat as an early Peeler – his role in the play suggesting a rather primitive type of police organisation.

The songs should be sung to folk-song airs. There are many available tunes which equally well suit the various songs – perhaps these are as good as any:

Sparky's song (Act One, Scene 1): 'Six Jolly Wee Miners' – Scottish.

Sparky's song and chorus (Act Two, Scene 2): 'Blow away the Morning Dew' – English.

Sparky's song – (Act Two, Scene 3): 'The Black Horse' – Irish.

Attercliffe's song (Act Three, Scene 2): First three stanzas – 'John Barleycorn' – English Air. Final stanza – 'John Barleycorn' – Irish Air.

Musgrave's song (Act Three, Scene 1): proved in production to be more satisfactory if the words were spoken against a background of drum rolls and recorded music.

The characters perhaps need a few notes of description:

The Soldiers: these are regulars and seasoned men. They should all have moustaches and an ingrained sense of discipline. Musgrave is aged between thirty and forty, tall, swart, commanding, sardonic but never humorous; he could well have served under Cromwell. Attercliffe is aged about fifty, grey-haired, melancholy, a little embittered. He is the senior O.R. of the party and conscious of his responsibility. Hurst, in his twenties, is bloody-minded, quick-tempered, handsome, cynical, tough, but not quite as intelligent as he thinks he is. Sparky, also in his twenties, is easily led, easily driven, inclined to hide from himself behind a screen of silly stories and irritating clownishness. The Dragoon Officer is little more than the deus-ex-machina at the end of the play.

All he needs to be is tall, calm, cold, and commanding. His Trooper is a tough, reliable soldier.

The Townsmen: The Mayor is a bustling, shrewd, super-ficially jovial man with a coarse accent and an underlying inclination to bully. The Parson is very much a gentleman: he is conscious of the ungentlemanly nature of the community in which he lives. He must have the accent and manners of a balked aristocrat rather than a stage-clergyman. He too has some inclination to bully. The Constable has a continual inclination to bully, except when in the presence of his superiors. He is as inefficient as he is noisy. The Colliers are all embittered but not so as to make them unpleasant. Walsh is a strong man, physically and morally. He knows what he wants and is entirely impatient with those who are not so single-minded. The Slow Collier is not particularly intelligent but has a vacuous good humour. The Pugnacious Collier is pugnacious, and very quick to show it. The Bargee is something of a grotesque, a hunchback (though this should not be over-emphasised), very rapid in his movements, with a natural urge towards intrigue and mischief.

The Women: The Landlady is a large, immobile widow of about fifty. She sits behind her bar and watches everything that happens. She is clearly a woman of deep sympathies and intelligence, which she disguises with the normal north-country sombre pessimism. Annie is a big-boned girl, not particularly attractive, but in an aggressive sort of way she provokes the men. Her emotional confusion expresses itself in a deliberately enigmatic style of speech and behaviour. Her voice is harsh.

As for the 'Meaning of the Play': I do not think that an introductory note is a suitable place for a lengthy analysis of the work, but in view of the obvious puzzlement with which it was greeted by the critics, perhaps a few points may be made. This is not a nihilistic play. This is not (except perhaps unconsciously) a symbolistic play. Nor does it advocate bloody revolution. I have endeavoured to write about the violence that is so evident in the world, and to do so through a story that is partly one of wish-fulfilment. I think that many of us must at some time have felt an overpowering urge to match some particularly outrageous piece of violence with an even greater and more outrageous retaliation. Musgrave tries to do this: and the fact that the sympathies of the play are clearly with him in his original horror, and then turn against him and his intended remedy, seems to have bewildered many people. I would suggest, however, that a study of the roles of the women, and of Private Attercliffe, should be sufficient to remove any doubts as to where the 'moral' of the play lies. Accusations of nihilism seem to derive from the scene where the Colliers turn away from Musgrave and join in the general dance around the beer barrel. Again, I would suggest that an unwillingness to dwell upon unpleasant situations that do not immediately concern us is a general human trait, and recognition of it need imply neither cynicism nor despair. Complete pacifism is a very hard doctrine: and if this play appears to advocate it with perhaps some timidity, it is probably because I am naturally a timid man – and also because I know that if I am hit I very easily hit back: and I do not care to preach too confidently what I am not sure I can practise.

J.A.

Serjeant Musgrave's Dance was first performed at the Royal
Court Theatre on 22 October 1959, with the following cast:

Private Sparky	Donal Donnelly
Private Hurst	Alan Dobie
Private Attercliffe	Frank Finlay
Bludgeon, *a bargee*	James Bree
Serjeant Musgrave	Ian Bannen
The Parson	Richard Caldicot
Mrs Hitchcock	Freda Jackson
Annie	Patsy Byrne
The Constable	Michael Hunt
The Mayor	Stratford Johns
A Slow Collier	Jack Smethurst
A Pugnacious Collier	Colin Blakely
Walsh, *an earnest collier*	Harry Gwynn Davies
A Trooper of Dragoons	Barry Wilsher
An Officer of Dragoons	Clinton Greyn

Produced by Lindsay Anderson
Music by Dudley Moore
Decor by Jocelyn Herbert

The play is set in a mining town in the north of England
eighty years ago. It is winter.

Act One

Scene One

A canal wharf. Evening.

Hurst *and* **Attercliffe** *are playing cards on the top of a side-drum. A few yards away,* **Sparky** *stands, as though on guard, clapping himself to keep warm. There is a pile of three or four heavy wooden boxes with the WD broad arrow stencilled on them, and a lantern set on top.*

Sparky Brr, oh a cold winter, snow, dark. We wait too long, that's the trouble. Once you've started, keep on travelling. No good sitting to wait in the middle of it. Only makes the cold night colder. (*He sings.*)

> One day I was drunk, boys, on the Queen's Highway
> When a recruiting party came beating that way.
> I was enlisted and attested before I did know
> And to the Royal Barracks they forced me to go.

Brr! And they talk of the Crimea! Did I ever tell you that one about the field kitchens at Sebastopol? Well, there was this red-haired provost-sarnt, y'see . . . and then the corporal-cook – now *he'd* got no hair at all . . . now the Commissary in that Regiment was – oh . . . (*He finds no one paying attention.*) Who's winning?

Hurst I'm winning.

Attercliffe Oho, no you're not. The black spades carry the day. Jack, King and Ace. *We* throw the red Queen over. That's another shilling, you know. Let's have it.

Hurst All right. Deal agen, boy. Or no, no, *my* deal, this game. Now let's see if I can't turn some good cards on to my side for a difference. Here: one, two, three, four . . . (*He deals the cards.*)

Sparky How much longer we got to wait, I'd like to know. I want to be off aboard that damned barge and away.

What's happened to our Black Jack Musgrave, eh? Why
don't he come and give us the word to get going?

Attercliffe   He'll come on the stroke, as he said. He works
his life to bugle and drum, this serjeant. You ever seen him
late?

Sparky   No. (*He sings.*)

When first I deserted I thought myself free
Till my cruel sweetheart informed upon me –

Attercliffe (*sharply*)   I don't think you ought to sing *that*
one.

Sparky   Why not? It's true, isn't it? (*He sings.*)

Court martial, court martial, they held upon me
And the sentence they passed was the high gallows tree.

Hurst (*dropping cards and springing up in a rage*)   Now shut it,
will you! God-damned devil of a song to sing on this sort of
a journey! He said you didn't ought to, so don't! (*He glances
nervously around.*)

Sparky   Ha, there's nobody to hear us. You're safe as a
bloody blockhouse out here – I'm on the sentry, boy, *I'm*
your protection.

Attercliffe (*irritably*)   You make sure you are then. Go on:
keep watching.

Sparky (*returns to his guard*)   Ah. Ha-ha . . . Or did you
think *he* could hear you? (*He gestures towards the boxes.*) Maybe,
maybe . . . *I* thought I heard him laugh.

Attercliffe   Steady, boy.

Sparky (*a little wildly*)   Steady yourself, you crumbling old
cuckold. He might laugh, who knows? Well, make a rattling
any road. Mightn't he, soldier boy?

Hurst   Are you coming funny wi' me –

Sparky   Funny? About *him*? You don't tell me he don't
know what we're at. Why shouldn't he have a laugh at it, if
that's how he feels?

Hurst   Arrh, you're talking daft.

Sparky   Now don't you be nervous, boy: not for *you* to be
nervous. You're a man and a soldier! Or an old red rag
stretched over four pairs o' bones – well, what's the odds?
Eh?

Hurst (*after glaring angrily, sits down again*)   All right . . . All
right, play.

They play in silence. **Sparky** *hums and blows his knuckles. Then he
starts.*

Sparky   Who goes there!

The **Bargee** *enters with a lantern, whistling 'Michael Finnegan'.*

Bargee   Hooroar, my jolly buckos! It's only old Joe
Bludgeon, the Captain of the Lugger. Crooked old Joe.
Heh, heh. And what's the news with you? Are we ready yet,
are we?

Sparky   Ready for what?

Bargee   Ready for off, of course, what do you think? Are
we?

Attercliffe   No.

Bargee   Why not, then?

Attercliffe   'Cos it's not time, that's why not. Half-past
seven, you was told.

Bargee   Oh, it's as near as –

Attercliffe   No begod it's not, and he won't be here till it
is.

Bargee   Ah, the serjeant, eh?

Attercliffe   Aye, the serjeant. Is your barge up yet?

Bargee   It's up. And the old horse waiting.

Attercliffe   Then we'll start to load.

Hurst   Hey, we've not finished the game.

Attercliffe   Save it, mucker. You heard what Black Jack said.

Hurst   All right. All right.

Bargee   You can load these smaller cases 'side of the cabin. What you got in 'em, for Godsake? Ten ton and a half here.

Sparky (*kicking one of them*)   There's a Gatling gun in that one. You know what a Gatling gun is, friend?

Bargee   I don't, and I don't care neither, tell you truth of it. By Lordy, what a life, the bloody Army. Do they still tie you fellers up and stripe you across with the cat-o'-nine-tails, eh?

Hurst   No they don't.

Attercliffe *and* **Hurst** *start carrying the cases out.*

Bargee (*gloating*)   Heheh, when I wor a young lad they told me, they did. Whack, whack, whack. Ooh, cruel it was. You know what they used to call 'em in them days – soldiers, I mean? Eh?

Sparky   I know a lot o' names for calling soldiers.

Bargee   I'll bet you don't know this one, though. Heh. Bloodred roses, that was it. What d'you think o' that, eh? Whack, whack, whack. Bloodred roses, eh? (*He calls offstage.*) Not there, don't put it there, give me some room to swing me tiller, can't you! Soldiers. Get 'em aboard a barge, you'd be as well off wi' a row of deaf niggers from Peru. That's right, now leave it where you've dropped it, and come ashore before you capsize her – you bloodred bloody roses, you!

Hurst *re-enters.*

Hurst   That's enough of that, matey. Watch it.

Musgrave *enters.*

Musgrave (*to the* **Bargee**)   Aye, you watch it. Now I'll tell you just once, old man, and that's all. We travel on your barge, passengers: we pay our fare. So don't you talk to my men like they're deck-hands. Clear?

Bargee   Oh it's clear, serjeant, I only wanted a little joke.

Musgrave   Aye. And now you've had one. So be thankful.

Attercliffe *re-enters.*

Attercliffe (*as he and* **Hurst** *pick up the remaining smaller boxes*) We got the Gatling loaded on, serjeant, and we're fetching the rest of it. Then there's just the drum and the other box left. Any news?

Musgrave (*quietly to him*)   We're all right. Don't worry.

Attercliffe *and* **Hurst** *go out with their load.* **Musgrave** *taps the drum meditatively and turns to the* **Bargee**.

I say, you, Bargee. Is it going to snow again before tomorrow?

Bargee   Likely. There's ice coming on the water too. Give her another day and this canal'll be closed. They say the road over the moors is fast already with the drifts. You've chose a merry time o' year beating up for recruities, haven't you? What you got in here? Another Gatling gun? (*He smacks the last box*).

Musgrave   Why not? Show 'em all the best equipment, glamourise 'em, man, fetch 'em in like conies . . . Now get this last box loaded, and be careful. And then we're all ready. You can start.

Attercliffe *and* **Hurst**, *having returned, pick up the box and carry it out,* **Sparky** *going with them, the drum slung on his shoulder.* **Musgrave** *takes the soldiers' lantern and makes a rapid circuit of*

*the stage to see if anything is left. He stands for a moment looking out
in the direction from which he has come in.*

Bargee (*waiting for him*)   This your first trip to the coalmining towns, serjeant?

Musgrave   It is.

Bargee   Ooh, brr, bitter and bleak: hungry men for the
Queen. If you're used to a full belly, you'll want it when you
get there.

Musgrave (*curtly*)   It's not material. We have our duty. A
soldier's duty is a soldier's life.

Bargee   Ah, duty.

    The Empire wars are far away
    For duty's sake we sail away
    Me arms and legs is shot away
    And all for the wink of a shilling and a drink . . .

Come on, me cheery serjeant, you've not left nowt behind.

They go out after the soldiers.

Scene Two

The bar of a public house.

Mrs Hitchcock *is sitting in the body of the room, talking to the*
Parson, *who is very much at his ease, with a glass of brandy in his
hand.* **Annie** *is polishing glasses etc. behind the bar.*

Parson   No. No, madam, no. I cannot be seen to
countenance idleness, pauperism, beggary. If no one comes
to buy your drink, I am sorry for you. But the fact is,
madam, a little less drunkenness and disorder will do this
town no harm. The Church is not a speculative bank, you
know, to subsidise pot-houses.

Mrs Hitchcock (*sulkily*)   Always a respectable house.

Parson   What?

Mrs Hitchcock   Always a respectable house, reverend.
Aye, if not, why renew the licence? You're a magistrate, you
know. You could have spoken agen me on me application.
But you didn't.

Parson   That is not to the purpose, Mrs Hitchcock. The
Bench allows that there have to be public houses to permit
an outlet for the poorer sort of people, but in times of
regrettable industrial conflict it is better that as many of
them as possible remain empty. If the colliers cannot afford
drink because of the strike – because of their own stupidity –
then there is the less likelihood of their being inflamed to
acts of violence. I am not at all certain that the Bench ought
not to withdraw all licences altogether until the pits are
working.

Mrs Hitchcock   That'd be grand. See half a dozen
publicans going on the parish – beer-dregs from the
workhouse served to the Trade – ooh, talk of arsy-versy! (*She
laughs throatily.*)

Parson   I'm quite sure that would not be necessary.

Mrs Hitchcock (*reasonably*)   Now, look, reverend, you've
been taking me crossroads since the minute I began. All I
asked you in to say is this: this strike is bad for the town.
Well, I mean, of course, that means me. But it means you
too. *And* it means His Worship the Mayor: oh aye, aye:

> I am a proud coalowner
> And in scarlet here I stand.
> Who shall come or who shall go
> Through all my coal-black land?

(*She laughs again.*) Eh, if we can't have a laugh, we'll starve!

Parson   You are impertinent. I have nothing more to say.

Mrs Hitchcock   Ah, but I come to you because you're
Church, you're charity. Go on, reverend, you tell the Mayor
to agree with his men and give them a good price, then

they'll buy and sell in the town and they'll drink in this taproom, and – ho-hoo – who knows, they might even come to church! That'll be the day.

The **Parson** *turns irritably from her and goes to the door.*

The **Bargee** *enters and confronts him.*

Bargee (*touching his cap mockingly*)   Parson.

Parson (*coldly*)   Good afternoon.

Bargee   Cold enough for you, eh?

Parson (*trying to pass*)   It is cold, yes.

Bargee   How's the strike?

Parson   It is not yet settled.

Bargee   No, I bet it's not, and all. Hey missus!

Mrs Hitchcock   Hello.

Bargee   A quart o' taddy. Best!

Mrs Hitchcock (*impassive*)   Can you pay for it?

Bargee   'Course I can pay – wait a minute, Parson, just a minute, all under control – I'm not one of your colliery agitators, you know. *I'm* still in work. I've news for you.

Mrs Hitchcock (*to* **Annie**)   He says he can pay. Draw him his quart.

Bargee (*to the* **Parson**)   I didn't think, like, to find you here, but, eh, well, seeing as how here you are – canal's froze up, you know.

Parson   Well?

Bargee   Well. Last barge come in this morning. *My* barge. There was passengers.

Parson   I am not really interested.

Bargee (*significantly*)   Four on 'em, Parson. Soldiers.

Annie *hands the* **Bargee** *his tankard.*

Parson (*in some alarm*)   Soldiers! Already! Who sent for them? Why was I not told? This could be very dangerous –

Bargee   They're not here for what you think, you know. Not yet, any road. You see, they've come recruiting.

Parson (*relieved, but vexed*)   Oh . . . Well, what if they have? Why bother me with it? You're just wasting time, man. Come on, get out of my way . . .

Bargee (*still detaining him*)   Eh, but, Parson, you're a magistrate.

Parson   Of course I'm a magistrate.

Bargee   You're a power, you are: in a town of trouble, in a place of danger. Yes. You're the word and the book, aren't you? Well then: soldiers. Recruiting. Useful?

Parson (*beginning to follow his drift*)   H'm. I do not think the Bench is in any real need of *your* suggestions. But I am obliged to you for the news. Thank you.

He gives the **Bargee** *a coin and leaves.*

Bargee (*flipping the coin*)   Heh, heh, I said I could pay.

He gives it to **Annie** *and starts whistling 'Michael Finnegan'.* **Annie** *goes back to the bar.* **Mrs Hitchcock** *takes the coin from her and tests it between her teeth.*

Mrs Hitchcock   Soldiers. Annie, love, you could tell us what soldiers is good for.

Annie (*sullen*)   Why should I tell you?

Bargee (*gleefully*)   Go on, go on, lassie, tell us about the soldiers. She knows the good red coat button-to-back, I'll bet. Go on, it's a cold day, warm it up for us. Heh, heh, our strong Annie's the champion, eh?

He smacks her on the bottom. She swerves angrily.

Annie   When I've given you leave: and not afore. You bloody dog, sit down.

Bargee (*subsiding in mock terror*)   Ooh, sharp, sharp.

Mrs Hitchcock   Aye, so sit down . . . Go on, Annie, tell us.

Annie   I'll tell you for what a soldier's good:

> To march behind his roaring drum,
> Shout to us all: 'Here I come.
> I've killed as many as I could –
> I'm stamping into your fat town
> From the war and to the war
> And every girl can be my whore
> Just watch me lay them squealing down.
> And that's what he does and so do we.
> Because we know he'll soon be dead
> We strap our arms round the scarlet red
> Then send him weeping over the sea.
> Oh he will go and a long long way.
> Before he goes we'll make him pay
> Between the night and the next cold day –
> By God there's a whole lot more I could say –

What good's a bloody soldier 'cept to be dropped into a slit in the ground like a letter in a box. How many did you bring with you – is it four?

Bargee   Aye. Four.

Annie   That's four beds in this house?

Mrs Hitchcock   I should hope it's in this house. It's the best house in town.

Annie (*in a sudden outburst*)   Then you'd do well to see they stay four nights because I'll not go with more nor one in one night, no, not for you nor for all of Egypt!

She lets out a howl and rushes out of the door behind the bar, clattering a tin tray full of tankards on to the floor.

Bargee   Oooh, Lordy! Champion, strong, and sharp. Annie! Tell us some more!

Mrs Hitchcock (*crossly*)   Let her alone. She's said enough for you, hasn't she? It's not right to set her off . . . I suppose they *are* coming to this house?

Bargee   Oh surely, aye, surely. *I* told 'em: *I* took care.

A rat-tat-tat on the drum heard, off.

There, you see, they're coming.

Sparky *enters magnificently, beating the drum.*

Sparky   Ho-ho, atten-tion! Stand by your beds! Name of the Queen, missus – has he told you – there's four of us: we three, we'll settle for palliasses in the loft, but the serjeant he wants a big brass bed with knobs on, that's his fancy! Can you do it?

Mrs Hitchcock   So here they are, the gay recruiters. Aye, I can do it, young man. I've only one room in the house. The serjeant can have that. The three of you'll have to doss down in me old stable, out back, but there's a good stove, you'll be warm. Now, who's going to pay? You or the Queen?

Sparky   Oh, Queen at end of it all, I suppose.

Mrs Hitchcock   But you at beginning, eh?

Sparky   Oh-oh, chalk it up, you know . . . we've brought some gear with us too.

Bargee   Ten and a half ton. Nigh foundered the old barge, it did, I can tell you.

Sparky   But we got here, friend, didn't we? Like we get ourselves to everywhere we go, we do. No question o' that, y'see.

Bargee   Heh, heh, none.

Sparky (*calls to offstage*)   Serjeant! We're fixed!

Musgrave (*off*)   And the equipment?

Sparky   And the equipment, missus?

Mrs Hitchcock   There's a coach-house across the yard.

Sparky (*calls to offstage*)   Coach-house across the yard, serjeant! . . . While they're taking it round there, missus, let's have a pint apiece drawn ready. Like what *he* drinks, eh? Recommend it, friend?

Bargee   You could stand your bayonet up in this, you could.

Sparky   Right, then. And we'll give you another while we're at it. That's five on 'em, pints, unless *you're* drinking with us, too, are you?

Mrs Hitchcock   Why not, soldier? Queen as pays . . . Annie! Hey Annie!

As there is no reply, she goes herself behind the bar and starts filling the tankards. **Musgrave** *enters.*

Musgrave   Is the padlock on your coach-house door a strong one, ma'am?

Mrs Hitchcock   Likely so.

Musgrave   Valuable equipment, y'see. Your window in there's barred, I notice.

Mrs Hitchcock   That's right.

Musgrave (*picking up a tankard*)   Good . . . This for me?

Mrs Hitchcock   If you want it.

The other two soldiers enter.

Attercliffe   The cases are all locked up and safe, serjeant.

Musgrave (*indicates drinks*)   Very good. Here you are.

Hurst *and* **Attercliffe**   Thank you, serjeant.

Bargee (*raising his drink*)   Good health to Her Majesty; to
Her Majesty's wars; to the girls we leave behind us. Drink!

They all drink.

Mrs Hitchcock (*raising her drink*)

    Into the river, out of the river
    Once I was dry, now I am wet
    But hunger and cold they hold me yet.

They drink again, with a certain puzzlement at the toast.

Mrs Hitchcock   They hold this town today, any road,
serjeant; or had you been told?

Musgrave   What's the matter?

Mrs Hitchcock   No work in the colliery. The owner
calls it a strike, the men call it a lock-out, we call it
starvation.

The **Constable** *enters violently.*

Constable   His Worship the Mayor.

Mrs Hitchcock   Eh?

Constable   I said, His Worship the Mayor!

Bargee   Oho, *now*, me jolly buckos, give attention, stand-
to, to the present!

Constable (*to the* **Bargee**)   Sssh – ssh –

Bargee   Heh, heh, heh –

The **Mayor** *enters at speed, wearing his gold chain. After him comes
the* **Parson**. **Musgrave** *calls his men to attention.*

Mayor   Mrs Hitchcock, I'm seeking the soldiers. Ah, here
they are! Well, I'm the Mayor of this town, I own the
colliery, I'm a worried man. So I come seeking you when I
could send for you, what do you think of that? Let's have a
look at you . . . Ah. Haha . . . Clear the snug a minute,

missus. I want a private word with the Parson. Serjeant, be ready outside when I send for you.

Musgrave   At your service, sir . . . Come on.

Beckoned by **Mrs Hitchcock***, he leads his party out behind the bar.*

Constable (*propelling the* **Bargee** *to the street door*)   Go on, you, out this road.

Bargee (*dodging him*)   Oo-er –

> Constable, Constable alive or dead
> His head is of leather and his belly's of lead.

Go – whoops . . . How are you, Parson?

He ducks out, whistling 'Michael Finnegan'.

Mrs Hitchcock (*sourly, to the* **Mayor**)   Do you want a drink?

Mayor   No.

Mrs Hitchcock   *At* your service, when you do.

She curtsies and goes out behind the bar.

Mayor   What do you think to 'em, Parson?

Parson   Fine strong men. They make me proud of my country. Mr Mayor, Britain depends upon these spirits. It is a great pity that their courage is betrayed at home by skulkers and shirkers. What do *you* think?

Mayor (*looking at him sideways*)   *I* think we'll use 'em, Parson. Temporary expedient, but it'll do. The price of coal has fell, I've had to cut me wages, I've had to turn men off. They say they'll strike, so I close me gates. We can't live like that for ever. There's two ways to solve this colliery – one is build the railway here and cut me costs of haulage, *that* takes two years and an Act of Parliament, though God knows I want to do it. The other is clear out half the population, stir up a diversion, turn their minds to summat else. The

Queen's got wars, she's got rebellions. Over the sea. All right. Beat these fellers' drums high around the town, I'll put one pound down for every Royal Shilling the serjeant pays. Red coats and flags. Get rid o' the trouble-makers. Drums and fifes and glory.

Parson (*severely*)   The soldier's calling is one of honour.

Mayor   It's more than that. It's bloody convenient. Town Constable, fetch that serjeant in!

Constable (*nervously*)   Er, excuse me, Your Worship. A point. Soldiers, you see. Now, I've got a very small force in this town. Only one other regular officer, you know: the rest of them deputy-specials – I can't trust *that* lot to stand fast and fear nowt when the time comes.

Parson   What time?

Constable   There's been stone-throwing this morning. Two of my office windows is broke. And I'm nervous – that's frank, you know – I *am*.

Mayor   Well?

Constable   Your Worship. I want these soldiers added to my force. It's all right recruiting. But what we need's patrols.

Mayor   Not yet.

Constable   Your Worship. I'm asking you formal. You've got agitators here, and they won't stop at throwing stones: that's frank.

Mayor (*angrily*)   I said not yet. We'll try it my road first. Godsake, man, what's four soldiers agen the lot of 'em? This town's wintered up, you'll get no more help till there's a thaw. So work on that. Call in the serjeant.

Constable   Right, Your Worship. Serjeant! Come in here!

Musgrave *re-enters.*

Musgrave   Sir?

Mayor   Serjeant, we're very glad to have you. I speak for the Council, I speak for the magistrates. Now listen: there's loyal hearts and true here, and we're every man-jack of us keen to see our best lads flock to the colours. Isn't that so, Parson?

Parson (*taken a little by surprise*)   Ha-h'm – with great pride, yes.

Mayor   Right. For every Queen's Shilling you give out, I give out a golden sovereign – no, two. One for the recruit, and one to be divided among you and your three good lads. What do you say to that?

Musgrave   That's most handsome, sir.

Mayor   I should damn well think it is. How do you propose to work?

Musgrave   Sir?

Mayor   Aye, I mean, d'you tramp around the streets drumming, or set on your fannies in a pub – or what?

Musgrave   Depends what's most appropriate, sir, according to the type of town. I've not had time for a look at yours yet. But the pubs seem pretty empty, if this one's owt to go by.

Parson   They *are* empty.

Musgrave   Aye. Well, in that case, I'll have to make a reconnaissance, won't I? When I'm decided, I'll let you know.

Constable   And let me know, serjeant. I'll see you get facilities.

Musgrave   Thank you, mister.

Mayor   And while you're on about them facilities, constable, perhaps you might let in the serjeant on a few

likely names for his list, eh? Could you pick him some
passable strong-set men, could you?

Constable (*significantly*)   I could have a try, Your Worship.

Mayor   Right. Then if that's settled, I'll be off back to
town hall. I've not got time to waste wi' nattering, snug and
all though it is in here. Come along, Constable. I want a
little word wi' you about them stones.

Mayor *and* **Constable** *go out.*

Parson (*severely*)   I think I ought to make one thing clear,
serjeant. I know that it is customary for recruiting-parties to
impress themselves upon the young men of the district as
dashingly as possible, and no doubt upon the young women
also. Now I am not having any of that. There's enough
trouble in the place as it is. So remember.

Musgrave   Yes, sir. I'll remember.

Parson   I want no drunkenness, and no fornication, from
your soldiers. Need I speak plainer?

Musgrave   No, sir. There will be none. I am a religious
man.

Parson   Very well. Good day to you.

Musgrave   Good day, sir.

The **Parson** *goes.* **Musgrave** *sits down, takes out a small pocket
bible and reads.* **Mrs Hitchcock** *enters.*

Mrs Hitchcock   What, they've not all gone, already?

Musgrave   They have, ma'am.

Mrs Hitchcock   Just like, isn't it? Use my bar for a
council-parlour, leave nowt behind 'em but bad breath and
a shiny bench – *they* take care. I'm giving your three their
dinners in back. You eating with 'em?

Musgrave (*off-handed*)   No. I'll have a hand of bread and
cheese and eat it here.

Mrs Hitchcock   Drink with it?

Musgrave (*still at his book*)   No . . . Thanks, no. Just the cheese.

Mrs Hitchcock (*sourly*)   H'm, another on 'em . . . Hey, Annie! Slice o' bread and a piece o' cheese in here for this one! Pickles?

Musgrave   Eh?

Mrs Hitchcock (*annoyed*)   Pickles!

Musgrave   No . . . (*He looks up suddenly.*) Tell me, ma'am, is there many from this town lately have gone for a soldier?

Mrs Hitchcock   Some. It's not a common pleasure here – not as long as the coal wor right to sell, any road. But there was some. You'll know the sort o' reasons, I daresay?

> The yellow-haired boy lay in my bed
> A-kissing me up from me toes to me head.
> But when my apron it did grow too short
> He thought it good time to leave his sport.

Enter **Annie** *with the bread and cheese. She gives it to* **Musgrave**.

Musgrave   Thank you.

Annie (*confronting him*)   Serjeant you are.

Musgrave   That's right.

Annie   You seem a piece stronger than the rest of 'em.

He nods.

And they call you Black Jack Musgrave?

He looks at her.

Well, I'm looking at your face, mister serjeant. Now do you know what I'd say?

Musgrave   What?

Annie   The North Wind in a pair of millstones
Was your father and your mother
They got you in a cold grinding.
God help us all if they get you a brother.

She looks at him another minute, then nods her head and goes out.

Musgrave (*wryly*)   She talks a kind of truth, that lassie. Is she daft?

Mrs Hitchcock   No, no, no, I wouldn't say daft. But there's not many would let her bide in their house.

Musgrave   Tell me, ma'am. It sticks on my mind that I once had a sort of a comrade came from this town . . . Long, yellow-haired lad, like in your little verse. Name of, oh, Hickson, was it, Hickman?

Mrs Hitchcock (*astonished and disturbed*)   Ey, ey –

Musgrave   What was it now, his name – Billy – Billy –

Mrs Hitchcock (*very upset*)   Billy Hicks. Hicks. Aye, oh, strange, serjeant, strange roads bringing you along, I'd not wonder.

Musgrave   What do you mean? . . . It *was* Hicks – I remember.

Mrs Hitchcock (*reminiscently*)   Not what you'd call a bad young feller, you know – but he weren't no good neither. He'd come in here pissed of a Sat'dy night – I'd tell him straight out, 'You needn't reckon on to get any more here.' But he'd lean on this bar and he'd look at me, and he'd sing. You know – *hymns* – 'Uplift your heads, you gates of brass' – church hymns, he'd sing. Like he'd say to me, 'I'll sing for me drinking, missus' . . . hymns . . .

She hums the tune of 'Uplift your heads' and breaks off sharply.

He gave her a baby, and he went straight off to the war. Or the rebellions, they called it. They told us he was killed.

Musgrave (*without emotion*)   Aye, he was killed. He was
shot dead last year . . . Gave a baby to who?

Mrs Hitchcock (*jerks her thumb to door behind bar*)   Her.

Musgrave (*truly surprised*)   Go on?

Mrs Hitchcock   True. But when it wor born, it came a
kind of bad shape, pale, sick: it wor dead and in the ground
in no more nor two month. About the time they called him
dead, y'see. What d'you reckon to that?

Musgrave (*carelessly*)   It's not material. He was no great
friend to me. But maybe, as you said, strange. He did use to
sing. And yellow hair he had, didn't he? (*He goes to the door
behind the bar and calls.*) Have ye finished your dinners?
Because we'll take a look at the town before it gets dark.
(*Confidently to* **Mrs Hitchcock**.) What you've just been
telling me, don't tell it to these. Dead men and dead
children should bide where they're put and not be rose up
to the thoughts of the living. It's bad for discipline . . . (*He
calls again.*) Come on, let's be having you!

The **Soldiers** *come in.* **Musgrave** *points to each one as they
enter.*

East; south; west; I'll go north; I'm told it suits my nature.
Then meet at the churchyard rail and tell me what you've
seen. Let's make it sharp.

They go out.

Scene Three

The churchyard.

Sunset. **Hurst** *enters and walks about, whistling nervously. The*
Slow Collier *enters and looks at him. They pass each other, giving
each other good hard stares. The* **Slow Collier** *is about to leave the
stage when he turns round and calls.*

Slow Collier   Hey! Soldier!

Hurst   Aye?

Slow Collier   How many on you is there?

Hurst   Four.

Slow Collier   Four . . . Four dead red rooks and be damned.

Hurst   What? What's that?

Slow Collier (*contemptuously*)   Arrh . . .

He slouches out.

Hurst *makes to follow, but decides not to, and continues walking about.*

Musgrave *enters.*

Musgrave   Coldest town I ever was in. What did you see?

Hurst   Hardly a thing. Street empty, windows shut, two old wives on a doorstep go indoors the minute I come. Three men on one corner, two men on another, dirty looks and no words from any on 'em. There's one man swears a curse at me just now. That's all.

Musgrave   H'm . . .

He calls to offstage.

Hello! We're over here!

Attercliffe *enters.*

What did you see?

Attercliffe   Hardly a thing. Street empty, doors locked, windows blind, shops cold and empty. A young lass calls her kids in from playing in the dirt – she sees me coming, so she calls 'em. There's someone throws a stone –

Musgrave   A stone?

Attercliffe   Aye. I don't know who did it and it didn't hit me, but it was thrown.

Hurst   It's a cold poor town, I'm telling you, serjeant.

Musgrave   Coldest town I ever was in. And here's the fourth of us.

Enter **Sparky**.

What did you see?

Sparky   Hardly a thing. Street empty, no chimneys smoking, no horses, yesterday's horsedung frozen on the road. Three men at a corner-post, four men leaning on a wall. No words: but some chalked up on a closed-door – they said: 'Soldiers go home'.

Hurst   Go home?

Sparky   That's it, boy: home. It's a place they think we have somewhere. And what did *you* see, serjeant?

Musgrave   Nothing different from you . . . So, here is our town and here are we. All fit and appropriate.

Hurst (*breaking out suddenly*)   Appropriate? Serjeant, now we've come with you so far. And every day we're in great danger. We're on the run, in red uniforms, in a black-and-white coalfield; and it's cold; and the money's running out that you stole from the Company office; and we don't know who's heard of us or how much they've heard. Isn't it time you brought out clear just what you've got in mind?

Musgrave (*ominously*)   Aye? Is it? And any man else care to tell me what the time is?

Attercliffe (*reasonably*)   Now serjeant, please, easy – we're all your men, and we agreed –

Hurst   All right: if we *are* your men, we've rights.

Musgrave (*savagely*)   The only right *you* have is a rope around your throat and six foot six to drop from. On the run? Stolen money? I'm talking of a murdered officer, shot down in a street fight, shot down in one night's work. They put that to the rebels, but *I* know *you* were the man. We deserted, but you killed.

Hurst   I'd a good reason . . .

Musgrave   I know you had reason, else I'd not have left you alive to come with us. All I'm concerned about this minute is to tell you how you stand. And you stand in my power. But there's more to it than a bodily blackmail – isn't there? – because my power's the power of God, and that's what's brought me here and all three of you with me. You know my words and purposes – it's not just authority of the orderly room, it's not just three stripes, it's not just given to me by the reckoning of my mortal brain – well, *where* does it come from?

He flings this question fiercely at **Hurst**.

Hurst (*trying to avoid it*)   All right, I'm not arguing –

Musgrave   *Where!*

Hurst (*frantically defensive*)   I don't believe in God!

Musgrave   You don't? Then what's this?

He jabs his thumb into **Hurst**'s *cheek and appears to scrape something off it.*

Hurst   Sweat.

Musgrave   The coldest winter for I should think it's ten years, and the man sweats like a bird-bath!

Hurst (*driven in a moral corner*)   Well, why not, because –

Musgrave (*relentless*)   Go on – because?

Hurst (*browbeaten into coherence*)   All right, because I'm afraid. 'Cos I thought when I met you, I thought we'd got the same motives. To get out, get shut o' the Army – with its 'treat-you-like-dirt-but-you-do-the-dirty-work' – 'kill *him*, kill *them*, they're all bloody rebels, State of Emergency, high standard of turnout, military bearin' – so *I* thought up some killing, I said I'll get me own in. I thought o' the Rights of

Man. Rights o' the Rebels: that's *me*! Then I *went*. And
here's a serjeant on the road, he's took two men, he's
deserted same as me, he's got money, he can bribe a civvy
skipper to carry us to England . . . It's nowt to do wi' *God*. I
don't understand all that about God, why d'you bring God
into it! You've come here to tell the people and then there'd
be no more war –

Musgrave (*taking him up with passionate affirmation*)   Which *is*
the word of God! Our message without God is a bad belch
and a hiccup. You three of you, without me, are a bad belch
and a hiccup. How d'you think you'd do it, if I wasn't here?
Tell me, go on, tell me!

Hurst (*still in his corner*)   Why then I'd – I'd – I'd tell 'em,
Sarnt Musgrave, I'd bloody stand, and tell 'em, and –

Musgrave   Tell 'em *what*!

Hurst (*made to appear more stupid than he really is*)   All right:
like, the war, the Army, colonial wars, we're treated like
dirt, out there, and for to do the dirty work, and –

Musgrave (*with withering scorn*)   And they'd run you in and
run you up afore the clock struck five! You don't understand
about God! But you think, yourself, you, alone, stupid,
without a gill of discipline, illiterate, ignorant of the
Scriptures – you think you can make a whole town, a whole
nation, understand the cruelty and greed of armies, what it
means, and how to punish it! You hadn't even took the
precaution to find the cash for your travel. I paid your fare!

Hurst (*knuckling under*)   All right. You paid . . . You're the
serjeant . . . All right. Tell us what to do.

Musgrave (*the tension eased*)   Then we'll sit down, and we'll
be easy. It's cold atween these tombs, but it's private. Sit
down. Now: you can consider, and you can open your lugs
and you can listen – ssh! Wait a minute . . .

The **Slow Collier** *enters at one side, the* **Pugnacious** *and*
Earnest Colliers *at the other. All three carry pick-hefts as clubs.*

Slow Collier (*calls to the other two*)   Four on 'em, you see. They're all here together.

Pugnacious Collier   Setting in the graveyard, eh, like a coffin-load o' sick spooks.

Earnest Collier (*coming towards the soldiers*)   Which one's the serjeant?

Musgrave (*standing up*)   Talk to me.

Earnest Collier   Aye and I will too. There's a Union made at this colliery, and we're strong. When we say strike, we strike, all ends of us: that's fists, and it's pick-hefts and it's stones and it's feet. If you work in the coal-seam you carry iron on your clogs – see!

He thrusts up his foot menacingly.

Pugnacious Collier   And you fight for your life when it's needed.

Musgrave   So do some others of us.

Earnest Collier   Ah, no, lobster, *you* fight for pay. You go sailing on what they call punitive expeditions, against what you call rebels, and you shoot men down in streets. But not here. These streets is *our* streets.

Musgrave   Anything else?

Earnest Collier   No. Not this evening. Just so as you know, that's all.

Pugnacious Collier   Setting in the graveyard. Look at 'em, for Godsake. Waiting for a riot and then they'll have a murder. Why don't *we* have one *now*: it's dark enough, ent it?

Earnest Collier   Shut up. It'll do when it's time. Just so as they know, that's all.

The **Colliers** *turn to go.*

Musgrave   Wait a minute.

They pause.

Who told you we'd come to break the strike?

Earnest Collier   Eh?

Musgrave   Who told you?

Earnest Collier   Nobody told us. We don't need to be told. You see a strike: you see soldiers: there's only one reason.

Musgrave   Not this time there isn't. We haven't been sent for –

Pugnacious Collier   Get away wi' that –

Musgrave   And all soldiers aren't alike, you know. Some of us is human.

Slow Collier   } Arrh –
Pugnacious Collier } *(laughs)*

Musgrave   Now I'm in Mrs Hitchcock's bar tonight until such time as she closes it. There'll be my money on the counter, and if you want to find what I'm doing here you can come along and see. I speak fair; you take it fair. Right?

Earnest Collier   No it's not right, Johnny Clever. These streets is our streets, so you learn a warning . . . Come on, leave 'em be, *we* know what they're after. Come on . . .

The **Colliers** *go, growling threateningly.*

Attercliffe   They hate us, serjeant, don't they? Wouldn't you say that's good?

Musgrave   Because of the bad coal-trade they hate us; the rest just follows. True, there's one man talks of shooting rebels down in streets, but the others only think of bayonets turned on pitmen, and that's no good. At the present, they believe we've come to kill them. Soon they'll find we haven't, so they'll stop hating. Maybe even some o' them'll come and sign on. You'll see: His Worship's sovereigns – they'll fall too damned heavy into these boys' pockets. But we'll watch and take count, till we know the depth of the corruption. 'Cos all that we know now is that we've had to leave behind us a colonial war that is a war of sin and unjust blood.

Attercliffe (*sharply*)   All wars is sin, serjeant . . .

Musgrave (*impatient*)   I'm not discussing that. Single purpose at a single time: your generalities aren't material: this is particular – one night's work in the streets of one city, and it damned all four of us and the war it was part of. We're each one guilty of particular blood. We've come to this town to work that guilt back to where it began.

He turns to **Sparky**.

Why to this town? Say it, say it!

Sparky (*as with a conditioned reflex*)   Billy. Billy's dead. He wor my mucker, back end of the rear rank. He wor killed dead. He came from this town.

Musgrave (*relentless*)   Go on.

Sparky (*appealing*)   Serjeant –

Musgrave   Use your clear brain, man, and tell me what you're doing here! Go on.

Sparky (*incoherent with recollecting what he wants to forget*)   I'm doing here? I'm doing . . . Serjeant, you know it. 'Cos he died. That wor Billy. I got drunk. Four days and four nights. After work of one night. Absent. Not sober. Improperly dressed.

He tries to turn it into one of his jokes.

> Stick me in a cell, boys,
> Pull the prison bell
> Black Jack Musgrave
> To call the prison roll –

Sarnt, no offence – 'First ye'll serve your punishment,' he says. 'Then I'll show you how,' he says, the serjeant. I says,

'You'll show me what?' He says, 'I'll show you how your
Billy can be paid for.' . . . I didn't want to pay for him –
what had I to care for a colonial war? . . .

He meets **Musgrave***'s eye and takes a grip on his motives.*

But I *did* want to pay for him, didn't I? 'Cos that's why I'm
here. 'You go down, I'll follow' . . . You, serjeant, ent it?

> Black Jack Musgrave
> He always calls the roll.

He says:

> Go down to Billy's town
> Tell 'em how he died.

And that's what I'm doing here. The serjeant pays the fare.
Here I am, I'm paid for. Next turn's for Billy. Or all that's
left of Billy. Who'll give me an offer for his bones? Sixpence
for a bone, for a bone of my dead mucker . . .

He again avoids emotion by turning on **Hurst***, jeeringly.*

You didn't even know him when he lived, you weren't in his
squad, what do *you* care that he's dead? To you he's like
God, ent that the truth, you don't care and you're not
bothered!

Hurst (*angrily*)   Hold your noise, you dirty turd! Who are
you telling?

Sparky   You. Oh you, me boy, you. A man and a
soldier –

He meets **Musgrave***'s eye again, and his voice trails away.*

– a man and a soldier . . .

Musgrave (*emphatically*)   Aye. And *you're* a soldier. Don't
forget that. You're my man and you'll here me. You're not
on any drunk now. Now you've got discipline. You've got
grief, but good order, and it's turned to the works of God!

Sparky (*submissively*)   Yes, sarnt.

Musgrave (*to* **Hurst**)   Turned to the works of God!

Hurst (*submissively*)   Yes, sarnt.

Musgrave (*in a more encouraging voice*)   There was talk about danger. Well, I never heard of no danger yet that wasn't comparative. Compare it against your purposes. And compare it against my strategy. Remember: the roads are closed, the water's frozen, the telegraph wires are weighted down with snow, they haven't *built* the railway. We came here safe, and here we are, safe here. The winter's giving us one day, two days, three days even – that's clear for us to hold our time, take count of the corruption, then stand before this people with our white shining word, and let it dance! It's a hot coal, this town, despite that it's freezing – choose your minute and blow: and whoosh, she's flamed your roof off! They're trembling already into the strikers' riots. Well, their riots and our war are the same one corruption. This town is ours, it's ready for us: and its people, when they've heard us, and the Word of God, crying the murders that we've done – I'll tell you they'll turn to us, and they'll turn against that war!

Attercliffe (*gravely*)   All wars, Serjeant Musgrave. They've got to turn against all wars. Colonial war, do we say, no war of honour? I'm a private soldier, I never had no honour, I went killing for the Queen, I did it for me wages, that wor my life. But I've got a new life. There was one night's work, and I said: no more killing.

Hurst (*with excitement*)   It's time we did our *own* killing.

Attercliffe   No, boy, it isn't.

Hurst   Aye, and I mean it. We're all on the run, and we're all of us deserters. We're wild-wood mad and raging. We caught it overseas and now we've got to run around the English streets biting every leg to give it *them* – that can't be done without –

Musgrave (*interrupting*)   Listen to me!

Hurst (*subsiding*)   Serjeant.

Musgrave (*with angry articulation*)   We are here with a word. That's all. That's particular. Let the word dance. That's all that's material, this day and for the next. What happens afterwards, the Lord God will provide. I am with you, He said. Abide with Me in Power. A Pillar of Flame before the people. What we show here'll lead forward for ever, against dishonour, and greed, and murder-for-greed! There is our duty, the new, deserter's duty: God's dance on this earth: and all that we are is His four strong legs to dance it . . . Very well. That'll do. It's dark. We'll go in. Now we'll be likely buying drinks around and so on, in the public tonight. I don't want to see any o' you with more nor you can hold. When there's danger, there's temptation. So keep it gay, but that's all. Off you go now! Take 'em in.

Attercliffe (*as the senior*)   All right then, smartly now, walking up the street. Remember, we're recruiting. I'll give you the time – left right left right.

They walk out briskly, leaving **Musgrave** *alone. As they go, the* **Bargee** *enters, and gives them a parody salute in passing.* **Musgrave** *doesn't see him, walks downstage, crosses his hands on his chest and stands to pray. The* **Bargee** *parodies his attitude behind his back.*

Musgrave   God, my Lord God. Have You or have You not delivered this town into my hands? All my life as a soldier I've made You prayers and made them straight, I've reared my one true axe against the timber and I've launched it true. My regiment was my duty, and I called Death honest, killing by the book – but it all got scrawled and mucked about and I could not think clear . . . Now I have my duties different. I'm in this town to change all soldiers' duties. My prayer is: keep my mind clear so I can weigh Judgement against the Mercy and Judgement against the Blood, and make this Dance as terrible as You have put it into my brain. The Word alone is terrible: the Deed must be worse. But I know it is Your Logic, and You will provide.

He pauses for a moment, then turns sharply on his heel and strides away after the soldiers. He still fails to see the **Bargee**. *The latter has whipped off his hat at the conclusion of* **Musgrave**'s *prayer, and now he stands looking solemnly up to Heaven. He gives a sanctimonious smirk and breaths: 'Amen'.*

Act Two

Scene One

The bar of the public house.

A scene of noise and conviviality, crowded confusion. **Mrs Hitchcock** *is seated behind the bar, drinking tea with brandy in it.* **Annie** *is going backwards and forwards in the room carrying drinks and empties.* **Musgrave** *is sitting with a tankard, calmly watching.* **Sparky** *is wearing his drum and alternately beating it and drinking and singing. The* **Slow** *and* **Pugnacious Colliers**, *well-oiled, are drinking and dancing. The* **Bargee** *is drinking and dancing and playing a mouth-organ and beating time to the singing.* **Attercliffe** *is drinking and dancing and pinning cockades to the hats of the* **Colliers**. *At intervals one of the dancers grabs hold of* **Annie** *and swirls her around, but she retains a contemptuous aloofness and carries on with her work. As the scene opens the men (save* **Musgrave***) are all joining in the chorus:*

Chorus   Blow your morning bugles
          Blow your calls ey-ho
          Form platoon and dress the ranks
          And blow, boys blow!

This chorus is sung (with progressively less correctness) by most of the men at the end of each verse of the song.

Sparky (*singing*)

          When first I came to the barracks
          My heart is grieved full sore
          For leaving of my old true love
          That I would see no more.
                    chorus

Slow Collier (*to* **Musgrave**, *who is studying a notebook*)   I'm not signing nowt. Provisional, I said, provisional.

Musgrave   Aye, aye, provisional. No one makes it different.

Sparky (*sings*)

> They made us drill and muster
> And stand our sentries round
> And I never thought I'd lay again
> A girl upon the ground.

chorus

Pugnacious Collier (*to* **Attercliffe**)   That's *my* point, *my* point, too . . . all right enlisting, aye . . . but I'm a married man –

Sparky (*sings*)

> But soon we were paraded
> And marching to the war
> And in every town the girls lay down
> And cried out loud for more.

chorus

Pugnacious Collier (*to* **Attercliffe**)   I'm not so sure I like your looks, aye, *you*!

Sparky   Me?

Pugnacious Collier (*pointing to* **Attercliffe**)   You!

Sparky (*sings*)

> And when we'd lodge in billets
> We'd beer in every can
> And the landlord's wife and daughters learnt
> Just how to love a man.

chorus

Pugnacious Collier (*going at* **Sparky**)   I'm a married man, bedamn, I've got a wife, I've got a wife, a wife . . .

Sparky   No one's taking her from you.

Pugnacious Collier   Not you?

Sparky   No.

Musgrave (*interrupting*)   All right, steady, friend, *no one.*

Slow Collier   *I'll* take her from you when you go to the war, I'll take her –

Pugnacious Collier   You?

Slow Collier   Me! Or no, no, no: I'll make do with our Annie!

He makes a drunken lurch at her which she more or less evades.

Come on then, mucker!

Foiled by **Annie***, he seizes the* **Pugnacious Collier** *and they do a clog dance together while the* **Bargee** *plays.*

Chorus while they dance, and general cheer.

Bargee   Bring 'em in some more, Annie, it's all on the Queen tonight – how many have you listed, serjeant!

Musgrave   I'm not listing no one tonight. (*He bangs with his tankard for silence.*) Now then, boys, everybody –

Bargee (*officiously*)   Everybody listen!

A roll of the drum.

Bargee   Listen!

Musgrave (*expansively*)   This is Her Majesty's hospitality – that's *all* that it is, boys, on a soldier's honour, so! Any man that drinks tonight –

Bargee   Any man that drinks tonight –

Musgrave   He drinks at the Queen's pleasure, and none of you need fear to find a shilling in your mug at the end of it – that like o' lark's finished and gone with the old days – the Army only wants good men, that's free men, of your own true will for the Empire – so drink and welcome: and all men in this town –

Bargee   All men in this town –

Musgrave   When we hold our meeting and the drum beats and we bring out our colours, then you can make your return in the signing of your names – but only those men willing! That's all: drink and away!

A roll on the drum.

Bargee   Drink and away, me boys, hurray!

Pugnacious Collier   Serjeant, you're a bleeding lobster, but you're a man! Shake me by the hand!

The **Bargee** *gives a whoop and starts to dance, playing a mouth-organ. He stumbles, and everybody laughs.*

Annie (*scornfully*)   And what regiment's *that* one, serjeant? The Backwards-Mounted-Foot?

Bargee   I'll tell you, me lovely, why not? The Queen's Own Randy Chancers: or the Royal Facing-Both-Ways – hey, me clever monkeys:

Old Joe looks out for Joe
Plots and plans and who lies low?
But the Lord provides, says Crooked Old Joe.

Musgrave (*looking sharply at him*)   Eh?

The **Bargee** *shrugs and grins.* **Musgrave** *dismisses the question.*

Bargee   Just a little joke . . . little joke: little dog, I'll be with you . . .

He whistles 'Michael Finnegan' and ducks out of the pub. Meanwhile **Sparky** *has taken off his drum and come downstage to intercept* **Annie.** **Attercliffe** *is drinking with the* **Colliers** *and one or other of these plays the drum at intervals. The going of the* **Bargee** *has made the room somewhat quieter for a while.*

Sparky (*to* **Annie**)   Little dog – bow-wow, *I'm* a little dog, any trick for a bit of biscuit, Annie, bit o' meat – look:

He takes a pack of cards out of his pocket and presents it.

Take one, go on, take one.

She obeys.

Well?

Annie   Queen o' Spades.

Sparky (*laughing*)   That's a hell of a card to take: I think there's treacle on it, sticks to all fingers o' this pack, I call her Grandma, makes her gentle, y'see – hope she'll kiss me whiskers and leave it at that.

He has replaced the card and shuffles.

Now then, take the first four cards on top. Tell me what they are.

Annie (*obeying*)   Eight Nine Ten Jack, all spades.

Sparky (*triumphantly*)   Right, right, calls the roll straight up to the one you took, the Queen, and where's the one you took? On the bottom – take it!

Annie (*obeying*)   It is the Queen and all!

Sparky   'Course it is: I *told* you. That's what I call life – it all turns up in the expected order, but not when you expect it. And that's what sets your two teeth laughing, click-clack, doesn't it, ha ha ha! Oh I'm a clever lad, you see, they call me Sparky, lots o' games, lots o' jokes . . .

Annie (*not impressed*)   Lots of liquor too. Now get out of me road while I fetch some more – *I've* got *work*, you know.

Sparky (*going after her and again intercepting her*)   Hey, but lovey, listen: there was an Englishman, a Welshman and a bloody great Irish – all three of 'em on Defaulters, y'see, for drunk. Now the Orderly Sarnt, he says, 'One, Two, Three, all we want's a Scotchman.' And a voice in the guardroom-yard says: 'Hoots awa', man, I'm taking back the empties fairst.'

She avoids him and goes away to the bar, thus ruining the climax of his tale. He tries to follow her up, but this time he is intercepted by **Musgrave**. **Hurst** *appears in the doorway.* **Annie** *looks up at him and follows him with her eyes for the rest of this dialogue.*

Musgrave (*to* **Sparky**)   You've had enough.

Sparky   I'm not drunk.

Musgrave   No and you won't be neither. This is no time.

Sparky (*pointing to* **Hurst**)   No – and *here* he comes, look at him.

Musgrave (*striding angrily over to* **Hurst**)   Where have you been?

Hurst (*surlily*)   Down by the canal.

Musgrave   Why?

Hurst   All right, I'd got things on my mind. And I'll tell you this, serjeant, it isn't enough.

Musgrave   What isn't enough?

Hurst   What you and that old cuckold are reckoning to do. It's all soft, it's all flat, it's all – God and the Word! Tchah! What good's a word, what good's a bloody word, they can *all* talk bloody words – it isn't enough: we've got to be strong!

Musgrave   Leave it alone, boy. *I* hold the logic. *You* hold some beer and get on with your work.

Musgrave *walks away from* **Hurst**.

Hurst (*shouts after him*)   It isn't enough!

He turns to find **Annie** *standing at his elbow, looking into his face and handing him a tankard of beer. He takes it and drinks it rapidly, without looking at her.*

Mrs Hitchcock (*calling from the bar*)   The Queen's in debt, serjeant!

Musgrave   Hello, ma'am?

Mrs Hitchcock   I said the Queen's in debt!

Musgrave   Chalk it up, ma'am, and another round for us all.

Mrs Hitchcock   No more chalk.

Musgrave   Easily found though.

He plunges his hand in his pocket and pulls out a quantity of money. He does a rapid count, whistles in consternation, and selects a few coins.

Attercliffe (*watching him*)   Not so much of it left, is there?

Musgrave   Easy, easy.

He goes over to the bar and pays. **Sparky** *is now showing his card tricks to the* **Colliers**. **Annie** *plucks at the sleeve of the pensive* **Hurst**.

Annie (*simply*)   You're the best to look at of all the four, aren't you?

Hurst   Eh? What's that?

Annie   Tell you again? Why? You know it, don't you?

Hurst (*preoccupied*)   I'd forgot it. I'd other matter beyond wondering what you'd think to our looks.

He studies her closer, and snaps out of his gloomy mood into an attitude of lady-killing arrogance.

Why, I don't need to think o' women. I let them think of *me*. I've knocked greasier ones than you between me porridge and me bacon. Don't flatter yourself.

Annie   I'm not, soldier: I'm flattering you. I'll come to you tonight.

Hurst (*pleased, though trying not to show it*)   Will you? That's a good choice, you've got sense.

Annie (*meaningly*)   But you forget them other matters, eh?

Hurst (*decidedly warming to her*)   I'll try . . . I'd rather. I hope I can . . . Stand straight: let's see . . . Gay and greasy, like I like 'em! You're big and you're bonny. A good shape, I'd call it. And you've got good hair, but wants a comb in it.

You ought to wash your face. And your neck smells of soot,
don't it?

Annie (*accepting this in the spirit in which it's meant*)   I've been
blowing up the fire.

Hurst (*boastfully*)   Ah, the last I had was a major's
daughter. I've got standards. Lovely.

Attercliffe *comes across to them.*

Attercliffe   You said he was the best looker. I heard you.
But it's not true.

Annie   Then who is? You?

Attercliffe   I'll tell you a tale about that. That pitman
over there – he said to me he thought I'd steal his wife. By
God, I'd sooner steal his nightsoil . . . I've got a wife. Ask me
to tell you one o' these days – Sparky'd make a joke of it –
wouldn't you, Sparky!

The last phrases are shouted across the room.

Sparky (*shouts back*)   Not any more – we're all going too fast.

He turns back to the **Colliers**.

Down, down – any card, any card, mate – tell me its name –
down.

Pugnacious Collier   Six o' Hearts!

Sparky   Right, right – *and* we shuffle and cut –

Enter the **Bargee**.

Bargee (*shouts*)   Time, gennelmen please, everybody time,
last orders everybody!

Mrs Hitchcock (*angrily*)   Who's given *you* leave to do the
calling here!

Bargee (*singing*)

   Blow your morning bugles
   Blow your calls ey-ho –

If it's not me and it's not you, there'll be somebody else –
look!

Enter **Constable**.

Constable   All right, Mrs Hitchcock, it's time you closed
your bar.

Mrs Hitchcock   What are you talking about!

Constable   Magistrates' orders, missus. All public houses
to close at nine o'clock sharp, pending settlement of colliery
dispute.

Mrs Hitchcock   It's the first I've heard of it.

Slow Collier (*to the* **Constable**)   Get out of it.

Pugnacious Collier (*ditto*)   Go home, you closhy
bluebottle, and sweep your bloody chimney.

Constable   That'll do there.

Musgrave   That'll do, lads, keep it easy.

Pugnacious Collier (*to* **Musgrave**)   We're not in the
Army yet, y'know!

Attercliffe   Steady, matey, steady. All friends, y'know:
married men together.

Pugnacious Collier   But, serjeant, you're a man, and I'll
shake you by the hand.

Constable (*now things seem quiet again*)   Magistrates issued
the order only this evening, missus. I've let you stay open a
lot longer than the others – it's nigh on a quarter to ten
already – and I'm in my rights to allow an exception for this
house, on account of the Army. Question of facilities. I trust
you've made good use of the extra time, Sarnt Musgrave?

Musgrave   H'm.

Pugnacious Collier (*with great friendliness*)   Have the last
drink on me, bluebottle!

Constable (*curtly*)   The last drink's been had already.
Close your bar, please, missus.

Pugnacious Collier (*an angry idea occurring to him*)   Wait a
minute . . . Suppose I join your Army. Suppose I bloody
'list. What does my wife do?

Bargee   Cock-a-doodle-do!

Pugnacious Collier (*finding his own answer*)   She goes to
bed with the Peeler! I'll break his wooden head off.

He goes for the **Constable** *with a tankard, the* **Constable**
staggers backwards and falls, the **Collier** *raises his tankard to smash
it into his face.* **Attercliffe** *and* **Musgrave**, *being nearest, jump
to prevent him.*

Attercliffe (*pulling the* **Collier** *fiercely back*)   Hey, ey, ey, ey-
ey, hold it there, boy, hold it there! My God, you might ha'
killed him. No . . .

Attercliffe *is trembling all over.*

Slow Collier   Why shouldn't he if he wants to?

Attercliffe (*with great passion*)   We've had enough o' that
already – no more, no more, no more of it.

Musgrave (*holding* **Attercliffe** *to quiet him*)   Stop it there!

Constable (*getting up slowly*)   Stand back, stand back. By
God, it's *time* this place was closed. Turn out into the street,
go on with you, get home. D'ye want me to whistle up me
specials? Go on.

He hurls the **Colliers** *and* **Bargee** *out of the pub.*

Attercliffe   He was going to, serjeant. He would have,
he'd have killed him. It's always here. Kill him. Kill.

Musgrave (*roughly*)   That'll do . . . We've all had enough,
Mr Constable. I'll get this lot to bed.

Constable   All right then. And try and keep folk quiet. I know you've got to buy 'em drink and that – but . . . *you* know – easy?

Musgrave   Aye, aye, easy. We know the trends. Don't you worry: *we* stand for law-and-order too, don't we?

Constable   Well, I hope so –

He goes to the door and calls into the street.

I said home, no loitering, go on, go on, or I'll run you in!

He comes back to **Musgrave** *in a confidential conspiratorial sort of way.*

It's a sort of curfew, you see. I told His Worship: 'If there's trouble at night, you can't hold *me* responsible. I've done my best,' I said – I told him frank . . . Oh, and while we're on about His Worship, serjeant, I might as well take occasion to discuss some names with you. There's a few like I could tell you as'd look very convenient on a regimental muster.

Musgrave (*coldly*)   I'm here for volunteers only, you know.

Constable (*insinuatingly*)   Ah well, what's a volunteer? You, you and you – the old Army custom – eh, serjeant? Mrs Hitchcock! A couple o' pints o' taddy for me and the serjeant.

Mrs Hitchcock   We're closed.

Constable (*broad-mindedly*)   That's all right, missus. Serve to the Serjeant: hotel-resident. All above the board.

Mrs Hitchcock (*to* **Annie**)   So take 'em their drinks. Queen as pays.

She pours herself out another cup of tea. **Annie** *prepares the drinks and brings them to* **Musgrave** *and the* **Constable**, *who get into a huddle over a list the latter produces.*

Sparky (*to the other two* **Soldiers**)   Very commodious Queen. I say, a very commodious Queen, ha ha, if she'd drank all she paid for tonight, heh, Sponge by Appointment, they could swab out the Windsor Castle Guardhouse, ha ha, who'd be a Coldstream! I say, they could swab out –

Attercliffe   Oh shut up, man, for God's sake. We've had all we can take of your stinking patter.

Sparky (*aggrieved*)   Ey-ey, matey – ey-ey.

He withdraws, hurt.

Hurst (*to* **Attercliffe**)   Shut up yourself – what's got into you?

Attercliffe   Why, *you* were making enough carry-on earlier, weren't you? Are you so daft or so drunk you didn't see what just happened?

Hurst   There was nowt happened. Couple o' pitmen three parts pissed? What's the matter wi' that? You were near as bad yourself – don't tell *me*. *You* were on about your *wife*!

Attercliffe   There was all but a man killed. We've come to stop it, not to start it – go on, sing to us.

He sings, with savage emphasis.

Who'll give a penny to the poor blind man
Holds out his hand with an old tin can.

– 'Cos that's all you are and it curdles up my bowels. I'm going to the coach-house.

Hurst   The coach-house! What for?

Attercliffe   Where there's a man to talk to who don't talk like a fool.

He goes out of the door behind the bar.

Sparky   Here, what d'you think to *him*? What sort o' talk does he reckon he'll get.

Hurst   Keep your mind off that!

Sparky (*wildly*)   Rattling, clattering, old bones in a box?
Billy used to sing, d'you think he'll have a sing-song?

Hurst   I don't understand you. This don't make *me* laugh.
It fair makes me sick.

Sparky (*jeeringly*)   Sick and bloody scared. Hey-ey, that's
you, that's you truly.

Hurst   Well, I've got things on my mind. If you can call it
scared –

Sparky   You and me, we're a pair, boy.

Hurst (*savagely*)   All right. But you'll learn. All *right*.

He turns abruptly away, and broods.

Sparky (*beckoning* **Annie**, *who comes unenthusiastically*)   I say,
Annie – oh I'll tell you what, Annie, I don't know what I'm
doing here.

She looks at him questioningly; he waves the point aside.

Aha, for that . . . Look, we've made us our beds in the
stables – ha, loose-box for every man, but the serjeant in the
house.

Annie   Aye, I know.

Sparky   We call it the Discipline, y'see. Yes-sarnt-no-
sarnt, three-bags-full-sarnt – that's our merry lives. Ha ha.
Third box from the end tonight, the fastest racehorse of 'em
all. Oaks, Derby, I carry 'em away, boy: but I'm best at a
steeple-chase – *hup* and *hover*, hedge and ditch, dear, and not
by soldiers' numbers either . . . Come for a gallop.

It is clear from the tone of the last phrase he is not joking.

Annie (*unemotionally*)   Not tonight.

Sparky   Oh . . . Go on, tonight.

Annie (*with something of a sneer*)   Maybe next I will. I can't
tell from day to day.

Sparky   No more can I. You know, you've not yet give me one little laugh . . . But I'll contrive it: now, y'see, there was a butcher, a baker, and a cats'-meat-man, all on the edge of the river. And down this river comes this dead dog, floating.

Hurst (*whose head has dropped, suddenly jerks himself up again*) God, I was near asleep! I started a bad dream and it woke me.

Musgrave (*to the* **Constable**)   No, mister, it won't wash. We can't play pressgangs these days. If a man gets drunk and then signs, all right: but otherwise –

Constable (*vexed*)   You're not over-co-operative, are you?

Musgrave   I'm sorry. Oh, I'll see what I can do: but I won't promise more. Besides, agitators is agitators, in or out the Army. I'm not sure we want 'em. But I'll think. Good night.

He goes with the **Constable** *to the street door.*

Constable   Good night. Good night, missus.

Exit the **Constable**. **Musgrave** *comes down to the* **Soldiers**.

Musgrave (*calling* **Annie**)   Lassie.

Annie   Hello.

Musgrave   These are my men. They're here with their work to do. You will not distract them.

Annie   I won't?

Musgrave   No. Because *they* know, whether you know it or not, that there's work is for women and there's work is for men: and let the two get mixed, you've anarchy.

Annie (*rather taken aback*)   Oh? And what's anarchy? You, you clever grinder – words and three stripes –

Musgrave   Look, lassie, anarchy: now, we're soldiers. Our work isn't easy, no and it's not soft: it's got a strong name – duty. And it's drawn out straight and black for us, a clear plan. But if you come to us with what you call your life or love – *I'd* call it your indulgence – and you scribble all over that plan, you make it crooked, dirty, idle, untidy, *bad* – there's anarchy. I'm a religious man. I know words, and I know deeds, and I know how to be strong. So do these men. You will not stand between them and their strength! Go on now: take yourself off.

Annie   A little bit of wind and a little bit of water –

Mrs Hitchcock   Annie –

Annie   But it drowned three score of sailors, and the King of Norway's daughter. (*She smiles for the first time in the play.*)

She sings:

O mother O mother
It hurts me so sore
Sing dody-eye-dodo
Then ye daft little bitch
Ye should do it no more
For you've never left off
Since we sailed from the shore.

Mrs Hitchcock (*sharply*)   Annie, get to bed.

Musgrave (*to the* **Soldiers**)   You two, get to bed. And pay heed to what I say.

Annie *goes out behind the bar, with a satirical curtsy.* **Musgrave** *goes out by the street door.* **Hurst** *makes a move as though to speak to him, but is too late. He stands reflective.*

Sparky

To bed to bed says Sleepy-head
Tarry a while says Slow
Open the book, says the wise old Rook
We'll have prayers before we go.

He sways a little tipsily, and laughs.

Scene Two

A street. Night.

The **Pugnacious** *and* **Slow Colliers** *enter, drunk and marching, the* **Bargee** *drilling them. (This is a kind of 'Fred Karno' sequence which must be kept completely under control. At each command each of the three carries out, smartly, a drill movement; but each drill movement is different for each man, and none of them performs the movement shouted. They must not be so drunk that they cannot appear erect and alertly jerking. The effect should be, not so much of three incompetents pretending to be soldiers, but of three trained soldiers gone mad.) The* **Colliers** *carry pickhefts as rifles, and the* **Bargee** *an oar.*

Musgrave *enters, and stands quietly watching.*

Bargee   Right turn. Forward march. Left right left right left right left.

Pugnacious Collier   To the front present. Halt.

Bargee   About turn.

Slow Collier   One two three four.

Bargee   Order arms.

Pugnacious Collier   Present and correct. By the right, number.

Slow Collier   One two three four.

They are now at attention, together.

Pugnacious Collier   Present and correct.

Bargee (*this order is properly obeyed*)   Stand-at-ease. Easy . . .

Pugnacious Collier (*breaking the spell*)   I'll tell you what, we're bloody good.

Bargee (*with enthusiasm*)   Eh. Lordy, mucker – good! By, I've never seen the like – y'know, if you signed on they'd excuse you three weeks' drill on the spot. You make that serjeant look like Old-Mother-Bunch-in-the-Popshop, alongside o' you – love you, mucker, you're *born* to it!

Pugnacious Collier   Well, why didn't I think on it afore?

Slow Collier (*still on parade*)   One two three four.

Pugnacious Collier   I'd not ha' got wed if I'd known!

Slow Collier (*suddenly coming to attention and starting off*) Quick march. One two three –

He bumps against **Walsh**, *who has just entered.*

Arh and be damned.

Walsh   Where the hell are you going to?

Musgrave *starts to go out. He passes* **Walsh**, *who stops him with a hand on his chest.*

Walsh   So we was mistook, eh? You're not here for no riots after all, but catching up men: that's it, in'it? Guineas?

Musgrave   Sovereigns.

Pugnacious Collier (*suddenly indicating* **Musgrave** *to* **Walsh**)   Here. This one: three stripes, but he's a man.

Walsh   Aye? And what are you? Drunk on *his* money: marching and drilling like a pack o' nit-headed kids at a barrack-gate!

Pugnacious Collier   Better nor bloody starve for no coal-owners, any road!

Walsh (*with passion*)   I'll tell you, I'm that ashamed, I could spew.

Musgrave (*gripping* **Walsh** *by the lapel and drawing him away*) Now listen here. I can see you, and see *you* what you are. I wasn't given these – (*He touches his stripes.*) – for not knowing men from ninepins. Now I'm telling you one word and I'm telling you two, and that's all. (*He lowers his voice.*) You and me is brothers –

Walsh (*in high irony*)   Eh begod! A Radical Socialist! Careful, soldier, careful. D'ye want to be hanged?

Musgrave (*very seriously*)   No jokes. I mean this. I mean it. Brothers in God –

Walsh (*even more scornful*)   Oh, hoho, *that* –

Musgrave   – And brothers in truth. So watch. And wait. I said, *wait.*

Walsh (*jeering*)   Brothers in God.

> Gentle Jesus send us rest
> Surely the bosses knows what's best!

Get along with yer –

Musgrave (*calmly*)   Well: I said, wait. You'll see.

Exit **Musgrave**.

Slow Collier (*who has been marking time since his collision, now mutters*).

> One two three four
> Where's the man as lives next door?
> Five six seven eight
> Come on in, he's working late.

Walsh (*looking at him in disgust*)   Holy God, I'd never ha' dreamt it.

Slow Collier (*his muttering rising in volume*)

> Nine ten eleven twelve
> Take his place and help yourself,
> Thirteen fourteen fifteen sixteen –

Pugnacious Collier (*with a stupid laugh*)   He's talking about my wife.

Slow Collier (*annoyed at being interrupted*)

> Thirteen fourteen fifteen sixteen
> Into the bed and there we'll fix him!

Pugnacious Collier (*in rising rage*)   I couldn't do it to the soldiers, I couldn't do it to the Peeler, but by, I'll do it to you! I'll break your bloody head.

He goes for **Slow Collier**, *who hits him in the belly, lets off a yell and runs out.* **Pugnacious Collier** *follows with a roar.*

Bargee (*calling after them in glee*)   Watch out for the Constable! Heh heh heh.

Walsh   Holy God! My mates! My brothers!

Bargee (*kindly*)   Ah well, they're drunk.

Walsh   I know they're drunk, and I known who's helped 'em to it.

Bargee   I could help *you* to summat, and all.

Walsh   What's that?

Bargee   They won't stay drunk all week. Oh the soldiers gives 'em sport, they *need* a bit o' sport, cold, hungry . . . When you want 'em, they'll be there. Crooked Joe, he's *here*.

Walsh   Aye?

Bargee   Could you shoot a Gatling gun?

Walsh (*looking at him sideways*)   I don't know.

Bargee   If you really want a riot, why don't you go at it proper? Come on, I'll tell you . . . (*He hops out, whistling 'Michael Finnegan' and looking back invitingly.*)

Walsh (*considering*)   Aye, aye? Crooked clever keelman, eh? . . . Well – all right – then *tell* me!

He hurries after him.

Scene Three

Interior of the pub (stable and bedroom).

Night. The stage is divided into two distinct acting-areas. The downstage area represents the stable, and is supposed to be divided into three loose boxes. If it is not practicable for the partitions between these to be built, it should be sufficient to suggest them by the three mattresses which are laid parallel, feet to the audience. The actors must not appear to be able to see each other from box to box. The forestage represents the central passage of the stable and is the only access to the boxes. Entry to the forestage can be from both wings (one side leads to the house, the other to the yard and coach-house).

The upstage area, raised up at least a couple of feet, represents a bedroom in the house. It is only large enough to contain a brass-knobbed bedstead with a small table or other support for a candle. The two areas must be treated as completely separate. Access to the bedroom area should be from the rear, and the audience must not be allowed to think that the actors can see from one area to the other (except as regards the light in the window, which is supposed to be seen as if from across the yard).

Musgrave, *in shirt and trousers, is sitting on the bed, reading by candlelight. His tunic etc. lies folded beside the bed.*

Hurst *and* **Sparky** *come into the stable from the house carrying palliasses and blankets. They proceed to make up their beds (in the two end boxes, leaving the middle one empty.* **Sparky** *is at the house end,* **Hurst** *next to the yard). They also undress to their shirts (of grey flannel) and their (long woollen) underpants and socks. Their clothes are laid out neatly beside the beds.*

Sparky (*as he prepares for bed*)   I say . . . I say, can you hear me?

Hurst (*uninterested*)   I can.

Sparky   You know, I'll tell you: I'm a bit pissed tonight.

Hurst   Uh. What of it?

Sparky   What's that?

Hurst   I said what of it? We all are, aren't we? *I* want an hour or two's sleep, I don't know about *you*, so let's have less o' your gab.

Sparky   I say, there's a light on still in Black Jack's window.

Hurst *grunts*.

Musgrave *has now lain down on top of his blankets, but has not taken off his trousers, or put out his candle.*

Sparky   Aye, aye. God's awake. Ha, ha! Not only God neither. Y'know, I think there might be some of us mortal even yet . . . I said God's awake!

Hurst   I *heard* you, and be damned.

A pause.

Sparky   Hour or two's sleep . . . What do you want to *sleep* for, and a fine fat tart all promised and ready!

Hurst (*who has got undressed and under his blanket*)   That'll do. Now shut your row, can't ye, when you're asked! I said I wanted to sleep, so let me.

Sparky   Why, it's you she's promised, y'see – *you*, not me – wake up, mucker, wake up. She'll soon be here, y'see. She'll soon be here! (*He blows 'reveille' with his lips, then gets under his blanket.*) You, boy, *you*, not me! . . . Shall I sing you a song?

Hurst (*almost asleep, and woken again*)   Eh, what? Are you going to shut up, or aren't you?

Sparky   Well, are *you* going to shut up or aren't you, when she comes? It's all right the best-looker loving the girl, but his two mates along the row wi' nowt but a bit o' wainscot atween – hey-ey-ey, it'll be agony for *us* tonight, y'know – so keep it quiet.

A pause.

(*He starts to sing, softly.*)

She came to me at midnight
With the moonshine on her arms
And I told her not to make no noise
Nor cause no wild alarms.
But her savage husband he awoke
And up the stairs did climb
To catch her in her very deed:
So fell my fatal crime . . .

While he is singing, **Annie** *enters from the house, carrying a candle. She goes gently to* **Hurst**'s *box and stands looking down at him. When she speaks, he sticks his head out of the bedclothes and looks at her.*

In the bedroom, **Musgrave** *sits up, blows out his light, and goes to sleep.*

Annie (*with tender humour*)   Here I come. Hello. I'm cold. I'm a blue ghost come to haunt you. Brr. Come on, boy, warm me up. You'll not catch cold off *me*.

Hurst (*getting up*)   No . . . I daresay not . . .

They put their arms round each other.

But what about the morning?

Annie   Ah, the morning's different, ent it? I'll not say nowt about mornings, 'cos then we'll *all* be cold. Cold and alone. Like, stand in a crowd but every one alone. One thousand men makes a regiment, you'd say?

Hurst   Near enough.

Annie   But for all that, when you're with them, you're still alone. Ent that right? So huggle me into the warm, boy, now. Keep out the wind. It's late. Dark.

Hurst (*suddenly breaking away from her*)   No, I won't. I don't care what I said afore, it's all done, ended, capped – get away. Go on. Leave me be.

Annie (*astonished and hurt*)   What is it? What's the matter? Lovey –

Hurst (*with violence*)   Go on. As far as *my* mind goes, it's morning already. Every one alone – that's all. You want me to lose my life inside of you –

Annie   No. No. But just for five hours, boy, six –

Hurst   You heard Black Jack say what's right. Straight, clear, dark strokes, no scrawling, I was wrong afore, I didn't trust him. He talked about God, so I thought he wor just nowt. But what he said about *you*: there, that was truth. He's going to be *strong*!

Annie (*scornfully*)   So *you* take note of Black Jack, do you?

Hurst   Aye, and I do. It's too late tonight for anything else. He's got to be trusted, got to be strong, we've got no alternative!

Annie (*standing a little away from him*)   My Christ then, they *have* found him a brother! It was only this evening, warn't it, *I* saw you, down by the canal, all alone and wretched –

She sings with fierce emphasis:

All round his hat he wore the green willow – !

Hurst   All right.

Annie (*not letting him off*)   But it can't have been you, can it? 'Cos now you're just the same as the rest of 'em – the Hungry Army! You eat and you drink and you go. Though *you* won't even eat when it's offered, will you? So *sprawl* yourself on the straw without me, get up to your work tomorrow, drum 'em in and write 'em down, infect 'em all and bury 'em! I don't care.

Hurst   What are you on about, what's the matter, why don't you go when you're told? Godsake, Godsake, leave a man to his sleep!

Annie   You know what they call me?

Hurst   I'd call you a bloody whoor –

Annie (*savagely ironical*)   Oh, not just a whoor – *I'm* a
whoor-to-the-soldiers – it's a class by itself.

Attercliffe *has entered from the yard with his bedding. They do not
notice him yet.* **Annie** *turns to pleading again.*

Annie   Christ, let me stay with you. He called me life and
love, boy, just you think on *that* a little.

Hurst *pushes her away with a cry. She falls against* **Attercliffe**.

Attercliffe (*holding her up*)   Life and love, it is? I'm an old
soldier, girly, a dirty old bastard, me, and *I've* seen it all.
Here.

*He grips her and kisses her violently all over face and neck. He sneers
at* **Hurst**.

Hey-up there, son, get in your manger and sleep, and leave
this to the men.

Hurst   All right . . . and you're welcome.

He goes to his box and lies down again, huffily, trying to sleep.

Attercliffe (*still holding* **Annie**, *with a sort of tenderness*)   Now
then, what'll I do to you, eh? How d'you reckon you're
going to quench *me*? Good strong girly with a heart like a
horsecollar, open it up and let 'em all in. And it still
wouldn't be no good.

Annie (*hard and hostile*)   Wouldn't it? Try.

Attercliffe   Ah, no. Not tonight. What would *you* know of
soldiers?

Annie   More'n you'd think I'd know, maybe.

Attercliffe   I doubt it. Our Black Jack'd say it's not
material. He'd say there's blood on these two hands. (*He
looks at his hands with distaste.*) You can wipe 'em as often as
you want on a bit o' yellow hair, but it still comes blood the
next time so why bother, *he'd* say. And *I'd* say it too. Here.
(*He kisses her again and lets her go.*) There you are, girly: I've

given you all you should get from a soldier. Say 'Thank you, boy', and that's that.

Annie (*still hard*)   Thank you, boy . . . You know it, don't you? All I should get. All I ever have got. Why should I want more? You stand up honest, you do, and it's a good thing too, 'cos you're old enough.

Attercliffe (*with a wry smile*)   H'm. I am and all. Good night.

He starts making up his bed and undressing. **Sparky** *has sat up and is listening. As* **Annie** *is standing still,* **Attercliffe** *starts talking to her again.*

Attercliffe   Girly. When I was a young lad I got married to a wife. And she slept with a greengrocer. He was the best looker (like *he's* the best looker) – (*He points towards* **Hurst***'s box.*) – or any road that's what *she* said. *I* saw him four foot ten inch tall and he looked like a rat grinning through a brush; but he sold good green apples and he fed the people and he fed my wife. I didn't do neither. So now I'm a dirty old bastard in a red coat and blue breeches and that's all about it. Blood, y'see: killing. Good night.

He has now undressed and lies down to sleep immediately.

Annie *stands for a minute, then subsides to a crouching position, in tears.*

Sparky *creeps out of his box.*

Sparky   Tst, tst, tst, Annie. Stop crying: come here.

Annie   Don't talk to me, go to bed. I can't bear wi' no more of you.

Sparky   Annie, Annie, look now, I want to talk. I'm not deaf, y'know, and I'm not that drunk, I mean I've been drunker, I mean I can stand, ha ha, one foot and all, I'm a stork, look at me – (*He tries to balance on one foot.*) Him at the far end – don't you worry for *him*, Annie – why, he's not mortal any more, he's like God, ent he? And God – (*He looks towards* **Musgrave**'s *light.*) – hello, God's asleep.

Annie   God?

Sparky   He's put his light out. Look.

Annie   That's where the serjeant is.

Sparky   That's right. I never thought he'd sleep. *I* can't sleep . . . what have you got against me?

Annie (*surprised*)   Nowt that I know.

Sparky   But you didn't come to me, did you? I mean, you asked *him* and he said no, I asked *you* and you said no. That's all wrong. I mean, you know what the Black Musgrave'd call that, don't you – *he'd* say anarchy!

Annie   *He'd say*? He?

Musgrave *groans in his bed.*

Every one of you swaggering lobsters, that serjeant squats in your gobs like an old wife stuck in a fireplace. What's the matter with you all!

Sparky   Ssh, ssh, keep it quiet. Come down here . . .

He leads her as far as possible from the other two.

Listen.

Annie   What for?

Sparky   Snoring. Him? Him? Good, two snorings. They're asleep . . . I told you in the bar, y'know, they call me Sparky – name and nature – Sparky has his laugh . . . A man can laugh, because or else he might well howl – and howling's not for men but for dogs, wolves, seagulls – like o' that, ent it?

Annie   You mean that you're frightened?

Sparky (*with a sort of nervous self-realisation*)   Aye, begod, d'you know: I am. God's not here, he's put his light out: so I

can tell you, love: I *am*. Hey, not of the war, bullets in the far
Empire, that's not the reason, don't think it. They even give
me a medal, silver, to prove so. But I'll tell you, I'm – here,
kiss me, will you, quickly, I oughtn't to be talking . . . I think
I've gone daft.

Annie (*who is looking at him curiously but fascinated*)   All right, I
will . . .

She kisses him, and he holds her.

Musgrave (*in clear categorical tones, though in his sleep*)
Twenty-five men. Nine women. Twenty-five men. No
children. No.

Annie (*in a sudden uprush*)   Look, boy, there was a time *I*
had a soldier, he made jokes, he sang songs and all – ah, *he*
lived yes-sarnt no-sarnt three-bags-full-serjeant, but he
called it one damned joke. God damn you, he was killed!
Aye, and in your desert Empire – so what did *that* make?

Sparky   I don't know . . .

Annie   It made a twisted little thing dead that nobody
laughed at. A little withered clover – three in one it made.
There was me, and there was him: and a baby in the
ground. Bad shape. Dead.

She can say nothing more and he comforts her silently a moment.

Sparky (*his mind working*)   Why, Annie . . . Annie . . . you
as well: another one not paid for . . . O, I wish *I* could pay.
Say, suppose I paid for yours; why, maybe you could pay for
mine.

Annie   I don't understand.

Sparky (*following his thought in great disturbance of mind*)   It
wouldn't be anarchy, you know; he can't be right there! All it
would be, is: *you* live and *I* live – we don't need his duty, we
don't need his Word – a dead man's a dead man! We could
call it *all* paid for! Your life and my life – make our *own*
road, we don't follow nobody.

Annie What are you talking about?

Sparky (*relapsing into his despair again*)   Oh God, I don't know. God's gone to sleep, but when he wakes up again –

Annie (*bewildered but compassionate*)   Oh quiet, boy, be quiet, easy, easy.

She stoops over him, where he has crumpled into a corner, and they embrace again with passion.

Musgrave (*now shouting in his sleep*)   Fire, fire! Fire, fire, London's burning, London's burning!

Mrs Hitchcock, *in a nightdress and robe, and carrying a tumbler, hurries into his bedroom.*

Mrs Hitchcock   What's the matter?

She lights his candle.

Musgrave (*sitting up and talking very clearly as if it made sense*) Burning. Burning. One minute from now, and you carry out your orders – get *that* one! *Get* her! Who says she's a child! We've got her in the book, she's old enough to kill! You will carry out your orders. Thirty seconds. Count the time. (*He is looking at his watch.*) Twenty-six . . . twenty-three . . .

Mrs Hitchcock (*very alarmed*)   Serjeant – Serjeant –

Musgrave   Be quiet. Twenty . . . Eighteen . . . I'm on duty, woman. I'm timing the end of the world. Ten more seconds, sir . . . Five . . . three . . . two . . . one.

He lets out a great cry of agony and falls back on the bed. All in the stable hear and take notice. **Attercliffe** *turns over again to sleep.* **Hurst** *sits up in alarm.* **Annie** *and* **Sparky** *stand apart from each other in surprise.*

Annie   Sparky, it's your God. He's hurt.

Sparky *sits staring and gasping, till* **Annie** *pulls him to her again.*

Mrs Hitchcock   What are you playing at – you'll wake up the town!

Musgrave *shivers and moans.*

Mrs Hitchcock (*shaking him gently*)   Come on – it's a nightmare. Wake up and let's get rid of it. Come on, come on.

Musgrave   Leave me alone. I wasn't asleep.

Mrs Hitchcock   You warn't awake, any road.

Musgrave   Mind your own business.

Mrs Hitchcock   I thought you might be poorly.

Musgrave   No . . . No . . . (*Suddenly*) But it *will* come, won't it?

Mrs Hitchcock   What will?

Musgrave   The end of the world? You'll tell me it's not material, but if you could come to it, in control; I mean, numbers and order, like so many ranks this side, so many that, properly dressed, steadiness on parade, so that whether you knew you was right, or you knew you was wrong – you'd know it, and you'd stand. (*He shivers.*) Get me summat to eat.

Mrs Hitchcock   I got you a hot grog. Here. (*She gives him a tumbler.*)

Musgrave   What – what . . . ?

Mrs Hitchcock   I take it at nights for me bad back. I heard you calling so I brought it in. Have a biscuit.

She gives him a biscuit from her dressing gown pocket.

Musgrave   Aye, I will . . . (*He eats and drinks.*) That's better . . . You *do* understand me, don't you? Look, if you're the right-marker to the Company and you're marching to the right, you can't see the others, so you follow the orders you can hear and hope you hear them true. When I was a recruit I found myself once half across the square alone – *they'd* marched the other way and I'd never heard the word!

Mrs Hitchcock   You ought to lie down. You *are* poorly,
I can tell. Easy, serjeant, easy.

Musgrave (*relaxing again*)   Easy . . . easy . . .

She draws the blanket over him and sits soothing him to sleep.

Sparky (*with a sudden access of resolution*)   Annie, I don't care.
Let him wake when he wants to. All I'll do this time is to
stand and *really* laugh. Listen to this one, because here's
what I'll be laughing at. There was these four lads, y'see,
and they made it out they'd have a strong night all night in
the town, each boozer in turn, pay-day. And the first one in
the first boozer, he says: 'Each man drinks my choice,' he
says. 'One sup of arsenic to every man's glass' – and *that's*
what they've to drink. Well, one of them, he drinks and he
dies, next man drinks and *he* dies, what about the third? Has
he to drink to that rule? 'Cos they'd *made* it a rule – each
man to the first man's choice.

Hurst *has left his box and crept up and is now listening to this.*

Annie   I don't know –

Sparky   Neither do I. But I can tell you what *I'd* do.

Annie   What?

Sparky (*with a switch to hard seriousness*)   I'd get out of it,
quick. Aye, and with you. Look, love, its snowing, we can't
leave the town now. But you could bed me down
somewheres I mean, like, hide; bide *with* me while it's all
over, and then get me some clothes and we'd go – I mean,
like, go to London? What about London? You've never
been to London?

Annie   Bide hid while *what's* all over? What's going to
happen?

Sparky   Eh, that's the question. I wish I could tell you. It's
Black Jack's work, not mine.

Annie   Bad work, likely?

Sparky Likely . . . I don't know. D'you know, I never *asked*! You see, he's like God, and it's as if *we* were like angels – *angels*, ha, ha! But that's no joke no more for me. This is funnier nor *I* can laugh at, Annie, and if I bide longer here, I'm *really* wild-wood mad. So get me out of it, quick!

Annie (*decisively*) I will. I'm frightened. Pull your clothes on, Sparky. I'll hide you.

Sparky Good love, good –

Annie But you'll not leave me behind?

He has started dressing, very confusedly, putting his tunic on first.

Sparky No.

Annie Swear it.

He has his trousers ready to step into. He lets them fall while he takes her for a moment in his arms.

Sparky Sworn.

Hurst *nips in and seizes the trousers.*

(*Releasing* **Annie**) Now then, sharp. Hey, where's me trousers?

Hurst Here!

Sparky What's the goddamn – give 'em back, you dirty –

Hurst (*triumphantly*) Come and get 'em, Sparky! Hey, you'll be the grand deserter, won't you, running bare-arsed over the moor in six-foot drifts of snow!

Sparky Give me them!

He grabs one end of the trousers and a farcical tug-o'-war begins.

Hurst (*in high malice*) A man and a soldier! Jump, natter, twitch, like a clockwork puppet for three parts of the night, but the last night of all, you *run*! You little closhy coward.

Attercliffe *has woken and tries to intervene.*

Attercliffe   What the hell's the row – easy, easy, *hold* it!

Sparky   He's got my bloody trousers!

He gives a great tug on the trousers and pulls them away, **Hurst** *falling down.*

Hurst   I'm going to *do* you, Sparky.

His hand falls on **Sparky***'s belt, with bayonet scabbard attached, which is lying on the floor. He gets up, drawing the bayonet.*

Annie   No, no, stop him!

Attercliffe   Drop that bayonet!

Annie *mixes in, seizing* **Hurst***'s wrist and biting it. The bayonet drops to the floor.* **Attercliffe** *snatches it and* **Hurst** *jumps upon him. Together they fall against* **Sparky** *and all three crash to the floor.* **Sparky** *gives a terrifying, choking cry.*

Musgrave *leaps up in the bedroom. Those on the forestage all draw back, appalled, from* **Sparky***'s dead body.*

Musgrave (*to* **Mrs Hitchcock**)   Stay where you are.

He leaves the bedroom.

Hurst   He's dead. He's dead. *I* didn't do it. Not me. No.

Attercliffe   Dead?

Hurst   Of course he's dead. He's stuck in the gut. That's you. Your hand. You killed him.

Attercliffe   I can't have.

Hurst   You did.

Attercliffe (*stupidly*)   I've got the bayonet.

Hurst   Aye, and you've killed him.

Attercliffe   O Holy God!

Musgrave *enters from the house.* **Mrs Hitchcock** *has left the bedroom.*

Musgrave   What's going on?

Hurst   Sparky's been killed.

Musgrave   *What!* How?

Hurst   His own bayonet. He was deserting. I tried to stop him. Then *he* –

He points to **Attercliffe**.

Musgrave (*to* **Attercliffe**)   Well?

Attercliffe (*hopelessly*)   Here's the bayonet. I got holding it, serjeant. I did. It's always me. You can call it an accident. But *I* know what that means, it means that it –

Musgrave   Shut up. You said deserting?

Hurst *nods.*

What's *she* doing here? Was she with him?

Hurst *nods.*

Aye, aye . . . Desertion. Fornication. It's not material. He's dead. Hide him away.

Hurst   Where?

Musgrave   In the midden at back of the yard. And don't show no lights while you're doing it. Hurry.

Hurst (*to* **Attercliffe**)   Come on.

Attercliffe   Holy God, Holy God!

They carry the body out.

Musgrave (*to* **Annie**, *unpleasantly*)   Oh, you can shake, you can quiver, you can open your mouth like a quicksand and all – blubbering and trouble – but *I've* got to think and *I've* got to do.

Mrs Hitchcock *enters from the house. She is carrying* **Musgrave***'s tunic, hat, and boots, which she puts down.*

Missus, come here. There's things going wrong, but don't ask me what. Will you trust me?

She looks at him searchingly and gives a short nod.

Get hold of this lassie, take her upstairs, lock her in a cupboard, and keep quiet about it. I've got a right reason: you'll know it in good time. Do as I tell you and you won't take no harm.

Mrs Hitchcock   The end of the world, already?

Musgrave   What's that? D'ye hear what I say?

Mrs Hitchcock   Oh aye, I heard you.

She takes the shuddering **Annie** *by the hand, and then looks sharply at her fingers.*

Hey-ey-ey, this here, it's blood.

Musgrave   I know. I repeat it: don't ask me.

Annie *looks at* **Musgrave** *and at* **Mrs Hitchcock**, *then licks her hand, laughing in a childish fashion.*

Mrs Hitchcock   Come away in, Annie . . . Aye, I'll go and lock her up . . . It might be the best thing. I've got to trust you, haven't I? I've always praised religion.

She takes **Annie** *away, into the house.* **Musgrave** *sits down suddenly, with his head in his hands. The* **Bargee** *creeps in from the yard and sits beside him, in a similar attitude.*

Bargee (*singing softly*)

Here we set like birds in the wilderness,
birds in the –

Musgrave *sits up, looks at him, realises who it is, and grabs him by the throat.*

Bargee (*struggling free*)   It's all right, bully, it's only Old Joe.

Musgrave (*relaxing, but still menacing*)   Oh it is, is it? Well?

Bargee (*significantly*)   I was thinking, like, if I wor you, *I* wouldn't just set down in a stable, not now I wouldn't, no.

Musgrave   Why not?

Bargee   *I* see your jolly muckers, over there, mucking in the muck-pile, eh? But if they turned theirselves around and looked at the coach-house –

Musgrave *leaps up in alarm.*

Musgrave   What about the coach-house?

Bargee   There's bars at its windows: and there's a crowbar at the bars – listen!

A crash of glass offstage from the yard.

That's the glass gone now! If you're quick, you can catch 'em!

Musgrave *has run to the yard side of the stage.*

Musgrave (*calling to offstage*)   Get to the coach-house, get round the back! Quick! Quick!

He runs off in great excitement.

More crashes of glass, shouting and banging.

The **Bargee** *watches what is happening in the yard, leaping up and down in high delight.*

Bargee   Go on, catch 'em, two to the back and the serjeant to the door, open the padlock, swing back the wicket – one little laddie, he's trapped in the window – head in, feet out – pull him down, serjeant, pull him down, soldiers – boot up, fist down, tie him in a bundle – oh me pretty roses, oh me blood-red flowers o' beauty!

The two **Soldiers** *hurry back, with* **Walsh** *frogmarched between them, his hands bunched up and tied behind his back.* **Musgrave** *follows. All are panting. They throw* **Walsh** *down.*

Musgrave   What about the others?

Hurst   Run away, serjeant.

Attercliffe   Nigh on a dozen of 'em.

Hurst   Ran down the alley.

Musgrave   Let's have a look at this one! Oho, so it's *you*! What were you after?

Walsh (*grinning*)   What d'you think, lobster?

Musgrave   Our little Gatling? Isn't that right?

Walsh   That's right, boy, you're sharp.

Musgrave (*quieter*)   But *you're* not sharp, brother, and I'm going to tell you why.

Shouting and shrill whistles, off.

Hurst   It's that Constable's out, and his Specials and all – listen! Hey, we'd better get dressed.

He starts huddling on his tunic and trousers.

Musgrave (*to* **Walsh**)   Chasing your friends. He'll be coming here, shortly.

Whistles again.

Constable (*offstage, in the house*)   Open up, Mrs Hitchcock, open up – name of the Law!

Musgrave   Ah, here he is. Now he asked me this evening to kidnap you for the Army. But *I* told you we was brothers, didn't I? So watch while I prove it. (*To* **Hurst**.) Take him out and hide him.

Hurst (*taken aback*)   Him in the midden too?

Musgrave   Don't be a fool. Do as you're told.

Walsh   Wait – wait a minute.

Musgrave (*furiously*)   Go with him, you damned nignog. Would ye rather trust the Constable?

Walsh (*very puzzled*)   What are you on, for God's sake?

Musgrave   Don't waste time! (*He pushes* **Walsh** *and barks at* **Hurst**.) Get him in that woodshed. God, what a shower o' tortoises!

Hurst *hustles* **Walsh** *out to the yard.* **Musgrave** *turns on* **Attercliffe**.

You get your trousers on.

Attercliffe *obeys.* **Mrs Hitchcock** *comes in, very agitated.*

Mrs Hitchcock   The Constable's here, he's running through the house.

Musgrave   Then send him to me! It's in control, in control, woman. I *know* all about it.

Mrs Hitchcock *goes back into the house.*

Attercliffe   Musgrave, what are you doing?

Musgrave   I'm doing what comes next and that's all I've got time for.

Attercliffe (*in a gush of despair*)   But he was killed, you see, killed. Musgrave, don't you see, that wipes the whole thing out, wiped out, washed out, finished.

Musgrave   *No!*

Mrs Hitchcock *and the* **Constable** *hurry in from the house.*

Constable   Ah, serjeant, what's happened? Saw a gang breaking in at the back of this coach-house. What's kept in the coach-house? (*To* **Mrs Hitchcock**.)

Mrs Hitchcock   The serjeant's got his –

Musgrave   I've got my gear.

Mrs Hitchcock   Hello, here's the Parson.

The **Parson** *hurries in from the house.*

Parson   Constable, what's going on?

Constable   I think it's beginning, sir. I think it's the riots.

Parson   At this hour of the morning?

Constable   I've sent word to the Mayor.

He starts making a rapid report to the **Parson***. The* **Bargee** *sidles up to* **Musgrave***.*

Bargee   Don't forget Old Joe. I brought the warning. Let me in on a share of it, there's a bully.

Musgrave   Get out, or you'll get hurt!

The **Mayor** *hurries in from the house.*

Mayor   This is bad, it's bloody bad. How did it start? Never mind that now. What steps have you taken?

Constable   Me Deputy-Specials all around the streets, but I've not got enough of 'em and they're frightened – that's frank. I *warned* you, Your Worship.

Mayor   Question is this: can you hold the town safe while twelve o'clock mid-day?

Constable   Nay I don't know.

Mayor   The telegraph's working.

Musgrave   The telegraph!

Mayor   Aye, there's a thaw begun. Thank God for that: they've mended the broken wire on top of the moor. So I sent word for the Dragoons. They'll come as fast as they can, but not afore twelve I shouldn't think, so we've *got* to hold this town!

Musgrave   Six hours, thereabouts. Keep 'em quiet now, they may bide. Mr Mayor, I'll do it for you.

Mayor   How?

Musgrave   I'll do what I'm paid for: start a recruiting-meeting. Look, we had 'em last night as merry as Christmas in here, why not this morning? Flags, drums, shillings, sovereigns – hey, start the drum! Top o' the market-place, make a jolly speech to 'em!

Mayor   Me?

Hurst *begins beating the drum outside in the yard.*

Musgrave   You! You, Parson, too. Mrs Hitchcock, free beer to the crowd!

Parson   No!

Mayor (*catching the idea*)   *Aye*, missus, bring it! *I'll* pay for it and all!

Musgrave (*to the* **Bargee**)   *You*, if you want to help, you can carry a flag. (*To* **Attercliffe**.) Get him a flag!

Exit **Attercliffe**. *Enter* **Hurst**, *drumming furiously.*

We'll *all* carry flags. Fetch me me tunic.

Mrs Hitchcock   Here it is, I brought it.

Musgrave (*quite wild with excitement*)   Flags, ribbons, bunches o' ribbons, glamourise 'em, glory!

Attercliffe *hurries in from the yard, with his arms full of colours. He hands these out all round.*

Bargee   Rosebuds of Old England!

Mayor   Loyal hearts and true!

Parson   The Lord mighty in battle!

Musgrave   GOD SAVE THE QUEEN!

General noise, bustle and confusion.

Act Three

Scene One

The market-place.

Early morning. In the centre of the stage is a practicable feature – the centre-piece of the market-place. It is a sort of Victorian clock-tower-cum-lamppost-cum-market-cross, and stands on a raised plinth. There is a ladder leaning against it. On the plinth are the soldiers' boxes and a coil of rope. The front of the plinth is draped with bunting, and other colours are leaning against the centre-piece in an impressive disposition.

When the scene opens, the stage is filled with noise and movement. **Hurst** *is beating his drum, the* **Mayor,** *the* **Parson** *and* **Musgrave** *are mounting the plinth, and* **Attercliffe** *is up already, making the last arrangements. The* **Constable** *takes up his stand beside the centre-piece, as does* **Hurst.** *The* **Bargee** *is hopping about on the forestage.*

The **Soldiers** *are all now properly dressed, the* **Mayor** *has put on his cocked hat and red robe and chain, and the* **Parson** *his gown and bands, and carries a Bible. They are all wearing bright cockades.*

The role of the **Bargee** *in this scene is important. As there is no crowd, the speeches are delivered straight out to the audience, and the* **Bargee** *acts as a kind of fugleman to create the crowd-reactions. Noises-off indicated in the dialogue are rather unrealistic – as it were, token-noises only.*

At one side of the stage there is an upper-storey window.

Bargee (*casting his cap*)

Hip hip hooroar
Hark hark the drums do bark
The Hungry Army's coming to town
Lead 'em in with a Holy Book
A golden chain and a scarlet gown.

Here they are on a winter's morning, you've got six kids at
home crying out for bread, you've got a sour cold wife and
no fire and no breakfast: and you're too damn miserable
even to fight – if there's owt else at all to take your mind off
it – so here you are, you lucky people, in your own old
market-place, a real live lovely circus, with real live golden
sovereigns in somebody's pocket and real live taddy ale to
be doled out to the bunch of you!

Mrs Hitchcock *enters, trundling a beer-barrel.*

Oh, it's for free, you can be certain o' that, there's no strings
to this packet – let's lend you a hand wi' that, missus!

*He helps her roll the barrel to one side of the centre-piece, where she
chocks it level and sits down on it. She also has a hand-basket full of
tankards. The* **Bargee** *comes back downstage.*

There we are, then. And here *you* are, the streets is filling, roll
up, roll up, and wallow in the lot! I'll tell you the word when
to cheer.

*The platform party is now all in place. The drum gives a final roll.
The* **Mayor** *steps forward.*

Constable   Silence for the Mayor!

Bargee   Long live His Worship, who gives us food and
clothing and never spares to meet the people with a smile!
Hooroar!

Three boos, off.

Boo, boo, boo? Don't be so previous, now; he'll surprise us
all yet, boys. Benevolence and responsibility. Silence for the
Mayor!

Mayor   All right. Now then. It's been a hard winter. I
know there's a bit of a thaw this morning, but it's not over
yet, there may be worse to come. Although you might not
think it, I'm as keen and eager as any o' you to get the pits
working again, so we can all settle down in peace to a good

roast and baked 'taters and a good pudding and the rest of it. But I'm not here to talk strikes today.

A noise off.

Bargee (*interpreting*)   He says: 'Who says strikes, it's a bloody lockout.'

Constable   Silence for the Mayor!

Bargee   Silence for His Worship!

Mayor   I said I'm not up here to talk on that today. Serjeant Musgrave, on my right, has come to town to find men for the Queen. Now that's a good opportunity – it's a *grand* opportunity. It's up to you to take it. By God, if I was a young lad in a town without work, you'd not catch me thinking twice –

Bargee   He says: 'There's only one man drives the work away in this town.'

The **Constable** *steps forwards, but the* **Bargee** *forestalls him.*

Silence for the Mayor!

Mayor   All right. You think I'm playing it crooked all the time – *I* know.

A cheer off.

But listen to this: (*He holds up a jingling money-bag.*) Here's real gold. It rings true to me, it rings true to you, and there's one o' these for every lad as volunteers. That's straight. It's from the shoulder. It pulls no punches. Take it or throw it away – I'm set up here and waiting. (Parson, tell 'em *your* piece now.) And keep quiet while the Rector's at you: he talks good sense and you need it. It you can't give *me* credit, at least you can give *him* some, for considering what's best for the community. Go on, Parson: tell 'em.

He retires and the **Parson** *steps forward.*

Parson   'And Jesus said, I come not to bring peace but a sword.' I know very well that the times are difficult. As your minister of religion, and as a magistrate, it is my business to be aware of these matters. But we must remember that this town is only one very small locality in our great country.

Bargee   Very true, very true.

Two cheers off.

Parson   And if our country is great, and I for one am sure that it *is* great, it is great because of the greatness of its responsibilities. They are world wide. They are noble. They are the responsibilities of a first-class power.

Bargee   Keep 'em there, Reverend! First-class for ever! Give a cheer, you boys!

Three cheers, very perfunctory.

And the crowd roars! Every hat in the air, you've struck 'em in the running nerve, hooroar!

Parson   Therefore, I say, therefore: when called to shoulder our country's burdens we should do it with a glancing eye and a leaping heart, to draw the sword with gladness, thinking nothing of our petty differences and grievances – but all united under one brave flag, going forth in Christian resolution, and showing a manly spirit! The Empire calls! Greatness is at hand! Serjeant Musgrave will take down the names of any men willing, if you'll file on to the platform in an orderly fashion, in the name of the Father, the Son and mumble mumble mumble . . .

He retires. There is a pause.

Musgrave   Perhaps, Mr Mayor, before we start enrolling names, it might be as well if I was to say a few words first, like, outlining the type of service the lads is likely to find, overseas, and so forth?

The **Slow Collier** *slouches in, and up to the base of the plinth.*

Slow Collier   Have you got my name down?

Musgrave   No. Not yet.

Slow Collier   Are you sure of that?

Musgrave   Aye, I'm sure. D'you want me to take it?

Slow Collier   Some of us was a bit full, like, last night in the boozer.

Musgrave   A man's pleasuring, friend, that's all. No harm in that?

Slow Collier (*thrusting forward his hat with the cockade in it*) Then what's this? Eh? Someone gave me this.

Musgrave (*laughs*)   Oh I'll tell you what that means: you drank along of me – that's all that it means – and you promised you'd come and hear me this morning. Well, here you are.

Slow Collier   Ah. Provisional. Aye. I thought that's what it was. Provisional.

The **Pugnacious Collier** *slouches in.*

Pugnacious Collier   Provisional or not, we're not signing nowt without we've heard more. So go on then, soldier, tell us. Prove it's better to be shot nor starve, *we'll* listen to you, man, 'cos we're ready to believe. And more of us and all.

Cries off   Aye. Aye. Aye. Tell us.

Bargee   Go on, serjeant, tell us. It's a long strong tale, quiet while he tells it – quiet!

Musgrave   Now there's more tales than one about the Army, and a lot of funny jokers to run around and spread 'em, too. Aye, aye, we've all heard of 'em, we know all about 'em, and it's not my job this morning to swear to you what's true and what's not true. O' *course* you'll find there's an RSM here or a provost-sarnt there what makes you cut the grass wi' nail-scissors, or dust the parade-ground with a toothbrush. It's all the bull, it's all in the game – but it's not what sends me here and it's not what put *these* on my arm, and it's nowt at all to do with *my* life, or these two with me, or any o' yours. So easy, me boys, don't think it. (*To the* **Colliers**.) There was another lad wi' *you*, in and out last night. He ought to be here. (*To the* **Bargee**.) Go and fetch him, will you? You know where he is.

Bargee (*finger to nose*)   Ah. Ha ha. Aye aye.

He slips out conspiratorially.

Musgrave (*continues his speech*)   I said, easy me boys, and don't think it. Because there's *work* in the Army, and bull's not right work, you can believe me on that – it's just foolery – any smart squaddy can carry it away like a tuppenny-ha'penny jam jar. So I'll tell you what the *work* is – open it up!

Attercliffe *flings open one of the boxes. It is packed with rifles. He takes one out and tosses it to* **Musgrave**.

Musgrave   Now this is the rifle. This is what we term the butt of the rifle. This is the barrel. This here's the magazine. And this – (*He indicates the trigger.*) – you should know what *this is*, you should know what it does . . . Well, the rifle's a good weapon, it's new, quick, accurate. This is the bayonet – (*He fixes his bayonet.*) – it kills men smart, it's good and it's beautiful. But I've more to show than a rifle. Open it up!

Attercliffe *opens a second box. It contains a Gatling gun and tripod mounting.*

This is the newest, this is the smartest, call it the most beautiful. It's a Gatling gun, this. Watch how it works!

Attercliffe *secures the gun to its mounting.*

Attercliffe   The rounds are fed to the chambers, which are arranged in a radial fashion, by means of a hopper-shaped aperture, *here*. Now pay attention while I go through the preliminary process of loading.

He goes through the preliminary process of loading.

Musgrave (*his urgency increasing all the time*)   The point being that here we've got a gun that doesn't shoot like: *Bang,* rattle-click-up-the-spit-what're-we-waiting-for, *bang!* But: Bang-bang-bang-bang-bang-bang-bang-bang-*bang* – and there's not a man alive in the whole of this market-place. Modern times. Progress. Three hundred and fifty rounds in one minute – *flat!*

The **Bargee** *re-enters, soft-footed.*

Musgrave (*quickly to him*)   Is he coming?

The **Bargee** *nods, finger to lips.*

Attercliffe   Now then, you see, the gun's loaded.

Musgrave   It didn't take long, you see.

Attercliffe   No.

Hurst *gives a roll on the drums.*

Attercliffe *swivels the gun to face out into the audience.*

Musgrave *loads his rifle with a clip of cartridges.*

Musgrave (*his voice very taut and hard*)   The question remains as to the *use* of these weapons! (*He pushes his rifle-bolt home.*) You'll ask me: what's their purpose? Seeing we've beat the Russians in the Crimea, there's no war with France (there *may* be, but there isn't yet), and Germany's our friend, who do we have to fight? *Well*, the Reverend answered *that* for you, in his good short words. Me and my three lads – two lads, I'd say rather – we belong to a regiment is a few thousand miles from here, in a little country without much importance except from the point of view that there's a Union Jack flies over it and the people of that country can write British Subject after their names. And that makes us proud!

Attercliffe   I tell you it makes us proud!

Hurst   We live in tattered tents in the rain, we eat rotten food, there's knives in the dark streets and blood on the floors of the hospitals, but we stand tall and proud: because of why we are there.

Attercliffe   Because we're there to serve our duty.

Musgrave   A soldier's duty is a soldier's life.

Walsh *enters at the extreme rear of the stage and walks slowly up behind the others and listens.*

A roll on the drum.

Musgrave   A soldier's life is to lay it down, against the enemies of his Queen.

A roll on the drum.

against the invaders of his home,

A roll on the drum.

against slavery, cruelty, tyrants.

A roll on the drum.

Hurst   You put on the uniform and you give your life away, and who do you give it to?

Attercliffe   You give it to your duty.

Musgrave   And you give it to your people, for peace, and for honesty.

A roll on the drum.

Musgrave   That's *my* book. (*He turns on the* **Mayor**.) What's *yours*?

Mayor (*very taken aback*)   Eh? What? I'm not a reading man, but it *sounds* all right . . . strong. Strong . . .

Musgrave (*to the* **Parson**)   What about *yours*?

Parson (*dubiously*)   You speak with enthusiasm, yes. I hope you'll be listened to.

Musgrave (*at the top of his passion*)   By God, I hope I am! D'ye hear me, d'ye hear me, d'ye hear me – I'm the Queen of England's man, and I'm wearing her coat and I know her Book backwards. I'm Black Jack Musgrave, me, the hardest serjeant of the line – I work my life to bugle and drum, for eighteen years I fought for one flag only, salute it in the morning, can you haul it down at dark? The Last Post of a living life? Look – I'll show it to you all. And I'll *dance* for you beneath it – hoist up the flag, boy – up, up, *up*!

Attercliffe *has nipped up the ladder, holding the rope. He loops the rope over the cross-bar of the lamp-bracket, drops to the plinth again, flings open the lid of the big box, and hauls on the rope.*

Hurst *beats frantically on his drum. The rope is attached to the contents of the box, and these are jerked up to the cross-bar and reveal themselves as an articulated skeleton dressed in a soldier's tunic and trousers, the rope noosed round the neck. The* **People** *draw back in horror.* **Musgrave** *begins to dance, waving his rifle, his face contorted with demoniac fury.*

Musgrave (*as he dances, sings, with mounting emphasis*)

Up he goes and no one knows
How to bring him downwards
Dead man's feet
Over the street
Riding the roofs
And crying down your chimneys
Up he goes and no one knows
Who it was that rose him
But white and red
He waves his head
He sits on your back
And you'll never lose him
Up he goes and no one knows
How to bring him downwards.

He breaks off at the climax of the song, and stands panting. The drum stops.

That'll do. That'll do for *that*. (*He beckons gently to the* **People**.) You can come back. Come back. Come back. We're all quiet now. But nobody move out of this market-place. You saw the gun loaded. Well, it's on a very quick swivel and the man behind it's well trained. (*He gestures with his rifle towards the platform party.*) And *I've* won a regimental cup four years running for small-arms marksmanship. So be good, and be gentle, *all* of you.

That checks the **Bargee**, *who made a move. The* **Mayor** *seems to be about to speak.*

Right, Mr Mayor – I'll explain the whole business.

Parson (*in a smaller voice than usual*)   Business? What business, sir? Do you intend to imply you are *threatening* us with these weapons?

Mayor   The man's gone balmy. Constable, do summat, grab him, quick!

The **Constable** *makes an indecisive move.*

Musgrave   Be *quiet*. I shan't warn agen. (*To the* **Mayor** *and the* **Parson**.) You two. Get down there! Constable, *there*!

He gestures peremptorily and the three of them obey him, moving downstage to stand facing the platform and covered by the gun.

Now I said I'll explain. So listen. (*He points to the skeleton.*) This, up here, was a comrade of mine – of ours. At least, he was till a few months since. He was killed, being there for his duty, in the country I was telling you about, where the regiment is stationed. It's not right a colony, you know, it's a sort of Protectorate, but British, y'know, British. This, up here, he was walking down a street latish at night, he'd been to the opera – *you've* got a choral society in this town, I daresay – well, he was only a soldier, but North Country, he was full of music, so he goes to the opera. And on his way again to camp he was shot in the back. And it's not surprising, neither: there was patriots abroad, anti-British, subversive; like they didn't dare to shoot him to his face. He was daft to be out alone, wasn't he? Out of bounds, after curfew.

Attercliffe (*with suppressed frenzy*)   Get on to the words as matter, serjeant!

Musgrave (*turning on him fiercely*)   *I'm* talking now; you wait your turn! . . . So we *come* to the words that matter. He was the third to be shot that week. He was the fifteenth that month. In the back and all. Add to which he was young, he was liked, he sang songs, they say, and he joked and he laughed – he was a good soldier, too, else *I'd* not have bothered (we'll leave out his sliding off to the opera WOL, but by and large good, and I've got standards). So at twelve o'clock at night they beat up the drums and sounded the calls and called out the guard and the guard calls us *all* out, and the road is red and slippery, and every soldier in the camp no longer in the camp but in the streets of that city, rifle-butts, bayonets, every street cut off for eight blocks north and west of the opera-house. And that's how it began.

Hurst (*the frenzy rising*)   The streets is empty, but the houses is full. He says, 'no undue measures, minimum violence', he says. 'But bring in the killers.'

Attercliffe   The killers are gone, they've gone miles off in that time – *sporting* away, right up in the mountains, I told you at the time.

Musgrave   That's not material, there's one man is dead, but there's *everyone's* responsible.

Hurst   So bring the *lot* in! It's easy, they're all in bed, kick the front doors down, knock 'em on the head, boys, chuck 'em in the wagons.

Attercliffe   I didn't known she was only a little kid, there was scores of 'em on that staircase, pitch-dark, trampling, screaming, they're all of 'em screaming, what are we to do?

Hurst   Knock 'em on the head, boy, chuck 'em in the wagons.

Attercliffe   How was I to tell she was only a little kid?

Musgrave (*bringing it to an end*)   THAT'S NOT MATERIAL! You were told to bring 'em in. If you killed her, you killed her! She was just one, and who cares a damn

for that! Stay in your place and keep your hands on that
Gatling. We've got to have order here, whatever there was
there; and I can tell you it wasn't order . . . (*To* **Hurst**.) You,
take a rifle. Leave your drum down.

Hurst *jumps on the plinth, takes a rifle and loads.*

We've *got* to have order. So I'll just tell you quietly how
many there were was put down as injured – that's badly
hurt, hospital, we don't count knocks and bruises, any o'
that. Twenty-five men. Nine women. *No* children, whatever
he says. She was a fully grown girl, and she had a known
record as an associate of terrorists. That was her. Then four
men, one of them elderly, turned out to have died too.
Making five. Not so very many. Dark streets. Natural surge
of rage.

Hurst   We didn't find the killers.

Musgrave   Of course we didn't find 'em. Not *then* we
didn't, any road. We didn't even know 'em. But *I* know 'em,
now.

(*He turns on* **Walsh**.)   So what's *your* opinion?

Mayor   He's not balmy, he's mad, he's stark off his nut.

Parson   Why doesn't somebody do something?
Constable?

Noises off.

Musgrave (*indicates* **Walsh**)   I'm talking to *him*.

Constable (*very shakily*)   I shall have to ask you to – to
come down off this platform, Sarnt Musgrave. It looks to me
like your – your meeting's got out of hand.

Hurst (*covering the* **Constable**)   Aye, it has.

Musgrave (*to* **Walsh**)   Go on, brother. Tell us.

Walsh *climbs up at the back of the plinth.*

Walsh (*with a certain levity*)   My opinion, eh? I don't know why you need it. You've got *him*, haven't you? (*He waggles the skeleton's foot familiarly.*) What more d'you want? (*He comes forward and sits on the front of the plinth, looking at the other two* **Colliers**.) Aye, or you too, with your natty little nosegays dandled in your hatbands. Take 'em out, sharp! He's learnt you the truth, hasn't he?

They remove their cockades, shamefacedly.

Pugnacious Collier   All right, *that'll* do.

Walsh   Will it, matey, will it? If it helps you to remember what we've been fighting for, I daresay it will. Trade Unions aren't formed, you know, so we can all have beer-ups on the Army.

Slow Collier   He said that'll do. I'm sick and bloody tired – I don't know *what* it's all about.

Walsh (*drops down to the forestage*)   Come home and I'll tell you. The circus is over. Come on.

Musgrave   Oh no it's not. Just bide still a while. There's more to be said yet. When I asked you your opinion I meant about them we was talking about – them as did *this*, up here.

Walsh   Well, *what* about them – brother? Clear enough to me. You go for a soldier, you find yourself in someone else's country, you deserve all you get. *I'd* say it stands to reason.

Musgrave   And that's *all* you would say? I'd thought better of you.

Walsh (*irritated*)   Now look, look here, what *are* you trying to get? You come to this place all hollering for sympathy, oh you've been beating and murdering and following your trade boo-hoo: but we're not bloody interested! You mend your own heartache and leave us to sort with ours – we've enough and to spare!

Musgrave (*very intensely*)   This *is* for your heart. Take another look at *him*. (*Points to skeleton.*) Go on, man, both eyes, and carefully. Because you all used to known him: or most of you did. Private Billy Hicks, late of this parish, welcome him back from the wars, he's bronzed and he's fit, with many a tall tale of distant campaigning to spin round the fireside – ah, *you* used to know him, *didn't* you, Mrs Hitchcock!

Mrs Hitchcock *has risen in great alarm.*

Slow Collier   That's never Billy Hicks, ye dirty liar.

Pugnacious Collier   He wor my putter for two year, when I hewed coal in number five – he hewed there hisself for nigh on a year alongside o' my brother.

Slow Collier   He left his clogs to me when he went to join up – that's never our Billy.

Noises off   Never Billy. Never Billy.

Bargee   'Never Billy Hicks' – 'Never Billy Hicks' – they don't dare believe it. You've knocked 'em to the root, boy. Oh the white faces!

Mrs Hitchcock   She ought to be told. She's got a right to know.

Musgrave   Go along then and tell her.

Hurst (*to* **Musgrave**)   You letting her go?

Musgrave   Yes.

Hurst   But –

Musgrave (*curtly*)   Attend to your orders.

Mrs Hitchcock *goes out.*

When I say it's Billy Hicks, you can believe me it's true.

Walsh   Aye, I'll believe you. And you know what I think – it's downright indecent!

Musgrave   Aye, aye? But wait. Because here is the reason. I'm a religious man, and I see the causes of the Almighty in every human work.

Parson   That is absolute blasphemy!

Mayor   This won't do you a pennorth o' good, you know.

Musgrave   Not to me, no. But maybe to you? Now as I understand the workings of God, through greed and the world, this man didn't die because he went alone to the opera, he was killed because he had to be – it being decided; that now the people in that city was worked right up to killing soldiers, then more and more soldiers should be sent for them to kill, and the soldiers in turn should kill the people in that city, more and more, always – that's what I said to you: four men, one girl, then the twenty-five and the nine – *and* it'll go on, there or elsewhere, and it can't be stopped neither, except there's someone finds out Logic and brings the wheel round. You see, the Queen's Book, which eighteen years I've lived, it's turned inside out for *me*. There used to be my duty: now there's a disease –

Hurst   Wild-wood mad.

Musgrave   Wild-wood mad we are; and so we've fetched it home. You've had Moses and the Prophets – that's *him* – (*He points at* **Walsh**.) – 'cos he told you. But you were all for enlisting, it'd still have gone on. Moses and the Prophets, what good did they do?

He sits down and broods. There is a pause.

Walsh (*awkwardly*)   There's no one from this town be over keen to join up now. You've preached your little gospel: I daresay we can go home?

Musgrave *makes no reply. The* **Soldiers** *look at one another doubtfully.*

Hurst   What do we do now?

Attercliffe   Wait.

Hurst   Serjeant –

Attercliffe (*shushing him*)   Ssh-ssh!

A pause. Restive noises, off.

Hurst   Serjeant –

Attercliffe   Serjeant – they've heard your message, they'll none of them forget it. Haven't we done what we came for?

Hurst (*astonished, to* **Attercliffe**)   Done what we came for?

Attercliffe *shushes him again as* **Musgrave** *stirs.*

Musgrave (*as though to himself*)   One man, and for him five. Therefore, for five of them we multiply out, *and* we find it five-and-twenty. . . . So, as I understand Logic and Logic to me is the mechanism of God – that means that today there's twenty-five persons will have to be –

Attercliffe *jumps up in horror.* **Annie** *and* **Mrs Hitchcock** *appear at the upper window. When she sees the skeleton* **Annie** *gasps and seems about to scream.*

Musgrave (*cutting her short*)   It's true. It's him. You don't need to cry out; you knew it when he left you.

Annie   Take him down. Let me have him. I'll come down for him now.

Bargee   Away down, me strong Annie. I'll carry you a golden staircase – aha, she's the royal champion, stand by as she comes down.

As he speaks he jumps on to the plinth, takes away the ladder, nips across the stage and props it under the window.

Musgrave   No! Let her wait up there. I said: wait! . . . Now then, who's with me! Twenty-five to die and the Logic is worked out. Who'll help me? You? (*He points to* **Walsh**.) I made sure that you would: you're a man like the Black Musgrave, you: you have purposes, and you can lead. Join along with my madness, friend. I brought it back to England but I've brought the cure too – to turn it on to them that

sent it out of this country – way-out-ay they sent it, where
they hoped that only soldiers could catch it and rave! Well
here's three redcoat ravers on their own kitchen
hearthstone! Who do we start with? These? (*He turns on the*
Mayor.) 'Loyal hearts and true, every man jack of us.' (*To
the* **Parson**.) 'Draw the sword with gladness.' Why, *swords* is
for honour, carry 'em on church parade, a *sword'll* never
offer you three hundred and fifty bullets in a minute – and it
was no bright sword neither finished *his* life in a back street!
(*He points to* **Billy**, *and then at the* **Constable**.) Or what about
the Peeler? If we'd left it to *him, you'd* ha' been boxed away
to barracks six or eight hours ago! Come on now, let's have
you, you know I'm telling you truth!

Walsh   Nay: it won't do.

Hurst   It won't do? Why not?

Walsh   I'm not over clear why not. Last night there was
me and some others tried to whip away that Gatling. And
we'd ha' used it and all: by God, there was need. But that's
one thing, y'see, and this is another – ent it, you tell me?

He appeals to the **Colliers**.

Pugnacious Collier   Nay, I don't know.

Slow Collier   I think they're all balmy, the whole damn
capful's arse-over-tip –

Walsh   No it's not. *I'm* not. And it comes to this wi' me:
he's still in uniform, and he's still got his Book. He's doing
his duty. Well, I take no duties from no bloody lobsters. This
town lives by collieries. That's coal-owners and it's pitmen –
aye, and they battle, and the pitmen'll win. But not wi' no
soldier-boys to order our fight for us. Remember their trade:
you give 'em one smell of a broken town, you'll never get
'em out!

Musgrave (*with growing desperation*)   But you don't
understand me – all of you, listen! I told you we could *cure* –

Attercliffe   I don't think you can.

Musgrave (*flabbergasted*)   Eh? What's that? Stay by your weapon!

Attercliffe   No. (*He stands away from the gun.*)

Hurst *rapidly takes his place.*

Hurst (*to the crowd*)   Keep still, the lot of you!

Attercliffe   It won't do, Black Jack. You swore there'd be no killing.

Musgrave   No I did not.

Attercliffe   You gave us to believe. We've done what we came for, and it's there we should have ended. *I've* ended. No killing.

He deliberately gets down from the platform, and squats on the ground. **Musgrave** *looks around him, appealing and appalled.*

Bargee   I'm with you, general!

Musgrave   You?

Bargee   Nobody else! I'll serve you a lovely gun! Rapine and riot! (*He scrambles on to the plinth, picks up a rifle from the box and loads it.*) When do we start breaking open the boozers? Or the pawnshops and all – who's for a loot?

Musgrave   None of you at all? Come on, come on, why, he was your Billy, wasn't he? That you knew and you worked with – don't you want to revenge him?

Annie   Somebody hold the ladder. I'm going to come down.

The **Slow Collier** *does so.*

Musgrave (*urgently, to her*)   Billy Hicks, lassie: here: he used to be yours! Tell them what they've got to do: tell them the truth!

Annie *has started to come down the ladder. When she is down, the* **Collier** *lowers it to the ground.*

Hurst   Wait a minute, serjeant, leave me to talk to them! We've not got time bothering wi' no squalling tarts.

Musgrave   Keep you your place.

Hurst (*furiously*)   I'm in my bloody place! And I'll tell you this straight, if we lose this crowd now, we've lost all the work, for ever! And remember summat else. There's Dragoons on the road!

General sensation. Shouts off: 'Dragoons'.

Hurst (*to the crowd*)   So you've just got five minutes to make up your minds.

He grabs his rifle up, and motions the **Bargee** *violently to the Gatling. The* **Bargee** *takes over, and* **Hurst** *leaps off the plinth and talks straight into the* **Colliers**' *faces and at the audience.*

We've earned our living by beating and killing folk like yourselves in the streets of their own city. Well, it's drove us mad – and so we come back here to tell you how and to show you what it's like. The ones we want to deal with aren't, for a change, you and your mates, but a bit higher up. The ones as never get hurt. (*He points at the* **Mayor**, **Parson** *and* **Constable**.) Him. Him. Him. You hurt them hard, and they'll not hurt you again. And they'll not send *us* to hurt you neither. But if you let 'em, then us three'll be killed – aye and worse, we'll be forgotten – and the whole bloody lot'll start all over again!

He climbs back and takes over the gun.

Musgrave   For God's sake stand with us. We've *got* to be remembered.

Slow Collier   We ought to, you know. He might be right.

Walsh   I don't know. I don't trust it.

Pugnacious Collier   Ahr and be damned, these are just like the same as us. Why don't we stand with 'em?

Walsh (*obstinately*)   I've not yet got this clear.

Annie   To me it's quite clear. He asked me to tell you the truth. My truth's an easy tale, it's old true-love gone twisted, like they called it 'malformed' – they put part in the ground, and hang the rest on a pillar here, and expect me to sit under it making up song-ballads. All right.

> My true love is a scarecrow
> Of rotted rag and bone
> Ask him: where are the birds, Billy?
> Where have they all gone?

He says: Unbutton my jacket, and they'll all fly out of the ribs – oh, oh, I'm not mad, though you told us that *you* were – let's have that bundle!

Mrs Hitchcock *throws down a bundle.* **Annie** *shakes it out, revealing* **Sparky**'s *tunic.*

Take a sight o' this, you hearty colliers: see what they've brought you. You can match it up with Billy's. Last night there were four o' these walking, weren't there? Well, this morning there's three. They buried the other one in Ma Hitchcock's midden. Go on, ask 'em why!

Hurst   He's a deserter, is why!

Annie (*holding up the tunic*)   Hey, here's the little hole where they let in the bayonet. Eee, aie, easily in. His blood's on my tongue, so hear what it says. A bayonet is a raven's beak. This tunic's a collier's jacket. That scarecrow's a birdcage. What more do you want!

Walsh   Is this what she says true? Where *is* he, the fourth of you?

Musgrave   He was killed, and that's all. By an accident killed. It's barely materi –

Attercliffe   Oh, it's material. And no goddamned accident. I said it to you, Musgrave, it washes it all out.

Walsh   It bloody does and all, as far as I go. (*He turns to the other* **Colliers**.) If you want to stand by 'em when they've done for their own mucker and not one of the bastards can tell ye the same tale, well, you're at your damned liberty and take it and go!

The **Colliers** *murmur dubiously.*

Hurst (*frantic*)   I'm going to start shooting!

General reaction of fear: he clearly means it. He spits at **Musgrave**.

You and your everlasting Word – you've pulled your own roof down! But *I'll* prop your timber for you – I'll give a One, Two, and a Three: and I'm opening fire!

Attercliffe   No.

He jumps up and stands on the step of the plinth, below the gun and facing it, with his arms spread out so that the muzzle is against his breast.

Hurst (*distorted with rage*)   Get down! Get down off it, you old cuckold, I don't care who you are. I'll put the first one *through* you! I *swear* it, I will! One! Two! . . .

Mayor (*to the* **Constable**)   Go for that gun.

The **Constable** *is making a cautious move towards the gun, but he is forestalled by* **Musgrave**, *who flings himself at* **Hurst** *and knocks him away from the breach. There is a moment's tense struggle behind the gun.*

Musgrave (*as he struggles*)   The wrong way. The wrong way. You're trying to do it without Logic.

Then **Hurst** *gives way and falls back down the steps of the plinth. He recovers himself.*

Hurst (*panting with excitement*)   All right then, Black Jack. All right, it's finished. The lot. You've lost it. I'm off!

Musgrave (*stunned*)   Come back here. You'll come back, you'll obey orders.

Hurst *makes a grab forward, snatches his rifle from the platform and jumps back clear.*

Hurst (*to the crowd*)   Get out o' my road!

At the very instant he turns towards the wings to run away, a shot is fired offstage. His quick turn changes into a grotesque leap as the bullet hits him, and he collapses on the stage. A bugle blares from offstage.

Voices Off   Dragoons!

Orders shouted and general noise of cavalry coming to a halt and dismounting.

Mayor ⎱ (*one after another, rapidly*)
Constable ⎰ The Dragoons! The Dragoons!
Parson ⎰ Saved! Saved! Saved!

Voices Off   Saved! Saved! Saved!

Musgrave *is standing beside the gun, temporarily at a loss.*

Attercliffe *has jumped down beside* **Hurst** *and lifted his head. Everyone else stands amazed.*

Suddenly **Musgrave** *swings the gun to point towards the Dragoons. The* **Bargee** *ups with his rifle and sticks it into* **Musgrave***'s back.*

Bargee   Serjeant, put your hands up!

Musgrave *is pushed forward by the rifle, but he does not obey. The* **Trooper** *enters, clicking the bolt of his smoking carbine, and shouting.*

Trooper   Everybody stand where you are! You, put your hands up!

Musgrave *does so.*

Bargee   I've got him, soldier! I've got him! Crooked Joe's got him, Mr Mayor.

The **Officer** *strides in, drawing his sabre.*

Give a cheer – hooroar!

Cheers off.

The **Officer** *comes to attention before the* **Mayor** *and salutes with his sabre.*

Officer   Mr Mayor, are we in time?

Mayor   Aye, you're in time. You're *just* in bloody time.

Officer (*seeing* **Musgrave**)   22128480 Serjeant Musgrave, J.?

Musgrave   My name.

Officer   We've heard word you'd come here. You are under arrest. Robbery and desertion. There were *three* who came with you.

Attercliffe (*getting up from* **Hurst**, *whose head falls back*)   You can count me for one of them. One other's dead already. Here's the third.

Officer   You're under arrest.

Constable   Hold out your hands.

He takes out two pairs of handcuffs and fetters them.

Officer   Mr Mayor, my troopers are at your disposal. What do you require of us?

Mayor   Well, I'd say it was about all over by now, young man – wouldn't you?

Officer   Law and order is established?

Parson   Wiser counsels have prevailed, Captain.

Bargee   *I* caught him, *I* caught him, *I* used me strategy!

Officer   My congratulations, all.

Walsh (*with great bitterness*)   The community's been saved. Peace and prosperity rules. We're all friends and neighbours for the rest of today. We're all sorted out. We're back where we were. So what do we do?

Bargee

> Free beer. It's still here.
> No more thinking. Easy drinking.
> End of a bad bad dream. Gush forth the foaming stream.

He takes the bung out of the barrel and starts filling tankards.

Officer   The winter's broken up. Let normal life begin again.

Bargee   Aye, aye, *begin* again!

He is handing the mugs to the people. He starts singing, and they all join in, by degrees.

> There was an old man called Michael Finnegan
> He had whiskers on his chin-egan
> The wind came out and blew them in agen
> Poor old Michael Finnegan –
> Begin agen –
>
> There was an old man etcetera . . .

He gives out mugs in the following order: the **Mayor**, *the* **Parson**, *the* **Slow Collier**, *the* **Pugnacious Collier**, *the* **Constable**. *Each man takes his drink, swigs a large gulp, then links wrists with the previous one, until all are dancing round the centre-piece in a chain, singing.*

Annie *has climbed the plinth and lowers the skeleton. She sits with it on her knees. The* **Dragoons** *remain standing at the side of the stage.* **Musgrave** *and* **Attercliffe** *come slowly downstage. The* **Bargee** *fills the last two tankards and hands one to* **Walsh**, *who turns his back angrily. The* **Bargee** *empties one mug, and joins the tail of the dance, still holding the other. After one more round he again beckons* **Walsh**. *This time the latter thinks for a moment, then bitterly throws his hat on the ground, snarls into the impassive face of the* **Dragoon**, *and joins in the dance, taking the beer.*

The scene closes, leaving **Musgrave** *and* **Attercliffe** *on the forestage.* **Mrs Hitchcock** *retires from the window.*

Scene Two

A prison cell.

This scene is achieved by a barred wall descending in front of the dancers of the previous scene. After a while the sound dies away, and the lights change so that we can no longer see past the bars.
Musgrave *remains standing, looking into the distance with his back to the audience.* **Attercliffe** *sighs and sits down gingerly on the floor.*

Attercliffe Sit down and rest yourself, serjeant. That's all there is left . . . Go on, man, sit down . . . Then stand and the devil take you! It's *your* legs, not mine. It's my *hands* is what matters. They finished Sparky and that finished me, and Sparky finished you. Holy God save us, why warn't I a greengrocer, then I'd never ha' been cuckolded, never gone for no soldier, never no dead Sparky, and never none of this. Go on, serjeant, talk to me. I'm an old old stupid bastard and I've nowt to do now but fret out the runs of the consequence; and the whole croaking work it's finished and done. Go on, serjeant, talk.

Musgrave *does not move.*

A pause.

Mrs Hitchcock *enters, carrying a glass.*

Mrs Hitchcock (*to* **Musgrave**) It's port with a bit o' lemon. I often take it of a morning; like it settles me stummick for the day. The officer said I could see you, if I warn't no more nor five minutes. Sit down and I'll give it to your mouth – them wrist-irons makes it difficult, I daresay.

Musgrave (*without looking at her*) Give it to him. I don't want it.

Mrs Hitchcock He can have half of it. You take a sup first.

Musgrave *shakes his head.*

All right. How you like.

She goes to **Attercliffe** *and puts the glass to his mouth.*

Attercliffe   I'm obliged to you, missus.

Mrs Hitchcock   It's on the house, this one. Change from the Queen, ent it?

Musgrave   Numbers and order. According to Logic. I had worked it out for months.

He swings round to **Mrs Hitchcock**.

What made it break down!

Mrs Hitchcock   Ah, there's the moral of it. You ask our Annie.

Musgrave (*furiously*)   He was killed by pure accident! It had nothing to do –

Attercliffe   Oh by God, it had.

Mrs Hitchcock   The noisy one, warn't he? Pack o' cards and all the patter. You asked me to trust you – (*Her voice rises with rage and emotion.*) – he was only a young lad, for gracious goodness Christ, he'd a voice like a sawmill – what did you want to do it for, you gormless great gawk!

Attercliffe   *He* didn't do it.

Mrs Hitchcock   He did, oh he did! And he broke his own neck.

Musgrave   What's the matter with you, woman!

Mrs Hitchcock   All wrong, you poured it out all wrong! I could ha' told you last night if only I'd known – the end of the world and you thought you could call a parade. In control – *you*!

Musgrave (*very agitated*)   Don't talk like that. You're talking about my duty. Good order and the discipline: it's the only road I know. Why can't you see it?

Mrs Hitchcock   All I can see is Crooked Joe Bludgeon having his dance out in the middle of fifty Dragoons! It's time you learnt your life, you big proud serjeant. Listen: last evening you told all about this anarchy and where it came from – like, scribble all over with life or love, and that makes anarchy. Right?

Musgrave   Go on.

Mrs Hitchcock   Then *use* your Logic – if you can. Look at it this road: here we are, and we'd got life and love. Then *you* came in and you did your scribbling where nobody asked you. Aye, it's arsy-versey to what you said, but it's still an anarchy, isn't it? And it's all your work.

Musgrave   Don't tell me there was life or love in this town.

Mrs Hitchcock   There was. There was hungry men, too – fighting for their food. But *you* brought in a different war.

Musgrave   I brought it in to end it.

Attercliffe   To end it by its own rules: no bloody good. She's right, you're wrong. You can't cure the pox by further whoring. Sparky died of those damned rules. And so did the other one.

Musgrave   That's not the truth. (*He looks at them both in appeal, but they nod.*) That's not the truth. God was with me . . . God . . . (*He makes a strange animal noise of despair, a sort of sob that is choked off suddenly, before it can develop into a full howl.*) – and all they dancing – all of them – there.

Mrs Hitchcock   Ah, not for long. And it's not a dance of joy. Those men are hungry, so they've got no time for *you.* One day they'll be full, though, and the Dragoons'll be gone, and then they'll remember.

Musgrave (*shaking his head*)   No.

Mrs Hitchcock   Let's hope it, any road. Eh?

She presents the glass to his lips. This time he accepts it and drinks, and remains silent.

Attercliffe (*melancholy but quiet*) That running tyke of a
Sparky, he reckoned he wor the only bastard in the barracks
had a voice. Well, he warn't. There's other men can sing
when he's not here. So listen at this.

He sings.

> I plucked a blood-red rose-flower down
> And gave it to my dear.
> I set my foot out across the sea
> And she never wept a tear.
>
> I came back home as gay as a bird
> I sought her out and in:
> And I found her at last in a little attic room
> With a napkin round her chin.

At her dinner, you see. Very neat and convenient.

He sings.

> Oh are you eating meat, I said,
> Or are you eating fish?
> I'm eating an apple was given me today,
> The sweetest I could wish.

So I asked her where she got it, and by God the tune
changed then. Listen at what she told me.

He sings to a more heavily accented version of the tune.

> Your blood-red rose is withered and gone
> And fallen on the floor:
> And he who brought the apple down
> Shall be my darling dear.
> For the apple holds a seed will grow
> In live and lengthy joy
> To raise a flourishing tree of fruit
> For ever and a day.
> With a fal-la-la-the-dee, toor-a-ley,
> For ever and a day.

They're going to hang us up a length higher nor most apple-
trees grow, serjeant. D'you reckon we can start an orchard?

Joe Orton was born in Leicester in 1933 and was battered to death in August 1967. He left school at sixteen and went to RADA two years later. He spent six months in prison for defacing library books. In 1964 his first play, *The Ruffian on the Stair*, was broadcast and his first full-length piece, *Entertaining Mr Sloane*, was staged in the West End, as was *Loot* two years later. *The Erpingham Camp* was televised in 1966 and staged at the Royal Court in 1967 in double-bill with *The Ruffian on the Stair*. His television plays, *The Good and Faithful Servant* and *Funeral Games*, were shown posthumously in 1967 and 1968. His last play, *What the Butler Saw*, was not staged until 1969, though it was successfully revived by the Royal Court in 1975 in a season that also included important revivals of *Loot* and *Entertaining Mr Sloane*. These last two plays have been made into successful films. Orton also wrote a screenplay for the Beatles, *Up Against It*, which was never filmed. A novel, *Head to Toe*, was published posthumously in 1971. *The Orton Dairies* (ed. John Lahr) were published in 1986.

Loot

To Peggy

Lord Summerhays   Anarchism is a game at which the
Police can beat you. What have
you to say to that?

Gunner   What have I to say to it! Well I call
it scandalous: that's what I have to
say to it.

Lord Summerhays   Precisely: that's all anybody has to
say to it, except the British Public,
which pretends not to believe it.

Misalliance George Bernard Shaw

Introduction

Loot was completed in October 1964. The play raises the
stakes of Orton's comic attack and the tone of his laughter. In
his early public appearances, there had been flashes of the
grotesque and of the sensational detachment which was part
of Orton's hilarious comic view of things: the dead goldfish in
The Ruffian on the Stair, the murdering Sloane and his fleshy
predatory landlady who entertains him; the one-armed and
eponymous good and faithful servant Mr Buchanan. But, in
all these plays, the ferocity of Orton's disgust hadn't yet found
its proper theatrical form. 'When you can assume that your
audience holds the same beliefs as you do, you can relax a
little and use more normal means of talking to it,' Flannery
O'Connor writes about the grotesque. 'When you have to
assume that it does not, then you have to make your vision
apparent by shock – to the hard of hearing you shout and for
the almost blind you draw large and startling figures.' In *Loot*,
where both the just and the dead are mocked, the corrupt
detective Truscott, the credulous widower McLeavy, and the
rapacious souls around him are all startling figures, whose
outrageousness is meant to raise the stakes of laughter and to
call into question the received opinions and unexamined
emotions of the audience. 'It's a Freudian nightmare,' says
the son, Hal, who is about to dump his mother's corpse into
the wardrobe in order to hide money he's stolen in her coffin.
And so it is. Comedy always acts out unconscious wishes
suppressed in daily life; and Orton seized this liberation with
gusto. 'You're at liberty to answer your own doorbell, miss,'
says the notorious Detective Truscott. 'That is how we tell
whether or not we live in a free country.' Orton's laughter
was offensive, elegant, cruel, shocking, monstrous, hilarious,
and smart. 'Your style is simple and direct,' says the oafish
Detective Truscott of the nurse's confession of foul play. 'It's
a theme which less skilfully handled could've given offence.'
The joke lampoons the critical appraisal of Orton's style,

disarming an audience while sticking the boot further in.

Loot was launched with an all-star cast (Geraldine McEwen, Kenneth Williams, Duncan Macrae and Ian McShane) and directed by Peter Wood. It was scheduled for a short provincial tour and a West End run. But the plans came a cropper. The combination of frivolity and ferociousness which Orton had discovered as his mature comic milieu was new to the English stage and it was difficult for any troupe to find the correct playing style. The confusion in Peter Wood's concept was immediately visible in the elegant but cartoonish black and white sets; Kenneth Williams' outrageous mugging as Detective Truscott; and the continual demand on Orton for rewrites which never allowed the performers the security of the same script from one day to the next. *Loot*, which opened in Cambridge in February 1965 and closed in Wimbledon in March, was a notorious flop. No West End Theatre would take it. 'The play is clearly not written naturalistically, but it must be directed and acted with absolute realism,' Orton wrote about the stage production of *Ruffian* with the experience of *Loot*'s failure still vividly in his mind. 'No "stylization", no "camp". No attempt in fact to match the author's extravagance of dialogue with extravagance of direction.' The first production of *Loot* suffered and sank because of these excesses. '*Loot* is a serious play,' Orton wrote to his producers. 'Unless *Loot* is directed and acted perfectly seriously the play will fail. As it failed in its original touring version. A director who imagines that the only object is to get a laugh is not for me.'

Orton was angry and shattered by *Loot*'s failure. In the rest of 1965, he produced only one television play, his version of *The Bacchae*, a fun palace revolution set in a Butlin's holiday resort: *The Erpingham Camp*. The play was part of an ITV series on 'The Seven Deadly Sins'; and *The Erpingham Camp*, like all Orton's farces, satirized Pride. Orton had explored the notion as a film treatment for Lindsay Anderson and then developed it as a Brechtian epic complete (in early drafts) with illustrative banners such as SCENE 5: AN EXAMPLE OF THE ACTIVE LIFE OF THE CHURCH. ERPINGHAM PREPARES HIMSELF TO MEET THE PEOPLE. THEOLOGY DISCUSSED.

THE PADRE PROVES THAT CHRISTIANITY IS ESSENTIAL TO GOOD HEALTH. The television play, which was aired in 1966, was a tepid version of the drastically rewritten and dazzingly epigrammatic Royal Court production in 1967. '*Erpingham* is the best play of mine performed so far,' Orton noted in his diary after the ragged dress rehearsal. 'If only Arthur Lowe were playing Erpingham they'd all be raving.' Besides the television play, Orton made his first visit to Morocco where, in spite of boys and hash, he continued to brood about the fate of *Loot*. 'I think it's disgusting with so much utter shit put on in both the commercial and subsidized theatres that a play like *Loot* should have this difficulty. I'd understand it after Wimbledon, but not after a really pretty average Rep production which succeeded in attracting a glowing notice in the *Telegraph*,' Orton wrote to his agent, Peggy Ramsay, who was having difficulty finding another London production for the play. 'I'm sick, sick, sick of the theatre . . . I think you'd better warn Oscar [Lewenstein] that if the *Loot* option runs out in January with no signs of the play being put on I shan't renew the option. I shall throw the play on the fire. And I shan't write a third stage play. I shall earn my living on T.V. I'm really quite capable of carrying out this. I've always admired Congreve who, after the absolute failure of *The Way of the World*, just stopped writing. And Rimbaud who turned his back on the literary world after writing a few volumes of poems . . .'

However, Orton did see his play remounted in London by Charles Marowitz. On 27 September 1966 at the Jeanetta Cochrane Theatre, *Loot* reopened; both the times and Orton's luck had changed. The play was an overwhelming hit.

Well, the sound and fury is over. And LOOT and JOE ORTON (as you can see from the reviews) are a great success. [Orton wrote to an American friend.] I feel exhausted. 18 months of struggling to vindicate the honour of my play (my own is beyond vindication) have left me weak at the knees.

There were other reviews which I haven't enclosed

because I can't lay my hands on a spare copy. The *Express*, for instance, is a rave. Which pleases the management; it's supposed to sell a lot of tickets. The *Financial Times* was excellent. We had two bad ones. The *Mail* (not exactly bad, but sniffy) and the *Birmingham Post* (which doesn't sell a seat anyway, but was furious . . .). But who cares. We've scooped the pool with the rest.

Loot won the *Evening Standard* Award and *Plays and Players* Award for the best play of the year. Orton was, to his delighted surprise, a new star. 'I'm now engaged in writing a film [*Up Against It*, commissioned by the Beatles but unproduced] for which I'm being paid (the equivalent) of 30,000 dollars,' Orton wrote to a friend in 1967. 'I'm going up, up, up.' Despite *Loot*'s success, Orton was never thrilled with the production. 'In general the tone of the London production is OK. Of course a lot of lines are muffed. This is the fault of having inexperienced actors in the parts . . .' Orton wrote to his producers about *Loot*'s forthcoming Broadway production. 'The way it was done was on the right lines. Ideally, it should be nearer *The Homecoming* rather than *I Love Lucy*. Don't think I'm a snob about *I Love Lucy*. I've watched it often. I think it's very funny. But it's aimed purely at making an audience laugh. And that isn't the prime aim of *Loot* . . . I also think it might be wise to reconsider Marowitz as a director. God knows I'm not a fan of his. I think a lot of the direction in *Loot* was atrocious. But on the principle of better the Devil you know than the Devil you don't, I'd think about it. With a stronger cast his direction wouldn't stick out so much. And it is a success in London!! Remember that.'

In its capering with 'human remains' and its gleeful celebration of police corruption, *Loot* attacked the most deep-seated myths of English culture. 'I never understand why [people are offended],' Orton said mischievously. 'Because, if you're absolutely practical – and I hope I am – a coffin is a box. One calls it a coffin and once you've called it a coffin it immediately has all sorts of associations.' Orton's art, as his diary recounts, had a curious way of haunting his life. Reality was the ultimate outrage:

Monday 26th December. I began writing *What the Butler Saw* at eleven o'clock this morning. At twenty past the telephone rang. It was from a call-box and the caller had difficulty getting through. When they did it was George [Barnet, Orton's brother-in-law]. He said, 'I've rung to tell you that your mum died this morning. It was very quick. She had a heart attack.' He didn't say anything else.

My father, who has just come out of hospital having been run over by a car, is staying with Leoni [Barnet, Orton's youngest sister]. The funeral is Friday . . .

Tuesday 27th December. . . . Leoni hasn't rung. I'll have to send a telegram to find out details of my mother's funeral. I can't go home if there's nowhere to sleep.

And I don't fancy spending the night in the house with the corpse. A little too near the Freudian bone for comfort . . .

Wednesday 28th December. . . . Leoni rang at about six. I'd sent a telegram earlier today. She'd just got it from work. She said that Dad has gone back home. Sleeps in my mother's bed downstairs with the corpse. After his accident he can't piss straight and floods the lavatory with it whenever he goes. She said, 'Well, I'm shocked by our Marilyn, you know.' I said, 'Why, what's she done?' Leoni said, 'Oh, you know, she behaves very ignorantly all round. And when I told her Mum was dead all she said was – "I'm not surprised." Well, you know, what kind of remark is that?' Dougie [Orton's younger brother] was upset. Remarkable how those without hearts when young suddenly develop them in later life.

I promised to go home tomorrow. Leoni and George will come round in the evening. As the corpse is downstairs in the main living room it means going out or watching television with death at one's elbow. My father, fumbling out of bed in the middle of the night, bumped into the coffin and almost had the corpse on the floor.

Peggy Ramsay said how dreadfully reminiscent of *Loot* it all was.

Thursday 29th December. I arrived in Leicester at four thirty. I had a bit of quick sex in a derelict house with a labourer I picked up . . .

I got home at five-thirty. Nobody in the house. My father was across the road with friends. He can't see now. The accident has affected his walking. He trembles all the time. I said I'd take him to the doctor's tomorrow. He should be in a hospital. Later on George and Leoni came round. We went to see Mum's body. It isn't at home as I supposed. It's laid out in a Chapel of Rest. Betty [Orton, his sister-in-law] came round with Susan and Sharon [his nieces]. Both very giggly. Dougie was also with them. He wasn't coming to see the body. He said he'd lifted Mum from the chair where she died and put her into the bed. He didn't want to see her again.

We all went to the Chapel of Rest. It's a room, bare white-washed. Muted organ music from a speaker in the corner. The coffin lid propped up against the wall. It said 'Elsie May Orton aged 62 years'. Betty said, 'They've got her age wrong, see. Your Mum was 63. You should tell them about that. Put in a complaint.' I said, 'Why? It doesn't matter now.' 'Well,' said Betty, 'You want it done right, don't you? It's what you pay for.'

Mum was quite unrecognizable without her glasses. And they'd scraped her hair back from her forehead. She looked fat, old and dead. They'd made up her face. When I asked about this the mortician said, 'Would you say it wasn't discreet then, sir?' I said, 'No. It seems all right to me.' 'We try to give a lifelike impression,' he said. Which seems to be a contradiction in terms somehow. I've never seen a corpse before. How cold they are. I felt Mum's hand. Like marble. One hand was pink, the other white. I suppose that was the disease of which she died. The death certificate said, 'Coronary thrombosis, arteriosclerosis and hyper-tension'.

Great argument as we left. The undertaker gave Marilyn a small parcel containing the nightgown Mum was wearing when she died. Nobody wanted it. So the undertaker kept it. Not for himself. 'We pass it on to the old folks,' he said. 'Many are grateful, you know.'

Didn't sleep much. Awful bed. Damp. And cold. House without Mum seems to have died.

Friday 30th December. I got up at eight o'clock. I went downstairs to the kitchen. My father appeared in the doorway of the living room dressed only in a shirt. He looks thin and old. Hardly more than a skeleton. He weighs six stone four. I said, 'Hallo.' He peered blindly for a second and said, 'Hallo.' After a pause he said, 'Who are you?' 'Joe,' I said. He couldn't remember I'd come last night. Then he said, 'D'you know where my slippers are?' I said, 'What do you mean – where are my slippers?' He got down on his knees and began feeling around. 'I can't find my slippers,' he said. 'They're on your feet,' I said. And they were. He'd been wearing them all the time.

. . . At ten the undertaker arrived. 'What about the flowers?' he said. I said I'd no idea what to do with the flowers. 'Where's father's tribute?' he said. 'I think just father's tribute on the coffin.' He found my father's wreath and put it on the coffin. Then we all got into the cars. My aunt Lucy was upset because strict protocol wasn't observed. 'They're all walking wrong,' she said. 'They shouldn't be with husbands and wives. Just immediate circle should be in the first car.' Several women were at their garden gates as the cortège passed. I noticed two old women weeping on each other's shoulders.

At the chapel in the cemetery they held a brief burial service. They didn't carry the coffin into the chapel. They wheeled it in on a trolley. The vicar, very young and hearty, read the service in a droning voice. And then the coffin was wheeled out and to the graveside. It was a cold, bright morning. My mother's grave was a new one. Her last wish was to be buried with Tony my nephew who was drowned aged seven, eighteen months ago, but Pete and Marilyn refused to have the grave reopened and so my mother's last wish was ignored.

The coffin was lowered. The vicar said his piece. The earth was sprinkled over the coffin. My father began to cry. And we walked back to the waiting cars. Immediately the mourners left the graveside a flock of old women descended on the grave, picking over the wreaths and shaking their heads.

We got back home at half-past ten. Sandwiches had been prepared by a neighbour. The party got rather jolly later . . . My father sat through the party looking very woebegone. The only person who seemed to be at the funeral, Mrs Riley, Mum's lifelong friend, was crying quietly in a corner and drinking endless cups of tea. 'I don't except I'll see you again,' she said as she left. 'Your mother was very dear to me. I've known her all my life. I shan't come up here now she's gone. Goodbye,' she said, kissing my cheek. 'I hope you have a happier life than your Mum did.'

Leoni and I spent part of the afternoon throwing out cupboardsful of junk collected over the years: magazines, photographs, Christmas cards. We burnt eight pairs of shoes. I found a cup containing a pair of false teeth and threw it in the dustbin. Then I discovered that they belonged to my father. I had to rescue them. I found my mother's teeth in a drawer. I kept them. To amaze the cast of *Loot* . . .

Monday 2nd January. Spent the day working on *What the Butler Saw*. In the evening Peter Willes [Yorkshire Television producer] rang . . . I told him about the funeral. And the frenzied way my family behave. He seemed shocked. But then he thinks my plays are fantasies. He suddenly caught a glimpse of the fact that I write the truth . . .

Wednesday 4th January. . . . I'd taken my mother's false teeth down to the theatre. I said to Kenneth Cranham [who played Hal], 'Here, I thought you'd like the originals.' He said. 'What.' 'Teeth,' I said. 'Whose?' he said. 'My mum's,' I said. He looked very sick. 'You see,' I said, 'It's obvious that you're not thinking of the events of the play in terms of reality if a thing affects you like that.' Simon Ward [who played Dennis] shook like a jelly when I gave them to him . . .

Buoyed by *Loot*'s success, Orton's writing took on a new verve and complexity. His idiom and stage effects became more brazen. It was an exciting, fecund period in his writing career fed also by the emotional tensions between himself and Halliwell who was oppressed by his own inadequacy and increasingly distressed at Orton's celebrity. Between October 1966 and August 1967, Orton wrote his ghoulish capriccio about the Church, *Funeral Games*, for television; a film script; the major revisions of *Ruffian* and *Erpingham*, published as they were produced under the title *Crimes of Passion*; and his farce masterpiece *What the Butler Saw*. *Butler* consolidated all the verbal and visual experiments Orton had made haltingly in his one-act plays. Originally, he had subtitled *Loot* 'a farce' but edited out the phrase from the final script. Strictly speaking, *Loot* is not pure farce; it is still pure pleasure. The play bears witness both to a buoyant brief moment in British culture and to the bumptious life of its short-lived, disenchanted master.

John Lahr, 1976, 2001

The first London production of *Loot* was given at the Jeanetta Cochrane Theatre by the London Traverse Theatre Company on 29 September 1966, with the following cast:

McLeavy	Gerry Duggan
Fay	Sheila Ballantine
Hal	Kenneth Cranham
Dennis	Simon Ward
Truscott	Michael Bates
Meadows	David Redmond

Directed by Charles Marowitz
Designed by Tony Carruthers

Loot was revived as part of the 'Joe Orton Festival' at the Royal Court Theatre, London, on 3 June 1975, with the following cast:

McLeavy	Arthur O'Sullivan
Fay	Jill Bennett
Hal	David Troughton
Dennis	James Aubrey
Truscott	Philip Stone
Meadows	Michael O'Hagan

Directed by Albert Finney
Designed by Douglas Heap
Costumes by Harriet Geddes

Act One

A room in **McLeavy**'s *house. Afternoon.*

Door left with glass panel. Door right. A coffin stands on trestles.
McLeavy, *in mourning, sits beside an electric fan.*

Fay, *in a nurse's uniform, enters from the left.*

Fay   Wake up. Stop dreaming. The cars will be here soon.
(*She sits.*) I've bought you a flower.

McLeavy   That's a nice thought. (*Taking the flower from her.*)

Fay   I'm a nice person. One in a million.

She removes her slippers, puts on a pair of shoes.

McLeavy   Are those Mrs McLeavy's slippers?

Fay   Yes. She wouldn't mind my having them.

McLeavy   Is the fur genuine?

Fay   It's fluff, not fur.

McLeavy   It looks like fur.

Fay (*standing to her feet*)   No. It's a form of fluff. They
manufacture it in Leeds.

*She picks up the slippers and takes them to the wardrobe. She tries to
open the wardrobe. It is locked. She puts the slippers down.*

You realize, of course, that the death of a patient terminates
my contract?

McLeavy   Yes.

Fay   When do you wish me to leave?

McLeavy   Stay for a few hours. I've grown used to your
company.

Fay   Impossible. I'm needed at other sickbeds. Complain
to the Society if you disagree with the rules.

She picks up his coat, holds it out for him to put on.

You've been a widower for three days. Have you considered a second marriage yet?

McLeavy (*struggling into his coat*)   No.

Fay   Why not?

McLeavy   I've been so busy with the funeral.

Fay   You must find someone to take Mrs McLeavy's place. She wasn't perfect.

McLeavy   A second wife would be a physical impossibility.

Fay   I'll hear none of that. My last husband at sixty came through with flying colours. Three days after our wedding he was performing extraordinary feats.

She takes the coathanger to the wardrobe. She tries to open the wardrobe door, frowns, puts the coathanger beside her slippers.

You must marry a girl with youth and vitality. Someone with a consistent attitude towards religion. That's most important. With her dying breath Mrs McLeavy cast doubt upon the authenticity of the Gospels. What kind of wife is that for you? The leading Catholic layman within a radius of forty miles. Where did you meet such a woman?

McLeavy   At an informal get-together run by a Benedictine monk.

Fay *takes the flower from his hand and pins it on to his coat.*

Fay   Was she posing as a Catholic?

McLeavy   Yes.

Fay   She had a deceitful nature. That much is clear. We mustn't let it happen again. I'll sort out some well-meaning young woman. Bring her here. Introduce you. I can visualize her – medium height, slim, fair hair. A regular visitor to some place of worship. And an ex-member of the League of Mary.

McLeavy   Someone like yourself?

Fay   Exactly. (*She takes a clothes brush and brushes him down.*) Realize your potential. Marry at once.

McLeavy   St Kilda's would be in uproar.

Fay   The Fraternity of the Little Sisters is on my side. Mother Agnes-Mary feels you're a challenge. She's treating it as a specifically Catholic problem.

McLeavy   She treats washing her feet as a Catholic problem.

Fay   She has every right to do so.

McLeavy   Don't Protestants have feet then?

Fay   The Holy Father hasn't given a ruling on the subject and so, as far as I'm concerned, they haven't. Really, I sometimes wonder whether living with that woman hasn't made a free thinker of you. You must marry again after a decent interval of mourning.

McLeavy   What's a decent interval?

Fay   A fortnight would be long enough to indicate your grief. We must keep abreast of the times.

She takes the brush to the wardrobe and tries to open it.

(*Turning, with a frown.*) Who has the key to this cupboard?

McLeavy   Harold.

Fay   Why is it locked?

McLeavy   He refused to give a reason.

McLeavy *shakes the wardrobe door.*

Fay   Your son is a thorn in my flesh. The contents of his dressing-table are an indictment of his way of life. Not only firearms, but family-planning equipment. A Papal dispensation is needed to dust his room.

She goes out left. **McLeavy** *follows her. She can be heard calling:*

(Off.) Harold! *(Farther off.)* Harold!

Hal *enters right. He goes to the wardrobe, unlocks it, looks in, and locks the wardrobe again. He stands beside the coffin and crosses himself.* **Fay** *and* **McLeavy** *re-enter left.*

Fay *(pause, with a smile)* Why is the wardrobe locked?

Hal I've personal property in there.

McLeavy Open the door. There's enough mystery in the universe without adding to it.

Hal I can't. You wouldn't wish to see. It's a present for your anniversary.

McLeavy What anniversary?

Hal Your being made a knight of the Order of St Gregory.

McLeavy I'm not convinced. Open the wardrobe.

Hal No.

Fay *(to* **McLeavy***)* You see how far things have progressed? Your son won't obey you. *(To* **Hal***.)* Are you still refusing to attend your mother's funeral?

Hal Yes.

Fay What excuse do you give?

Hal It would upset me.

Fay That's exactly what a funeral is meant to do.

McLeavy He prefers to mourn in private.

Fay I'm not in favour of private grief. Show your emotions in public or not at all.

Hal *(to* **McLeavy***)* Another wreath has arrived.

McLeavy   Is it roses?

Hal   Roses and fern.

McLeavy   I must look.

He goes out left.

Fay   I sometimes think your father has a sentimental attachment to roses.

Hal   Do you know what his only comment was on my mother's death?

Fay   Something suitable, I'm sure.

She takes the mattress cover from the mattress and folds it.

Hal   He said he was glad she'd died at the right season for roses. He's been up half the night cataloguing the varieties on the crosses. You should've seen him when that harp arrived. Sniffing the petals, checking, arguing with the man who brought it. They almost came to blows over the pronunciation.

Fay *hangs the folded mattress cover over the screen.*

If she'd played her cards right, my mother could've cited the Rose Growers' Annual as co-respondent.

Fay   The Vatican would never grant an annulment. Not unless he'd produced a hybrid.

Hal (*at the coffin, looking in*)   Why was she embalmed?

Fay   She asked to be scientifically preserved after her last attack.

Hal *stares into the coffin, deep in thought.* **Fay** *joins him.*

You couldn't wish her life. She was in agony since Easter.

Hal   Yes, the egg I presented to her went untouched.

Fay   On doctor's orders, I can tell you in confidence.

Pause.

Sit down, Harold. I want a word with you. Your father can't be expected to help at the moment.

Hal *sits.* **Fay** *sits opposite him.*

(*Folding her hands in her lap.*)   The priest at St Kilda's has asked me to speak to you. He's very worried. He says you spend your time thieving from slot machines and deflowering the daughters of better men than yourself. Is this a fact?

Hal   Yes.

Fay   And even the sex you were born into isn't safe from your marauding. Father Mac is popular for the remission of sins, as you know. But clearing up after you is a full-time job. He simply cannot be in the confessional twenty-four hours a day. That's reasonable, isn't it? You do see his point?

Hal   Yes.

Fay   What are you going to do about this dreadful state of affairs?

Hal   I'm going abroad.

Fay   That will please the Father. Who are you going with?

Hal   A mate of mine. Dennis. A very luxurious type of lad. At present employed by an undertaker. And doing well in the profession.

Fay   Have you known him long?

Hal   We shared the same cradle.

Fay   Was that economy or malpractice?

Hal   We were too young then to practise, and economics still defeat us.

Fay   You've confirmed my worst fears. You have no job. No prospects. And now you're about to elope to the Continent with a casual acquaintance and not even a baby as justification. Where will you end? Not respected by the world at large like your father. Most people of any influence will ignore you. You'll be forced to associate with young men like yourself. Does that prospect please you?

Hal   I'm not sure.

Fay   Well, hesitation is something to be going on with. We can build on that. What will you do when you're old?

Hal   I shall die.

Fay   I see you're determined to run the gamut of all experience. That can bring you nothing but unhappiness. You've had every chance to lead a decent life and rejected them. I've no further interest in your career. (*She rises to her feet.*) Call your father. He's surely had enough of the company of plants for the present.

Hal *goes to the door left.*

Hal (*calling*)   Eh, Dad!

Fay   Shhh! This is a house of mourning.

Hal *returns and sits.*

The priest that came to pay his condolences had such quiet tones that at first I thought they'd sent along a mute.

McLeavy *enters carrying a large wreath marked off into numbered squares.*

McLeavy   The Friends of Bingo have sent a wreath. The blooms are breathtaking.

He puts the wreath down. Sits. Takes out a newspaper. **Fay**, *standing beside the coffin, looking into it, silently moves her lips in prayer, a rosary between her fingers.*

(*With a loud exclamation.*)   Another catastrophe has hit the district! Bank robbers have got away with a fortune.

Fay (*looking up*)   Which bank?

Mcleavy   Next door to the undertakers. They burrowed through. Filled over twenty coffins with rubble.

Fay   Rubble?

McLeavy   From the wall. Demolished the wall, they did.

Fay   People are so unbalanced these days. The man sitting next to you on the bus could be insane.

McLeacvy   Where the money has gone is still occupying the police. It's one of the big gangs, I expect.

Hal   What do you known of the big gangs? It's a small gang. Minute.

Fay   Do you know the men concerned?

Hal   If I had that money, I wouldn't be here. I'd go away.

Fay   You're going away.

Hal   I'd go away quicker.

Fay   Where would you go?

Hal   Spain. The playground of international crime.

Fay   Where are you going?

Hal   Portugal.

Pause.

You'll have to get up early in the morning to catch me.

Door chimes. **Hal** *goes to the window, draws back the curtains and looks out.*

Dennis is here with the cars.

Fay   Is he driving?

Hal   Yes. He looks impressive. Close proximity to death obviously agrees with him.

He goes out left.

McLeavy (*putting away the newspaper*)   What's the plan for the afternoon?

Fay   The funeral will occupy you for an hour or so. Afterwards a stroll to the house of a man of God, a few words of wisdom and a glance through the Catholic Truth Society's most recent publication should set your adrenalin flowing. Then a rest. I don't want you overstrained.

McLeavy   When did you say you were leaving? I don't wish to cause you any inconvenience.

Fay   I'll decide when you've inconvenienced me long enough.

McLeavy   You're very good to me.

Fay   As long as you appreciate my desire to help. My own life has been unhappy. I want yours to be different.

McLeavy   You've had an unhappy life?

Fay   Yes. My husbands died. I've had seven altogether. One a year on average since I was sixteen. I'm extravagant you see. And then I lived under stress near Penzance for some time. I've had trouble with institutions. Lack of funds. A court case with my hairdresser. I've been reduced to asking people for money before now.

McLeavy   Did they give it to you?

Fay   Not willingly. They had to be persuaded. (*With a bright smile.*) I shall accompany you to your lawyers. After the reading of your wife's will you may need skilled medical assistance.

McLeavy (*with a laugh*)   I don't think there are any surprises in store. After a few minor bequests the bulk of Mrs McLeavy's fortune comes to me.

Fay   I've also arranged for your doctor to be at your side. You've a weak heart.

Dennis *enters left.*

Dennis   Good afternoon. I don't want to be too formal on this sad occasion, but would you like to view the deceased for the last time?

Fay *takes out a handkerchief.*

Hal *enters.*

(*To* **Hal**.)   Give us a hand into the car with the floral tributes.

Hal *takes out several wreaths,* **Dennis** *picks up the rest.*

(*To* **Fay**.)   We'll need help with the coffin. (*Nods to* **McLeavy**.) He's too near the grave himself to do much lifting.

Fay   Harold can carry his mother to the car.

Dennis   A charming suggestion. (*To* **McLeavy**.) If you'll be making your last good-byes while I give them a hand?

Takes the wreaths to the door. **Hal** *enters left.*

(*Passing* **Hal** *in the doorway.*)   I want a word with you.

Dennis *goes out left.* **Hal** *is about to follow him.*

Fay (*calling*)   Come and see your mother, Harold. You'll never see her again.

McLeavy, **Hal** *and* **Fay** *stand beside the coffin, looking in.*

She looks a treat in her W.V.S. uniform. Though I'd not care to spend Eternity in it myself.

Hal   She's minus her vital organs, isn't she?

Fay   It's a necessary part of the process.

McLeavy   Where are they?

Fay   In the little casket in the hall. Such tranquillity she has. Looks as though she might speak.

McLeavy (*taking out a handkerchief, dabbing her nose*)   God rest the poor soul. I shall miss her.

Fay   Death can be very tragic for those who are left.

They bow their heads in silence.

Hal   Here, her eyes are blue. Mum's eyes were brown. That's a bit silly, isn't it?

Fay   I expect they ran out of materials.

McLeavy   Are her eyes not natural, then?

Fay   No. (*With a smile, to* **Hal**.) He's such an innocent, isn't he? Not familiar with the ways of the world.

McLeavy   I thought they were her own. That surprises me. Not her own eyes.

Dennis *enters with a screwdriver.*

Dennis   The large harp we've placed on top of the motor. On the coffin we thought just the spray of heather from her homeland.

McLeavy   It's going to take me a long time to believe she's dead. She was such an active sort of person.

Fay (*to* **Dennis**)   You're going abroad, I hear?

Dennis   Yes.

Fay   Where did you get the money?

Dennis   My life insurance matured.

McLeavy (*to* **Dennis**)   Tragic news about your premises. Was the damage extensive?

Dennis   The repair bill will be steep. We're insured, of course.

McLeavy   Was your Chapel of Rest defiled?

Dennis   No.

McLeavy   Human remains weren't outraged?

Dennis   No.

McLeavy   Thank God for that. There are some things which deter even criminals.

Dennis   I'm concerned with the actual furnishings damaged – I mean, the inside of the average casket is a work of art – time and labour, oh, it makes you weep.

McLeavy   The bodies laid out. Waiting for burial. It's terrible thoughts that come to me.

Dennis   It broke my heart. Dust and rubble.

McLeavy   What a terrible thing to contemplate. The young men, thinking only of the money, burrowing from the undertakers to the bank. The smell of corruption and the instruments of death behind them, the riches before them. They'd do anything for money. They'd risk damnation in this world and the next for it. And me, a good man by any lights, moving among such people. They'll have it on their conscience. Even if they aren't caught, they'll suffer.

Dennis   How?

McLeavy   I don't know. But such people never benefit from their crimes. It's people like myself who have the easy time. Asleep at nights. Despite appearances to the contrary, criminals are poor sleepers.

Fay   How do you sleep, Harold?

Hal   Alone.

Dennis   We'll be leaving in a short time, Mr McLeavy. I'd like to satisfy myself that everything is as it should be. We pride ourselves on the service.

McLeavy   What clothes would they wear, d'you suppose? Dust is easily identified. They'd surely not work in the nude? God have mercy on them if they did. Even to avoid the hangman I'd not put up with precautions of that nature.

Fay   They'd wear old clothes. Burn them after.

McLeavy   If you could get a glance between their toes you'd find the evidence. But to order a man to remove his clothes isn't within the power of the police. More's the pity, I say. I'd like to see them given wider powers. They're hamstrung by red tape. They're a fine body of men. Doing their job under impossible conditions.

Hal   The police are a lot of idle buffoons, Dad. As you well know.

McLeavy   If you ever possess their kindness, courtesy and devotion to duty, I'll lift my hat to you.

Dennis   I'm going to batten down the hatches now.

McLeavy (*glancing into the coffin*)   Treat her gently. She was very precious to me.

He goes out left.

Fay (*following* **McLeavy**, *turning in the doorway*)   I'll be consoling your father if I'm needed. Be careful what you talk about in front of the dead.

She goes out left.

Dennis *opens a packet of chewing-gum, puts a piece in his mouth, takes off his hat.*

Dennis   Lock the door.

Hal   It won't lock.

Dennis   Put a chair under the handle. We're in trouble.

Hal *wedges a chair under the handle.*

We've had the law round our house.

Hal   When?

Dennis   This morning. Knocked us up they did. Turning over every bleeding thing.

Hal   Was my name mentioned?

Dennis   They asked me who my associate was. I swore blind I never knew what they were on about. 'Course, it's only a matter of time before they're round here.

Hal   How long?

Dennis   Might be on their way now. (*He begins to screw down the lid of the coffin.*) Don't want a last squint, do you? No? Where's the money?

Hal *taps the wardrobe.*

In there? All of it? We've got to get it away. I'll lose faith in us if we get nicked again. What was it last time?

Hal   Ladies' overcoats.

Dennis   See? Painful. Oh, painful. We were a laughing-stock in criminal circles. Banned from that club with the spade dancer.

Hal   Don't go on, baby. I remember the humiliating circumstances of failure.

Dennis   We wouldn't have been nicked if you'd kept your mouth shut. Making us look ridiculous by telling the truth. Why can't you lie like a normal man?

Hal   I can't, baby. It's against my nature.

He stares at the coffin as **Dennis** *screws the lid down.*

Has anybody ever hidden money in a coffin?

Dennis *looks up. Pause.*

Dennis   Not when it was in use.

Hal   Why not?

Dennis   It's never crossed anybody's mind.

Hal   It's crossed mine.

He takes the screwdriver from **Dennis**, *and begins to unscrew the coffin lid.*

It's the comics I read. Sure of it.

Dennis (*wiping his forehead with the back of his hand*)   Think of your mum. Your lovely old mum. She gave you birth.

Hal   I should thank anybody for that?

Dennis   Cared for you. Washed your nappies. You'd be some kind of monster.

Hal *takes the lid off the coffin.*

Hal   Think what's at stake.

He goes to wardrobe and unlocks it.

Money.

He brings out the money. **Dennis** *picks up a bundle of notes, looks into the coffin.*

Dennis   Won't she rot it? The body juices? I can't believe it's possible.

Hal   She's embalmed. Good for centuries.

Dennis *puts a bundle of notes into the coffin. Pause. He looks at* **Hal**.

Dennis   There's no room.

Hal *lifts the corpse's arm.*

Hal (*pause, frowns*)   Remove the corpse. Plenty of room then.

Dennis   Seems a shame really. The embalmers have done a lovely job.

They lift the coffin from the trestles.

There's no name for this, is there?

Hal   We're creating a precedent. Into the cupboard. Come on.

They tip the coffin on end and shake the corpse into the wardrobe. They put the coffin on the floor, lock the wardrobe and begin to pack the money into the coffin.

Dennis   What will we do with the body?

Hal   Bury it. In a mineshaft. Out in the country. Or in the marshes. Weight corpse with rock.

Dennis   We'll have to get rid of that uniform.

Hal (*pause*)   Take her clothes off?

Dennis   In order to avoid detection should her remains be discovered.

Hal   Bury her naked? My own mum?

He goes to the mirror and combs his hair.

It's a Freudian nightmare.

Dennis (*putting lid upon coffin*)   I won't disagree.

Hal   Aren't we committing some kind of unforgivable sin?

Dennis   Only if you're a Catholic.

Hal (*turning from the mirror*)   I am a Catholic. (*Putting his comb away.*) I can't undress her. She's a relative. I can go to Hell for it.

Dennis   I'll undress her then. I don't believe in Hell.

He begins to screw down the coffin lid.

Hal   That's typical of your upbringing, baby. Every luxury was lavished on you – atheism, breast-feeding, circumcision. I had to make my own way.

Dennis   We'll do it after the funeral. Your dad'll be with the priest.

Hal   O.K. And afterwards we'll go to a smashing brothel I've just discovered. Run by a woman who was connected with the Royal Family one time. Very ugly bird. Part Polish. Her eyes look that way. Nice line in crumpet she has. (*He sits astride the coffin.*)

Dennis   I can't go to a brothel.

Hal   Why not?

Dennis   I'm on the wagon. I'm trying to get up sufficient head of steam to marry.

Hal   Have you anyone in mind?

Dennis   Your mum's nurse.

Hal   She's older than you.

Dennis   An experienced woman is the finest thing that can happen to a lad. My dad swears by them.

Hal   She's three parts Papal nuncio. She'd only do it at set times.

Dennis   Oh, no. She does it at any time. A typical member of the medical profession she is.

Hal   You've had her? (**Dennis** *grins.*) Knocked it off? Really?

Dennis   Under that picture of the Sacred Heart. You've seen it?

Hal   In her room. Often.

Dennis   On Wednesday nights while you're training at St Edmund's gymnasium.

They lift the coffin back on to the trestles.

I'd like to get married. It's the one thing I haven't tried.

Hal   I don't like your living for kicks, baby. Put these neurotic ideas out of your mind and concentrate on the problems of everyday life. We must get the corpse buried before tonight. Be in a tricky position else. And another stretch will be death to my ambitions. I put my not getting on in life down to them persistently sending me to Borstal. I might go permanently bent if this falls through. It's not a pleasant prospect, is it?

The coffin is back upon the trestles.

Dennis *takes the chewing-gum from his mouth and sticks it under the coffin. He puts on his hat.* **Hal** *sits.*

Was it Truscott searched your house?

Dennis   Yes. And he had me down the station for questioning. Gave me a rabbit punch. No, I'm a liar. A rabbit-type punch. Winded me. Took me by the cobblers. Oh, 'strewth, it made me bad.

Hal   Yes, he has a nice line in corporal punishment. Last time he was here he kicked my old lady's cat and he smiled while he did it. How did he get into your house?

Dennis   He said he was from the sanitary people. My dad let him in. 'Course, I recognized him at once.

Hal   Did you tell him?

Dennis   Yes.

Hal   What did he say?

Dennis   Nothing. He kept on about testing the water supply. I asked him if he had a warrant. He said the water board didn't issue warrants.

Hal   You should've phoned the police. Asked for protection.

Dennis   I did.

Hal   What did they say?

Dennis   They said that one of their men called Truscott was at our house and why didn't we complain to him?

Hal   What did Truscott say?

Dennis   He said he was from the water board. My nerves were in shreds by the end of it.

Fay *approaches the door left. Her shadow is cast on the glass panel.*

Fay (*off*)   What are you doing, Harold?

Hal *goes to the coffin and kneels in prayer.*

Hal   That brothel I mentioned has swing doors. (*He bows his head.*) You don't often see that, do you?

Dennis *takes the chair from under the door handle and opens the door quietly.*

Dennis   We're ready now.

Fay *enters in mourning with a veil over her hair. She carries an embroidered text. Her dress is unzipped at the back. She goes to the wardrobe and tries to open the door. She sees in the mirror that her dress is unzipped, comes to the coffin and bows her head over it.* **Hal**, *still kneeling, zips her dress up.* **McLeavy** *enters blowing his nose, a sorrowful expression upon his face.*

McLeavy (*to* **Dennis**)   Forgive me being so overwrought, but it's my first bereavement.

Dennis   The exit of a loved one is always a painful experience.

Fay, *the dress zipped, straightens up.*

Fay   Here – (*She puts the embroidered text on to the coffin.*) – the Ten Commandments. She was a great believer in some of them.

Hal *and* **Dennis** *lift the coffin.*

McLeavy (*greatly moved, placing a hand on the coffin*)   Good-bye, old girl. You've had a lot of suffering. I shall miss you.

Hal *and* **Dennis** *go out with the coffin.* **Fay** *throws back her veil.*

Fay   She's gone. I could feel her presence leaving us. Funny how you know, isn't it?

McLeavy   That dress is attractive. Suits you. Black.

Fay   It's another piece of your late wife's finery. Some people would censure me for wearing it. (*She puts a hand on his arm, smiles.*) Are you feeling calmer now?

McLeavy   Yes. I've a resilient nature, but death upsets me. I'd rather witness a birth than a death any day. Though the risks involved are greater.

Truscott *enters left.*

Truscott   Good afternoon.

Fay   Good afternoon. Who are you?

Truscott   I am attached to the metropolitan water board. I'm on a fact-finding tour of the area. I'd like to inspect your mains supply.

McLeavy   It's outside.

Truscott   Is it?

Pause, ruminates.

I wonder how it came to be put out there. Most ingenious. You're sure there isn't a tap in this cupboard?

He tries the wardrobe door and smiles.

McLeavy   It's in the garden.

Truscott   Where?

McLeavy   I don't know.

Truscott   I suggest, then, that you find it, sir. Any property belonging to the council must be available on demand. The law is clear on that point.

McLeavy   I'll find it at once, sir. I wouldn't wish to place myself outside the law.

He goes off right.

Truscott (*turning to* **Fay**)   Who has the key to this cupboard?

Fay   The son of the house.

Truscott   Would he be willing to open it? I'd make it worth his while.

Fay   I've already asked for it to be opened. He refused point-blank.

Truscott   I see. (*Chews his lip.*) Most significant. You'll be out of the house for some considerable time this afternoon?

Fay   Yes. I'm attending the funeral of my late employer.

Truscott   Thank you, miss. You've been a great help. (*He smiles, goes to window.*) Who sent the large wreath that has been chosen to decorate the motor?

Fay   The licensee of the King of Denmark. I don't think a publican's tribute should be given pride of place.

Truscott   You wouldn't, miss. You had a strict upbringing.

Fay   How do you know?

Truscott   You have a crucifix.

Fay's hand goes to the crucifix on her breast.

It has a dent to one side and engraved on the back the words: 'St Mary's Convent. Gentiles Only.' It's not difficult to guess at your background from such tell-tale clues.

Fay   You're quite correct. It was a prize for good conduct. The dent was an accident.

Truscott   Your first husband damaged it.

Fay   During a quarrel.

Truscott   At the end of which you shot him.

Fay (*taken aback*)   You must have access to private information.

Truscott   Not at all. Guesswork mostly. I won't bore you with the details. The incident happened at the Hermitage Private Hotel. Right?

Fay (*a little alarmed*)   This is uncanny.

Truscott   My methods of deduction can be learned by anyone with a keen eye and quick brain. When I shook your hand I felt a roughness on one of your wedding rings. A roughness I associate with powder burns and salt. The two together spell a gun and sea air. When found on a wedding ring only one solution is possible.

Fay How did you know it happened at the Hermitage Private Hotel?

Truscott That particular hotel is notorious for tragedies of this kind. I took a chance which paid off.

He takes out his pipe and chews on it.

Has it never occurred to you to wonder why all your husbands met with violent deaths?

Fay They didn't!

Truscott Your first was shot. Your second collapsed whilst celebrating the anniversary of the Battle of Mons. Your third fell from a moving vehicle. Your fourth took an overdose on the eve of his retirement from Sadler's Wells. Your fifth and sixth husbands disappeared. Presumed dead. Your last partner suffered a seizure three nights after marrying you. From what cause?

Fay (*coldly*) I refuse to discuss my private life with you.

Truscott For ten years death has been persistently associated with your name.

Fay You could say the same of an even moderately successful undertaker.

Truscott Undertakers have to mix with the dead. It's their duty. You have not that excuse. Seven husbands in less than a decade. There's something seriously wrong with your approach to marriage. I find it frightening that, undeterred by past experience, you're contemplating an eighth engagement.

Fay How do you know?

Truscott You wear another woman's dress as though you were born to it.

Fay (*wide-eyed with wonder*) You amaze me. This dress did belong to Mrs McLeavy.

Truscott   Elementary detection. The zip is of a type worn by elderly women.

Fay   You should be a detective.

Truscott   I'm often mistaken for one. Most embarrassing. My wife is frequently pestered by people who are under the impression that she is a policeman's wife. She upbraids me for getting her into such scrapes. (*He laughs.*) You recognize the daily bread of married life, I'm sure. (*He chews on his pipe for a moment.*) When do you intend to propose to Mr McLeavy?

Fay   At once. Delay would be fatal.

Truscott   Anything taken in combination with yourself usually results in death.

Fay   How dare you speak to me like this! Who are you?

Truscott *takes out his notebook and pencil.*

Truscott (*pleasantly*)   I'm a council employee who has let his imagination wander. Please forgive me if I've upset you.

He tears a page from the notebook and hands it to **Fay**.

Sign this chit.

Fay (*looking at it*)   It's blank.

Truscott   That's quite in order. I want you to help me blindly without asking questions.

Fay   I can't sign a blank sheet of paper. Someone might forge my name on a cheque.

Truscott   Sign my name, then.

Fay   I don't know your name.

Truscott   Good gracious, what a suspicious mind you have. Sign yourself Queen Victoria. No one would tamper with her account.

Fay *signs the paper and gives it back to* **Truscott**.

I think that's all I want from you, miss.

Fay   Will you do one thing for me?

Truscott   What?

Fay   Let me see you without your hat.

Truscott (*alarmed*)   No. I couldn't possibly. I never take my hat off in front of a lady. It would be discourteous.

McLeavy *enters right.*

Have you been successful in your search, sir?

McLeavy   Yes. Next to my greenhouse you'll find an iron plaque. Under it is a tap.

Truscott   Thank you, sir. I shall mention your co-operation in my next report. (*He touches his hat.*) Good afternoon.

He goes off right.

McLeavy   I hope he finds what he's looking for. I like to be of assistance to authority.

Fay   We must watch that he doesn't abuse his trust. He showed no credentials.

McLeavy   Oh, we can rely on public servants to behave themselves. We must give this man every opportunity to do his duty. As a good citizen I ignore the stories which bring officialdom into disrepute.

Hal *enters left.*

Hal   There's a delay in starting the car. A flat tyre. (*Taking off his coat.*) We're changing the wheel.

McLeavy   I hardly think it proper for a mourner to mend the puncture. Is your mother safe?

Hal   Dennis is guarding the coffin.

McLeavy   Be as quick as you can. Your mother hated to miss an appointment.

Hal   The contents of that coffin are very precious to me. I'm determined to see they get to the graveyard without mishap.

He goes off left.

McLeavy (*with a smile, shaking his head*)   It's unusual for him to show affection. I'm touched by it.

Fay   Mrs McLeavy was a good mother. She has a right to respect.

McLeavy   Yes. I've ordered four hundred rose trees to help keep her memory green. On a site, only a stone's throw from the church, I intend to found the 'Mrs Mary McLeavy Memorial Rose Garden'. It will put Paradise to shame.

Fay   Have you ever seen Paradise?

McLeavy   Only in photographs.

Fay   Who took them?

McLeavy   Father Jellicoe. He's a widely travelled man.

Fay   You mustn't run yourself into debt.

McLeavy   Oh, Mrs McLeavy will pay for the memorial herself. The will is as good as proven.

Fay *sits beside him, takes his hand.*

Fay   I don't know whether you can be trusted with a secret, but it would be wrong of me to keep you in the dark a moment longer. Your wife changed her will shortly before she died. She left all her money to me.

McLeavy   What! (*Almost fainting.*)   Is it legal?

Fay   Perfectly.

McLeavy   She must've been drunk. What about me and the boy?

Fay   I'm surprised at you taking this attitude. Have you no sense of decency?

McLeavy   Oh, it's God's judgement on me for marrying a Protestant. How much has she left you?

Fay   Nineteen thousand pounds including her bonds and her jewels.

McLeavy   Her jewels as well?

Fay   Except her diamond ring. It's too large and unfashionable for a woman to wear. She's left that to Harold.

McLeavy   Employing you has cost me a fortune. You must be the most expensive nurse in history.

Fay   You don't imagine that I want the money for myself, do you.

McLeavy   Yes.

Fay   That's unworthy of you. I'm most embarrassed by Mrs McLeavy's generosity.

McLeavy   You'll destroy the will?

Fay   I wish I could.

McLeavy   Why can't you?

Fay   It's a legal document. I could be sued.

McLeavy   By whom?

Fay   The beneficiary.

McLeavy   That's you. You'd never sue yourself.

Fay   I might. If I was pushed too far. We must find some way of conveying the money into your bank account.

McLeavy   Couldn't you just give it to me?

Fay   Think of the scandal.

McLeavy   What do you suggest then?

Fay   We must have a joint bank account.

McLeavy   Wouldn't that cause an even bigger scandal?

Fay   Not if we were married.

McLeavy   Married? But then you'd have my money as well as Mrs McLeavy's.

Fay   That is one way of looking at it.

McLeavy   No. I'm too old. My health wouldn't stand up to a young wife.

Fay   I'm a qualified nurse.

McLeavy   You'd have to give up your career.

Fay   I'd do it for you.

McLeavy   I can give you nothing in return.

Fay   I ask for nothing. I'm a woman. Only half the human race can say that without fear of contradiction. (*She kisses him.*) Go ahead. Ask me to marry you. I've no intention of refusing. On your knees. I'm a great believer in traditional positions.

McLeavy   The pains in my legs.

Fay   Exercise is good for them. (**McLeavy** *kneels.*) Use any form of proposal you like. Try to avoid abstract nouns.

Hal *enters left.*

Hal   We're ready. The leader of the Mother's Union has given the signal for tears. (*He picks up his coat.*) We must ride the tide of emotion while it lasts.

Fay   They'll have to wait. Your father is about to propose to me. I think you may stay.

McLeavy (*struggling to his feet*)   I'm giving no exhibition. Not in front of my son.

Hal   I'm surprised he should wish to marry again. He couldn't do justice to his last wife.

Car horn. **Dennis** *enters left.*

Dennis Would everybody like to get into the car? We'll have the priest effing and blinding if we're late.

McLeavy (*to* **Fay**) This is so undignified. My wife isn't in her grave.

Fay And she never will be if you insist on prolonging the proceedings beyond their natural length.

McLeavy I'll propose to you on the way to the cemetery, Nurse McMahon. Will that satisfy you?

Dennis (*to* **Fay**) You can't marry him. You know the way I feel about you.

Fay I couldn't marry you. You're not a Catholic.

Dennis You could convert me.

Fay I'm not prepared to be both wife and missionary.

Hal (*putting his arm round* **Dennis**) He's richer than my dad, you know.

Fay Has he his bank statement on him?

Dennis I came out without it.

Car horn.

McLeavy Mrs McLeavy is keeping her Maker waiting. I'll pay my addresses to you after the interment.

Prolonged car horn.

Come on! We'll have a damaged motor horn to pay for next!

Fay I've decided not to attend. I shall wave. Show my respects from afar.

McLeavy The number of people staying away from the poor woman's funeral is heartbreaking. And I hired a de luxe model car because they're roomier. I could've saved myself the expense.

He goes off left.

Dennis (*to* **Fay**)   I'd slave for you.

Fay (*pulling on her gloves*)   I can't marry boys.

Hal   He'd grow a moustache.

Fay   It really doesn't concern me what he grows. Grow two if it pleases him.

Hal   Would it please you? That's the point.

Fay   The income from fairgrounds might interest me. Otherwise a man with two has no more fascination than a man with one.

Dennis   A fully productive life isn't possible with a man of Mr McLeavy's age.

Fay   We shall prove you wrong. He'll start a second family under my guidance.

Hal   You're wasting your time. He couldn't propagate a row of tomatoes.

Car horn.

Fay (*to* **Dennis**)   Get in the car! I've no intention of marrying you.

Dennis (*to* **Hal**, *in tears*)   She turned me down. She's broken my heart.

Hal   She doesn't know what she's missing, baby.

Dennis   But she does! That's what's so humiliating. (*He wipes his eyes with the back of his hand.*) Well, the funeral is off as far as I'm concerned.

Hal   You're driving the car. People will notice your absence.

Fay *is at the wardrobe.*

Fay (*pause*)   Where did you get your money?

Dennis   My auntie left it to me.

Fay Is that true, Harold?

Hal (*after an inner struggle*) No.

Dennis I mean my uncle.

Fay (*to* **Hal**) Is that true?

Hal (*desperate, looking at* **Dennis**) No.

Dennis You make our life together impossible. Lie, can't you?

Hal I can't, baby. It's my upbringing.

Car horn.

Dennis Try to control yourself. If I come back and find you've been telling the truth all afternoon – we're through!

He goes off left. **Fay** *takes two black-edged handkerchiefs from her handbag, shakes them out, gives one to* **Hal**.

Fay Blow your nose. People expect it.

She lowers her veil. They both go to the window. They wave. Sound of a car receding. Pause. **Fay** *turns from the window. She goes to the wardrobe. She throws off her veil.*

Come here. Open this cupboard.

Hal *puts his handkerchief into his pocket.*

Don't hesitate to obey me. Open this cupboard.

Hal Why are you so interested?

Fay I've a coatee in there.

Hal Really?

Fay I bought it three days ago. I must change. Mourning gets so grubby if you hang around in it for long.

She looks at **Hal** *in silence.*

I've got a key. I could see in. Quite easy.

Hal I've got something in there.

Fay What?

Hal A corpse.

Fay You've added murder to the list of insults heaped upon your family?

Hal One doesn't have to murder to acquire a corpse.

Fay You're running a private mortuary, then?

Pause.

Where are you concealing the money?

Hal In my mother's coffin.

Fay That'd be an unusual hiding-place.

Pause.

Where is it now? Answer at once. I shan't repeat my question.

Hal The money is putting on incorruption. The flesh is still waiting.

Fay Where is it waiting?

Hal In that cupboard.

Fay Open it.

Hal You have a key.

Fay I haven't.

Hal You were lying?

Fay Yes.

Hal *gives her the key. She opens the wardrobe, looks in, closes the door and screams.*

This is unforgivable. I shall speak to your father.

Pause.

She's standing on her head.

Hal I concealed nothing from you.

Fay Your explanation had the ring of truth. Naturally I disbelieved every word.

Hal I want her buried. Are you prepared to help me?

Fay Oh, no! I couldn't. This is a case for the authorities.

Hal You'll never make it to the altar without my help.

Fay I need no help from you to get a man to bed.

Hal My father holds it as a cherished belief that a whore is no fit companion for a man.

Fay As a creed it has more to offer than most.

Hal My mate Dennis has done you. He speaks of it with relish.

Fay Young men pepper their conversation with tales of rape. It creates a good impression.

Hal You never had the blessing of a rape. I was with him at his only ravishment. A bird called Pauline Ching. Broke a tooth in the struggle, she did. It was legal with you. While Jesus pointed to his Sacred Heart, you pointed to yours.

Fay I never point. It's rude.

Hal If I tell my father, he'll never marry you.

Fay I haven't decided whether I wish to marry your father. Your friend is a more interesting proposition.

Hal He won't be if you grass to the police.

Fay (*pause*) Blackmail? So early in the game.

Hal *takes out a comb and goes to the mirror. He combs his hair.*

Hal I want the body stripped. All I ask is an hour or two of Burke and Hare. It isn't a thing someone of the opposite sex can do. And I'm a relative, which complicates the issue.

Fay You intended a country burial?

Hal   Yes.

Fay   Suppose a dog were to discover her? When they were out hunting for foxes. Do you set no store by the average foxhound?

Hal   Perfectly preserved body of a woman. No sign of foul play. The uniform we'll burn. The underwear you can keep.

Fay   Your mother's underclothes?

Hal   All good stuff.

Fay   I couldn't. Our sizes vary.

Hal   For the bonfire then. Her teeth can go in the river.

Fay   We're nowhere near the river.

Hal   We can borrow your car.

Fay   Provided you pay for the petrol.

Hal   Right.

Fay   Where will she be?

Hal   In the back seat. (*He puts the comb away.*) She always was a back-seat driver.

He opens the wardrobe and wheels the bed to the wardrobe door.

Fay   What about payment?

Hal   Twenty per cent.

Fay   Thirty-three and a third.

Hal   You can keep her wedding ring.

Fay   Is it valuable?

Hal   Very.

Fay   I'll add it to my collection. I already have seven by right of conquest.

Hal *puts the screen round the bed.*

Thirty-three and a third and the wedding ring.

Hal   Twenty per cent, the wedding ring and I pay for the petrol?

Fay   Thirty-three and a third, the wedding ring and you pay for the petrol.

Hal   You drive a hard bargain.

Fay   I never bargain.

Hal   Done.

He throws the mattress cover to her.

Put her in that.

Fay *goes behind the screen.*

Fay   I need help to get her out of the cupboard.

Hal *goes behind the screen.*

I'm not taking the head end.

Hal   She won't bite. You have your gloves on.

They lift the corpse from the wardrobe and lay it on the bed. Something drops from it and rolls away.

Fay   What's that?

Hal *(appearing from behind the screen, searching)*   Nothing, nothing.

Fay *(poking her head over the screen)*   A screw from the coffin, perhaps?

Hal   Was it the wedding ring?

Fay *(looking)*   No. Nothing important.

Hal   I'm inclined to agree.

Fay *goes behind the screen.* **Hal** *takes a sheet from off the screen and spreads it on the floor.*

Fay (*from behind the screen*)   Lovely-shaped feet your mother had. For a woman of her age.

She hands a pair of shoes across the screen. **Hal** *places them in the centre of the sheet.*

What will you do with the money?

She hands a pair of stockings over the screen.

Hal   I'd like to run a brothel. (*He pushes the stockings into the shoes.*) I'd run a two-star brothel. And if I prospered I'd graduate to a three-star brothel. I'd advertise 'By Appointment'. Like jam.

Fay *hands a w.v.s. uniform across the screen.* **Hal** *folds it up and puts it into the sheet.*

I'd have a spade bird. I don't agree with the colour bar. And a Finnish bird. I'd make them kip together. To bring out the contrast.

Fay *hands a slip across the screen.* **Hal** *puts it into the pile.*

I'd have two Irish birds. A decent Catholic. And a Protestant. I'd make the Protestant take Catholics. And the Catholic take Protestants. Teach them how the other half lives. I'd have a blonde bird who'd dyed her hair dark. And a dark bird who'd dyed her hair blonde. I'd have a midget. And a tall bird with big tits.

Fay *hands across the screen in quick succession, a pair of corsets, a brassiere and a pair of knickers.* **Hal** *puts them into the pile.*

Fay   Are you committed to having her teeth removed?

Hal   Yes.

Pause.

I'd have a French bird, a Dutch bird, a Belgian bird, an Italian bird –

Fay *hands a pair of false teeth across the screen.*

– and a bird that spoke fluent Spanish and performed the dances of her native country to perfection. (*He clicks the teeth like castanets.*) I'd call it the Consummatum Est. And it'd be the most famous house of ill-fame in the whole of England.

Fay *appears from behind the screen.* **Hal** *holds up the teeth.*

These are good teeth. Are they the National Health?

Fay   No. She bought them out of her winnings. She had some good evenings at the table last year.

Fay *folds up the screen. The corpse is lying on the bed, wrapped in the mattress cover, tied with bandages.*

Hal (*approaching the bed, bowing his head*)   She was a great lady. Nothing was too good for her. Which is why she had to go.

Fay (*taking a key from her handbag, gives it to* **Hal**)   Fetch the car. Pay cash. It's not to be charged to my account.

Truscott *approaches the door left. His shadow is cast upon the glass panel. He knocks on the door.* **Hal** *picks up the sheet with the clothes in it. He looks for somewhere to put them.* **Fay** *opens the door.* **Truscott** *stands outside, smiling.*

Truscott (*touching his hat*)   I'm back again, miss.

Fay *slams the door.* **Hal** *stuffs the sheet and clothes into the bedpan attached to the invalid chair.* **Hal** *pulls the screen round the bed.*

(*Calling.*) Might I have a word with you.

Hal *closes the lid of the bedpan, concealing the clothes.*

Fay (*calling, answering* **Truscott**)   Yes.

Truscott   Let me in, then, I can't hold a conversation through a keyhole. I'm a council employee. I might lose my pension.

Hal *sits in the invalid chair.* **Fay** *opens the door.* **Truscott** *enters.*

What's going on in this house?

Hal   Nothing.

Truscott   You admit it? You must be very sure of yourself. Why aren't you both at the funeral? I thought you were mourners.

Fay   We decided not to go. We were afraid we might break down.

Truscott   That's a selfish attitude to take. The dead can't bury themselves, you know.

He takes his pipe from his pocket and plugs it with tobacco.

Fay   What are you doing here?

Truscott (*smiling*)   I've been having a look round your charming house. Poking and prying.

Hal   Have you a search warrant?

Truscott   What for?

Hal   To search the house.

Truscott   But I've already searched the house. I don't want to do it again.

Fay   It's common knowledge what police procedure is. They must have a search warrant.

Truscott   I'm sure the police must, but as I've already informed you, I am from the water board. And our procedure is different.

He puts the pipe into his mouth, lights it, draws on it.

(*Chewing on his pipe.*) Now, I was sent on a fool's errand a few minutes ago. Unless I'm much mistaken, the object of my search is in that cupboard.

Pause.

Open it for me.

Hal   It isn't locked.

Truscott   I can't take your word for it, lad.

Hal *opens the wardrobe door.* **Truscott** *puts on a pair of spectacles, and stares in. He shakes his head. He takes off his spectacles.*

This puts an entirely different complexion on the matter.

Fay   It's empty.

Truscott   Exactly. There's still a lot of routine work to be done, I can see that. Would you mind waiting outside, miss? I'd like a word with this lad alone. I'll let you know when you're wanted.

Fay *and* **Hal** *exchange bewildered glances.* **Fay** *goes off left.*

(*Laughing pleasantly.*) I always have difficulties with the ladies. They can't accept a *fait accompli.*

Pause. He takes the pipe from his mouth and stares speculatively at **Hal**.

What do you know of a lad called Dennis?

Hal   He's a mate of mine.

Truscott   You don't want to spend your time with a youth like him. He's not your type. He's got five pregnancies to his credit.

Hal   Anyone can make a mistake.

Truscott   Maybe. But he's obviously getting into the habit of making mistakes. Where does he engender these unwanted children? There are no open spaces. The police patrol regularly. It should be next to impossible to commit the smallest act of indecency, let alone beget a child. Where does he do it?

Hal   On crowded dance floors during the rhumba.

Fay *enters left.*

Truscott (*removing his pipe patiently*)   I'm a busy man, miss. Do as you're told and wait outside.

Fay   What's your name?

Truscott   I prefer to remain anonymous for the present.

Fay   Your Christian name.

Truscott   I'm not a practising Christian.

Fay   Is it Jim?

Truscott   No.

Fay   A man at the door says it is.

Truscott   I'd like to help him, but I'm not prepared to admit to any name other than my own.

Fay   He says his name is Meadows.

Truscott (*pause, nods his head sagely*)   One of my names is Jim. Clearly this fellow is in possession of the fact and wishes to air his knowledge. I shall speak to him.

Truscott *goes off left.*

Fay (*closing the door, whispers*)   There's a uniformed policeman at the door! They're on to us.

Hal   It's bluff.

Fay   No. God works for them. They have Him in their pockets like we've always been taught.

Hal   We've got to get rid of him. He'll find the body next.

He opens the wardrobe door and puts **Fay***'s shoes and the coathanger inside. He closes the door quickly and turns to* **Fay***.*

Remember when we were wrapping her up?

Fay   It's not something I care to reminisce about.

Hal   Something dropped out? We couldn't find it?

Fay   Yes.

Hal   I know what it was.

Fay   What?

Hal   One of her eyes!

They drop to their knees. They search. **Truscott** *enters. They stand.*

Truscott (*smiling*)   Just a bobby making a nuisance of himself.

He goes to the screen and glances behind it. Pause. He takes the pipe from his mouth.

The theft of a Pharaoh is something which hadn't crossed my mind.

He folds the screen revealing the corpse, swathed in the mattress cover and tied with bandages.

Whose mummy is this?

Hal   Mine.

Truscott   Whose was it before?

Hal   I'm an only child.

Truscott   A word of warning. Don't take the mickey. You'll make me angry. (*He smiles.*) O.K.?

Fay   It's not a mummy. It's a dummy. I used to sew my dresses on it.

Truscott   What sex is it?

Fay   I call it 'she' because of my sewing. The garments were female and because I'm literal-minded I chose to believe I was making them on a lady.

Truscott   Splendid. Excellently put.

Hal   No actual evidence of sex can be given. It's contrary to English law.

Truscott   Yes, a tailor's dummy provided with evidence of sex would fill the mind of the average magistrate with misgiving. Why is it wrapped?

Hal   We were taking it in the car.

Fay   To a carnival. She's part of a display.

Truscott   What part?

Fay   A sewing-class. Prewar. The difference in technique is to be demonstrated.

Truscott   Is this dummy a frequent visitor to exhibitions?

Fay   Yes.

Truscott   When is the object's outing to take place?

Fay   It isn't going now.

Truscott   The treat has been cancelled?

Fay   Yes.

Truscott   Why?

Hal   My mate Dennis was to have arranged transport. He let us down.

Truscott   I can believe that. From all I've heard of your friend I'd say he was quite capable of disappointing a tailor's dummy.

He puts his pipe into the corner of his mouth. He takes out his notebook and makes notes.

You claim this object is awaiting transport to a carnival where it will be used to demonstrate the continuity of British needlework?

Fay   Yes.

Truscott   Sounds a reasonable explanation. Quite reasonable.

He puts the notebook away and chews on his pipe. He observes **Hal** *narrowly.*

What were you doing on Saturday night?

Pause as **Hal** *tries to avoid telling the truth. He stares at* **Fay** *in an agony.*

Hal (*at last*)   I was in bed.

Fay *breathes a sigh of relief.*

Truscott   Can you confirm that, miss?

Fay   Certainly not.

Truscott (*to* **Hal**)   What were you doing in bed?

Hal   Sleeping.

Truscott   Do you seriously expect me to believe that? A man of your age behaving like a child? What was your mate doing on Saturday night?

Hal   He was in bed as well.

Truscott   You'll tell me next he was sleeping.

Hal   I expect he was.

Truscott (*to* **Fay**)   What a coincidence, miss. Don't you agree? Two young men who know each other very well, spend their nights in separate beds. Asleep. It sounds highly unlikely to me. (*To* **Hal**.) What is your excuse for knowing him.

Hal   He's clever. I'm stupid, see.

Truscott   Why do you make such stupid remarks?

Hal   I'm a stupid person. That's what I'm trying to say.

Truscott   What proof have I that you're stupid. Give me an example of your stupidity.

Hal   I can't.

Truscott   Why not? I don't believe you're stupid at all.

Hal   I am. I had a hand in the bank job.

Fay *draws a sharp breath.* **Hal** *sits frozen.* **Truscott** *takes his pipe from his mouth.*

(*With a nervous laugh.*) There, that's stupid, isn't it? Telling you that.

Truscott (*also laughing*)   You must be stupid if you expect me to believe you. Why, if you had a hand in the bank job, you wouldn't tell me.

Fay   Not unless he was stupid.

Truscott   But he is stupid. He's just admitted it. He must be the stupidest criminal in England. Unless – (*He regards* **Hal** *with mounting suspicion.*) – unless he's the cleverest. What was your motive in confessing to the bank job?

Hal   To prove I'm stupid.

Truscott   But you've proved the opposite.

Hal   Yes.

Truscott (*baffled, gnawing his lip*)   There's more to this than meets the eye. I'm tempted to believe that you did have a hand in the bank job. Yes. I shall inform my superior officer. He will take whatever steps he thinks fit. I may be required to make an arrest.

Fay   The water board can't arrest people.

Truscott   They can in certain circumstances.

Fay   What circumstances?

Truscott   I'm not prepared to reveal the inner secrets of the water board to a member of the general public. (*To* **Hal**.) Where's the money?

Hal (*closing his eyes, taking a deep breath*)   It's being buried.

Truscott   Who's burying it?

Hal   Father Jellicoe, S.J.

Truscott   Come here! Come here!

Hal *goes over, his hands trembling as they button up his coat.*

I'm going to ask you a question or two. I want sensible answers. None of your piss-taking. Is that understood? Do I make myself plain? I'm talking English. Do you understand?

Hal   Yes.

Truscott   All right then. As long as we know.

A pause, in which he studies **Hal**.

Now be sensible. Where's the money?

Hal *looks at his watch.*

Hal   By now I'd say it was half-way up the aisle of the Church of St Barnabas and St Jude.

He half turns away. **Truscott** *brings his fist down on the back of* **Hal***'s neck.* **Hal** *cries out in pain and collapses on to the floor rubbing his shoulder.*

Fay (*indignant*)   How dare you! He's only a boy.

Truscott   I'm not impressed by his sex, miss. (*To* **Hal**.) I asked for the truth.

Hal   I'm telling the truth.

Truscott   Understand this, lad. You can't get away with cheek. Kids nowadays treat any kind of authority as a challenge. We'll challenge you. If you oppose me in my duty, I'll kick those teeth through the back of your head. Is that clear?

Hal   Yes.

Door chimes.

Fay   Would you excuse me, Inspector?

Truscott (*wiping his brow*)   You're at liberty to answer your own doorbell, miss. That is how we tell whether or not we live in a free country.

Fay *goes off left.*

(*Standing over* **Hal**.) Where's the money?

Hal   In church.

Truscott *kicks* **Hal** *violently.* **Hal** *cries out in terror and pain.*

Truscott   Don't lie to me!

Hal   I'm not lying! It's in church!

Truscott (*shouting, knocking* **Hal** *to the floor*)   Under any other political system I'd have you on the floor in tears!

Hal (*crying*)   You've got me on the floor in tears.

Truscott   Where's the money?

Hal   I've told you. In church. They're quoting St Paul over it.

Truscott   I don't care if they're quoting the Highway Code over it. One more chance. Where is it?

Hal (*desperate, trying to protect himself*)   In church! In church. My dad's watching the last rites of a hundred and four thousand quid!

Truscott *jerks* **Hal** *from the floor, beating and kicking and punching him.* **Hal** *screams with pain.*

Truscott   I'll hose you down! I'll chlorinate you!

Hal *tries to defend himself, his nose is bleeding.*

You'll be laughing on the other side of your bloody face.

Fay *enters left, supporting* **McLeavy** *who is heavily bandaged.*

Fay   They've had an accident!

Truscott *leaves* **Hal**, *pulls the bed from the wall and shoves it to* **McLeavy**, *who faints on to it, just missing the corpse.* **Hal** *drags the corpse from the bed and shoves it behind the screen.*

Truscott (*to* **McLeavy**)   Have you reported the accident?

McLeavy *opens his mouth. He is too overcome with emotion to speak.*

Fay   It's the shock. Taken away his power of speech, it has.

Truscott   Has this happened before?

Fay   Yes. Six or seven times.

Truscott   If he's going to make a habit of it he ought to learn a sign language. (*To* **McLeavy**.) Do you understand me, sir?

McLeavy *closes his eyes, shudders.* **Truscott** *straightens up.*

I've known people communicate with the dead in half this time.

McLeavy (*moaning*)   Oh . . . Oh . . .

Truscott   What has happened, sir?

McLeavy   I've had an accident.

Truscott   I shall have to make a full report.

He takes out his notebook.

McLeavy   Are you qualified?

Truscott   That needn't concern you at present, sir. I shall let you know later. Now give me a full statement.

McLeavy *passes a hand across his brow and clears his throat.*

McLeavy   We set off in high spirits. The weather was humid, a heat mist covered the sky. The road to the graveyard lay uphill. It was a sad occasion for me. In spite of this I kept a tight hold on my emotions, refusing to show the extent of my loss. Along the route perfect strangers had the courtesy to raise their hats. We got admiring glances for the flowers and sympathetic nods for me.

Pause.

The dignity of the event was unsurpassed.

He bows his head, everyone waits. **Truscott** *taps sharply on the bedrail with his pencil.*

Then, as the solemn procession was half-way up the hill, a lorry, clearly out of control, came hurtling down on top of us. It struck the first car, holding the remains, and killed the undertaker.

Hal   Not Dennis!

McLeavy   No. Mr Walter Tracey. The hearse was a wreck within seconds. Meanwhile the second part of the cortège crashed into the smoking wreckage. I was flung to one side, hitting my head on the bodywork of the vehicle. The next thing I knew I was being helped out by passers-by. The road looked like a battlefield. Strewn with the injured and dying. Blood, glass.

He chokes. Pause.

Several fires were started.

Hal   Was the actual fabric of the coffin damaged?

McLeavy   No. Your mother is quite safe.

Hal   No dents? No holes?

McLeavy   No. People remarked on the extreme durability of the lid. I was about to give the undertaker a recommendation. Then I remembered that he wasn't capable of receiving one.

Truscott   Surely he understood when he took on the job that he couldn't make capital out of his own death?

Fay   Where is the coffin?

McLeavy   Outside.

Fay (*to* **Truscott**)   Can it be brought in?

Truscott   By all means. We mustn't keep a lady waiting.

Hal *goes off.* **Truscott** *turns to* **McLeavy**.

Why are you bandaged? Is that a result of the accident?

McLeavy   Indirectly. My wounds stem from a fear-crazed Afghan hound that was being exercised at the time. I was bitten about the face and hands. In my nervous state I was an easy target.

Truscott   Did you take the owner's name?

McLeavy   No.

Truscott   It all seems highly irregular. The dog will have to be destroyed.

McLeavy   I don't hold it responsible for its actions. It was frightened.

Truscott   I've been frightened myself on occasions. I've never bitten anyone. These people should learn to control their pets.

McLeavy   The woman who owned the dog had fainted.

Truscott   She sounds an unstable kind of person to me.

Hal *and* **Dennis** *enter with the coffin. It is charred, blackened and smoking.*

Fay   Who'd think she'd be back so soon?

McLeavy   She could never make up her mind in life. Death hasn't changed her.

Dennis   Your wreaths have been blown to buggery, Mr McLeavy. We might manage a repair job on that big harp.

Hal   What are we going to do for the replay?

McLeavy   Buy fresh ones, I suppose. Always some new expense.

The coffin is set down. The side falls away, revealing the banknotes inside. **Dennis** *stands in front of the coffin, shielding the contents from* **Truscott** *and* **McLeavy**. **McLeavy** *holds out a hand and tries to shake* **Dennis**'s *hand.*

(*To* **Truscott**.) You must congratulate this boy. He rescued the coffin from the blazing car at considerable personal risk.

Truscott (*drily*)   If he behaves with such consideration to a dead woman, what might we not expect with a live one?

Hal   We need a finishing touch. Know what it is? A holy image. Centre. Between candles.

Fay   I have a Madonna.

Hal   What could be better? Make a gesture. She knew what disappointment was, didn't she? Same as us. A little imagination. What wonders can't it accomplish.

Dennis   Oh, yes. We've found in the trade that an impression can be created with quite humble materials: a candle, half a yard of velvet and a bunch of anemones and the effect is of a lying in state.

McLeavy   My photo of His Holiness would enhance the scene, only it's three Popes out of date.

Fay   Mrs McLeavy won't mind. She wasn't a woman who followed the fashions. Go and get it.

McLeavy *stands, moves to the door.* **Truscott** *bars his path.*

Truscott   I must ask you to remain where you are. No one is to leave without my permission.

McLeavy   Why?

Truscott   When you disobey my orders, sir, you make my job doubly difficult.

McLeavy   On what authority do you give orders?

Truscott   You'd be considerably happier if you allowed me to do my duty without asking questions.

McLeavy   Who are you?

Truscott   I'm an official of the metropolitan water board, sir, as I've already told you.

McLeavy   But the water board has no power to keep law-abiding citizens confined to their rooms.

Truscott   Not if the citizens are law abiding.

McLeavy   Whether they're law abiding or not the water board has no power.

Truscott   I don't propose to argue hypothetical cases with you, sir. Remain where you are till further notice.

McLeavy   I shall take legal advice.

Truscott   That is as may be. I've no power to prevent you.

McLeavy   I want to telephone my lawyer.

Truscott   I can't allow you to do that. It would be contrary to regulations. We've no case against you.

Truscott *chews on his pipe.* **McLeavy** *stares in fury.*

Fay   Can't he fetch the Pope's photo?

Truscott   Only if some responsible person accompanies him.

Hal   You're a responsible person. You could accompany him.

Truscott   What proof have I that I'm a responsible person?

Dennis   If you weren't responsible you wouldn't be given the power to behave as you do.

Truscott *removes his pipe, considers.*

Truscott   That is perfectly correct. In which case I shall accompany you, sir. Come with me.

Truscott *and* **McLeavy** *go off left.*

Hal (*closing the door*)   We must return the remains to the coffin and the money to the cupboard.

Dennis   Why?

Fay   Mr McLeavy may ask for the coffin to be opened. Formaldehyde and three morticians have increased his wife's allure.

Dennis   But a corpse is only attractive to another corpse.

Hal   We can't rely on him having heard that.

Dennis *begins to unscrew the coffin lid.* **Fay** *and* **Hal** *drag the corpse from behind the screen.*

Dennis (*looking up*)   What's that!

Fay   Mrs McLeavy.

Dennis (*to* **Hal**)   How much have you told her?

Hal   Everything.

Dennis   We've never involved a woman in anything unsavoury before.

He takes the lid off the coffin. **Fay** *piles money into his arms.* **Hal** *does the same.*

(*To* **Fay**.) Half of this money is mine. Will you marry me?

Hal   We're splitting the money three ways now, baby. You'll have thirty-four thousand.

Dennis (*to* **Fay**)   Is that enough?

Fay   You've a slight lead on Mr McLeavy at the moment.

She kisses him. **Dennis** *trembles and drops the money back into the coffin.*

Hal (*angry*)   Hurry up! What's the matter with you?

Dennis   My hands are trembling. It's excitement at the prospect of becoming engaged.

Hal   You're too easily aroused. That's your trouble.

McLeavy's *shadow appears on the glass panel.* **Dennis** *tips the money into the coffin.*

McLeavy (*off*)   I'll complain to my M.P. I'll have you reported.

Hal *shoves the lid on to the coffin.* **McLeavy** *enters.*

He's turned the water off. I've just been trying to use the toilet –

Fay (*standing in front of him, preventing him seeing the corpse*)   Oh, please! You don't have to explain.

Hal *tries to drag the corpse away.* **Dennis** *opens the wardrobe.*

McLeavy   I don't believe he's anything to do with the water board. I was handcuffed out there. D'you know that? Handcuffed.

He sees the corpse. He gives a shriek of horror.

What in Heaven's name is that!

Fay   It's my appliance.

McLeavy   I've never seen it before.

Fay   I kept it in my room. It was personal.

McLeavy   What is it doing down here?

Fay   I'm going to do some work. For charity.

McLeavy   What kind of work?

Fay   I'm making the vestments for Our Lady's festival. I was commissioned. My altar cloth at Easter brought me to the attention of the Committee.

McLeavy   My congratulations. You'll want plenty of room to work. (*To* **Dennis**.) Take Nurse McMahon's applicance to my study.

Fay (*anxious, with a smile*)   It's most kind of you, Mr McLeavy, but I'd prefer to work down here. Mrs McLeavy's presence will bring me inspiration.

McLeavy   Very well, you have my permission to work down here. I look forward to seeing the finished results.

Truscott *enters.*

Truscott (*to* **McLeavy**)   Do you still want your padre's photograph, sir?

McLeavy   Yes.

Truscott   You'll find a policeman outside. He will accompany you. Off you go.

McLeavy   I resent your manner of speaking! I'm the householder. I can't be ordered about like this.

Truscott (*shoving him to the door*)   Don't make my job any more tiring than it is, sir. Fetch the photograph in question and wait outside until I call.

McLeavy *goes off left.*

(*To* **Dennis**.) I want a word with you. (*To* **Hal** *and* **Fay**.) The rest of you outside!

Hal   Can't I stay with him? He's the nervous type.

Truscott   I'm nervous as well. I'll be company for him –

Fay   It'd be better if I was present. He's more relaxed in the company of women.

Truscott   He'll have to come to terms with his psychological peculiarity. Out you go!

Fay *and* **Hal** *go off left.*

(**Truscott** *faces* **Dennis**, *the corpse between them.*) Now then, I'm going to ask a few questions. I want sensible answers. I've had enough fooling about for one day. (*He observes* **Dennis** *narrowly.*) Have you ever been in prison?

Dennis   Yes.

Truscott   What for?

Dennis   Stealing overcoats and biting a policeman.

Truscott   The theft of an article of clothing is excusable. But policemen, like red squirrels, must be protected. You were rightly convicted. What do you know of paternity orders?

Dennis   Is that when birds say you've put them in the club?

Truscott   Don't try to evade the issue. How many women have you made pregnant?

Dennis   Five.

Truscott   You scatter your seed along the pavements without regard to age or sex. (*He taps the corpse.*) What are you doing with this? Have you taken up sewing?

Dennis   I was putting it in the cupboard.

Truscott   Why?

Dennis   To keep it hidden.

Truscott   Don't try to pull the wool over my eyes. I've been told the whole pathetic story. You ought to be ashamed of yourself.

Dennis (*pause, with resignation*)   Am I under arrest, then?

Truscott   I wish you were. Unfortunately what you've done isn't illegal.

Dennis (*pause, with surprise*)   When did they change the law?

Truscott   There was never any law.

Dennis   Has it all been a leg-pull? My uncle did two years.

Truscott   What for?

Dennis   Armed robbery.

Truscott   That is against the law.

Dennis   It used to be.

Truscott   It still is.

Dennis   I thought the law had been changed.

Truscott   Who told you that?

Dennis   You did.

Truscott   When?

Dennis   Just now. I thought there'd been a reappraisal of society's responsibilities towards the criminal.

Truscott   You talk like a judge.

Dennis   I've met so many.

Truscott   I'm not impressed by your fine friends.

*He chews on his pipe and watches **Dennis** closely.*

Where's the money from the bank job?

Dennis   What bank job?

Truscott   Where's it buried?

Dennis   Buried?

Truscott   Your mate says it's been buried.

Dennis (*indignant*)   He's a liar!

Truscott   A very intelligent reply. You're an honest lad. (*He smiles and puts an arm around **Dennis**'s shoulders.*) Are you prepared to co-operate with me? I'll see you're all right.

Dennis *edges away.*

I'll put a good word in for you.

Dennis (*nervous, laughing to hide his embarrassment*)   Can't we stand away from the window? I don't want anybody to see me talking to a policeman.

Truscott   I'm not a policeman.

Dennis   Aren't you?

Truscott   No. I'm from the metropolitan water board.

Dennis   You're the law! You gave me a kicking down the station.

Truscott   I don't remember doing so.

Dennis   Well, it's all in the day's work to you, isn't it?

Truscott   What were you doing down the station?

Dennis   I was on sus.

Truscott   What were you suspected of?

Dennis   The bank job.

Truscott   And you complain you were beaten?

Dennis   Yes.

Truscott   Did you tell anyone?

Dennis   Yes.

Truscott   Who?

Dennis   The officer in charge.

Truscott   What did he say?

Dennis   Nothing.

Truscott   Why not?

Dennis   He was out of breath with kicking.

Truscott   I hope you're prepared to substantiate these accusations, lad. What evidence have you?

Dennis   My bruises.

Truscott   What is the official version of those?

Dennis   Resisting arrest.

Truscott   I can see nothing unreasonable in that. You want to watch yourself. Making unfounded allegations. You'll find yourself in serious trouble.

He takes **Dennis** *by the collar and shakes him.*

If I ever hear you accuse the police of using violence on a prisoner in custody again, I'll take you down to the station and beat the eyes out of your head.

He shoves **Dennis** *away.*

Now, get out!

Dennis *is about to leave the corpse.*

And take that thing with you. I don't want to see it in here again.

Dennis *goes off left with the corpse.*

Truscott *closes the door and, as he does so, sees something on the floor. He puts his pipe into the corner of his mouth and picks up the glass eye. He holds it to the light in order to get a better view. Puzzled. He sniffs at it. He holds it close to his ear. He rattles it. He takes out a pocket magnifying-glass and stares hard at it. He gives a brief exclamation of horror and surprise.*

Curtain.

Act Two

Truscott, *by the window, is examining the eye under a pocket magnifying-glass.*

McLeavy *enters carrying a photograph of Pope Pius XII.* **Fay** *follows him.*

McLeavy   Is it possible to use the toilet, sir?

Truscott (*putting the eye into his pocket*)   The water is off.

Fay   Who turned it off?

Truscott   My men did.

McLeavy (*handing the photograph to* **Fay**)   I'm getting on the phone. I'll have your particulars filed.

Truscott   I've disconnected the telephone.

McLeavy   Why?

Truscott   You always begin your sentences with 'Why?' Did they teach you to at school?

McLeavy   Now, look here – I've a right to know – are you from the sanitary people? I never knew they had power over the post office. Aren't they separate entities? (*To* **Fay**.) The water board and the post office? Or have they had a merger? (*To* **Truscott**.) They'd never connect up the water board and the post office, would they?

Truscott   I'm not in a position to say, sir.

McLeavy   Produce your warrant and you're justified. If not, get out of my house. Even a Government department should take account of death.

Truscott   Less of that. I must ask you to respect my cloth.

McLeavy (*to* **Fay**)   Is he a priest?

Fay   If he is he's an unfrocked one.

McLeavy (*stares at* **Truscott**, *goes closer to him, wonderingly*)
Who are you?

Truscott   My name is Truscott.

McLeavy   What in Hell kind of a name is that? Is it an
anagram? You're not bloody human, that's for sure. We're
being made the victims of some kind of interplanetary rag.
(*To* **Fay**.) He's probably luminous in the dark. (*To*
Truscott.) Come on, I don't care what infernal power you
represent. I want a straight answer.

Truscott *regards* **McLeavy** *calmly and in silence.*

I'll go next door – they're Dubliners. If you're the Angel of
the Lord Himself, they'll mix it with you.

Truscott   I've warned you already about leaving this
room. Do as you're told or take the consequences.

McLeavy   I'll take the consequences.

Truscott   I can't allow you to do that.

McLeavy   You've no power to stop me.

Truscott   I must disagree. I'm acting under orders.

McLeavy   Whose?

Truscott   My superior officer's.

McLeavy   I don't believe he exists!

Truscott   If you don't control yourself, I shall have to
caution you.

McLeavy   I know we're living in a country whose respect
for the law is proverbial: who'd give power of arrest to the
traffic lights if three women magistrates and a Liberal M.P.
would only suggest it; but I've never heard of an employee
of the water board nicking a kid for stealing apples, let alone
a grown man for doubting whether he had any right to be
on the planet.

Silence. **Truscott** *removes his pipe from his mouth slowly, weighing his words before he speaks.*

Truscott   If you'll give me your undivided attention for a few moments, sir, I promise you we'll have this whole case sorted out. It isn't a game we're playing. It's my duty, and I must do it to the best of my ability.

The door right is flung open, **Dennis** *and* **Hal** *burst in with the corpse.* **Truscott** *looks steadily and searchingly at them. He points to the corpse with his pipe.*

What are you doing with that thing?

Dennis   We were taking it outside.

Truscott   Why? Did it need the air?

Hal   We were putting it in the garage.

Truscott   This isn't the garage. What do you mean by bringing it back into this room?

Hal   A police sergeant was in the garage.

Truscott   I'm sure he has no particular aversion to sharing a garage with a tailor's dummy.

Hal   He wanted to undress it.

Truscott   What possible objection could there be to an officer undressing a dummy?

Dennis   It isn't decent.

Hal   It's a Catholic.

Truscott (*with contempt*)   The things you say are quite ludicrous, lad. (*He laughs mirthlessly.*) Ho, ho, ho. Take it to the garage. The bobby won't interfere with it. He's a married man with children.

No one moves. **Truscott** *chews on his pipe; he takes pipe from his mouth.*

Go on! Do as I say.

Fay   No! I'd rather it didn't go. I want it here.

Truscott   Why?

Fay   It's valuable.

Truscott   Has its value increased during the last few minutes?

Fay   No.

Truscott   If it's your usual custom to encourage young men to run up and down garden paths with tailor's dummies, you must be stopped from exercising such arbitrary power.

Fay   I did want it in the garage, but after what has been said I feel I can't allow her out of my sight.

Truscott   Really, miss, your relationship with that object verges on the criminal. Has no one in this house any normal feelings? I've never come across such people. If there's any more of it, I shall arrest the lot of you.

McLeavy   How does the water board go about making an arrest?

Truscott   You must have realized by now, sir, that I am not from the water board?

McLeavy   I have. Your behaviour was causing me grave concern.

Truscott   Any deception I practised was never intended to deceive you, sir. You are – if I may so – an intelligent man. (*He laughs to himself.*) You saw through my disguise at once. It was merely a ruse to give me time to review the situation. To get my bearings on a very tricky assignment. Or two tricky assignments. As you will shortly realize. (*He smiles and bows to* **McLeavy**.) You have before you a man who is quite a personage in his way – Truscott of the Yard. Have you never heard of Truscott? The man who tracked down the limbless girl killer? Or was that sensation before your time?

Hal   Who would kill a limbless girl?

Truscott   She was the killer.

Hal   How did she do it if she was limbless?

Truscott   I'm not prepared to answer that question to anyone outside the profession. We don't want a carbon-copy murder on our hands. (*To* **McLeavy**.) Do you realize what I'm doing here?

McLeavy   No. Your every action has been a mystery to me.

Truscott   That is as it should be. The process by which the police arrive at the solution to a mystery is, in itself, a mystery. We've reason to believe that a number of crimes have been committed under your roof. There was no legal excuse for a warrant. We had no proof. However, the water board doesn't need a warrant to enter private houses. And so I availed myself of this loophole in the law. It's for your own good that Authority behaves in this seemingly alarming way. (*With a smile.*) Does my explanation satisfy you?

McLeavy   Oh, yes, Inspector. You've a duty to do. My personal freedom must be sacrificed. I have no further questions.

Truscott   Good. I shall proceed to bring the crimes to light. Beginning with the least important.

Hal   What is that?

Truscott   Murder.

Fay (*anxiously*)   Murder?

Truscott   Yes, murder. (*To* **McLeavy**.) Your wife passed away three days ago? What did she die of?

Fay   The death certificate is perfectly legible.

Truscott   Reading isn't an occupation we encourage among police officers. We try to keep the paper work down to a minimum. (*To* **McLeavy**.) Have you no grumble at the way your wife died?

McLeavy   None.

Truscott   You're easily satisfied, I see. I am not.

Fay   Mrs McLeavy's doctor signed the death certificate.

Truscott   So I understand. But he'd just come from diagnosing a most unusual pregnancy. His mind was so occupied by the nature of the case that he omitted to take all factors into consideration and signed in a fuzz of scientific disbelief. Has anyone see Mrs McLeavy since she died?

Hal   How could we?

Truscott   Can all of you swear you've had no commerce with the dead?

Dennis   We're not mediums.

Truscott   That's a pity. It would have considerably simplified my task if you had been.

Fay   I wasn't going to mention it, but I had a psychic experience last night. Three parts of Mrs McLeavy materialized to me as I was brushing my hair.

Truscott   Was her fate discussed?

Fay   Yes. In great detail.

McLeavy   I never knew you had visions.

Truscott (*to* **Fay**)   Mrs McLeavy and I are perhaps the two people most closely involved in her death. I'd be interested to hear her on the subject.

Fay   She accused her husband of murder.

Sensation.

McLeavy   Me? Are you sure she accused me?

Fay   Yes.

McLeavy   Complete extinction has done nothing to silence her slanderous tongue.

Truscott   Was anyone with her at the end? (*To* **Hal**.) Were you?

Hal   Yes.

Truscott   Was she uneasy? Did she leave no last message?

Hal   No.

Truscott   Was this her usual custom?

Hal   She hadn't died before.

Truscott   Not to the best of your knowledge. Though I've no doubt our information isn't as up to date as we supposed. Did she whisper no last words? As you bent to kiss her cheek before she expired?

Hal   She spoke of a book.

Truscott   Which?

Hal   A broken binding recurred.

Truscott   Was it a metaphor?

Hal   I took it to be so.

Truscott *goes to the bookcase. He takes down a book.*

Truscott   Apart from Bibles, which are notorious for broken bindings, there is this – *The Trial of Phyllis McMahon.* Nurse accused of murdering her patient.

He fixes **Fay** *with a steely look; she turns pale.*

One of my own cases.

He turns over pages, staring hard and with recognition at the photograph.

Look at this photograph.

Hal   It's you.

Truscott Yes, most unflattering, isn't it? They always choose the worst. I cannot get them to print a decent picture.

He tears the photograph from the book, screws it into a ball and stuffs it into his pocket.

Dennis Is there a photo of the nurse?

Truscott Unfortunately not. Someone has torn every picture of the nurse from the book.

Once again he turns his piercing gaze upon **Fay**; *she looks uncomfortable.*

However, we have something equally damning – the handwriting of the accused.

He opens the book at a page of handwriting.

And here – (*Triumphantly he takes a sheet of paper from his pocket.*) – the evidence on which I propose to convict: a recent specimen of the handwriting of your late wife's nurse. Identical in every respect.

McLeavy (*staring at the sheet of paper*) But this is signed Queen Victoria.

Truscott One of her many aliases.

McLeavy *stares in amazement at the evidence.*

Hal If it was one of your own cases, how is it she didn't recognize you?

Truscott Two very simple reasons. I conduct my cases under an assumed voice and I am a master of disguise. (*He takes off his hat.*) You see – a complete transformation. (*To* **McLeavy**.) You've had a lucky escape, sir. You'd've been the victim of a murder bid inside a month. We've had the tabs on her for years. Thirteen fatal accidents, two cases of suspected fish poisoning. One unexplained disappearance. She's practised her own form of genocide for a decade and called it nursing.

Fay (*staring at him, agitatedly*)   I never killed anyone.

Truscott   At the George V hospital in Holyhead eighty-seven people died within a week. How do you explain that?

Fay   It was the geriatric ward. They were old.

Truscott   They had a right to live, same as anybody else.

Fay   I was in the children's ward.

Truscott   How many innocents did you massacre – Phyllis?

Fay   None.

Truscott   I fail to see why you choose to cloak the episode in mystery. You can't escape.

Fay   Mrs McLeavy accused her husband.

Truscott   We can't accept the evidence of a ghost. The problems posed would be insuperable.

Fay   You must prove me guilty. That is the law.

Truscott   You know nothing of the law. I know nothing of the law. That makes us equal in the sight of the law.

Fay   I'm innocent till I'm proved guilty. This is a free country. The law is impartial.

Truscott   Who's been filling your head with that rubbish?

Fay   I can't be had for anything. You've no proof.

Truscott   When I make out my report I shall say that you've given me a confession. It could prejudice your case if I have to forge one.

Fay   I shall deny that I've confessed.

Truscott   Perjury is a serious crime.

Fay   Have you no respect for the truth?

Truscott   We have a saying under the blue lamp: 'Waste time on the truth and you'll be pounding the beat until the day you retire.'

Fay (*breaking down*)   The British police force used to be run by men of integrity.

Truscott   That is a mistake which has been rectified. Come along now. I can't stand here all day.

Fay (*drying her eyes*)   My name is Phyllis Jean McMahon alias Fay Jean McMahon. I am twenty-eight years of age and a nurse by profession. On the third of December last I advertised in the trade papers for a situation. Mr McLeavy answered my request. He wished me to nurse his wife back to health: a task I found impossible to perform. Mrs McLeavy was dying. Had euthanasia not been against my religion I would have practised it. Instead I decided to murder her. I administered poison during the night of June the twenty-second. In the morning I found her dead and notified the authorities. I have had nothing but heartache ever since. I am sorry for my dreadful crime. (*She weeps.*)

Truscott (*looking up from his notebook*)   Very good. Your style is simple and direct. It's a theme which less skilfully handled could've given offence. (*He puts away his notebook.*) One of the most accomplished confessions I've heard in some time.

He gives **McLeavy** *a police whistle.*

I'll just arrange transport. Blow that if she should attempt to escape. My men will come to your aid immediately. The sooner we get a spoonful of Mrs McLeavy on a slide the sooner McMahon faces that murder rap.

He goes off left.

McLeavy (*to* **Fay**)   How could you rob me of my only support?

Fay   I intended to provide a replacement.

McLeavy I never knew such wickedness was possible.

Fay You were aware of my character when you employed me. My references were signed by people of repute.

McLeavy You murdered most of them.

Fay That doesn't invalidate their signatures.

McLeavy Pack your bags! You're not being arrested from my house.

Fay *dabs at her eyes with a handkerchief.*

Dennis I've never seen you in adversity. It's an unforgettable experience. I love you. I'll wait for you for ever.

Fay No, you'll tire of waiting and marry someone else.

Hal He won't be able to. (*He runs his hand along the coffin lid.*) Not when the Inspector asks to see mum's remains. He'll have us by the short hairs, baby.

Truscott *re-enters left with* **Meadows**.

Truscott We're ready when you are, McMahon.

Fay *holds out her hand to* **Hal**. **Hal** *shakes it and kisses her.*

Hal (*kissing* **Fay***'s hand*)   Good-bye. I count a mother well lost to have met you.

Dennis *kisses* **Fay***'s hand.*

Dennis I shall write to you. We're allowed one letter a week.

Fay How sweet you are. I'd like to take you both to prison with me.

Truscott They'd certainly do more good in Holloway than you will. Take her away, Meadows.

Meadows *approaches* **Fay** *with the handcuffs. She holds out her hands.* **Meadows** *hesitates, bends swiftly and kisses* **Fay***'s hand.*

Meadows!

Meadows *handcuffs* **Fay**, *and leads her out.*

Nothing but a miracle can save her now.

Meadows *goes off with* **Fay**.

(*To* **McLeavy**.) I understand your wife is embalmed, sir?

McLeavy   Yes.

Truscott   It's a delicate subject, sir, but for the post-mortem we shall want Mrs McLeavy's stomach. Where are you keeping it?

McLeavy   Is the little casket.

Truscott   Where is it?

Hal   In the hall.

Truscott   Fetch it, will you?

Hal *goes off left.*

Dennis   I have something to say which will be a shock to you, Inspector.

Truscott (*nodding, taking out his pipe*)   What is it? Tell it to your uncle. (*He smiles.*)

Dennis   After I'd removed the coffin I went back for the little casket. As I reached it a violent explosion occurred. The lid of the casket was forced open and the contents dispersed.

Hal *enters left. He carries the casket. He turns it upside down. The hinged lid swings free.*

It's well known in the trade that the viscera, when heated, is an unstable element.

Hal   The contents of my mother's stomach have been destroyed.

Truscott *shakes his head, bowled over.*

Truscott   What an amazing woman McMahon is. She's got away with it again. She must have influence with Heaven.

Hal   God is a gentleman. He prefers blondes.

Truscott   Call her back! Look sharp! She'll sue us for wrongful arrest.

Hal *and* **Dennis** *go off left.*

McLeavy (*to* **Truscott**)   I'm sorry, sir, but I'm rather confused as to what has been said and in answer to whom.

Truscott   Briefly, sir, without your wife's stomach we have no evidence on which to convict.

McLeavy   Can't you do a reconstruction job on my wife's insides.

Truscott   Even God can't work miracles, sir.

McLeavy   Is the world mad? Tell me it's not.

Truscott   I'm not paid to quarrel with accepted facts.

Fay *enters with* **Hal** *and* **Dennis**.

Well, McMahon, you've had another twelfth-hour escape?

Fay   Yes. I shall spend a quiet hour with my rosary after tea.

McLeavy (*to* **Fay**)   I know one thing, you'll be black-listed. I'll see you never get another nursing job.

Truscott   There's no need to be vindictive. Show a little tolerance.

McLeavy   Is she going to get away with murder?

Truscott   I'm afraid so, sir. However, I've an ace up my sleeve. The situation for law and order, though difficult, is by no means hopeless. There's still a chance, albeit a slim one, that I can get McMahon as accessory to another crime.

And one which the law regards as far more serious than the taking of human life.

McLeavy   What's more serious than mass murder?

Truscott   Stealing public money. And that is just what your son and his accomplices have done.

McLeavy   Harold would never do a thing like that. He belongs to the Sons of Divine Providence.

Truscott   That may make a difference to Divine Providence, but it cuts no ice with me.

He takes the eye from his pocket.

During the course of my investigations I came across this object. Could you explain to me what it is?

He hands the eye to **McLeavy**.

McLeavy (*examining it*)   It's a marble.

Truscott   No. Not a marble. (*He regards* **McLeavy** *calmly.*) It looks suspiciously to me like an eye. The question I'd like answered is – to whom does it legally belong?

McLeavy   I'm not sure that it is an eye. It think it's a marble which has been trod on.

Truscott   It's an eye, sir. (*He takes the eye from* **McLeavy**.) The makers' name is clearly marked: J. & S. Frazer, Eye-makers to the Profession.

Fay   It's mine. My father left it to me in his will.

Truscott   That's a strange bequest for a father to make.

Fay   I always admired it. It's said to have belonged originally to a well-loved figure of the concert platform.

Truscott   You're a clever woman, McMahon. Unfortunately you're not quite clever enough. I'm no fool.

Fay   Your secret is safe with me.

Truscott   I've a shrewd suspicion where this eye came from. (*He smiles.*) You know too, don't you?

Fay   No.

Truscott   Don't lie to me! It's from your sewing dummy, isn't it?

Fay (*laughing*)   It's no good, Inspector. You're too clever by half.

Truscott   I'm glad you've decided to tell the truth at last. We must return the eye to its rightful owner. Unwrap the dummy.

Fay   No, no! You can't undress her in front of four men. I must do it in private.

McLeavy   One moment. (*To* **Truscott**.) Let me see that eye.

Truscott *gives it to him.*

(*To* **Fay**.) Who gave you this?

Fay   It's from my dummy. Didn't you hear the Inspector?

McLeavy (*to* **Truscott**)   Is it likely they'd fit eyes to a sewing machine? Does that convince you?

Truscott   Nothing ever convinces me. I choose the least unlikely explanation and file it in our records.

McLeavy (*to* **Fay**)   Who gave you this? Come on now!

Dennis   I gave it to her. A woman gave it to me as a souvenir.

McLeavy   Of what?

Dennis   A special occasion.

McLeavy   It must've been a very special occasion if she gave you her eye to mark it. Come along, I'm not the police. I want a sensible answer. Who gave it to you?

Hal   I did.

McLeavy (*shrieks*)   You! Oh, Sacred Heaven, no!

Truscott   We're open to serious discussion, sir, but not bad language.

McLeavy   This is stolen property. This eye belongs to my wife.

Truscott   On what do you base your assumption?

McLeavy   My wife had glass eyes.

Truscott   A remarkable woman, sir. How many were in her possession at the time of her death?

McLeavy   None.

Truscott   I see.

McLeavy   These were fitted after death. Her own were taken away.

Truscott   Where to?

McLeavy   I don't know.

Truscott   Did you never think to inquire?

McLeavy   No.

Truscott   You act in a singularly heartless manner for someone who claims to have been happily married.

McLeavy   Oh, Inspector – (*Brokenly.*) – my son, you heard him confess it, has stolen the eyes from the dead; a practice unknown outside of medical science. I have reared a ghoul at my own expense.

Silence. **Truscott** *considers.*

Truscott   What do you wish me to do, sir?

McLeavy   Fetch a screwdriver. The coffin must be opened. I want to know what else thievery stoops to. Her head may have gone as well.

Dennis   Might I advise caution, Mr McLeavy? From a professional point of view? The coffin took a pasting, you know.

Fay   She may be in pieces.

McLeavy   Fetch a screwdriver.

Hal   Couldn't we bury the eye separately?

McLeavy   I can't ask the priest to hold the burial service over an eye. Fetch a screwdriver.

Nobody moves. **Truscott** *draws a deep breath.*

Truscott   What good will it do, sir?

McLeavy   I'm not interested in doing good. There are organizations devoted to that purpose. Fetch a screwdriver! Do I have to repeat it like the muezzin?

Dennis *gives* **McLeavy** *a screwdriver.* **McLeavy** *hands the eye to* **Truscott** *and begins to unscrew the coffin lid.*

Truscott   This is unwarranted interference with the rights of the dead. As a policeman I must ask you to consider your actions most carefully.

McLeavy   She's my wife. I can do what I like with her. Anything is legal with a corpse.

Truscott   Indeed it is not. Conjugal rights should stop with the last heartbeat. I thought you knew that.

McLeavy *begins to unscrew the second side of the coffin.*

I must say, sir, I'm aghast at this behaviour. Equivalent to tomb robbing it is. What do you hope to gain by it? An eyeless approach to Heaven is as likely to succeed as any. Your priest will confirm what I say.

McLeavy *bows his head, continues his work.*

You strike me, sir – I have to say this – as a thoroughly irresponsible individual. Always creating unnecessary trouble.

Hal We'll have the house full of the law. Half our fittings will be missing. That's why they have such big pockets on their uniforms.

Truscott Your son seems to have a more balanced idea of the world in which we live than you do, sir.

McLeavy My duty if clear.

Truscott Only the authorities can decide when your duty is clear. Wild guesses by persons like yourself can only cause confusion.

McLeavy *lifts the coffin lid.*

Hal He's going to be shocked. See him preparing for it. His generation takes a delight in being outraged.

McLeavy *looks into the coffin, gives a grunt of disbelief, staggers back, incredulous.*

Dennis Catch him! He's going to faint.

He and **Fay** *support* **McLeavy** *and help him to the bed.* **McLeavy** *sinks beside the corpse in a state of shock.*

McLeavy Where? (*Bewildered.*) Where? (*He follows* **Hal**'*s glance to the corpse and recoils in horror.*) Oh, the end of the world is near when such crimes are committed.

Truscott The opening of a coffin couldn't possible herald Armageddon. Pull yourself together, sir.

Fay (*to* **Truscott**) The condition of the corpse has deteriorated due to the accident. Do you wish to verify the fact?

Truscott (*shuddering*) No, thank you, miss. I receive enough shocks in the line of duty without going about looking for them.

Fay (*to* **Dennis**) Replace the lid on the coffin.

Dennis *does so.*

McLeavy (*to* **Hal**)   I shall disown you. I'll publish it abroad that I was cuckolded.

Fay (*to* **Truscott**)   It's been a harrowing experience for him.

Truscott   He was warned in advance of the consequences of his action.

Hal (*kneeling to* **McLeavy**)   I'm in a bit of a spot, Dad. I don't mind confessing. Don't get stroppy with me, eh?

McLeavy   I'm sorry I ever got you. I'd've withheld myself at the conception if I'd known.

Truscott   Such idle fantasies ill become you, sir.

McLeavy *chokes back his sobs.*

Fathers have discovered greater iniquities in their sons than the theft of an eye. The episode isn't without instruction.

McLeavy   Where did I go wrong? His upbringing was faultless. (*To* **Dennis**.) Did you lead him astray?

Dennis   I was innocent till I met him.

Hal   You met me when you were three days old.

McLeavy (*to* **Hal**)   Where are your tears? She was your mother.

Hal   It's dust, Dad.

McLeavy *shakes his head in despair.*

A little dust.

McLeavy   I loved her.

Hal   You had her filleted without a qualm. Who could have affection for a half-empty woman?

McLeavy (*groaning*)   Oh Jesus, Mary, Joseph, guide me to the end of my wits and have done with it.

Hal   You've lost nothing. You began the day with a dead wife. You end it with a dead wife.

McLeavy   Oh, wicked, wicked. (*Wildly.*) These hairs – (*Points.*) – they're grey. You made them so. I'd be a redhead today had you been an accountant.

Truscott (*removing his pipe from his mouth*)   We really can't accept such unlikely explanation for the colour of your hair, sir.

McLeavy *wails aloud in anguish.*

Your behaviour indicates a growing lack of control. It's disgraceful in a man of your age and background. I'm half inclined to book you for disturbing the peace.

Fay *hands* **McLeavy** *a handkerchief. He blows his nose. He draws himself up to his full height.*

McLeavy   I'm sorry, Inspector. My behaviour must seem strange to you. I'll endeavour to explain it. You can then do as you think fit.

Fay   Consider the consequences of telling the truth. It will kill Father Jellicoe.

Dennis   My pigeons will die if I'm nicked. There'll be nobody to feed them.

Silence. **Truscott** *opens his notebook and looks at* **McLeavy**.

McLeavy   I wish to prefer charges.

Hal (*desperate*)   If my Aunt Bridie hears of this, she'll leave her money to an orphanage. You know how selfish she is.

Truscott   Whom do you wish to charge, sir?

McLeavy (*pause, struggles with his conscience, at last*)   Myself.

Truscott (*looking up from his notebook*)   What crime have you committed?

McLeavy   I – I – (*Sweating.*) I've given misleading information to the police.

Truscott   What information?

McLeavy   I told you that the eye belonged to my wife. It
doesn't. (*Conscience stricken.*) Oh, God forgive me for what I'm
doing.

Truscott   If the eye doesn't belong to your wife, to whom
does it belong?

McLeavy *is unable to answer; he stares about him, perplexed.*

Fay (*with a smile*)   It belongs to my sewing dummy,
Inspector. Your original deduction was quite correct.

Truscott *slowly puts away his notebook and pencil.*

Truscott   I ought to have my head examined, getting
mixed up in a case of this kind. (*To* **McLeavy**.) Your
conduct is scandalous, sir. With you for a father this lad
never stood a chance. No wonder he took to robbing banks.

McLeavy (*in shame*)   What are you going to do?

Truscott   Do? I'm going to leave this house at once. I've
never come across such people. You behave as though
you're affiliated to Bedlam.

McLeavy   But – the bank robbery – is the case closed?

Truscott   No, sir, it's not closed. We don't give up as
easily as that. I'm going to have this place turned upside
down.

McLeavy   Oh, dear, what a nuisance. And in a house of
mourning, too.

Truscott   Your wife won't be here, sir. I shall take
possession of the remains.

Fay   Why do you need the remains? You can't prove Mrs
McLeavy was murdered.

Truscott   There's no cause for alarm. It's a mere
formality. You're quite safe. (*He smiles. To* **McLeavy**.)
There's no one more touchy than your hardened criminal.

(*He puts his pipe away.*) I'll be back in ten minutes. And then, I'm afraid, a lot of damage will be done to your property. You'll be paying repair bills for months to come. One unfortunate suspect recently had the roof taken off his house.

McLeavy   Isn't there anything I can do to prevent this appalling assault upon my privacy?

Truscott   Well, sir, if you can suggest a possible hiding-place for the money?

McLeavy *hangs his head.*

McLeavy (*almost in a whisper*)   I can't, Inspector.

Truscott   Very well. You must take the consequences of ignorance. (*He tips his hat.*) I'll be back soon.

He goes off left.

McLeavy   Oh, what a terrible thing I've done. I've obstructed an officer in the course of his duty.

Hal (*hugging him*)   I'm proud of you. I'll never feel ashamed of bringing my friends home now.

McLeavy   I shan't be able to face my reflection in the mirror.

Fay   Go to confession. Book an hour with Father Mac.

Hal   Oh, not him! Three brandies and he's away. The barmaid at the King of Denmark is blackmailing half the district.

McLeavy   I'll say nothing of what I've discovered if you return the money to the bank. You're not to keep a penny of it. Do you understand?

Hal   Yes, Dad. (*He winks at* **Dennis**.)

McLeavy   I'll go and ring Father Jellicoe. My soul is in torment.

McLeavy *goes off left.*

Hal (*closing the door, to* **Fay**)   Unwrap the body. Once we've got it back into the coffin we're home and dry.

Fay *pulls the screen round the bed. She goes behind the screen to unwrap the corpse.*

Dennis   What are we going to do with the money?

Hal   Put it into the casket.

Dennis   Won't he want that?

Hal   He knows it's empty.

Dennis *takes the lid from the coffin.*

Dennis   Why didn't we put it in there in the first place?

Hal   My mum's guts were in there. The damp would've got at the notes.

Hal *opens the casket.*

Got a hanky?

Dennis *throws a handkerchief over.* **Hal** *wipes the inside of the casket.*

Dennis   Oh, you've gone too far! Using my handkerchief for that. It was a birthday present.

Hal *throws him the handkerchief back.*

Hal   Relax, baby. You'll have other birthdays.

Dennis *throws the bundles of notes to* **Hal**. **Hal** *packs them into the casket.*

I shall accompany my father to Confession this evening. In order to purge my soul of this afternoon's events.

Dennis   It's at times like this that I regret not being a Catholic.

Hal   Afterwards I'll take you to a remarkable brothel I've found. Really remarkable. Run by three Pakistanis aged between ten and fifteen. They do it for sweets. Part of their religion. Meet me at seven. Stock up with Mars bars.

Fay *appears from behind the screen, folding the mattress cover.*

Fay   Don't look behind there, Harold.

Hal   Why not?

Fay   Your mother is naked.

She hangs the folded cover over the screen. **Hal** *packs the last bundle of notes into the casket.*

Hal   We're safe.

He bangs down the lid.

Nobody will ever look in there.

Truscott *enters left.*

Truscott   I've fixed everything to my satisfaction. My men will be here shortly. They're perfectly capable of causing damage unsupervised, and so I shall take my leave of you. (*He bows, smiles.*)

Fay (*shaking hands*)   Good-bye, Inspector. It's been nice meeting you again.

Truscott   Good-bye. (*He nods to* **Hal** *and* **Dennis**.) I'd better take the little casket with me.

Hal   It's empty!

Truscott   I must have it certified empty before I close my report.

Fay   We're having it de-sanctified. Mr McLeavy is on the phone to the priest about it.

Truscott   Our lads in forensic aren't interested in sanctity. Give me that casket!

McLeavy *enters left. He sees* **Truscott** *and cowers back.*

McLeavy   You're back already? Have you decided to arrest me after all?

Truscott   I wouldn't arrest you if you were the last man on earth. (*To* **Hal**.) Give me that casket! (*He takes the casket from* **Hal**. *To* **McLeavy**.) I'll give you a receipt, sir.

He looks somewhere to rest the casket, sees the empty coffin puts the casket down.

Where is Mrs McLeavy?

Fay   She's behind the screen.

Truscott *looks behind the screen and raises his eyebrows.*

Truscott   Did she ask to be buried like that?

McLeavy   Yes.

Truscott   She was a believer in that sort of thing?

McLeavy   Yes.

Truscott   Are you, sir?

McLeavy   Well no. I'm not a member myself.

Truscott   A member? She belonged to a group, then?

McLeavy   Oh, yes. They met a couple of times a week. They do a lot of good for the country. Raising money for charities, holding fêtes. The old folk would be lost without them.

Truscott   I've heard many excuses for nudists, sir, but never that one.

McLeavy (*pause*)   Nudists?

Truscott   Your wife was a nudist, you say?

McLeavy   My wife never took her clothes off in public in her life.

Truscott   Yet she asked to be buried in that condition?

McLeavy   What condition?

Truscott   In the nude.

McLeavy (*with dignity*)   You'd better leave my house, Inspector. I can't allow you to insult the memory of my late wife.

Truscott (*tearing a sheet of paper from his notebook*)   You give me a lot of aggravation, sir. Really you do. (*He hands the paper to* **McLeavy**.) You'll get your property back in due course.

He lifts casket, the lid swings away and the bundles of banknotes fall to the floor. **Truscott** *stares at the notes scattered at his feet in silence.*

Who is responsible for this disgraceful state of affairs?

Hal   I am.

Truscott (*stoops and picks up a bundle of notes*)   Would you have stood by and allowed this money to be buried in holy ground?

Hal   Yes.

Truscott   How dare you involve me in a situation for which no memo has been issued. (*He turns the notes over.*) In all my experience I've never come across a case like it. Every one of these fivers bears a portrait of the Queen. It's dreadful to contemplate the issues raised. Twenty thousand tiaras and twenty thousand smiles buried alive! She's a constitutional monarch, you know. She can't answer back.

Dennis   Will she send us a telegram?

Truscott   I'm sure she will.

He picks up another bundle and stares at them.

McLeavy   Well, Inspector, you've found the money and unmasked the criminals. You must do your duty and arrest them. I shall do mine and appear as witness for the prosecution.

Hal   Are you married, Inspector?

Truscott   Yes.

Hal   Does your wife never yearn for excitement?

Truscott   She did once express a wish to see the windmills and tulip fields of Holland.

Hal   With such an intelligent wife you need a larger income.

Truscott   I never said my wife was intelligent.

Hal   Then she's unintelligent? Is that it?

Truscott   My wife is a woman. Intelligence doesn't really enter into the matter.

Hal   If, as you claim, your wife is a woman, you certainly need a larger income.

Truscott *takes his pipe from his pocket and sticks it into the corner of his mouth.*

Truscott   Where is this Jesuitical twittering leading us?

Hal   I'm about to suggest bribery.

Truscott *removes his pipe, no one speaks.*

Truscott   How much?

Hal   Twenty per cent.

Truscott   Twenty-five per cent. Or a full report of this case appears on my superior officer's desk in the morning.

Hal   Twenty-five it is.

Truscott (*shaking hands*)   Done.

Dennis (*to* **Truscott**)   May I help you to replace the money in the casket?

Truscott   Thank you, lad. Most kind of you.

Dennis *packs the money into the casket.* **Fay** *takes* **Mrs McLeavy**'s *clothes from the bedpan on the invalid chair and goes behind the screen.* **Truscott** *chews on his pipe.* **Hal** *and* **Dennis** *take the coffin behind the screen.*

McLeavy   Has no one considered my feelings in all this?

Truscott   What percentage do you want?

McLeavy   I don't want money. I'm an honest man.

Truscott   You'll have to mend your ways then.

McLeavy   I shall denounce the lot of you!

Truscott   Now then, sir, be reasonable. What has just taken place is perfectly scandalous and had better go no farther than these three walls. It's not expedient for the general public to have its confidence in the police force undermined. You'd be doing the community a grave disservice by revealing the full frightening facts of this case.

McLeavy   What kind of talk is that? You don't make sense.

Truscott   Who does?

McLeavy   I'll go to the priest. He makes sense. He makes sense to me.

Truscott   Does he make sense to himself? That is much more important.

McLeavy   If I can't trust the police, I can still rely on the Fathers. They'll advise me what to do!

He goes off left. **Hal** *appears from behind the screen.*

Hal   You'll be glad to know that my mother is back in her last resting-place.

Truscott   Good. You've carried out the operation with speed and efficiency. I congratulate you.

Dennis *appears from behind the screen.*

Dennis   We're ready for the eye now. If you'd like to assist us.

Truscott *(taking the eye from his pocket)*   You do it, lad. You're more experienced in these matters than me.

He hands **Dennis** *the eye.*

Hal   You'd better have these as well.

He hands **Dennis** *the teeth.*

Dennis *takes the eye and teeth behind the screen.*

Truscott   Your sense of detachment is terrifying, lad. Most people would at least flinch upon seeing their mother's eyes and teeth handed around like nuts at Christmas.

Fay *appears from behind the screen.*

Fay   Have you given a thought to the priest?

Truscott   We can't have him in on it, miss. Our percentage wouldn't be worth having.

Fay   Mr McLeavy has threatened to expose us.

Truscott   I've been exposed before.

Fay   What happened?

Truscott   I arrested the man. He's doing twelve years.

Hal   If you wish to arrest my dad, you'll find me an exemplary witness.

Truscott   What a bright idea. We've vacancies in the force for lads of your calibre. (*To* **Fay**.) Are you with us, McMahon?

Fay   Yes, it seems the best solution for all of us.

Dennis *folds up the screen. The coffin is lying on the bed.*

Truscott (*to* **Dennis**)   And you?

Dennis   I've never seen the view from the witness box. It'll be a new experience.

The door left burst open. **McLeavy** *enters with* **Meadows**.

McLeavy (*pointing to* **Truscott**)   This is the man. Arrest him.

Truscott   Good afternoon, Meadows. Why have you left your post?

Meadows   I was accosted by this man, sir. He insisted that I accompany him to the Catholic church.

Truscott   What did you say?

Meadows   I refused.

Truscott   Quite rightly. You're a Methodist. Proceed with the statement.

Meadows   The man became offensive, sir. He made a number of derogatory remarks about the force in general and yourself in particular. I called for assistance.

Truscott   Excellent, Meadows. I shall see H.Q. hear of this. You have apprehended, in full flight, a most dangerous criminal. As you know, we've had our eye upon this house for some time. I was about to unmask the chief offender when this man left the room on some excuse and disappeared.

Meadows   He was making a bolt for it, sir.

Truscott   You have the matter in a nutshell, Meadows. Put the cuffs on him.

Meadows *handcuffs* **McLeavy**.

You're fucking nicked, my old beauty. You've found to your cost that the standards of the British police force are as high as ever.

McLeavy   What am I charged with?

Truscott   That needn't concern you for the moment. We'll fill in the details later.

McLeavy   You can't do this. I've always been a law-abiding citizen. The police are for the protection of ordinary people.

Truscott   I don't know where you pick up these slogans, sir. You must read them on hoardings.

McLeavy   I want to see someone in authority.

Truscott   I am in authority. You can see me.

McLeavy   Someone higher.

Truscott   You can see whoever you like, providing you convince me first that you're justified in seeing them.

McLeavy   You're mad!

Truscott   Nonsense. I had a check-up only yesterday. Our medical officer assured me that I was quite sane.

McLeavy   I'm innocent. (*A little unsure of himself, the beginnings of panic.*) Doesn't that mean anything to you?

Truscott   You know the drill, Meadows. Empty his pockets and book him.

McLeavy *is dragged away by* **Meadows**.

McLeavy   I'm innocent! I'm innocent! (*At the door, pause, a last wail.*) Oh, what a terrible thing to happen to a man who's been kissed by the Pope.

Meadows *goes off with* **McLeavy**.

Dennis   What will you charge him with, Inspector?

Truscott   Oh, anything will do.

Fay   Can an accidental death be arranged?

Truscott   Anything can be arranged in prison.

Hal   Except pregnancy.

Truscott   Well, of course, the chaperon system defeats us there.

He picks up the casket.

The safest place for this is in my locker at the station. It's a maxim of the force: 'Never search your own backyard – you may find what you're looking for.' (*He turns in the doorway, the casket under his arm.*) Give me a ring this evening. I should have news for you of McLeavy by then. (*He hands a card to* **Fay**.) This is my home address. I'm well known there.

He nods, smiles, and goes off left. Sound of front door slamming. Pause.

Hal (*with a sigh*)   He's a nice man. Self-effacing in his way.

Dennis   He has an open mind. In direct contrast to the usual run of civil servant.

Hal *and* **Dennis** *lift the coffin from the bed and place it on the trestles.*

Hal   It's comforting to know that the police can still be relied upon when we're in trouble.

They stand beside the coffin, **Fay** *in the middle.*

Fay   We'll bury your father with your mother. That will be nice for him, won't it?

She lifts her rosary and bows her head in prayer.

Hal (*pause, to* **Dennis**)   You can kip here, baby. Plenty of room now. Bring your bags over tonight.

Fay *looks up.*

Fay (*sharply*)   When Dennis and I are married we'd have to move out.

Hal   Why?

Fay   People would talk. We must keep up appearances.

She returns to her prayers, her lips move silently. **Dennis** *and* **Hal** *at either side of the coffin.*

Curtain.

Edward Bond was born and educated in London. His plays include *The Pope's Wedding* (Royal Court Theatre, 1962), *Saved* (Royal Court, 1965), *Early Morning* (Royal Court, 1968), *Narrow Road to the Deep North* (Belgrade Theatre, Coventry, 1968; Royal Court, 1969), *Black Mass* (Sharpeville Commemoration Evening, Lyceum Theatre, 1970), *Passion* (CND Rally, Alexandra Palace, 1971), *Lear* (Royal Court, 1971), *The Sea* (Royal Court, 1973), *Bingo* (Northcott, Exeter, 1973; Royal Court, 1974), *The Fool* (Royal Court, 1975), *The Bundle* (RSC Warehouse, 1978), *The Woman* (National Theatre, 1978), *The Worlds* (New Half Moon Theatre, London, 1981), *Restoration* (Royal Court, 1981), *Summer* (National Theatre, 1982), *Derek* (RSC Youth Festival, The Other Place, Stratford-upon-Avon, 1982), *The Cat* (produced in Germany as *The English Cat* by the Stuttgart Opera, 1983), *Human Cannon* (Quantum Theatre, Manchester, 1986), *The War Plays* (*Red Black and Ignorant, The Tin Can People* and *Great Peace*), which were staged as a trilogy by the RSC at the Barbican Pit in 1985, *Jackets* (Leicester, Haymarket, 1989), *September* (Canterbury Cathedral, 1989), *In the Company of Men* (Paris, 1992; RSC at the Barbican Pit, 1996), *At the Inland Sea* (toured by Big Brum Theatre-in-Education, 1995), *Coffee* (Rational Theatre Company, Cardiff and London, 1996), and *Eleven Vests* (toured by Big Brum Theatre-in-Education, 1997); *Olly's Prison (BBC2 Television, 1993), Tuesday* (BBC Schools TV, 1993). His *Theatre Poems and Songs* were published in 1978 and *Poems 1978–1985* in 1987.

Early Morning

A Manifesto for Other People

The censor returned my first plays with lines and sections
ruled out in light blue pencil. The lines reminded me of
prison bars: through them I could see the text of my play –
freedom. It was a small example of state violence – of
concentration camps, prisons, inquisitions, executions, mili-
tarism, social inequality and the vicious repression known as
law-and-order. The ultimate freedom is not to do and say
what you choose but to know yourself. Without that how can
you know what you do and say? – socially every act might be
a self-mutilation and every word a self-betrayal. Self-
knowledge is the most difficult freedom to achieve. Without it
there is no freedom. It is what makes censorship the
foundation of *all* state violence and ultimately the origin of
psychological violence.

If you are to know yourself you must know the world and
your society. To do that you must understand nature and
power. A simple image of power is a horse – it draws your cart
and this gives you power. Societies change historically
because technology gives them greater power. But there is a
paradox: in all collectivities the roles are reversed, the horse
is in the driving seat. Power sweeps us before it and we are
slow to adapt. History differs from evolution. In evolution
animals adapt to change in their environment, in their site. In
history, we change the site (which is our technological power)
but do not adapt to it because society's rulers (and owners)
resist change. That is the structural origin of injustice.
Revolution is the effort made to get the horse (or rather, the
ass) out of the driving seat. It is awkward and not a pretty
sight: the past is the coffin in which the present is born. I wish
the epigram were not so neat because – as our technological
power increases – the relation it defines may decide our fate.

How is knowledge created? Science tells us only about
things. Even when it explores people it treats them as things.
This is its strength. Science has internal instrumental values
but no moral guide. A scientific discovery may lead to better
hospitals or to gas chambers. All scientific changes to society

are mediated through social power. To use science humanely you have to change social power to make it more human. Science cannot do that because it has no conception of what humanness is – nor should it have: the idea is an abomination. Contemporary ideology teaches genetic determinism: we are the product of our genes. As human history has been largely disastrous, the theory of genetic determinism is pessimistic, an equivalent to the medieval doctrine of original sin. It leads to the idea of scientifically designing out the 'bad' genes and creating perfect people. But science has no conception of human perfection. It could only design perfect things: things incapable of the struggle to be human. The scientifically perfect human would be a monster of inhumanness.

We are not born human. Infants enter into humanness when they enter a culture. Our genes enable us to do that – but we acquire, become, our culture's virtues and faults, its humanness and inhuman corruptions. In evolution animals struggle to survive, but in cultures humans do not. To say they do is pseudo-science and reactionary clap-trap. Survival is often surprisingly incidental. It is easily 'postponed' by ideological demands. Only one thing creates humanness: drama. And by drama I mean all art, formal and informal. If humanness does not exist, it has to be created. Each generation must create it in its changed 'site'. To that extent it is like a technology, but it has no science to found itself on, no world of things to define it. Drama's subject is not a thing, it is a no-thing – the nothing out of which we created everything that makes us human. We create it in defiance of the indifference of the universe and the cruelty of our streets. At the heart of cruelty and injustice there is emptiness. But nothingness is the source of humanness. It is what forces us to give a meaning to the world – and it forces us to become that meaning.

To be self-conscious you must have imagination. The two are one. In politics and culture the difference between right and left derives from the imagination. Pessimism of the imagination is conservative and reactionary, the horse in the driving seat. Optimism of the imagination is creative and human. What causes the difference? Imagination seeks reason – it is a structural necessity of the neonate and infant. I cannot explain this in a preface, it flies in the face of the teachings of ideology, common sense, religion – the distortions which are at first necessary for the creation of humanness but which in time become its most dangerous enemies. As society is unjust its philosophy and practices, its culture, are pessimistic – but art is optimistic (even when that is against its stated intention, even when it is absurd and nihilistic – you do not write a suicide note unless you intend it to be read). So there is a conflict between inhumanness and humanness which science cannot resolve because humanness is never a thing and must be *created*. If that were not so the distortions of ideology would be impossible. Unjust cultures teach irrationality, it is their ideology – but imagination seeks reason: and there is a logic of imagination. The logic is elucidated through the agon of drama, in which the conflicts are reconciled at least to the degree that we may live in them less destructively. This is the slow process of civilization – the human world, human subjectivity and the human image do not exist but must constantly be recreated. The dramatic agon is a structure which may – but need not – be cathected with great emotion and even the tragic. It is the site of the paradox out of which, in the world of things, we respond to the demands that nothingness imposes on our imaginations. Nothingness is the gap in us which we fill with the 'self' we create – and that self is never anything other than the meaning we give to the world. The psyche is an empty stage until we create a self on it. That is the imperative of drama in practical life and in theatre.

When I wrote my first plays there were two tendencies in drama: a murky mysticism and a reductive materialism. The former would be dismissable as jejune, except that when it itself joins forces with materialism it becomes fascism. The latter – reductive materialism (often miscalled scientific materialism) – regards people, structurally, as things, or (as this is absurd unless you create Piscator's match-stick people) as colourful, often lovably quixotic, facades over things. It saw humanness as something extra to be learnt when other human problems were resolved. No, the struggle for humanness is the foundation of the human psyche: which is the site of the self *and* the world. The human being is not a soul, there is not even a human mind – there is a gap: we are the gap in which we create our humanness or inhumanness. Which it is, depends precisely on how we understand our 'site': our society and the world. We should not be puzzled that people may behave inhumanly. There is no 'human nature', and neither history nor culture guarantee our humanness. We are formed as part of our culture's unresolved conflicts. Because we are not born human each generation must resolve these conflicts as humanly as it can, each person must become the assessor and judge of reality.

Imagination is not fantasy and its logic is not transcendental – it is of this world. Without the logic of imagination no materialism is possible – instead what is presented as materialism is an empty transcendentalism, a living nightmare to be enforced with knouts, prison vans and censors. We need a theatre which might be betrayed (it could not be otherwise in our society) but which could not betray itself. It would be the Rational Theatre.

When I started to write, most plays were made trivial by censorship. Now young writers are honest, serious and accurate about the frustrations of living in our society and even try to write about the obscurities of time and place and creation. But they have lost society itself, they write the Theatre of Symptoms. Many of their plays are like Rattigan written with obscenities or Coward written in rage. When you lose society you lose the world. The mysticism of the past was cant, and reductive materialism was an abortive short-cut. But when you ignore the problems they tried to deal with – the ordering of society (and the enigmas of time and space, which are also part of our paradox) – you hand them back to ideology. Human existence has no purpose so we must give it a human meaning. If we do that the great existential problems become part of human dignity, resolve and sanity. Ideology can only make them repressive – and then drama becomes anecdotal and empty. Really, if you lose the world you lose yourself.

In 1995 I saw Sarah Kane's *Blasted*. I knew I was in the presence of theatrical greatness. I might have been in the Theatre of Dionysus or the Globe, not the little theatre of the Royal Court. It is a strange feeling. I have had it sometimes watching young people's dramas: it has the weight of darkness and the freedom of light, you are manacled and released, you are shown reality and it is the ability to show it that lets you survive it with greater strength. All Sarah Kane's plays are revelations, but after *Blasted* they often concentrate on the search for the perfect person who would give you a reason to live. It is as pointless to search for a human god as it is to search for a divine god. There is no such person, you must live for others – with their imperfections. Sarah Kane said you could learn everything about dramatic technique from my play *Saved*. That is not true. You must know many more things if you are to write about society and the world. Sarah Kane lost both when she killed herself. You might say that was the last symptom of the Theatre of Symptoms, when stage and street became one. But that would be glib, theatre is always its own reality. Sarah Kane's plays belong to the future. She wrote about the conflicts of her time because she lived them. But they are only instances of conflicts common to all human generations. Her plays are part of the human desire to make the world our home – it is that imperative which makes imagination optimistic. That is why drama may be defined as the tradition of the future.

My first plays – *The Pope's Wedding* and *Saved* – have been called social realism. They are about small communities. To fully understand the conflicts in these communities and analyse them in a way that could be theatrically understood – enact them in the reality of imagination – I needed to go beyond social realism and write dramas of imaginative realism. I needed to show how ideology corrupts humanness and turns justice into revenge. Otherwise I could not show why the strongest prisons are in the mind, and how it is easy to make freedom a form of imprisonment. I needed to find many ways to reproduce the complexities of the social world in the simplicities of drama.

The editor of this book wanted to put *Saved* in it. Instead I chose *Early Morning*. None of my plays are social realism though they have been misunderstood as such. Social realism must be part of drama but drama must not be reduced to it. Social realism is where imagination should begin. If it doesn't, drama is reduced to performance art, ritual and other modish kitsch. No one could reduce *Early Morning* to social realism, reductive materialism or fantasy. It is simply too real for that. That is what makes it a useful text for the times.

Young writers need to re-find society and the world. Theatre is against them. It is deeply complicit in the economic imperative to exploit. Directors become sales people and stage designers part of the advertising industry. Often acting is reduced to the tics and gimmicks of performing to cameras. Most dangerous of all, young writers are exploited and then condemned to TV and the golden muckheaps of Hollywood. They do not have the time or places in which to develop their craft, to learn how to radically challenge directors and actors. Without that challenge theatre dies. It is as if everything had to be learnt from the beginning again. This should be a time of great creativity. Instead theatre is committing suicide even as it falls into the hands of its murderers.

Edward Bond, July 2001

The events of this play are true

Early Morning was first presented by the English Stage
Society at the Royal Court Theatre, London, on 31 March
1968 with the following cast:

Albert	Nigel Hawthorne
Disraeli	Malcolm Tierney
Arthur	Peter Eyre
George	Tom Chadbon
Lord Chamberlain	Roger Booth
Lord Mennings	Norman Eshley
Queen Victoria	Moira Redmond
Florence Nightingale	Marianne Faithfull
Len	Dennis Waterman
Joyce	Jane Howell
Jones	Hugh Armstrong
Griss	Harry Meacher
Doctor	Gavin Reed
Gladstone	Jack Shepherd
Ned	Bruce Robinson

Directed by William Gaskill

Characters

Prince Arthur	20 years
Prince George, *Prince of Wales*	20 years
Albert, *Prince Consort*	45 years
Disraeli, *Prime Minister*	50 years
Gladstone, *Prime Minister*	50 years
Lord Chamberlain	old
Lord Mennings	young
Len, **Joyce**'s *boyfriend*	18 years
Corporal Jones	35 years
Private Griss	19 years
Doctor	50 years
Ned, *a drummer boy*	16 years
Queen Victoria	45 years
Florence Nightingale	20 years
Joyce, **Len**'s *girlfriend*	50 years

Mob, **Courtiers**, **Footman**, **Officers**, **Soldiers**, **Wounded**, **Firing Squad**, **Ghosts**, **Jurors**, **Bodies**, etc.

Most of the smaller parts may be doubled, and played by some of the mob, etc.

The play is in twenty-one scenes. It may be played in four parts, with intervals after scenes five, ten and fifteen: or in three parts, with intervals after scenes five and fifteen.

Very little scenery should be used, and in the last six scenes probably none at all. Whenever possible the place should be suggested by clothes and actions.

Scene One

A corridor in Windsor Castle. **Prince Albert** *and* **Disraeli** *come on.*

Albert (*looks round*)   This is safe.

Disraeli   Victoria's going to announce the Prince of Wales' engagement. Victoria's not popular. She's frightened. She knows a royal wedding will pacify the people, so we must strike now.

Albert   Exactly.

Disraeli   You've been saying exactly for five years.

Albert   It's my sons. Not George – when we kill Victoria he'll come to heel, he's just her tool – it's Arthur. I want him to join us.

Disraeli   I hoped he would. He's heir after Prince George. It would have given our coup the appearance of legality. But there's no more time.

Albert   I'll talk to him.

Disraeli   Again?

Albert   Tonight. I'll tell him about the engagement. That'll shock him.

Disraeli   All right, but tomorrow I start secret mobilisation. Tonight I'll bring the black list up to date. I was going to shoot them – to demonstrate our military support, you understand. But I've decided on hanging – that will emphasise our respectability. I'll keep the numbers down.

Albert   How many?

Disraeli   We don't know all our enemies till we start. So far, eight hundred and thirteen.

Albert   Make it fourteen. People are superstitious. (*Looks off. Loudly.*) I shouldn't be surprised if it doesn't rain.

They go.

Scene Two

Windsor Castle. The Princes' bedroom. Dark. **George** *isn't seen till he wakes up.* **George** *and* **Arthur** *in bed.* **Albert** *comes in. He carries a candle.*

Arthur George is asleep.

Albert If I could talk to you alone for once – just for five minutes – we'd clear up all our misunderstandings.

Arthur Be quick!

Albert It's not easy, Arthur. Help me. Try to –

Arthur Sh! (**Albert** *starts to go.*) No, he's asleep.

Albert He spoke.

Arthur He wants some water. He thinks he's in a desert. He always dreams that when he's frightened.

Albert Why's he frightened?

Arthur He's getting married.

Albert (*annoyed*) Who told you?

Arthur Who's the woman?

Albert We don't know. Disraeli's going to mobilise. I can't put him off any longer.

Arthur He wants to make himself dictator.

Albert Of course. But we can use him for a time. Your mother's the first danger. We must stop her before she causes the wrong revolution. She should have been a prison governess. She's afraid of people. She thinks they're evil. She doesn't understand their energy. She suppresses it.

Arthur If you give Disraeli his head he'll end up by standing us all against the wall.

Albert No. Let him establish the new constitution, and then blame him for using force – because force is going to be necessary, let's be realistic – and stage a counter revolution. But you must be in from the start. You must accept responsibility. I mean personally, between ourselves. That's what I want.

Arthur   How many will you kill?

Albert   A few. Every time you open a bridge you know people will throw themselves off it.

Arthur   A purge.

Albert   No.

Arthur   Mother?

Albert   A place in the country.

Arthur   And George?

Albert   That's up to you.

Arthur   He'd have to accept it.

Albert   Good.

Arthur   So, have your revolution, get rid of Disraeli when he's done the dirty work, and make yourself Regent. I won't interfere.

Albert   No, you don't understand. I'm not doing this because I hate your mother. Hate destroys, I want to build. The people are strong. They want to be *used* – to build empires and railways and factories, to trade and convert and establish law and order. I know there'll be crimes, but we can punish them. The good will always outweigh the bad – in the end perhaps there won't be any bad, though I don't believe that. Arthur I can't do this alone. That would be tragic. You must promise to carry on my work.

Arthur   The trouble with the world is it's run by politicians.

Albert   I'm going to tell Disraeli you've joined us. That will give you time to think, and when you decide to join us – we need a code – you must say you've solved the riddle!

George *sits up in bed. He drinks some water.*

George   I thought I was in a desert. (*He sees* **Albert**.) Who's that?

Albert   I'm tying my shoe.

George   You're wearing slippers.

Albert   They don't fit. Good night. (**Albert** *goes out.*)

George   I shall have to tell mother about this.

Arthur   He has these little talks because he's jealous of you and mother. She should stop sending you notes.

George   They're state secrets. Goodnight. (*He lies down.*)

Arthur   We shouldn't quarrel. It can't be all my fault, and –

George   I try, I shall keep trying, but you'll never respond.

Arthur   That's not true! I always give way if it helps. I try to put myself in your shoes: it's not easy being Prince of Wales . . . One day you'll have to marry.

George   Yes.

Arthur   I shan't object.

George   Thank you!

Arthur   *I* can't marry! Have you thought of that?

George   That's up to you.

Arthur (*angrily*)   No it isn't! How could I involve a woman in this unless I was forced to? (*Slight pause.*) When you do marry we must stop quarrelling. She'll have enough to put up with without –

George (*suddenly realizing*)   You know!

Arthur   You talked about it in your sleep.

George   I did not! I've trained myself not to talk in my sleep. *He* told you!

Arthur   Who is she?

George   That's no concern of yours.

Arthur   This is impossible!

George   Goodnight!

Arthur (*angrily*)   I have no rights – not even the right to surrender. I'm sick of secrets and arguments. I'd like to be happy – just for the experience! That's all. And if that's all you wanted there wouldn't be any trouble. Instead I'm trapped!

George   . . . Water . . .

Scene Three

Windsor Castle throne room. The **Lord Chamberlain**, **Lord Mennings**, *a* **Footman**, *other* **Lords** *etc.*

Chamberlain   Her Majesty will be here directly.

Mennings   This trial should be a real jazz. Is it true the woman's a lot older than him?

Chamberlain   Yes.

Mennings   You can't get tickets. The black market's sold out.

Chamberlain   I'm as modern as anyone but I'm all for holding trials in secret and executions in public. That simplifies government and satisfies the people. We should never have abolished hanging. It was something to live up to.

Albert *comes in. Bows.*

Footman   The Prince Consort.

Disraeli *comes in.*

Footman   The Prime Minister.

Albert (*quietly to* **Disraeli**)   Why's she summoned us here?

Disraeli   I don't know.

Footman   The Prince of Wales and Prince Arthur.

Arthur *and* **George** *come on. It is seen that they are siamese twins. Bow.*

Albert   Have you solved the riddle?

George   What riddle? (*To* **Arthur**.) Well?

Arthur   What burns in water, drowns in fire, flies through the ground, and lies in the sky?

George   Well what?

Arthur   I don't know.

Footman   The Queen.

Victoria *comes in. Bows.*

Victoria   Albert, dearest, where have you been since breakfast?

Albert (*kisses her cheek*)   My love.

Victoria   Thank you. You've cured my headache. (*She makes a formal address.*) Our kingdom is degenerating. Our people cannot walk on our highways in peace. They cannot count their money in safety, even though our head is on it. We cannot understand most of what is called our English. Our prisons are full. Instead of fighting our enemies our armies are putting down strikers and guarding our judges. Our peace is broken. You know that the Prince of Wales poses certain constitutional questions. Because of this the

anarchists and immoralists say that the monarchy must end
with our death, and so they shoot at us. They are wrong.
Our son will follow in our footsteps, with his brother at his
side, and in time his son will follow him. Our line began at
Stonehenge, and we shall not fall till Stonehenge falls. We
shall not abandon this kingdom to anarchy. That is why our
son will have a normal marriage. His bride will be Miss
Florence Nightingale.

Florence Nightingale *comes in. She curtsies to* **Victoria** *and
then to* **George**. **Victoria** *gives a note to her and a note to*
George.

George (*reads his note*)   Dear Miss Nightingale, I welcome
you to Windsor and hope you will be happy here.

Florence (*reads her note*)   Thank you.

Victoria   Miss Nightingale is an expert sanitarian. We
believe that to be a branch of eugenics.

Arthur   Why wasn't I warned?

Victoria   Warned is not diplomatic. Gentlemen, you may
go.

Mennings   May I say how delighted –

Victoria   Thank you.

The others go. **Victoria**, **Albert**, **George**, **Arthur**, **Disraeli**
and **Florence** *are left.*

Victoria   I will not permit family bickering in public! (*To*
Arthur.) Of course this will call for some slight personal
adjustment. But the country must come first. (*To* **Disraeli**.)
He'll make that girl's life a tragedy – and one day she'll hate
me, poor child.

Disraeli (*going with* **Victoria**)   Ma'am, you wear a crown
of thorns.

Disraeli *and* **Victoria** *go out.* **Albert** *follows them. Slight
pause.*

George   I'd better show you the castle.

Arthur   He's inspired.

Florence   Why don't you cut . . .

Arthur   We can't. I have the heart – he hasn't got one.

George   There was a mistake. I'll show you the castle.

Arthur   I'm not in a sightseeing mood.

George   Well we are! (*He tries to pull* **Arthur** *with him. A brief, silent struggle. He stops.*) You! . . . He wants you to think I'm impotent without him.

Florence   Isn't it nice here!

Arthur   I'm going to sit down. Join me. Talk. I won't listen. You'd better decide how many children you're going to have. Then you can warn me.

George   Bastard.

Arthur   Did mother tell you he swore?

Florence   I'm so pleased to be here. I ought to tell you something . . . I love you.

Arthur   Another note.

Florence   I was eleven when it happened. You were going down the street in a big carriage. You wore a sailor suit. You looked very . . . clean and kind and lonely. I prayed for you. I dream about you . . . I'm sorry.

Arthur (*to* **George**)   Don't get too excited. It's bad for my heart.

George (*holds her hands*)   Mother's clever. I knew she'd choose best.

Arthur   Warn me if you're going to kneel.

Florence (*to* **Arthur**)   I hope I won't get in your way.

Arthur   Break off your engagement. That's the best advice you've had since you got engaged. You don't know what you're letting yourself in for.

Florence   I do – I'm a nurse. Can we look at the castle?

Slight pause.

Arthur (*unsmiling*)   If you like.

They go out.

Scene Four

Windsor Castle throne room. The stage is bare except for some chairs or a bench, upstage, and downstage two chairs or a smaller bench, by an open trap. **Disraeli** *and* **Albert** *alone.*

Disraeli   Next Monday there's a picnic in the Great Park. I'll dress my soldiers as servants. During the picnic the Queen will be shot together with anyone who helps her. I hope Prince Arthur –

Albert   He sees himself as a shrewd politician. He's not going to join us till we've seized power. But one thing: he'll never accept our hand in the killing. He's peculiar about his mother. It must look as if some stray fanatic kills her. We just step in to keep the peace. We close the ports and airfields, take over the power stations, broadcast light classics and declare martial law. The important thing is she mustn't recover: she must be shot dead.

Disraeli   Well, shoot her more than once. Who's the assassin? You wanted to pick him. (**Albert** *puts his hands on the back of one of the chairs by the trap.*) Congratulations.

Albert   Oddly enough Arthur was talking about him. He said he'd murder his mother for five shillings, if he hadn't done it already for the experience. Victoria will tear him to pieces today – and I shall promise him his freedom. It gives us a motive – revenge – and it guarantees a good job.

*The **Lord Chamberlain** comes in. He has a pile of old clothes, tagged as exhibits. He puts them down.*

Chamberlain (*calls*)   Bring up the prisoner.

Len *and* **Joyce** *are brought up through the trap by* **Jones** *and* **Griss**.

Mennings   There he is!

Chamberlain   Rise.

Victoria, **Florence**, **George**, **Arthur** *and* **Doctor** *come on. They sit upstage.* **Victoria** *is in the centre.*

Victoria (*to* **Florence**)   Pass me that hat, dear. I'm sitting in a draught. (**Florence** *hands her the black hanging cap. She puts it on.*) Black's my lucky colour. (*To* **Lord Chamberlain**.) Read the charge. Place?

Chamberlain   Outside the State Cinema, Kilburn High Street.

Victoria   Day?

Chamberlain   A week last Wednesday.

Victoria   Time?

Chamberlain   Evening.

Victoria   What happened?

Chamberlain   The accused killed Joseph Hobson, and then ate him.

Joyce   'E pushed in the queue.

Len   I –

Victoria   Silence.

Joyce (*to* **Len**)   What did I tell yer? I tol' yer wait, ain' I? Yer can't take 'im nowhere.

Victoria   If he'd listened to you before he wouldn't be here.

Joyce   Thanks, lady. I'll shut 'im up for yer. (*To* **Len**.) Shut it. – Me best bet's ask for a separate trial.

Len   I –

Victoria   Silence.

Joyce   You tell 'im, dearie. (*To* **Len**.) An' keep it shut.

Victoria   I shall proceed to sentence.

Len (*to* **Joyce**)   'Ere, I thought yer said I'd get me say?

Joyce   Well what yer wan'a go an' antagonise 'er for?

Victoria   Put him on oath, but don't let him touch the Bible. King James would turn in his grave. (**Lord Chamberlain** *holds the Bible in front of* **Len**.)

Len   I swear to tell the truthwholetruthnothingbuttruth.

Chamberlain   Amen.

Joyce   Go on.

Len   We –

Joyce   Louder.

Len
Joyce } We was stood in the queue for the State –

Len   T' see *Buried Alive on 'Ampstead 'Eath* –

Joyce   No, *Policeman in Black Nylons*. *Buried Alive* was the coming attraction.

Len   Fair enough. We was stood in the queue for –

Len
Joyce } *Policeman in Black Nylons* –

Joyce   – an I'd like t' know why chair accommodation ain' provided. They don't wan'a know yer in this country. Thass 'ow yer get yer trouble. Yer pays enough. Not that I pay. Me entertainments never cost me a penny, not that I

wan'a boast. Well, next thing this fella's pushed in up front.
'E weren't there when we looked before, was 'e?

Len   Never looked.

Joyce   Don't I always tell yer count the queue in front?
That could 'ang yer.

Len   'E –

Joyce   'E crep' in with 'is 'ead in 'is paper.

Victoria   This? (**Lord Chamberlain** *holds up a blood-stained newspaper.*)

Len   Picture a Manchester United page six?

Joyce   Seven.

Victoria   The page doesn't matter.

Len   Course it matters, it's United.

Chamberlain   There's a football team on page eight.

Joyce   I was thinking a the earlier edition.

Victoria   Does he recognise the blood?

Joyce (*sniffs*)   'Is.

Victoria   Go on.

Len   We'd bin stood there 'ours and me guts starts t'
rumble. 'Owever, I don't let on. But then she 'as t' say 'I
ain' arf pecky'.

Joyce   Thass yer sense a consideration, ain' it! I'd 'eard
your gut.

Len   I 'ad an empty gut many times, girl. That don't mean
I'm on the danger list. But when you starts rabbitin' about
bein' pecky I –

Joyce   Now don't blame me, love.

Len   Truth ain' blame, love.

Joyce   Then wass all this 'she says' for? Anyway the 'ole queue turned round for a good look! 'Ow'd they know it ain' me? O, no, I ain' –

Len   Wrap it!

Joyce   I never 'eard that.

Len   You're a rabbitin' ol' git! 'Ear that?

Joyce   O it's different names when he puts the light out.

Victoria   We'll leave that for the medical report.

Len   Look, we're stood outside the State for *Buried Alive on 'Ampstead 'Eath* – right? – me gut rumbles an' there's this sly bleeder stood up front with 'is 'ead in 'is paper – right? – so I grabs 'is ears, jerks 'im back by the 'ead, she karate-chops 'im cross the front of 'is throat with the use of 'er 'andbag, and down 'e goes like a sack with a 'ole both ends – right? – and she starts stabbin' 'im with 'er stilettos, in twist out, like they show yer in the army, though she ain' bin in but with 'er it comes natural, an 'e says ' 'Ere, thass my place', an' then 'e don't say no more, juss bubbles like a nipper, an' I take this 'andy man'ole cover out the gutter an' drops it on 'is 'ead – right? – and the queue moves up one.

Joyce   *Policeman in Black Nylons.*

Len   Yer can't win.

Joyce   Me catch went. They don't 'ave the workmanship in 'em. I paid best money.

Victoria   Who cut him up?

Len   Don't remember. (*To* **Joyce**.) You remember? It was my knife. She 'ad the wishbone.

Joyce   I know I stripped him. I kep' 'is knickers on. I don't 'old with this rudery yer get. Speak ill a the dead, but 'e weren't worth the bother. Still, it makes a change. Yer don't know what t' get in for a bit of variety. I suppose you don't 'ave 'ouse-keepin' problems. 'E 'as t' 'and 'im round, a coursc.

Len   Yer can't nosh an' not offer round, can yer? Some a the fellas off the queue give us a 'and, an' I 'ad a loan a this 'atchet from some ol' girl waitin' t' cross the street. Yer 'ad t' offer 'im.

Joyce   'Oo said anythin' about the queue or the ol' lady? I don't begrudge no pensioners. All I say is, there was a leg on the pavement one minute and when I turned round it's gone. Someone goin' up the street 'ad that an' dodged round the corner, sharpish. Thass was wrong. They ain' even paid t' go in!

Len   Then the commissionaire blows 'is whistle an' the queue starts t' move.

Joyce   Thievin' ol' grabber. I know 'oo 'ad the pickins when we was gone. Anyway, I played it crafty. I drops a few bits in me 'andbag an' we 'as a little nosh when the lights went down. I don't 'old with that stuff they bring round on sticks. Give yerself a nasty mouthful a splinters in the dark.

Chamberlain   That's our case.

Victoria   I shall sum up.

Arthur   Where's the defence?

Victoria   Silence.

Albert   It would look better.

Victoria   Albert, you are always right. (*She turns to* **Arthur**.) You defend them.

Arthur   Has a doctor seen them?

Albert   Yes.

The **Doctor** *is nudged. He stands. His stethoscope is in his ears. Pause.*

Arthur   Have you seen these two? (*Someone removes his stethoscope.*) Have you seen these two?

Doctor   I have examined the accused. Loosely speaking one was male and the other was – I made a note of it at the time . . . (*He finds his note. He stares at it. He realizes that he is reading it upside down. He turns it up the right way.*) I see, it's a diagram . . . female.

Victoria   That explains most crimes. (*Appreciative laughter.*)

Mennings   There are others. (*A frozen silence.*)

Arthur   But did you find anything that would help us?

Doctor   Most definitely. Both the accused have stomachs.

Arthur   Yes?

Doctor   That suggests – I wouldn't care to put it any higher than that – that the accused would experience from time to time . . . (*To his stethoscope.*) What? I'm so sorry, I thought you spoke . . . Pangs.

Victoria   Exactly!

Doctor   I protest! I was forcibly prevented from making an autopsy. Had I been given full academic freedom my evidence would have hanged them. (*He sits.*)

Victoria   I shall sum up: guilty.

Len   Leave t' appeal.

Victoria   Granted.

Len   I put the man'ole cover back.

Joyce   It *was Policeman in Black Nylons*. I remember because I like a good musical.

Victoria   Appeals dismissed. The sentence of the court upon you is that you be taken from this place to a lawful prison and that you be there kept until you are dead, and that your bodies be afterwards handed over to the doctors, and your souls to our lady novelist royal.

Parson (*low*)   Eureka.

Len
Joyce } Lord George hanged my father
Dad fell through the trap
But he started bouncing
Dad's neck wouldn't snap
Lord George said to father
Play the game my lad
But he kept on bouncing
You can't hang my dad.

There is a scuffle.

Victoria   Put them down.

Len *and* **Joyce** *are forced apart. It is seen that they are handcuffed together.*

Arthur   No! (*He goes towards them.* **George** *moves reluctantly.* **Arthur** *stops by the pile of exhibits.*) You're handcuffed together!

Len   She likes t' keep an eye on me.

Arthur   Why did you kill him?

Len   'E pushed in the queue.

Arthur   Why?

Len   It's 'is 'obby.

Florence   George is too close.

Victoria   Don't be frightened, Florence. I'll take care of you.

Arthur   Why did you kill him –

Len   No fancy questions. I ain' bein' mucked about!

Arthur   You're sure these are his clothes?

Len   Yeh!

Joyce   Mr 'Obson's.

Arthur   Shoes. Socks. Trousers. Pants. Vest. Shirt. Mac. No tie. The cuffs are gone.

Joyce   Thass 'im.

Arthur   Why did you kill him –

Len   I said it ain' I? 'Is shirt! 'Is shoes! 'Is vest! (*He kicks the exhibits at* **Arthur**.) I done it! Thass that! Get, mate, get! They're 'is! 'Is! I got a right a be guilty same as you! An' you next, matey! You ain' out a reach!

Some of the exhibits fall on **Arthur**. *He's draped in them.*

Arthur   Why did you kill him –

Florence   George!

Victoria   You're trembling. You're so young. Let me take you away.

Joyce   Be'ave. Yer'll land yerself in trouble one day.

Florence   My arm!

Victoria   Darling, I won't hurt you.

Victoria *goes out with* **Florence**. **Len** *and* **Joyce** *are bundled down the trap.* **Len** *sings 'Lord George' as he goes.* **Arthur**, **George** *and* **Albert** *are left alone.*

George (*referring to* **Arthur**)   Typical.

Arthur (*holds mac*)   Can I keep this for a while?

Albert   I suppose you can.

Arthur   Mother will ban queues.

Albert   And films. (*He starts to go out through the trap.*)

Arthur   I've solved the riddle.

Albert (*surprised*)   I thought you would.

Florence (*off*)   George!

George (*calls*)   Yes!

Albert   Don't go to the picnic.

George   I'm going!

Arthur (*to* **Albert**)   Why not?

Albert   Nothing. I didn't mean anything . . . (**Albert** *goes out through the trap*.)

Florence (*off*)   O!

Arthur   I feel as if I'd eaten too much.

George (*he starts to go. Calls*)   Florence!

They go out.

Scene Five

Windsor Great Park. A picnic chair. A hamper with a rug on it. The men wear flannels, blazers and boaters, except for the servants and the **Lord Chamberlain**. *He wears regalia or a uniform.* **Florence** *wanders on.*

Florence (*distraught*)   I'm changed. Queen Victoria raped me. I never dreamed that would happen. George will know. I'll disgust him . . . I've started to have evil thoughts. Her legs are covered in shiny black hairs.

Lord Mennings *comes in. He carries a silver hip flask. Distant shots.*

Florence   What was that?

Mennings   Shots. Aren't you well?

Florence   Yes, yes.

Mennings   I like picnics. (*Laughs.*) Drink?

Florence   No. No.

Mennings (*he pours himself a drink from the hip flask*)   Bottoms up!

Florence (*before he can drink*)   I want that chair.

Mennings (*surprised*)   Yes. (*He brings the chair to her. She sits.*) You're tired.

Florence   Give me that. (*He hands her his drink. She takes off her shoe and pours the drink into it.*)

Mennings (*on his knees*)   I knew it! (*He kisses the shoe on her other foot.*) Governess!

Florence   You dare touch me before you've earned permission! I own all the shoes in the world!

Mennings   I'm evil.

Florence   Don't make excuses. You're a grovelling little pervert. I'll cauterize your lips where they touched me.

Mennings   Oh shoe-boss!

Florence   Deposit my marching weapon on the floor. (*He does so.*) Drink. (*He starts to drink like a dog. Immediately.*) Did you say grace?

Mennings   I've sinned.

Florence   I shall withdraw all shoes.

Mennings   No. No. More! One drop!

Florence   I might allow you half a drop.

Mennings   O ma'am-boss-miss! (**Victoria** *and the* **Lord Chamberlain** *come on upstage behind* **Florence** *and* **Lord Mennings**.) May – may –

Florence   Stuttering?

Mennings   MayIdrinkitfromthetoe?

Florence   If it comes in three. (*She holds the shoe over his mouth, with the open toe pointing downwards.*) One. Two. Thr – (*It trickles into his mouth. He is convulsed.*)

Victoria   That reminds me I'm thirsty.

Florence *stands.* **Lord Mennings** *lies on the ground.*
Victoria *comes down and takes the shoe.*

Victoria (*to* **Florence**)   Please pour.

Florence   I'd like to go home. I've had a fainting spell.

Victoria   I'm thirsty. (**Florence** *fills the shoe.*)

Chamberlain   Ma'am, I can fetch a cup.

Victoria   Lord Chamberlain, you are like the bishop who
always said amen after he'd lain with his wife. She became
frigid. (*To* **Florence**.) Cheers. (*She drinks and throws the shoe
over her shoulder.*)

Florence   My shoe . . . (*She goes upstage and looks for her shoe.*)

Mennings (*watches* **Florence** *on his hands and knees*)   My
shoe . . .

Victoria   Lord Mennings, they're coming. I'll have you
flogged.

Mennings   Thank you, ma'm-sir. By the shoe owner . . .

Victoria   Disgraceful. (*She swats a fly with a flyswat.*)
Eighteen.

Albert, **George** *and* **Arthur** *come on.* **Albert** *carries a rifle,*
and **George** *dead birds.*

Albert   Is there enough shade for you, dearest?

Victoria   It's perfect. (**Len**, **Jones** *and* **Griss** *come on*
dressed as rustics. **Victoria** *clasps* **Albert**'s *hands to her breast.*)
Such pretty costumes! (*The rustics lay the picnic.*)

Arthur   Why is Florence limping? She's only been with us
a week.

Victoria   She's lost her shoe.

Arthur   D'you dance?

Florence   Dance?

Arthur (*sarcastically*)   You dance with one shoe and I dance with four legs. It's called the hobble.

Florence   I don't know that one.

Arthur   It's a new dance in honour of your engagement. She's very well brought up. She only dances to hymn tunes.

Florence   Why is he rude to me?

Arthur (*surpised*)   Rude?

Florence   I can't find my shoe. (*She goes upstage.* **Arthur** *and* **George** *go to* **Albert***, by the hamper, and* **George** *puts down the birds.*)

Victoria (*loudly*)   I think it went over here . . . (*She takes* **Florence** *aside.*) Freddie –

Florence   George will –

Victoria   Darling.

Florence   No.

Victoria   Call me Victor.

Florence   Not here.

Victoria   Tonight.

Florence   No.

Victoria   I've never had a girl with such deep feelings – you've seen my maids of honour.

Florence   Victor.

Victoria   I shall cherish that moment when I felt you were a virgin. Will you do something for me?

Florence   Yes, yes.

Victoria   Kill my husband.

Florence   Why?

Victoria   He wants to kill me.

Florence   That's wicked!

Victoria   O, you look for it in a husband. (*She swats a fly.*) Twenty. He'll propose the loyal toast in a minute – that's one of his pompous habits. You hand him his drink – and pour the powder from this earring into it. (*She takes off an earring and gives it to* **Florence**.) No one will suspect you. You look so innocent.

Florence   It's pretty.

Victoria   Wear it, and I'll wear the other. That will make us blood brothers.

Florence   Victor, is it right to kill?

Victoria   You'll always be attractive because you're so pure.

George (*calls*)   Florence, what are you doing?

Victoria (*calls back*)   Lady's talk. (*To* **Florence**.) Till tonight. (**Victoria** *and* **Florence** *join the others. Loudly.*) It's hot. You must all be thirsty. (**Len** *passes. He whistles 'Lord George'.* **Arthur** *notices this.*)

George   Florence, did the trial upset you?

Florence   Yes.

George   Is that why mother took you out?

Florence   I fainted.

George   But why did you scream?

Victoria (*interrupting* **George**, *swats*)   Twenty-one! O, twenty and a half. I once scored 187. (*Swats.*) Twenty-one.

Albert   I want to give you a toast. (*He holds a filled glass.*)

Victoria   Dearest, drink it from Florrie's shoe.

George   No!

Albert   Of course! You youngsters don't understand romantic gestures.

Florence *holds the shoe and a rustic fills it.*

Victoria   Full. (*The rustic puts more in.* **Florence** *poisons it and takes it to* **Albert**. *Swats.*) Twenty-three! Two at one go!

Albert   Ladies and gentlemen, I offer you the loyal toast – and Florence. And then we will pass the shoe round, like a loving cup. (**Victoria** *chokes. He drinks.*) Victoria. (*He offers her the shoe.*)

Victoria   I've signed the pledge. I'm teetotal. Drink is the ruin of the country.

Albert   But you must drink to our daughter-in-law!

Lord Mennings *runs to* **Albert**. *As he passes the rustics* **Len** *whips out a pistol.* **Lord Mennings** *snatches the cup and drinks.*

Mennings   Nightingales! Eagles!

Florence   He's drunk it all. (*Laughter.* **Len** *tries to hide the pistol.*)

George   That man's armed!

Victoria   Treason!

Len   Keep still a minute.

Albert (*goes to* **Len**)   Please give me that gun. (*Aside.*) Shoot her, you fool!

Len   Well make up yer mind!

Arthur *stands in front of* **Victoria**.

Jones   Contact base, sir?

Albert   Base?

Griss   Wilco. (*He converts the hamper into a radio set by pulling out an aerial and plugging in earphones.*) Dead Queen to base. Are you receiving me? Over.

Chamberlain   It's highly organized.

Jones (*to* **Griss**)   Gettin' anythin'?

Griss   Dead Queen t' base.

Len (*to* **Arthur**)   Move, sonny.

Arthur (*to* **Albert**)   You said you wouldn't kill her!

Albert   But I knew nothing about this! You heard me ask for his gun. He's crazed with revenge.

Victoria   Liar! This is your doing!

Griss   Dead Queen to –

Albert   Put that bloody thing away!

Jones   O 'e's got a make contact, sir.

Griss   They're all 'anging on down the other end.

Victoria (*quietly*)   George, keep him talking.

Albert (*quietly to* **Len**)   Shoot her – or I'll have you court martialled!

Len   'Ow can I shoot 'er with 'im stuck in front? Yer said don't touch 'im.

Victoria   I'm ready to die. I shall make a final speech. I need thirty minutes to arrange my thoughts.

Albert   Arthur, I'm your father. Help me!

Arthur   You're a liar!

Albert   I'm running a revolution. You have to lie. (*He looks at his watch.*) I'm not well.

Victoria   At last! You've been poisoned.

Mennings   The shoe!

Florence   That's not possible.

Albert (*staggers*)   It hurts.

Griss   Dead Queen to base.

Jones   Try the other channel.

Albert *falls.*

Victoria   Take off his garter.

Chamberlain (*goes to* **Albert**)   I beg your pardon. (*He tries to take the garter sash from* **Albert**. **Albert** *struggles and the* **Lord Chamberlain** *hits him with his hat.*) I only want to look after it for you, sir. (*He takes the sash.*)

Griss   I'm getting somethin'.

Victoria (*swats*)   Twenty-four. (**Lord Mennings** *falls.*) I shall pass my highest score. (**Albert** *tries to crawl away.*)

Chamberlain   Shall I put my foot on him, ma'am?

Victoria   Let him crawl, it circulates the poison. You can't crawl out of your hearse.

Griss (*to* **Len**)   You any good with these things?

Len *holds one headphone against his ear.*

Albert (*still crawling*)   Shoot her, you –

Len (*listening to the set*)   You nutter! Thass Radio One!

Victoria (*comes from behind* **Arthur**)   I don't like to see them linger – I'm a patron of the RSPCA. (*She strangles* **Albert** *with the garter sash.*)

Arthur (*tries to pull* **Victoria** *off.* **George** *tries to stop him*) No! No! Stop it!

Len (*listens to the set. Clicks his fingers*)   Thass my favourite number!

Albert   O dear. (*Dies.*)

Victoria   Let that be a lesson to you. (*Examines her swat.*) He broke my swat!

Arthur *kneels by* **Albert**. **Disraeli** *comes on and stands behind* **Len** *and the two* **Soldiers**.

Griss (*listening to the earphones*)   Dead Queen to base!

Disraeli   She isn't dead!

Griss   I got 'em! I got 'em! (*Into set.*) Spot of tech' trouble, sir. Delay in –

Disraeli   I'm here!

Len *and the* **Soldiers** *turn to face* **Disraeli**. *They come to attention.* **Griss** *salutes.* **Victoria** *picks up* **Albert***'s rifle. She points it at* **Disraeli***'s back. She fumbles with the catch.*

Len *sees her with the rifle, drops his pistol and puts up his hands. There are no other weapons on stage.*

Len   Permission to speak sir.

Disraeli   Parade, shun!

Arthur (*takes the sash from* **Albert***'s neck*)   You stupid little fool.

Len   Permission t' –

Disraeli (*to* **Jones**)   Parade, report!

Jones   Dead Queen reportin', sir, all present an –

Disraeli   But she's not dead yet!

Jones   Set konked out, sir.

Len   Permission t' –

Jones   Battery went.

Disraeli   I shall have something to –

Len   'Scuse me, sir, she's pointin' 'er gun at yer.

Disraeli (*turns to face* **Victoria**)   A counter attack. I'll fetch reinforcements. (**Disraeli** *goes out.*)

Victoria (*points to* **Len***'s pistol on the floor*)   He dropped his gun! Get it! (**Len** *and* **George** *both go for the pistol at the same time.* **Victoria** *fires the rifle at* **Len**. *It clicks.*)

George   Push the safety catch!

Len *and* **George** *reach the pistol at the same time. There is a scuffle between* **Len**, **George** *and* **Arthur**. *They interlock in a bundle.*

Victoria   Where's the safety catch? (**Victoria** *and* **Florence** *examine the rifle. The* **Soldiers** *pack up the radio set.*)

Florence   Is that it?

Victoria   Yes. (*She pulls the trigger. The rifle fires over the soldiers.*)

Griss   They're closin' in.

Jones   Better warn the others. (**Jones** *and* **Griss** *go out.*)

George, **Arthur** *and* **Len** *mill slowly round.* **Victoria** *walks round them trying to aim the rifle at* **Len**. **Florence** *tries to swat at him with the broken swat.*

Chamberlain (*brushes his regalia with a small pocket brush*) I'll be with you in a minute. The late prince unintentionally soiled my clothes when I was giving him artificial respiration. If you don't go into battle neat and clean you never win. One guardsman with polished boots is worth fifty American rockets.

Off. A whistle blows.

Victoria (*prodding*)   Is that you George?

There is a shot inside the group. They stop struggling. They fall apart.

Arthur (*groans*)   Pain.

Florence   Arthur's shot!

Len (*looks for the* **Soldiers**)   They bloody scarpered! (*He goes out.*)

Victoria   Is George all right?

George *is holding his head in his hands.* **Arthur** *lifts it up. It is covered in blood. Off: a whistle blows.*

Arthur   He's shot. I feel his pain.

Disraeli (*off*)   Double! Double!

Victoria   I knew it was going too well! (**Arthur** *winces harshly. To* **Florence**.) We must run.

Florence   I can't leave George!

Victoria (*hustling* **Florence** *out*)   Quickly. We'll be shot!

Off: a whistle blows. **Victoria** *and* **Florence** *go out.*

Mennings (*he holds the shoe to his mouth*)   If you're dying you might as well enjoy it. The last drop.

Chamberlain   My job is to serve the head of the country. But who is the head? Uncertainty always leads to ineffectiveness. I shall go to bed for a few weeks. By then my duty should be clear. (*He bows to* **George** *and goes out.*)

George *is unconscious with pain. His head is on* **Arthur**'s *chest.* **Arthur** *has his eyes shut. Several* **Soldiers** *come on. They carry rifles.* **Disraeli** *comes on.*

Mennings (*diminuendo*)   Shoe. Shooe. Shoooe. (*Dies.*)

Disraeli   The day's catch?

Scene Six

A room in Windsor Castle. **Disraeli**, **Doctor**, **George**, **Arthur**. *The* **Doctor** *has a field dressing case with a red cross on it.* **George** *and* **Arthur** *sit.*

Doctor   The Prince of Wales is dying.

Disraeli   What about Prince Arthur?

Doctor   I shall cut him free.

Arthur (*looks at* **George**)   He'll die.

Doctor   Yes. I give you my word.

Arthur   And I'll live? (**Disraeli** *makes a sign to the* **Doctor**.)

Disraeli   Yes?

An **Officer** *comes in.*

Officer   Sir, the mob's collecting outside.

Disraeli   Good.

Officer   Sir. Permission to fire.

Disraeli   No. Don't knot the sack till it's full. I'll be down soon. (*The* **Officer** *starts to go.*) Have you found the Queen?

Officer   Sir, not yet.

Doctor   He's not coming round. (**Disraeli** *gestures to the* **Officer** *to go.*)

Officer   Sir. (*He goes out.*)

Doctor   Watch my finger. (*He moves his finger in front of* **George***'s face.*)

George (*snaps at the finger. Misses*)   Bone.

Doctor   His brain's gone.

Disraeli   Good. He'll be better off out of his misery. (*To* **Arthur**.) So you're King. The mob's outside. I'll read the riot act in your name.

The crowd is heard in the distance.

Arthur   I won't cut my brother off.

Disraeli (*an angry pause. Calls*)   Officer. (*To* **Arthur**.) You always said you wanted to get rid of him!

The **Officer** *comes in.*

Disraeli   What's happening?

Officer   They're throwing stones.

Disraeli   I'll come down. Doctor, stay and look after your patients. (*To* **Officer**.) Put more sentries on this door. We must protect their highnesses.

Officer   Sir. (**Disraeli** *and the* **Officer** *go out. The* **Doctor** *opens his satchel.*)

Doctor   I'll give you an injection.

Arthur   No.

Doctor   You're in pain.

Arthur   It's gone.

Doctor   As your doctor I – (*Breaking glass. The mob sounds nearer.*) What's that?

Arthur   Glass.

Doctor   O.

Arthur   They'll break the doors next.

Doctor   They sound like animals.

Arthur   They'll be all right once they've lynched someone.

Doctor   If they're lynching they'll need death certificates. Is there a back way out?

Arthur   Down the corridor.

Doctor   The sentries will look after you.

The **Doctor** *goes out.*

George (*frightened*)   Cut.

Arthur   No.

George   Breadboard.

Arthur   Walk.

George   Knifeboard.

Arthur   We'll slip out through the secret passage.

George   Cut.

Arthur (*opens trap*)   You'll be all right. It's easy. (*He sits on the edge of the trap. Winces.*) O God. (*He climbs down.*)

George (*going down*)   Cut . . . Cut . . . Cut. (**Arthur** *helps him. They go.*)

Scene Seven

Forest clearing. A large flat gravestone. Otherwise the stage is bare.

George *and* **Arthur** *come on.* **George** *looks white.*

George   Eat.

Arthur   There was a battle. Bang field, yes? We must keep going.

George   Eat. (*He stops.*)

Arthur   No. (**George** *won't move.* **Arthur** *is too tired to struggle much.*) All right. I haven't heard the guns for an hour. Sit down. (*They sit on the gravestone.* **Arthur** *takes a cake from his pocket.* **George** *snatches.*) Wait! (**Arthur** *breaks the cake and gives some to* **George**.) Slowly! (**George** *gulps at it. Immediately his mouth slackens. Cake dribbles down his chest.*) Eat.

George   Sleep.

Arthur   You were hungry!

George   Sleep.

Arthur   If you don't eat you can't walk! (*He picks up the cake that* **George** *dribbled on the floor. He eats this. He puts fresh cake in* **George**'s *mouth.* **George** *leaves it there.*) It's good cake. A lot of people are starving.

George   Sleep.

Arthur (*looks round*)   . . . I'm tired too. (*He scoops the cake from* **George**'s *mouth with his finger. He holds it in his hand.* **George** *lies down.*) Goodnight. At least it's quiet here. (*He covers* **George** *with a coat. He eats the cake in his hand. He stares in front of him and chews slightly.*)

George   Hic . . . Cold. Pain. Sleep. Eat. Sick. Cut. Die. Hic. Jacet.

Arthur   Hic jacet . . . (*He reads the gravestone.*) This is our father's grave. (*He half rises, but* **George** *won't move.*) We've walked in a circle. (*He tries to stand.*)

George   Cold! Cold!

Albert *comes out of the grave. He wears a brown shroud.*

George   . . . Wha'? . . . (*He sees* **Albert**.) Death here! Death come! Run!

Albert   Shut up. – Arthur, no flowers? I've waited a long time.

George   Run!

Albert   Listen to it! (*He gestures* **Arthur** *to the open grave.*) That's the pit. I lie there and you tramp round and round on top of me. There's no peace. The living haunt the dead. You will learn that. (*He lifts his arms. Heavy chains run from them into the grave.*) I dragged these with me. Help me.

Arthur   How? How?

Albert   Kill the Queen. Make yourself King. Let the country live in peace. Let us die in peace.

Arthur   George is King!

Albert   Kill him too!

Arthur   No!

Albert   This is why you came here.

Arthur   No! It was an accident. We came in a circle –

Albert   You came so that I could cut him off! (**George** *whimpers.* **Albert** *comes slowly down from the gravestone as he talks.*) I had a state funeral. The Queen changed my will – I didn't know. It said I was to lie with my hands on my stomach holding a bible. So they laid me out like that. But when they closed their eyes to pray I reached out and took

my sword. You can't face heaven with a bible in your hands.
(*He takes his sword from under his shroud. There is no scabbard.*)

Arthur No.

Albert You were first in the womb. Your mother
screamed and struggled and your brother thrashed his way
out in front.

George Run!

Albert *groans and shakes his shroud and lunges with the sword. The
chains still run back into the grave and hamper him. He stamps and
lunges.*

Arthur (*to* **George**) My arm! Keep still!

George (*shouts*) Cut! Cut!

Albert *lunges round* **George**. *Some of the lunges seem to hit him.*

Albert Die! Die! Die!

George Cock-a-cock-aroo!

Albert Kill!

George Cock-a-cock-aroo!

Albert (*stands on his grave. He gathers his shroud round him*)
Cock crow!

Arthur It's him.

Albert Cock crow! (*He flays with his sword.*)

George Ding-dong. Ding-dong.

Albert Bells! (**George** *giggles with fright.*) Bells! Bells! My
sword . . . My sword won't . . . (*It droops in his hands.*)

Arthur It's him! Father, don't go!

George Cock-cock-creewww! (**Albert** *goes down into the
grave.* **George** *looks down into it.*) Ding-dong-bell, pussie's in
the – (**Albert**'s *arm comes out of the grave. He reaches towards*
George.)

Albert (*off*)   I'll frighten him to death! (*His arm goes down out of sight.* **George** *tries to pull away.*)

Arthur   Come here! He's gone!

George (*gasping. Struggling*)   No!

Arthur   Don't pull!

George   You!

Arthur   He's gone.

George   Kill.

Arthur   No!

George   Let – let – go!

Arthur (*shouting ironically*)   Let go! Let go!

George   You – glad – doctor – kill – me – but scared – Dis – Disra' – kill you – you run – save *you* – not me – you hate – always.

Arthur   Keep still! Father can't hurt you! He's dead!

George   Dead. (*Dies.*)

Pause.

Arthur (*looks up*)   . . . How long have I been here? I must cut him off. Your blood's like ice. I'm free. Tomorrow I'll look at a map. I must sleep (*He lies down on the grave.*)

Scene Eight

Windsor Great Park. A lynching mob comes in. **Gladstone**, **Joyce**, **Jones**, **Griss** *and* **Len**. **Len**'s *arms are tied behind him. His feet are shackled. He hobbles and jumps along.*

Griss   Wass best?

Jones   The lot.

Joyce   The lot plus extras.

Gladstone   This tree was made for it.

Jones   'Oo's got the ball a string?

Gladstone   'Old it, brothers. Trial first.

Griss   Stick yer trial.

Gladstone   Yer 'ave t' 'ave yer trial t' make it legal. Yer
don't wan' a act like common criminals. Trial first, death
after: yer got a copy a the book. Wass the charge?

Jones   'E – (*He pushes* **Len**.) let that bitch scarper – (*He
pushes* **Len**.) when we –

Griss   'Ere-'ere!

Jones   –'ad 'er teed up nice for 'im. (*He pushes* **Len**.)

Gladstone   So, brother, less 'ear your side. Speak out –
we don't tolerate no totalitarian larkins 'ere. Only keep it
sharp. We don't want our brothers on overtime. They need
their leisure same as you.

Joyce   I was a virgin mother a nine an' 'e seduced me. 'E
showed me the bright lights an' I neglected me offspring.
Five died. Give me back me babies.

Gladstone   An old story.

Joyce   'E ought a be castrated.

Griss   Castrated as well.

Joyce   By the offended party.

Jones   This I got a see.

Gladstone   Is it in the book, brothers?

Griss   Stick the book!

Gladstone   Now, brothers, don't get excited. Rules are
made t'abide by. One foot off the straight an narrer an yer
never know what yer'll tread in. The proper procedure is
vote an amendment. 'Ands up for castration.

All except **Len** *put their hands up.*

Griss　My vote's as clean as the next man's.

Joyce　One woman one vote.

Gladstone (*counts the hands silently*)　Castration in. Rule 98.

Joyce　By offended party.

Gladstone (*counts the hands silently*)　In. Sub rule 98 little i. Right, brothers. The book now gives us a clear guidance. (*To* **Len**.) Well, less 'ear yer plead.

Griss　'E'll *plead* all right.

Gladstone　All right, brother. It's a good joke – don't spoil it by over indulgin'. Yer get too worked up. (*To* **Len**.) Well, brother? (**Len** *spits at him.* **Jones** *knocks him down and puts his boot across his mouth.*)

Jones　Spit on that. It could do with a clean.

Gladstone　Thank yer, brother. Spit I don't mind – it's a natural expression a feelin' – but yer're quite right t'protect the dignity a the court. Well, 'e's put the block right on. Yer can't 'ang 'im till yer've 'eard 'is version. Rule 53. (*He turns to* **Len**.) Brother – (**Len** *spits at him again.*) I'll 'ave yer spittin' out a the ends a yer finger tips before I done. (*To* **Jones**.) Explain the legal situation to 'im, brother.

Jones　Will do, dad. (*He stands* **Len** *on his feet and starts kicking his legs.*)

Gladstone (*strolls round the stage*)　Life! Life! The sparrer falls, the mountain turns t'dust, we spit into the wind, an the ash blows back into our face. (**Griss** *gives* **Len** *a kick.*) Do my mincers see right? Yer can't do that, brother. Where's yer uniform?

Griss　What uniform? I got a right a do me duty same as 'im. Change the rules.

Gladstone.　Not twice in one day, brother. Rule nineteen. Drive slow an yer'll never bump into yerself comin' back. 'Oo uses a nose rag. (**Joyce** *gives him a handkerchief.*) Thank yer, sister. I like me women folk t'be clean in their 'abits. (*He ties the handkerchief round* **Griss***'s arm.*) Yer'll do now yer got yer armband up, brother.

Griss   Cor thanks, pop. (*He salutes.*)

Gladstone   Now less see yer get stuck into a bit a team work. Four feet is one more than a yard. (**Griss** *and* **Jones** *start kicking* **Len** *again.* **Gladstone** *strolls round the stage.*) Time! Time! Suddenly the birds come, it's spring, suddenly they mate, suddenly they 'atch, the young fly, a few days and they're gone, the sickle's already in the corn, the fruit falls, the old man leans on 'is 'oe, suddenly 'e looks up, it's winter, an' the skull's already on the window-sill.

Joyce   'E ought t' be on telly. (**Len** *groans.*) 'E'd give a lovely epilogue.

Gladstone   'E speak?

Griss   Nah. Somethin' broke.

Gladstone   I ain't the one t'criticise the workin' man, as yer well know, brothers. But yer're too excitable. Yer lack yer discipline. Let an old 'and show yer – or should I say an old boot?

Joyce   'E's 'ysterical!

Gladstone   The secret is: move from the thigh an' let the weight a the tool do the work. That economizes yer effort so yer can keep it up longer. (*He demonstrates without touching* **Len**.) Watch that toe. Keep a good right angles t' the target. The other way looks good but it's all on the surface. Yer don't do yer internal damage. Study yer breathin': in when yer go in, out when yer come out. Got it? (*He swings his boot back.*) Out – thigh – toe – in! (*He kicks* **Len** *once.*) Child's play.

Griss   Gor, 'e travelled 'alf a yard!

Joyce   I'll give yer a 'and.

Gladstone   Dodgy, darlin'.

Joyce   Fair shares for –

Gladstone (*explaining*)   It's the uniform, ain' it?

Joyce   I ain' got no arm band, but I got a leg band. (*She shows him the top of her stockings.*)

Gladstone   It's stretchin' a point, but it'll do for an emergency.

Griss   It'll do for my emergency.

Gladstone   Can yer squeeze in a little one?

Jones   I could squeeze in somethin'.

Joyce (*lining up*)   Ain' it a giggle?

Gladstone   One, two, three!

They kick **Len**. **Arthur** *and* **George** *come in*. **George**'s *skin is white and looks wet*. **Arthur** *supports him*.

Gladstone   'Old up.

Joyce (*kicking*)   Yer pus-brained, murderous git! There won't be nothin' left t'castrate.

Gladstone   Later, sister.

They stop kicking.

Arthur   'Morning. (*Points ahead of him.*) Which way is this? (*Sees* **Len**.) Ah. What's wrong with him?

Jones   Nothin' yet.

Griss   We're killin' 'im.

Gladstone   Allow me t'introduce meself. William Ewart Gladstone. You're wanted for war crimes.

Arthur   Don't touch me. I've got Porton Plague.

Gladstone (*steps back*)   It's a try-on.

Arthur   I caught it on your battlefields. My brother's died of it.

Gladstone   Leave off.

Joyce   No – they look like that. I was late out for bingo one night an' I 'ad t' smother three a me nippers. I never 'ad time t'get 'em t'bed. They look juss like that when I come 'ome next week. I'll get the doctor. (*She goes out.*)

Jones   I'll see she's all right.

Gladstone   Stay put.

Jones (*taking off his belt*)   Yer got a protect the ladies. Never know 'oo's roamin' about. (*He throws the belt to* **Griss**.) Cop 'old a that. (*He goes out.*)

Griss   I'd better give 'im a 'and. (*He goes out, undoing his flies.*)

Gladstone (*calls*)   I'll court-martial the lot a yer!

Arthur   Help him up.

Gladstone   Let him lie. 'E's my son. Ain' many could a took 'is 'ammerin'. When 'e dies I'll be the first t'cry. I ain' ashamed a tears. Till then he lives by the book. Rule 5. Me an' brother Disraeli's formed a national government. We want you – so take my advice an' scarper. I can't nab yer on me jack, but I'll be back an' yer'll need yer runnin' pumps t'dodge me then. I'll see yer later. (*He goes out.*)

Arthur Get up.

Len (*sways to his feet*)   O, Laws a cricket is it? Don't shoot till the umpire's scratched 'is balls. (*He tries to stand in a fighting pose.*) Less 'ave yer. (*Sways, looks round.*) Where's all the rocks? . . . (*His arms fall to his sides.*) Chriss guv, be quick. Finish us off, guv. I 'ad enough. Be quick.

Arthur   I'm glad it's you. I had something to ask you. Why did you kill that man?

Len   What man?

Arthur   Go home.

Len   'Ome?

Arthur   He's fetching troops.

Len   Turn me back an' yer knife's in it. I 'eard a you blokes: can't look yer in the eye when they do it.

Arthur (*going. To* **George**)   We must find somewhere for the night, George.

Len (*realizes*)   You're a gent, guv! I won't forget yer, sir. (*He touches his cap.*) You'll need a 'and someday – an' I 'ope I'm in reachin' distance. God bless yer, guv.

Arthur *goes out, still supporting* **George**.

Len (*coughs blood*)   I've landed on me feet 'ere! If I was t' go t' the Queen an' tell 'er I knows where 'er boys is – thass worth two quid any day! Three if a play me cards right! Four if me luck's in! (*Slyly.*) . . . an' then if I was t' . . . (*Gestures left.*) . . . an' then if I was t' (*Gestures right.*) . . . I'd be rollin' in clover – if me internal 'aemorrhagin' 'olds out . . . (*He goes out cunningly after* **Arthur** *and* **George**.)

Scene Nine

Windsor Castle. **Victoria** *and* **Florence**. **Victoria** *sits and knits a union jack.* **Florence** *stands beside her dressed as John Brown.*

Florence (*in her own voice*)   The Lord Chamberlain's here.

Victoria   I'll see him.

Florence *goes out. She returns immediately with the* **Lord Chamberlain**. *She now walks and talks as John Brown.*

Florence   The ol' wuman'll see ye noo.

Chamberlain (*bows*)   Congratulations, ma'am. I hear the enemy's been driven into Wales. They won't be any more trouble, they'll go native. The doctor says I should be in bed. But I've been away from my post long enough.

Victoria   John keeps an eye on me. (**Florence** *and* **Lord Chamberlain** *exchange nods.* **Victoria** *knits.*) Lady Flora says you got her with child.

Chamberlain   Accidently, ma'am. It was dark. My wife and I don't converse during intimacy, apart from the odd remark about the weather. It was only afterwards that I discovered she was not my wife. (*Aside to* **Florence**.) What's up that kilt?

Florence   Did ye address me, laddie?

Victoria   John, I'm out of wool.

Florence   Theer's enough sheepies heer in yon baggie tay nat wavies far yeer 'hae armee, wuman. As ma faither sayed: eek muckle the wuman, and the nattin wull sluther. That's wisdum.

Victoria   Help me wind.

Florence (*holds the skein of wool on her wrists.* **Victoria** *winds the wool*)   Wend, wend, wend, the loom a' leef a' wendit. If yor brack yeer thrud, aluck! ye'll nayer ment it. That was ma maither's constant reply.

Victoria   Thank you, John. Your thoughts are a comfort. I wonder if they'd make you archbishop.

Chamberlain (*aside to* **Florence**)   What's up that kilt? Am I your type?

Victoria (*drops the ball of wool*)   It's dropped. (**Florence** *bends to pick it up.*)

Chamberlain (*aside to* **Florence**)   What's up that kilt? When's your night off?

Len *is brought in by a* **soldier**. *His hands and feet are shackled again. He hobbles and jumps.*

Victoria (*still winds the wool, but looks at* **Len**)   Good! You've caught him. Dear Albert stood in front of me and took the bullet. You were tried in absentia and sentenced to be shot.

Len   I never ment t' shoot yer, lady. I was going t' miss. I can prove it. I juss give meself up. 'Ow about a pardon an' five nicker?

Victoria (*stops winding*)   Why should I give you money?

Len   I know where yer boys is, luv.

Victoria   Where?

Len   I need the money t' pay me legal expenses.

Victoria   Only a hero could find the Prince of Wales. You're pardoned. (*She counts out the money.*) D'you mind all silver? One, two, three, four. I'll owe you one. (*The* **Soldier** *unties* **Len**. *To* **Lord Chamberlain**.) When he's shot see my money's returned to me. (*To* **Len**.) How is George? (*To* **Lord Chamberlain**.) And don't let him spend any in the meantime.

Len   'E's dead.

Victoria (*stands. Her knitting falls to the ground. To* **Florence**) Pick up my knitting. (*She goes upstage.* **Florence** *stoops and starts to gather up the knitting.*)

Chamberlain   Allow me. (*He helps her.*) You're a fine figure of a scotsman. What's up that kilt? D'you know that one about the horizontal sporran? I can introduce you to a lot of nice people.

Victoria (*upstage*)   The court will go into mourning.

Scene Ten

Near Bagshot. A cave. **George** *and* **Arthur** *sit on a box.* **George**'s *skin is wet and blotchy, and he is set in an awkward, hunched position. The* **Soldiers** *are formed in a firing squad on the other side. Their rifles point at* **Arthur**. *The breeches are open. The* **Officer** *goes along the line and puts a bullet into each rifle. After he has done so the* **Soldier** *closes the bolt. There is silence except for the noise of the closing bolts.*

Disraeli *takes a few steps towards* **Arthur**.

Disraeli   I shall protect your name for history. Your mother's assassins shot you. Your last words were 'St George and Disraeli for England'.

The Firing Squad takes aim.

Arthur (*to* **George**)   Ignore them and they'll go away.

Griss (*listening on headphones*)   Forward party's sighted Queen.

Disraeli   Good. My plan works. This can wait. (*To* **Griss**.) Remind the men to keep under cover. We'll ambush her when she's inside. (*To* **Arthur**.) If you warn her, I'll put a bullet through your brother's head. (**Arthur** *shudders slightly*.)

Disraeli *and his men hurry out.* **Arthur** *and* **George** *are alone. Immediately* **Victoria**, **Florence** *and the* **Lord Chamberlain** *hurry in.*

Victoria   So, you've finally killed my heir.

Arthur   He's got the queen's evil.

Florence   What the devil's that?

Arthur   An old disease. Once the queen cured you. She kills.

Florence   I mind noo I heard tell a yon. Try it some day, wuman. I'm awful partial tay experimentation.

Victoria   I'm a constitutional monarch, so far as medicine is concerned.

Arthur   Try.

Victoria   What am I supposed to do? He's dead.

Arthur   And now you'll kill me.

Victoria   The law does.

Arthur   Cure him. Try! – What's the use? You never –

Victoria   That's not true. You hate me so you think I have no feelings. He was born first but they said he'd have to die. Kill that poor little boy? I wouldn't let them, and you've never forgiven me. You exploited your position to come between us. You set Albert against me. I had to find happiness where I could: d'you think I like that?

Arthur (*to* **George**)   I'll tell you a riddle. What drowns in water, burns in fire, lies in the ground and falls out of the sky?

Victoria (*dabs at her eyes. She reaches out to* **George** *and touches his shoulder*)   Arise, my son! George, this is mother, I want you back. (*Slight pause.*) Good. (*To* **Arthur**.) You've been tried and I've dismissed your appeal.

Arthur   Blindfold him. (*He ties the scarf round* **George**'s *head.* **Len** *comes on.*)

Len   All set? (**Victoria** *nods. He gestures to the offstage. The* **Officer** *marches back with the firing squad.*)

Officer   Squad halt. Right turn. Order arms.

Arthur (*at the same time*)   She answers riddles. Who came first, the man or his shadow? The shadow, of course. I undressed a shadow once: it was white underneath and cried: it was cold.

George   Where am I?

Florence   Take it off! (*She removes his blindfold.*)

George   Who are you?

Florence   It's Florence! Florence! You were dead.

George   Why's she got a moustache?

Victoria   George, congratulations. I knew everything would come out all right. I hope you cut your father.

George   Why are you wearing those clothes?

Florence   It's fancy dress.

Victoria   We're going to a party. To raise money for war wounded.

Arthur   What was it like? It's better than here?

Victoria   Be quiet. Let him thank me.

Florence   I'm so happy again!

George (*touches his head*)   My head. (*Tries to stand. Realizes.*) O. I forgot.

Arthur   We'll both stand.

George (*to* **Victoria**)   Did you do this?

Victoria   Yes.

George   You had no right to!

Victoria   Arthur said –

George   Of course! It's you! Only you would drag me back to this misery!

Arthur   Misery?

George   Misery! You taught me that, why can't you learn it? – and let me die in peace! (*To* **Victoria**.) You should have made him cut me off! (*To* **Arthur**.) Help! – look at my head! That's blood!

Florence   I'll stop it.

George   I don't want it stopped! I want to die!

Victoria   That's enough. You haven't benefited from your experience. (*She turns away.*) Government must continue. Arthur must be shot.

Florence   Not now!

Victoria   The court found he'd poisoned Albert's champagne. I'd like to pardon him, but governments must keep their word. Officer! (*She takes* **Florence** *aside.*) Listen, Florence. I'll tell them not to hit George.

Florence   If Arthur dies he dies!

Victoria   Will he? The doctors say he will – that means he probably won't. And if he does I'll bring him back to life.

Florence   But he's got no heart!

Victoria   He's got yours.

Florence   Yes. I'll always love you – but I still love him.

Victoria   You did right to tell me. (*She turns away and goes to the squad.*) Splendid turnout. How's Mrs Smith?

Officer   Mrs Jones, ma'am?

Victoria   I thought so, Major Jones.

Officer   Captain, ma'am.

Victoria   Nonsense, I've just promoted you. I have a favour to ask in return. Shoot them both. (*Aside.*) I shan't resurrect him. I'll say my power's gone. Florence has only herself to blame. I can't share her – certainly not with my son. It's worse than incest, and I'm head of the church.

Len   Could I have a loan a yer pistol, mum?

Victoria   Why?

Len   Give 'im the last rites in the back a the neck.

Victoria   Yes, you might as well earn your five pounds. (*She laughs without opening her mouth. She gives her pistol to* **Len**.) On your marks. (*The squad point their rifles at* **Arthur**.) Get set. Fire. (*The squad point their rifles at* **Victoria**.) . . . Let me warn you: I fire the last shot.

Disraeli *comes on.*

Disraeli   Good morning, ma'am.

Victoria   Private Jones, you're cashiered . . .

Disraeli (*gives* **Len** *money*)   Well done. I'll make you a life peer. Line them up. Ma'am, I trust we part friends. You stare death in the face magnificently. It must flinch.

The **Soldiers** *move* **Victoria**, **George**, **Arthur** *and* **Florence** *upstage.*

Chamberlain   I shouldn't be out. I'll fetch my doctor's certificate. It won't take –

Jones   Up. (*He moves the* **Lord Chamberlain** *up with the others.*)

Florence (*to* **George**)   I'm afraid.

Arthur (*looks at her*)   Try not to scream.

Victoria (*to the other prisoners*)   Play for time. Something always turns up. (*To* **Disraeli**.) I have the right to die like a queen. I shall give the orders. On your marks. (*Pause.*) Get set. (*Pause.*) God save the Queen. (*Pause.*) Rule Britannia. (*Pause.*) Unaccustomed as I am. (*Pause.*) In moments of crisis. (*Pause. She shrugs.*) Fire! (*Silence.*) Mutiny even now!

Jones   She makes yer piss run cold.

Disraeli   On your marks. Get set. Fire! (*They shoot him.*) Betrayed! (*He falls dead.*)

Gladstone *comes in.*

Gladstone   Mornin', all. Mornin', ma'am.

Victoria   We are not amused.

Gladstone   Tyranny shall be cast down. Beware thy left 'and in the night.

Len   Squad shun!

Gladstone   Thank yer son, I knew yer'd see yer ol' dad right. (*Gives* **Len** *money.*)

Len   Three cheers for the people's William! 'Ip-'ip!

They cheer.

Gladstone   One's enough. We'll celebrate after openin' time.

Victoria   Dear Mr Gladstone –

Gladstone   Did yer know 'e wore corsits, ma'am? I ain'
ambitious, but I thought no man in a corsit, 'oo puts 'is 'air
in curlers, ain' good enough for Britain, even for the tories.

Victoria   William – may we call you William? – come
over to our side and we'll drive together to St Paul's –

Gladstone   No drives, ol' lady. It's the chopper.

Victoria   I have one card left to play: prayer. (*She kneels in
prayer.*)

Chamberlain   Bill – it is Bill, isn't it? My doctor says
fresh air is bad for me, so I'll just –

Gladstone   Ours is a complete cure, brother. I'll address
my army. (*He turns to the squad.*) Brothers, yer're now owned
by the people's William. Up from the gutter, selfmade, shine
like a new penny. Me secret is take it slow. Take it calm.
Take it natural. The slower yer go the sooner yer get there.

Victoria   Amen. (*Slight pause while the prisoners look at*
Gladstone.) O.

Arthur   Her gift doesn't work in reverse. A pity – that
would be more useful to a politician.

Victoria   I never abandon God. (*She prays.*)

Gladstone   Remember me motto, boys: moderate it.
What yer spend on beer yer can't spend on riney, but yer
still get yer money's worth if yer take yer time. William
knows. (*The squad laugh.*)

Len   Three cheers for the people's William. 'Ip-'ip! (*They
cheer.*) 'Ip-'ip! (*They cheer.*) –

Gladstone   Two'll do, bretheren. Moderate it. Ready
then. Nice and slow. Never run through the door, it might
be locked . . . Steady aim . . . Comfy grip . . . Wait on the
word . . . One . . . Two . . . Two-an'-a-'alf –

He falls dead.

Len (*goes to* **Gladstone**)   'Is 'eart! (*He puts his pistol on the ground and looks in* **Gladstone**'s *pockets.*) Where's yer pills, yer silly ol' bugger? Dad? I tol' 'im the cheerin' would go to 'is 'ead. – 'E's landed us right in it!

Victoria (*goes to* **Gladstone**)   Authority shall be lifted up. The sun rises on the Lord's dead.

George *picks up* **Len**'s *pistol.*

Jones   Watch 'im. 'E's nicked a gun.

Griss   We're surrounded.

Len   Best warn our mates.

Jones, **Griss**, *the rest of the squad and* **Len** *go out.*

Florence   Don't George! Please!

Arthur (*holds* **Florence** *off*)   Let him do it! (**George** *shoots himself.*)

Florence   O God!

George   Death again. (*He slumps.*)

Florence   It's happened! It's happened!

Victoria   No time to cry! They'll be back.

Florence (*sobs*)   George! No hope! Nothing to live for.

Victoria   Now, now – we must count our blessings.

Victoria *tries to take* **Florence** *out.* **Florence** *breaks away and runs out ahead of her.* **Victoria** *follows quickly.*

George (*dying*)   Yes, I remember . . . We weren't joined together there, we were free . . . when you die *you*'ll be . . . free and happy . . . when you die. (*Dies.*)

Scene Eleven

A clearing. The stage is bare, but there is something down left that looks like a pile of old clothes. **Arthur** *comes in.* **George** *is still attached to him, but he is now a skeleton.* **Arthur** *and* **George** *sit on a box, or can, and talk.*

Arthur I did not give your foot to the dog! – Well why say I did? The dog took it. – I did not give it to him! I'd have given him a leg! (*Pause.*) All right, I'm sorry. I'm tired. You're not easy to carry. – I didn't say it's easy to walk on one foot . . . You don't eat. That's your trouble . . . At least you sleep. (*He drapes a coat round* **George**.) You're good at that. And you're wrong about the dog. (*Pause. Suddenly.*) I know I gave your clothes away! They were beggars! They'd been fighting. They were cold. – I did not! (*Pause.* **George***'s head is pointing down left.*) What are you staring at? (**Arthur** *stands, goes down left, stops, looks, turns, goes back to his box, and sits. Calmly.*) It's a body. (*Slight pause.*) We'll take turns to sleep. I'm not being blamed if you lose your other foot. (*Softly.*) Don't stare. Would you like to be stared at? . . . Is it someone we know? (**Arthur** *goes to the body. He stoops and looks closely at it.*) Him. I thought they'd get him. Undo his flies. (*He does so.*) She got her souvenirs. He wouldn't like that. (**Arthur** *has accidently uncovered* **Len***'s face. His features are blurred. His hair is plastered. He doesn't grin. His eyes are shut.* **Arthur** *turns and starts to walk back to his box. He stops.* **Len** *has spoken to him.*) I'm sorry. (*He goes to* **Len** *and fastens his flies.*) I thought you wouldn't mind. – I know it's a liberty. Is that better? – Could we sit with you? Thank you. (*He sits. Pause.*) Travelling mostly. It's nice to hear some intelligent conversation. (*He looks at* **George**. *In tears.*) So many bones to be broken . . . (*To* **Len**.) He can't hear. I pretend he hears because I'm lonely. – You noticed? Sh, I gave it to a dog. I woke up and this brute was slinking off with its tail down and its ears back and his foot in its mouth. I threw a stone and it dropped it . . . Then I thought no. So I called it back and gave it to him. I'm a limited person. I can't face another hungry child, a man with one leg, a running woman, an empty house. I don't go near rivers when the bridges are burned. They look like the bones of charred hippopotamuses. I don't like maimed cows, dead horses, and wounded sheep. I'm limited. (*He looks at* **George**.) He won't miss it. (*Longer pause.*) I talk too much – D'you dream? – so do I. D'you dream about the mill? There are men and women and children and cattle and birds and horses pushing a mill. They're grinding other cattle and people and children: they push each other in. Some fall in. It grinds their bones, you see. The ones pushing the wheel, even the animals, look up at the horizon. They stumble. Their feet get caught up in the rags and dressing that slip down from their wounds. They go round and round. At the end they go very fast. They shout. Half of them run in their sleep. Some are trampled on. They're sure they're reaching the horizon . . . Later I come back. There's a dust storm. White powder everywhere. I find the mill and it's stopped. The last man died half in. One of the wooden arms dropped off and there's a body under it. (*He looks off right.*) We're being watched. (*Slight pause.*) Some of my dreams are better. In one, each man slaughters his family and cattle and then kills himself.

The **Doctor** *comes in. He is covered with oil and smoke stains. His clothes are torn. His satchel is dirty and empty. The flap is open.*

Arthur   Doctor.

Doctor (*going*)   No supplies. Keep still. Try to sleep.

Arthur   Is this the way to Windsor?

Doctor (*points*)   There.

Arthur   Who won?

Doctor   We're regrouping. (*He walks round the stage, looking off.*)

Arthur   Was Napoleon there?

Doctor   I didn't see him.

Arthur   Hitler? Einstein?

Doctor   Try to sleep.

Arthur   Doctor, you're a medical man. Why do men hate life? Is it the light? Is it more comfortable to be mud and ashes? (*The **Doctor** crosses to the other side and looks off.*) Why do the good men work for the bad men? Doctor? (*He turns to **Len**.*) Not many people rise to the heights of Hitler. Most of them only nurse little hates. They kill under licence. Doctor, Hitler had vision. He knew we hated ourselves, and each other, so out of charity he let us kill and be killed.

Doctor   No supplies. (*He crosses the stage and looks off.*)

Arthur   Heil Hitler! Heil Einstein! Hitler gets a bad name, and Einstein's good. But it doesn't matter, the good still kill. And the civilized kill more than the savage. That's what science is for, even when it's doing good. Civilization is just bigger heaps of dead. Count them.

Doctor (*crossing the stage*)   Try to sleep.

Arthur   It's unfair to Hitler. With this insight he could have killed himself at twenty. Instead he stayed alive and did his duty. He must have known it would lead to misunderstandings. Well, saints expect the cross. Doctor, why don't you ask me something? Ask me why doesn't everyone just kill himself? That's simplest. But you see, they don't just hate their own life – they hate life itself. It's a matter of conscience, like duty in the blood: they stay alive to kill. They can't die in peace till they've seen the world dead first. That's why they have doctors and drugs and anti-famine weeks and scientists and factories and comfort to keep them alive – when their only happiness is being dead. It's tragic. But not for long. They're clever. They'll soon learn how to grant their own wishes. (*He sees that the **Doctor** has gone.*) Pity. I wanted to tell him why I'm going back to Windsor. The world's been lucky: there's always been enough dictators to ease its misery. But even Hitler had his limitations. He pretended – in my dark moments I even think he pretended to himself – that he killed for the sake of something else. But I've discovered the logical thing for men to do next. It's a real step in human progress. For the first time in my life I can be useful. Hitler protected his own people. What we need now is the great traitor: who kills both sides, his and theirs. I'm surprised no one's seen it. It lets you kill twice as many. He wants to congratulate me. (*He takes* **George***'s hand.*) First I'll take over the mob – it's easy now they've lost their old leader. Then we'll go on to Windsor. Shake. (*He shakes* **George***'s hand.*)

Scene Twelve

The Long Walk at Windsor. Three corpses hang on a gallows upstage. Another corpse is tied to a gallows-post. And two other corpses to the other gallows-post. These last three have been blindfolded and shot. **Victoria** *and* **Florence**.

Florence   I was better today. It's a question of taking it calmly and getting all your things ready beforehand. Like cooking.

Victoria   You make me proud.

Florence (*looks off*)   What does Arthur want?

Victoria   We'll soon know. I've told the sentries to bring him straight up. Florrie, you're not wearing your kilt again.

Florence   No.

Victoria   I wish you would.

Florence   I can't do the accent.

Victoria   Try. If they knew you were a woman there'd be a scandal.

Arthur *comes on.* **George** *is still attached to him, but a leg, an arm and half the ribs are gone.*

Victoria   I got your letter. I don't usually receive war criminals.

Arthur (*looks at the gallows*)   Who were they?

Victoria   They were all called Albert. I can't take chances.

Florence   I didn't shoot the ones on the posts but I hanged the others.

Arthur (*looks across at them*)   Good, good.

Florence   I'm the first hangwoman in history – public hangwoman, that is. It's part of our war effort. We take over any man's job that's suitable.

Arthur   I'm sure *they* prefer it.

Florence   Victoria knits the hoods.

Victoria   I run a knitting circle for ladies. They like to be useful.

Florence   I use a new hood each time. It adds that little touch of feminine sensibility. That's very precious in war.

Arthur   What d'you charge?

Florence   Pin money.

Arthur *goes to the gallows. He unblindfolds one of the shot men. He looks at him. A long silent pause.* **Florence** *tip-toes to the gallows. She takes hold of the feet of one of the hanging men and swings the body so that it kicks* **Arthur**.

Florence   Penny for them.

Arthur   Just admiring . . .

Victoria   You call yourself King.

Arthur   Yes.

Victoria   And you tell your men they're winning.

Arthur   I want to betray them.

Victoria   Why?

Arthur   You were right and I was wrong. I had no
political experience. Now I've learned that justice depends
on law and order, unfortunately. The mob's sadistic, violent,
vicious, cruel, anarchic, dangerous, murderous, treacherous,
cunning, crude, disloyal, dirty, destructive, sadistic –

Florence   You said that.

Victoria   Foulmouthed.

Arthur   Yes.

Victoria   And unwashed. I'm delighted! There's nothing
like political responsibility for educating a man.

Arthur   The animals would blush to call him brother. The
earth isn't his – he stole it, and now he messes in it. Even
lice crawl off him, like rats abandoning a doomed ship. He
has no pity. He can't see further than his own shadow. He
eats his own swill and makes his own night and hides in it.
That's what's wrong with the world: it's inhabited. To live!
Live is evil spelt backwards. It is also an anagram of vile.

Victoria   Yes. We must keep a sense of proportion. Hate
is an anagram of . . . Death is an anagram of . . . I'm always
kind when I can be. It makes you liked. Your letter
mentioned a plan.

Arthur   I've brought a long rope. I'll arrange a tug-of-war
between our armies. We'll say it's the final effort. We'll put
everyone on the rope: every man, woman, child, horse, dog,
cat, bird – even the sick. I'll choose a site and line my side
up with a precipice behind them. We'll start pulling in the
normal way, and when everyone's pulling flat out I – or you
– give a signal. Immediately everyone on your side drops the
rope. My side will be pulling flat out. They'll rush back over
the precipice and be killed. It's very deep.

Victoria   It sounds sensible.

Arthur   I said I was going for a stroll. They'll miss me. Let me send you the details later. (*Suddenly, to* **Florence**.) Why are you staring at him? Didn't you like him?

Florence   Yes.

Arthur (*hesitates*)   He always talks about you. It's irritating. (*He goes out.*)

Victoria   I prayed for this to happen! He's mad. But that doesn't matter. If we can just get his side together, we'll beat them. And perhaps he *will* get rid of them – and then we'll get rid of him. This is what I've dreamed of: peace.

Florence   I'm going to the front.

Victoria   No.

Florence   That's why I've been unhappy. I knew it when I saw those bones. Men are dying.

Victoria   I need you! (**Florence** *starts to go.*) Florrie! Fred! You'll be killed! You're all I live for. (**Florence** *goes out.*) Again, again! Things seem to go better, and then suddenly I lose everything. Freddie, don't leave me! Don't! Don't!

Victoria *follows* **Florence** *out.*

Scene Thirteen

Slough. A hospital ward. The stage is bare. Men lie in blankets on the floor. **Ned**, *a drummer boy,* **Jones** *and other soldiers.* **Griss** *is being brought in.*

Jones   What copped you, mate?

Griss   Leg off.

Ned   Juss the one?

Griss   Yeh.

Ned   So far.

Griss   That true?

Jones   About this ward?

Griss   Yeh!

Ned   It's true. But she don't let yer in till you're down for dyin'.

Griss   What a way t' go.

Ned   I'm 16 but I'll die 'appy.

Griss   Wass 'e lost?

Jones   'Is cherry.

Ned   So long as you ain' 'ad it, yer grotty ol' 'oodlum. (*He drums a roll.*) I got a lot a give thanks for. If I was 'ome I'd still be developin' the muscles in me right wrist. 'Ere I've 'ad more 'ole than the ol' fella ever 'ad off the ol' lady an' they're celebratin' their silver bung-up. (*He drums a roll.*)

Florence *comes on. She carries a lamp.*

Voices   Bless yer mum. God bless yer mum. Angel a Mons. Angel a mercy. 'Underneath the lamp light dum-di-dum-di-dum.'

Florence   Good evening, boys. (*To* **Griss**.) You're the new man?

Griss   Permission t' touch yer skirt, lady.

Ned   'Or! They're scrapin' the barrel – they're sendin' out fetishists. Another one t' jerk off in 'er shadder.

Florence   Ned.

Ned   It still hurts.

Florence   Where?

Ned   Give us yer 'and an' I'll take yer on a guided tour.

Florence   I have a letter from the Queen.

Ned   Don't ask me t' stand by me bed. There'd be sensation.

Jones   We wouldn't notice, sonny.

Florence (*reads*)   Dear men, I want you to know you are always in my thoughts, night and day. I too have made my sacrifice to this war, and I know what suffering is. (*She holds the letter nearer the lamp.*) I can't see.

Ned   Wan'a loan a bigger wick?

Florence   I have planned a tug-of-war against the enemy. You will all take part. (*Groans.*) Crutches and wheel chairs will be provided. After the victory you may go home. (*Cheers, laughter, whistles.*) I have a large stock of knitted material and this is being made into bed-jackets for you. (*A wolf-whistle.*) Miss Nightingale has you in good hands. (*Groans.*) God bless you all, Victoria RI.

Griss   Could I keep it, mum. (**Florence** *gives him the letter.*)

Ned   'Ere, 'e's a sentimentalist under all that dirt.

Jones   Wrap up.

Ned   Watch it. I'll be over there and stick me drumsticks where yer 'ide yer wallet. Both of 'em. (*He drums a roll.*)

Jones (*immediately*)   I'm still waitin'.

Griss   An' me, mate.

Ned (*to* **Griss**)   O matey, you wan' a watch yerself. 'E fancies one-legged corpses. 'E ought to be in quarantine. (*He drums a roll.*) Remember the drummer boy! (*To* **Florence**.) Come on, luv, less 'ave the names out the 'at. (*He gives her a military cap.*) 'Oo's first bash t'night. Give it a good shake. (*He drums a roll as he picks out a twist of paper and unfolds it. He stops and she reads the name.*)

Florence   Ned.

Jones   Stone me!

Ned She's chuffed! Thass what we like. A drop a keenness is like salt on chips.

Jones Don't know what yer see in 'im, ol' girl. Yer got me 'ere.

Ned I take 'er mind off 'er murky past.

Florence He's the purest person I know. He has most of the virtues of Christ and none of his vices.

Ned An' I do it all on one ball. The Light Brigade charged over the other one. Could a bin a lot worse. Could a bin the 'Eavy Brigade. Less 'ave the light out.

Jones 'Old on, give 'er time to read the other names.

Florence (*reads*) Ned, Ned, Ned –

Griss 'E's put 'is bleedin' moniker on every bleedin' slip. The scabby little –

Jones (*to* **Griss**) All right, lad. We'll write the names t'morra.

Jones *lowers the lamp as* **Florence** *goes to* **Ned**. *She stands by him. The light is almost out. She goes back to* **Jones**.

Florence Give me the lamp. (*He gives her the lamp. She turns it full up and goes back to* **Ned**. *She looks at him.*) He's dead . . .

Silence.

Griss Stroll on . . .

Jones The silly little . . . 'Ow many times I told 'im take it easy?

Florence I'll tell the men to –

Jones No. Let 'im be. 'E's all right for a bit. It's cold in the corridor.

Scene Fourteen

Beachy head. Bare stage. The two sides are lining up on the rope. Some are on crutches and in splints. **George** *is still attached to* **Arthur**, *but he is now only a skull and a few bones, like a ragged epaulette, on* **Arthur***'s shoulder.*

Victoria (*upstage*)   Let us thank God for granting us victory.

Her men   Amen.

Jones   'E ain't give us it yet.

Arthur (*downstage. He talks to the skull*)   Have you guessed? This riddle isn't hard. When my men go over the side what will hers do? What can you trust them to do? What would you expect them to do? What's the natural thing, the normal thing, the human thing to do? Run to the edge and watch the others die. Her whole army will stand along the edge. That's why I chose it. It's weak, it'll give, and her men will fall down on top of my men and they'll all be killed, both lots together. Don't grin, she'll see.

Florence *takes her place on the rope.*

Arthur *to* **Victoria**   They know the signal.

Victoria   Yes. They let go when I shout peace.

Arthur   Good. One – two – pull!

Victoria   Pull! (**Victoria** *and* **Arthur** *shout 'pull' while the teams pull.*)

Hers   Pull.

His   Heave.

Hers   Groan.

His   Grunt.

Hers   Onward!

His   Forward!

Hers   Upward!

His   To the future!

Hers   The dawn!

His   Freedom! Justice!

Hers   Culture! Democracy!

His   Science! Civilization!

Hers   Our future! Our past!

His   Our children! Our home!

Hers   Fraternity! Brotherhood! Love! Mankind!

Victoria   Peace!

Victoria's *side let the rope go.* **Arthur**'s *side run backwards over the cliff. For a moment* **Victoria**'s *side stand in silence. Then they cheer, and rush to the edge. They stand along it. They look down, laugh, wave, the cliff roars and gives.*

Scene Fifteen

Foot of the cliff. The stage is littered with bodies. Some of these are broken dummies. A rope curls round the stage and under and over and between the bodies. **Arthur** *comes down. He has lost the skull but the bones are still on his shoulder.*

Arthur   Over. Finished. Now I can die in peace. (*He takes out a pistol.*)

Florence *comes in. She is dirty and untidy. She carries the red cross satchel.*

Arthur   Why didn't you fall?

Florence   Victoria ran to the edge, so I stayed behind.

Arthur   I ought to kill you. It's not fair to leave you out. George would think I hate you. But I've done enough good for one life. Will you do something for me?

Florence　What?

Arthur　Close my eyes.

Florence　Why?

Arthur　I have some weaknesses. (*A line of ghosts rises upstage. They are in black cowls. They stand close together.*) Look. Ghosts. (*The ghosts move down a few steps. They stop.*) Don't stop. I'm not afraid. Look. (*He shoots himself.*) Ah! That's blood. Nearly spot on: it won't take long . . . (*To the ghosts.*) . . . I feel better now. Stand here. Hup! Hup! Salute! I'm proud. I've lived a good life. Arthur the Good. I set you free. You'll always be free. (*The ghosts move apart. They are joined together like a row of paper cut-out men.*) No! That's not true! That's a lie! No! I killed you! You're free! – This is all right, my mind's going, I'm seeing things . . . You've no right to come here like this! Florence, stop them!

Florence　Who?

Arthur　Them!

Florence　They're dead!

Arthur　No, no. Help them.

Florence　It's burning oil from tanks.

Arthur　O god! The pit! The pit! Give them the kiss of life! Him! Him! (*He breathes into a man's mouth.* **George** *comes from the line of ghosts. He holds himself as if he was still attached to* **Arthur**.) My blood! Give them my blood! (*He wets his hand on his head.*) My – (*He sees* **George**. *He steps back. He falls down.*)

Florence　He's dead.

George *goes to* **Arthur**. *He bends down and starts to fasten himself to* **Arthur**. **Arthur** *shudders and groans.*

Arthur (*groaning*)　No. No. No. No. No.

Scene Sixteen

Heaven. The stage is bare. The wheeled hamper, which is used several times in the remaining scenes, is a trolley with two large hamper-baskets on it. It has a handle for pushing and pulling. The whole cast except **Victoria**, **Albert** *and* **Florence**. **Arthur** *and* **George** *sit downstage. They are joined as before. The others are upstage, under a pulley.*

Arthur (*repeats in surprise*)   Where?

George   Heaven.

Arthur   What d'you do?

George   Nothing. We're all happy in heaven.

Arthur   We're still joined.

George   Till the trial?

Arthur   What trial?

George   Everyone's tried. Then they cut us free.

Arthur   I saw some men chained together.

George   Imagination! – that's just a habit.

Albert *and* **Victoria** *come on.*

Albert   Arthur, this is nice!

Victoria   Yes, I'm surrounded by my family again. But you're very late – we were here long ago. Let's start the Trial.

Albert (*to* **Arthur**)   The father prosecutes and the mother defends.

Victoria   Arthur v God.

During the trial people, including the **Jury**, *wander backwards and forwards between the court and the pulley. At one time all the* **Jury** *are under the pulley. There are bursts of noise and laughter from the people at the pulley.*

Arthur (*points to the pulley*)   What's that?

Victoria   What's the charge?

The **Lord Chamberlain** *whispers in* **Victoria**'s *ear.*

Victoria   O. Well, we have the perfect defence. (*She brings out a huge pile of papers.*)

Albert   Swear the jury.

The **Jurors** *raise their hands one after the other and say one of the following lines. Some say more than one line, but not two lines consecutively. They smile and nod at* **Arthur** *while they speak. One waves.*

He rapes little girls.
He rapes little boys.
He rapes grey haired grannies.
He rapes grey haired grandads.
He rapes dogs.
He rapes anything.
He rapes himself.
He likes to flog.
He gives babies syphilis.
He drinks before breakfast.
He wastes electricity.
He's mean.
He gives gonorrhoea syphilis.
He kills.
He's a nose-picker.
He looks at dirty pictures.
He picks his nose while he looks at dirty pictures.
He kills.
He can't control his natural functions.
He's only got unnatural functions.
He kills.
He eats dirt.
He is dirt.
He dreams about killing.
They ought to name a venereal disease after him.

Victoria   No objections.

Albert   First witness.

Len comes down from the group under the pulley.

Len   I admit that when 'is brother wen' a kill 'is-self 'e reckons let 'im. An' whass more, 'e poisoned 'is cake. (*The* **Jury** *clap.*) *But* – when 'is brother died 'e wen' an' dragged 'im back t' life! – I'm top a the queue. (*He goes upstage to the pulley.*)

Arthur   I wanted to make him happy. (*The* **Jury** *laugh.*) I was confused.

Foreman   The accused must not speak out of turn.

Victoria (*to* **Arthur**)   Hush. (*To* **Foreman**.) No questions. (*She sorts her papers.*)

Albert   A last world. I can smell his finger-prints from here.

Victoria   We call no evidence. (*She grabs her papers.*) Members of the jury, we speak to the mothers among you. (*They are all men.*) My son used to be a disappointment to me. Then he killed us all. For the first time I was able to call him son. The defence confidently asks for a verdict of guilty. (*She puts her papers away.*)

Albert   Members of the jury, your verdict. (*The* **Jury** *put their heads together.*)

Foreman   We order trial by ordeal.

Arthur   This is –

Victoria   The usual formality.

The **Lord Chamberlain** *comes down from the pulley with* **Albert**'s *sword. The* **Foreman** *tests the blade.*

Foreman   White hot.

Albert   Let me unbutton your shirt.

Albert *undoes* **Arthur**'s *shirt. The people under the pulley have been making a steady noise. They now chant: 'Heave-heave-heave.'*

Albert *sticks the sword into* **Arthur**. **Arthur** *does not react. A slight pause.* **Albert** *pulls the sword out.*

Victoria (*sniffs*)   Do I smell burning?

Albert   The verdict?

Foreman   Guilty and admitted to heaven.

Albert *cuts* **Arthur** *from* **George** *with the sword. There are loud shouts from the crowd at the pulley.* **Len** *runs downstage carrying a leg. It is torn off at the thigh and still wears its sock and shoe. The stump is ragged and bloody.* **Len** *chews it. The crowd fight round him like sparrows.*

Crowd   Me! Me! Me!

Len (*fights them off by kicking at them and by swinging the leg*) Lay off! 'Ang about! Get the other one! (*He chews.*)

Albert   You're interrupting a trial.

Victoria   It's disgraceful. If you must make that noise make it elsewhere.

Crowd   Me! Me! Shares!

Len   'Old on, 'old on. (*He turns to* **Arthur**.) Yer once did me a good turn. Welcome t' 'eaven. It's all yourn – (*He wrenches a bite from the leg.*) – wass left of it. (*He puts the leg into* **Arthur**'s *hands and steps back shyly. Then he shyly rubs the palms of his hands on the seat of his trousers. Shyly and pleasantly.*) An' I 'ope it chokes yer.

Joyce   O – I didn't know 'e 'ad it in 'im. (*Some of the crowd pat him on the back.*)

Albert   In heaven we eat each other.

Victoria   It doesn't hurt.

Albert   And it grows again.

George   Like crabs.

Victoria   Nothing has any consequences here – so there's no pain. Think of it – no pain. Pain is just a habit. You forget all your habits here. Bon appetite. (*She sniffs suspiciously.*) I could have sworn I smelt burning.

A one-legged man stands up under the pulley. He has a rope round his neck. The other end is slung over the pulley. He pulls it free.

Victoria (*sniffs*)   I could have sworn –

The one-legged man starts to hop out. The rope hangs from his neck and dances along behind him.

Len   'E's off.

Chamberlain   Bring him down!

George   Tally-ho!

They shout and chase the man out. **Arthur** *is alone. He has been in one position since the leg was put in his hand. He holds it vertical with the stump up. Slight pause. He seems to whisper. Then he speaks with difficulty.*

Arthur   I'm not dead. O God, let me die.

Scene Seventeen

Heaven. **George** *writhes on the floor with his knees up.* **Victoria** *brings* **Albert** *in.*

Victoria   It's his second attack today.

Albert   Perhaps he's eaten something that disagreed with him.

Victoria   I hoped you'd say something sensible! – I know what's behind this. (*She turns away.*) I haven't seen Arthur since the trial, and that was weeks ago.

Florence *comes on.*

Victoria Florence!

Albert How nice!

Victoria We were just talking about you. How did you get here?

Florence O, after the catastrophe I had to earn my living. (**Victoria** *clicks her tongue.*) I opened a brothel, and business was so brisk I didn't have time to get up. I catered for ministers, probation officers, WVS hierarchy, women police chiefs. – Well, there I was, in bed with Disraeli and Gladstone. They always shared a booking. They got very excited as usual and just then Gladys (a nom d'amour) said 'Listen'. There was a newsboy shouting in the street. Mafeking had been relieved. That on top of the rest was too much. They got over excited – and here I am.

Victoria I'm pleased about Mafeking.

George Hungry.

Victoria George, you can't feel pain in heaven! (*She takes* **Florence** *aside.*) I'm giving a little garden party, dear. I expect it of myself. My other guests will be here soon. I've managed to store a little food away, but I didn't tell George.

Arthur *comes on and crosses upstage.* **George** *immediately goes and stands by him.*

Victoria Arthur.

Arthur (*turns vaguely*) Florence . . .

Victoria Arthur. (*He turns to her.*) George isn't well. He's hungry. Are *you* hungry? (*Slight pause.*) Arthur, dear?

Arthur No.

Victoria I've got some sweets left from when I was alive.

Arthur (*his hands shoot out*) Yes! (*The others stare at him.* **George** *groans.*)

Victoria   So you're not eating! That's what's making George hungry.

George (*still standing next to* **Arthur**)   Starving!

Victoria   Aren't you happy here?

Albert   Of course he is! It's heaven. Anyway, you only die once. He can't starve himself to death.

George   For God's sake eat! You couldn't stand this agony.

Arthur   I feel it too.

Victoria   Arthur, what's wrong? Is there something you don't like? Some little thing we've overlooked? Is it me? Don't be afraid to tell me.

Arthur *goes out.*

George (*following* **Arthur** *closely*)   Eat! Eat! (*He goes out.*)

Victoria   Good – they'd have spoiled my party. Albert, go and keep an eye on them, and don't let them back till it's over.

Albert   But I was . . .!

The mob start to come on. **Albert** *goes out. The mob's clothes are not rags, but most of them are worn and dirty.* **Victoria** *greets them but they ignore it.*

Victoria   I'm so glad you could come.

Len   Glad t' do a favour.

Victoria   I'm so glad you could come.

Griss   Where's the grub?

Florence (*to* **Victoria**)   You're upset. You should have cancelled it.

Victoria   I died fighting. I won't give in now. – I'm so glad you could come.

Len   Whass this garden-whass-it caper?

Joyce   Picnic.

Griss (*at the hamper*)   This the grub? (*Opens the hamper.
Surprised.*) She must be runnin' 'er own farm! (*Sniffs.*) Don't it
pong, though?

Len (*sniffs*)   Thass off!

Victoria   It's game.

Griss   Game?

Victoria   It's hung – to give it flavour.

Joyce   Naturally. (*To* **Len**.)   Thass game. (*To* **Victoria**.)
Ta, luv. (*Eats.*) It's all right, en it? It *is* person?

Victoria   O yes.

Griss   English.

Victoria   Well, British.

Griss   I wouldn't fancy no black and yeller imported
muck.

Len   Well, it's freeman's. (*Eats.*) Strewth. (*Eats.*)

Griss   'S all right if yer 'old yer nose an swaller quick.

Arthur *comes on.* **George** *follows him closely.*

Victoria   I wanted you to stay away!

George (*to* **Arthur**)   Eat!

Joyce   Wass up?

George   Eat! Eat!

Arthur (*in pain*)   O God.

Len   Whass 'is caper?

George (*sees the others eating*)   Food! (*He runs to the hamper and
takes food.*) Ah!

As **George** *eats* **Arthur** *starts to retch and this automatically makes* **George** *retch.*

Griss   'Oo you shuvin'?

George *rolls on the floor and eats and retches. The mob stare at them.*

Joyce   'Ere! They're poisoned.

Griss   Do what?

Len   I knew it tasted funny.

Griss   You kiddin'?

Joyce   No, me ol' gran was 'aving a knees-up one night when I wanted a watch telly. I 'ad t' put drain-cleaner in 'er meths t' quieten 'er down. She rolled down the stairs juss like that.

George (*eating and retching*)   Arthur, stop it! Let me eat!

Len (*drops his food*)   'Er word's good enough for me!

Griss (*drops his food*)   Me gut!

Victoria   You can't be poisoned in heaven!

George   Aahh! Arthur!

Arthur   I can't eat!

Griss   'E can't eat!

Joyce   Thass yer confirmation! (*The mob groans and doubles up.*)

Victoria *and* **Florence** *run out.*

Joyce (*alarmed*)   Whass goin' a 'appen to us?

Len   It's worse'n the double cramps!

Joyce   We ain' goin' a die again? We ain' goin' a lose all this?

Albert *comes in. He sees* **George** *and* **Arthur**.

Albert   There you are! But where's Victoria! (*He takes a piece of body from the hamper.*)

Joyce   'E's one a 'em! (*The mob stops.*)

Griss   Out the same sty! (*The mob surrounds* **Albert**.)

Joyce   Take 'is bone away! (**Griss** *takes the food from* **Albert**.)

Albert   I thought my wife was here. I'd better –

Griss   Up the pulley!

Griss *takes a rope from his shoulder. The mob push* **Albert** *into the hamper and tie the rope on him.* **Griss** *walks away tugging on the rope. The mob crowd round the hamper holding* **Albert** *in. They shout.* **Griss** *tugs.* **George** *runs between* **Griss** *and the mob encouraging and trying to help.*

George   Food! Food!

Arthur (*quickly. In pain*)   No! No! No more pain, no more war, no more suffering – we're in heaven!

Joyce (*calling to* **Arthur**)   All right luvy, we'll settle 'im for yer!

Arthur   Why can't I let them alone in peace!

Len (*calling to* **Arthur**)   Yeh yer deserve a gong for flushin' 'im out!

Arthur (*quickly*)   Let me die! (*The mob shouts, the rope slackens, and* **Griss** *sits down with a thump.*) Stop it! No more! I'll eat! I'll eat! (**George** *runs from the hamper, eating a piece of* **Albert**. **Arthur** *takes a piece of* **Albert** *from the hamper. He bites from it.*)

Arthur   I'll eat! I'll be good! Good! Good!

Joyce (*at the hamper*)   Drag 'im up our end.

Len (*helping her*)   'Ow's yer gut?

Joyce   Bit better.

Len   We'll eat 'er next. She'll purge it for yer!

They drag the hamper out. The trolley is left on stage. **George** *sits alone and eats.*

Arthur (*eats*)   Eat and be good. Be good and die. Die and be happy. (*They chew in silence for a few moments.*) O God, let me die. Let me die – and everyone will be happy.

Scene Eighteen

Heaven. **Victoria** *and* **Florence** *come on.* **Florence** *looks over her shoulder.* **Victoria** *has a black eye. Her hair is undone.*

Victoria (*stops*)   Rest for five minutes.

Florence (*looks back*)   They should keep up. It's dangerous. (*Calls.*) George!

Victoria   If there's pain in heaven, why isn't there love? (*After reflection.*) I can't say I love you. D'you love me?

Florence   No.

Victoria   D'you feel pain?

Florence   No.

Victoria   Nor do I. Nor does the mob. Crowds believe anything.

George *wheels* **Albert** *in on the trolley.* **Albert** *has no legs.*

George (*groans*)   I can't go on. (*Stops pushing.*) It's getting worse! I thought it would go when he started to eat.

Victoria   He must have stopped again. We can't keep running away. We must do something.

Albert   Yes.

Victoria   There was peace in heaven till Arthur got here. He doesn't belong! He hasn't got the gift of happiness. We must get rid of him. (**George** *is groaning.*)

Albert (*defeated*)   You can't kill people in heaven.

Victoria   We could eat him.

Albert (*shrugs*)   He'd grow again.

Victoria   We could eat him again. Keep his bones and chew off every sign of life the moment it appears.

Albert   That's a brilliant idea!

Victoria   But we can't do it.

Albert   Why not?

Victoria   You'd never catch him. The mob protects him. He's infected them with his lunacy – they *all* think they're in pain. He's their messiah.

George   Use Florence.

Victoria   What?

George   She could put a ring through his nose and bring him here on his knees.

Florence   Could I?

Victoria   I see. I've just understood something. (*To* **George**.) I've underrated you. (*To* **Florence**.) Get him away from the mob – take him for a walk. Then it'll be four against one.

Florence   No. I'm afraid of the mob.

George   He won't let them touch you. (*Groans.*)

Victoria   At least you'll stand a chance. If we go on like this we'll all be caught. And think what it means: peace.

Florence   I'll try.

Victoria (*going*)   Let's go back.

Florence   Now?

Victoria   Now! I feel lucky again.

George (*groans*).

They go out.

Scene Nineteen

Heaven. **Arthur** *sits upstage.* **Len**, **Joyce**, **Jones** *and* **Griss** *sit a little apart from him. They moan.* **Arthur** *has long, dirty hair and a long, dirty beard. He wears rags. The others are not so dirty and ragged.* **Florence** *stands downstage. She looks at* **Arthur**.

Arthur   Yes?

Florence   I wasn't sure it was you.

Len (*stands*)   Whass 'appenin'?

Arthur   Sit down. (**Len** *sits.*) How's my brother?

Florence   Can we go somewhere?

Len   'E ain' t' be bothered.

Griss   I got pain all over.

Joyce   This ain' 'eaven. It's prison.

Jones   We want civilized grub.

Arthur   I'd like a walk.

Len (*shrugs*)   On yer pins then. (*He helps* **Arthur** *to stand.*)

Arthur   I'll be back soon.

Arthur *and* **Florence** *walk downstage. All the others go out.*

Arthur   Sit here. (*Sits.*)

Florence   Not here.

Arthur   I'm tired.

Florence (*sits*)   Why aren't you happy?

Arthur   I'm in pain.

Florence   I'm sorry, you can't be. Not in heaven.

Arthur   You don't feel pain.

Florence   Sometimes I'm hungry. That's all. – They ate my arm. It didn't hurt. Eat me. Part of me.

Arthur   No.

Florence   You do eat. Sometimes George's pain's a bit better.

Arthur   I eat myself.

Florence   O.

Arthur   When it's too bad. I eat my arm. (*He moves the back of his forearm across his mouth and chews.*)

Florence   Does it hurt?

Arthur   Less than hunger.

Florence (*pause*)   You're old.

Arthur   My beard grew overnight. The night I ate my father. I ate some of him. I don't know what. When I woke up I was old. My hair was white and I had a beard. It was white when it came, and wet – I must have been crying. I felt very tired, as if I'd been born with a beard. (*A slight pause.*) Why did you come?

Florence   I'm not sure.

Arthur   I'm going to ask you something. First, I'm not staying in heaven.

Florence   There is nowhere else.

Arthur   I'm not staying here. (*He reaches for her hand. She stands and looks round.*) What is it?

Florence   What were you going to ask me?

Arthur   Don't eat.

Florence   I –

Arthur   Most people die before they reach their teens. Most die when they're still babies or little children. A few reach fourteen or fifteen. Hardly anyone lives on into their twenties.

Florence   Thank God.

Arthur   Bodies are supposed to die and souls go on living. That's not true. Souls die first and bodies live. They wander round like ghosts, they bump into each other, tread on each other, haunt each other. That's another reason why it's better to die and come here – there *must* be peace when you're dead. Only I'm not dead.

Florence   You are! Just believe in yourself!

Arthur   No. Not quite. I've tried but I can't die! Even eating didn't kill me. There's something I *can't* kill – and they can't kill it for me. Pity – it must be nice to be dead. Still, if I can't die I must live. I'm resigned to my curse! I accept it. I'll probably even end up being happy. (**Florence** *moves.*) O God, don't go! You're looking for something.

Florence   I'm hungry! I'm hungry!

Arthur   Don't go back to my family!

Florence   I must!

Arthur   Come with me.

Florence   Where?

Arthur   Somewhere.

Florence   There is nowhere!

Arthur (*desperately*)   We'll find somewhere!

Florence   What good is that? You still won't eat!

Arthur   We'll eat ourselves!

Florence   No!

Arthur   We'll eat each other!

Florence   You said you wouldn't!

Arthur   Well – well – yes if you stay!

Florence   You won't! You know you won't! You talk about life when you mean pain! That's why you cause trouble – you can't let them die in peace. The mob, your mother – wherever you go – someone will always want to kill someone, and they can't and so it goes on and on! I'm hungry! They're hungry! You're hungry! We're all dead and hungry! And it's the same wherever you go!

Arthur   You keep me alive.

Florence   You're not alive! This is heaven! You can't live or laugh or cry or be in pain! You can't love! You can't torture people! Let me alone! You're a ghost! Ghost! Ghost! You're haunting me – O stop it!

Arthur   You're crying.

Florence   No, no, no, no.

Arthur   My hand's wet.

Florence   Too late. Why didn't you tell me this before? What d'you think I did while I waited? I'm not crying. Perhaps I'm alive, perhaps we needn't be like this. I'm trying to think.

Victoria *runs in.*

Victoria (*calls*)   Albert! We've got him!

Florence (*trying to make* **Victoria** *leave*)   We must go. The mob's here.

Victoria   No. The moment he left they went hunting for food.

Albert *and* **George** *come on.* **Albert** *has legs again. He limps.*

Victoria (*takes hold of one of* **Arthur**'s *arms. To* **Albert**) Take that arm.

George (*rubs his hands together*)   I told you!

Victoria (*to* **George**)   Keep watch! (**George** *goes upstage.* **Albert** *limps across to* **Arthur**.)

Arthur   Florence, help me!

George   I'm hungry!

Victoria   Albert, don't just stand there –

George (*goes to* **Arthur**)   Food! –

Victoria (*to* **George**)   Go and keep watch.

George (*going upstage*)   Hurry!

Victoria   Now Albert, we'll –

Arthur (*to* **Florence**)   Help me!

Albert   They'll hear!

Florence   We can't eat him!

Victoria (*to* **Albert**)   Gag him!

Albert   But I didn't bring any –

Arthur   Florence!

Victoria   Strangle him!

Albert   But I didn't bring any –

Victoria   With his beard!

Albert   His –!

Victoria   Beard! Like this. (*She winds the beard round* **Arthur***'s throat.*) And so. Two. Three. (*To* **Arthur**.) This is for *your* good. Six. Seven. Eight.

George (*upstage, looking off*)   Be quick!

Victoria   Nine. Ten. (*She stops strangling.*) He'll be out for a good ten minutes.

George (*going back to the others*)   They must have heard!

Victoria   Keep calm! Calm. (*To* **Albert**.) Put him across your back.

Victoria *and* **George** *help* **Albert** *to get* **Arthur** *on to his back.*

Florence (*walking round*)   He feels pain, you see . . .

Victoria   Walk. Don't run.

Albert *starts to carry* **Arthur** *out.*

George (*groans*)   I'm starving!

Albert, **George** *and* **Victoria** *go out.*

Florence   Why didn't he talk to me before? You have to pay for waiting.

Florence *follows the others out.*

Scene Twenty

Heaven. **Victoria**, **Albert** *and* **Florence** *resting.* **Florence** *sits on the hamper.*

Albert   Where's George?

Florence   Picking up the bones.

Victoria   He left a trail of them behind us. He hopes he'll find some meat on them.

Albert (*licks his fingers*)   He won't find much.

George *comes on. He chews a bone and he has a stack of bones under his arm.*

George   I'm still starving!

Victoria   It should have gone when we ate him.

George (*chews and groans*)   It didn't.

Victoria   Give me those bones. (*He gives her the bones but keeps the one he is chewing.*) And that.

George   I'm hungry.

Victoria   And that. (*He gives her the bone.*) We must keep them together. (*She stands them in a large box and arranges them like flowers.*) Where's his head?

George   I haven't got it. (*He picks his teeth and chews hungrily.*)

Victoria   Florence?

Florence   No.

Victoria   Albert?

Albert   No.

Victoria   You don't just lose a head.

Albert   O lor'.

Victoria (*annoyed*)   That's why you're still in pain.

George (*stands by the bones and eyes them*)   It can't have gone far.

Victoria (*to **Florence***)   You're not sitting on it, dear?

Florence   No.

Victoria   Well who remembers eating it?

George   I don't.

Victoria   You wouldn't.

George (*groans*)   That's not fair! Starving's bad enough without –

Victoria   Well we'll have to search. It's got to be found. He might sprout a new body!

Florence   Can he?

Victoria   It's the sort of perverse thing he would do. We'd end up with two Arthurs on our hands. I couldn't cope. (*To **Albert** and **George**.*) Come on. – Florence.

Florence   I'll stay and mind the bones.

Victoria (*going*)   You don't just lose a head.

George *groans.* **George**, **Albert** *and* **Victoria** *go out.*
Florence *waits. Then she uncovers her lap.* **Arthur**'s *head is in it.*

Florence   O dear.

Arthur   Don't. I love you.

Florence   They're looking for you.

Arthur   I know.

Florence (*shudders*)   O dear.

Arthur   This is the first time I've been happy. I'm not hungry now.

Florence   Something's going to fall in your eyes. (*She removes it.*)

Arthur   It's a hair.

Florence   Keep still.

Arthur   My beard. Mother tore it out when she strangled me.

Florence   Why are you smiling?

Arthur   It's nice here.

Florence   What?

Arthur   In your lap?

Florence   O.

Arthur   Don't shake. When they cut off a man's leg he still feels it. I'm like that. They've cut off my body – but I'm alive. I could make love to you. Now. I can feel it. Hard. That's why I like it in your lap.

Florence (*laughs. Bewildered*)   I don't know what to do.

Arthur   You keep worrying because you ate me.

Florence   Victoria was watching.

Arthur   It's all right. I love you.

Florence   But what can I do?

Arthur   Don't eat.

Florence   You always say that! –

Arthur   Tell Victoria you love me. She won't stand for that: it's treason. She'll make them eat you and then you'll be like me.

Florence   What good is that?

Arthur   You'll be alive.

Florence   Where? How?

Arthur   With me.

Florence   But you're nothing. They've eaten you.

Arthur   I'm alive. Or I'm beginning to live!

Florence   Where? How?

Arthur   I don't know. I can't tell you, you must find out. I'm like a fire in the sea or the sun underground. I'm alive. You love me.

Florence   It's too late. Love, love – I don't know what it means now. You talk about sun and fires – and I'm hungry!

Arthur   Of course you are! The dead are always hungry!

Florence   I've told you, I don't understand.

Arthur   You do!

Florence   I want to, but I don't.

Arthur   It's why you're hiding me.

Florence   I don't know why!

Arthur   I'm in your lap! That's proof!

Florence   I'll see. I'll try. I'll try.

Arthur   Kiss me.

Florence   Let me think.

Arthur Kiss me! Lift my head in your hands and hold it against your mouth. Then it will be all right. We'll be alone, and happy.

Florence Yes . . . Yes. (*She slightly bends her head towards him. She takes his head in her hands and starts to raise it.*)

Victoria (*off*) You don't just lose a head.

Florence *covers* **Arthur**'s *head*. **Victoria** *comes in.*

Florence Did you find it?

Victoria I will.

Albert *and* **George** *come on.* **Albert** *has his hands in his pockets.* **George**'s *pain is obviously worse. He chews a bone.*

Albert Tch, tch, tch!

George O God! (*He drops the bone in the tin.*) A microbe couldn't feed on that. (*He hunts through the other bones.*) If we had a fire we could boil soup.

Victoria You don't just lose a head.

Florence I expect it's rolled off on its own somewhere. It doesn't matter.

Victoria (*to* **George**) Put those bones down. (*She takes the tin to* **Florence**.) I'm not losing any more. Albert, you can't think with your hands in your pockets. No wonder we lost his head. (*To* **Florence**.) Look after those, dear.

Florence Yes. (*She puts the tin on the floor.*)

Albert Dear-o-dear-o-lor!

George (*suddenly*) I can't stand it! Ah! (*He rolls on the floor.* **Albert** *looks at him.*)

Victoria He's just trying to attract attention. Florence, we'll go for a walk.

Florence It's nice here.

Victoria It's nicer walking.

Albert (*looking at* **George**)   Victoria, this is serious. I didn't realise how bad he was!

Victoria (*looks at* **George**)   Hm. – Florence, come and look at him.

Florence   I don't think I could help.

Victoria   Nonsense, you're a nurse. (*She bends down and looks at* **George**. **Florence** *starts to walk towards them.*)

Albert   Shall I rub his wrists?

Victoria   Put something between his teeth. George, we're going to put something between your teeth. (*To* **Florence**.) Fetch a bone, dear.

Florence   What?

Victoria   A bone. To put between his teeth.

Florence   Yes. (*She starts to walk back to the hamper.*)

Victoria   George, try saying the National Anthem backwards. It calms the nerves.

Florence (*stops. To* **Arthur** *under her skirt*)   Stop it! (*She smacks him.*)

Victoria   What, dear?

Florence   I twisted my back. (**Florence** *starts to walk again.*)

Victoria   What's wrong with your legs?

Florence   They went to sleep. (*She reaches the tin of bones. She takes out a bone and starts walking back to* **Victoria**. **Victoria** *is saying the National Anthem backwards.*)

Albert   Take off his shoes.

Victoria   Why?

Albert   You always take the shoes off the sick.

Florence Stop it! (*She slaps* **Arthur**'s *head under her skirt. She wriggles and grimaces.*)

Victoria Is that your leg, dear?

Florence My leg?

Victoria It went to sleep.

Florence It's worse. I'll sit down. (*She turns to go.*)

Victoria Try jumping.

Florence I don't think I –

Victoria It helps the circulation.

Florence I've got a headache.

Victoria It's invaluable for headaches and for twisted backs. Up you go! (**Florence** *jumps once.*) You call that up? Again. Higher. Up! (**Florence** *jumps once.*) Nurses never look after themselves. I'll massage it.

Florence (*moves quickly away*) It's gone now.

Victoria There you are. Jumping cures everything.

Arthur *laughs.* **Florence** *slaps him under her skirt.*

Victoria George, don't laugh. You're supposed to be ill.

George (*points at* **Florence**) I didn't laugh. It was – (**Florence** *puts the bone in his mouth. He talks through the bone.*) – bla bla bla.

Victoria And don't talk with your mouth full.

George (*pointing at* **Florence**) Bla bla bla!

Florence *backs away from* **George**. *She trips over the hamper. She falls with her feet in the air.* **Victoria** *sees the head between her legs. She grasps* **Florence**'s *legs and holds them up. She twists her head round so that it is in line with* **Arthur**'s *head.*

Victoria Arthur! I said you don't just lose a head.

George (*takes the head*) Meat!

Victoria   Give that back!

George   No!

George *takes a bite from the head.* **Arthur** *laughs loudly.*

George (*stops*)   He laughed!

Victoria   George give me that head!

George   No. (*He puts the head under his jacket.*)

Victoria   Albert, speak to him.

Albert   George –

George *runs upstage. He takes a bite from the head.* **Arthur** *laughs loudly.*

George   O!

George *runs out with the head. Silence.*

Florence   Why did Arthur laugh?

Victoria (*to* **Albert**)   Pick up the bones.

Albert (*to* **Victoria**)   It's no use being bitter. We've all had a trying day.

George *runs on with the head. It is half eaten.*

George (*chewing*)   It's a miracle! My pain's going!

Victoria   Albert!

Albert   George, I'm very cross with –

George *goes out.*

Florence   Why did he laugh when George ate him?

George *runs back. He carries a skull.*

George   My pain's gone! Gone! All gone!

Albert (*takes the skull from* **George**)   And when he grows again you won't have one bite!

George   I'm free! I'm free! (*He runs out.*)

Victoria   He won't grow again.

Albert   Why not?

Victoria   He's dead.

Albert   How?

Victoria   If George's pain is gone, Arthur's gone.

Florence   Where?

Victoria   I don't know. I don't want to know. He's dead –
that's good enough for me. Give me his skull. (**Albert** *gives
her the skull. She puts it in the tin, on top of the other bones.*) Now
we've got a complete set.

George (*off*)   Yippee!

Albert   What will happen?

Victoria   We'll wait and see.

Florence   Will he grow again?

Victoria   He might. But it'll be dead meat. Not fit for
human consumption. And there'll be no more pain.

George (*off*)   Yippee!

Victoria   We must keep him quiet. I don't want to face
the mob till I can show them the body.

They all go out. The bones are left onstage in the tin.

Scene Twenty-One

Heaven. **Arthur** *is lying with one foot in the tin. The bones are gone.*
Joyce *sleeps near him.* **Victoria**, **Albert**, **George** *and*
Florence *come on.*

Albert   He's grown.

Victoria (*pokes* **Arthur**)   But he's dead. (*To* **George**.) And
you're not in pain?

George   No.

Victoria   Good. Fetch a coffin. (**George** *and* **Florence** *go out.*)

Victoria (*shakes* **Joyce**)   Wake up, dear!

Joyce   You killed the master!

Victoria   He said you'd say that. Run and fetch your friends, dear.

Joyce   I will! (**Joyce** *runs out.*)

Albert   What are you going to do?

Victoria   Settle it.

George *and* **Florence** *come in with a coffin. They set it down by* **Arthur**.

Victoria (*to* **Albert**)   Get the food, but don't bring it on till I go like this. (*She makes a gesture.*)

Joyce (*off*)   Yoooeee!

Victoria (*to* **Florence**)   Hammer? (**Florence** *goes out.*) I have to think of everything. It'll be interesting to see if she brings the nails.

Joyce, **Len**, **Jones**, **Griss** *and the rest of the mob come on.*

Len (*to* **Joyce** *as he comes in*)   An' yer reckoned 'e's bin poisoned?

Joyce   For keeps.

Victoria (*goes to meet them*)   You can't kill people in heaven. They can only kill themselves.

Griss   No speeches.

Victoria   You're hungry.

Len   'Oo says?

Victoria   He did. That's why he killed himself.

Joyce   Do what?

Victoria   He told you not to eat each other.

Len   Right.

Victoria   But he knew he was asking something unnatural and impossible. Something quite, quite impossible. And because he loved you – and he only attacked you out of love – he wouldn't ask you to eat yourself, as he did. (**Len** *puts his arm behind his back.*) So he died, to let you eat each other in peace.

Griss   Fact?

Len   Never.

Victoria   His last words were 'Feed them'. (*She gives* **Albert** *the signal.*)

Griss   Stroll on! (**Albert** *comes in with the hamper.* **Florence** *comes on with him.*)

Griss   That grub?

Victoria   Yes.

Joyce   One thing.

Jones   What?

Joyce   That trial.

Griss   Yeh.

Joyce   'E singed when they put the knife in. I smelt burnin'.

Jones   Thass a fact.

Griss   Thass what I said.

Joyce   Never belonged, see.

Len   Nosh now or later?

Victoria   After we've put him in the box. (**Albert** *and* **George** *put* **Arthur** *in the coffin.*) Lid. (**Len** *puts the lid on the*

coffin.) Hammer. (**Florence** *hands her the hammer.*) Nails.
(**Florence** *drops her hands to her sides.*) I'll use my teeth. (*She pulls out a tooth and looks at it.*) That'll hold better. (*She knocks it into the coffin.*) One. (*She pulls out another tooth and knocks it in.*) Two. Be putting the food out. (*She pulls out another tooth.*)

Len   It ain' none a that fancy stuff, ma?

Victoria (*knocking*)   No.

Joyce   Shame. I enjoy anythin' exotic. They ain' got the taste for it.

Victoria   One more.

Griss   Don't pull the lot.

Victoria (*knocks*)   I've got handy gums.

Len   She's a girl!

Albert (*aside to* **Victoria**)   Will it be all right?

Victoria (*to* **Albert**)   Of course. I pride myself on my common touch. – Put the nosh on the lid, boys. (*They lay the food on top of the coffin.* **Disraeli** *and* **Gladstone** *come in.*) How nice! We were just talking about you.

Disraeli   Ah, ma'am. Having no teeth suits you.

Gladstone (*looks at the food*)   We timed it nice!

Disraeli (*to* **Florence**)   I'm sorry about that.

They all sit round the coffin, except **Florence**. *She sits a bit on one side and faces the audience.*

Victoria   Quiet please. For what we are about to receive.

Two voices   Amen. (*All except* **Florence** *eat.*)

Len   I'll 'ave that bit.

Disraeli   Allow me. (*He hands the food to* **Victoria**.)

Joyce (*to* **Len**)   Yer already got two bits, guts.

Arthur *steps out of the coffin. He stands on the lid. He looks a bit cleaner, but his hair and beard are still dirty and uncombed. He is draped in a long white smock or shawl. Parts of his old clothes are seen underneath. He arranges the smock so that it hangs more comfortably. The others don't see him. They eat and talk.*

Griss   'E weren' a bad bloke. Juss couldn't keep 'is-self to 'is-self. Thass a fault – but it don' make yer wicked.

Victoria   I'll miss him. But he's better gone. I could never help him, otherwise things would have been different. I'm working out a roster for the order in which we're eaten. Then there'll be no arguments. My name comes first.

Arthur *starts to rise in the air. His hands are half raised against his chest. The shawl hangs behind him. His feet are seen.* **Florence** *doesn't see him. She cries silently.*

Victoria   Florence? (*Offers her food.*)

Florence   There's something in my eye.

Victoria   Take it out.

Jones   Bit a dirt.

Victoria   There's no dirt in heaven. There's only peace and happiness, law and order, consent and co-operation. My life's work has borne fruit. It's settled.

Len (*to* **Joyce**)   Pass us that leg.

Peter Barnes is a writer and director whose work includes *The Ruling Class* (Nottingham and Piccadilly Theatre, London, 1968), *Leonardo's Last Supper* and *Noonday Demons* (Open Space Theatre, London, 1969), *The Bewitched* (Royal Shakespeare Company at the Aldwych Theatre, London, 1974), *Laughter!* (Royal Court Theatre, London, 1978), *Red Noses* (RSC, Barbican, London, 1985), *Sunsets and Glories* (West Yorkshire Playhouse, Leeds, 1990), *Dreaming* (Manchester Royal Exchange and Queens Theatre, London, 1999) and *Jubilee* (RSC, Swan Theatre, Stratford, 2001). He has won the *Evening Standard* Award and the John Whiting Award 1969; Laurence Olivier Award 1985; Sony Best Radio Play Award 1981; Royal Television Society Award for Best TV Play 1987; and was nominated for an Oscar in 1993.

The Ruling Class

For Charlotte

A Chronology

of First Performances

Introduction

This introduction is something of a problem. It should be personal to some extent. But I have always seen the world of the strictly personal as shallow, tending to break life up into little closed cells. I have therefore tried, as far as possible, to keep any conscious autobiographical element out of my plays.

I can remember being evacuated to the country during the war and waiting outside our cottage, for my father to come home from night work at a nearby factory. He would come up the hill coughing loudly in the cold morning light and have two eggs for breakfast. It has no significance; it's just personal history. What is important in my life will not necessarily be so for an audience. Write what you know is good advice for journalists. I write what I imagine, believe, fear, think.

If there is one certain way of achieving absolute unpopularity it is by writing against the prevailing modes and pieties. With each new play I presented to disinterested parties I felt I was always starting from scratch. Here, the fact one may have written a number of major plays over the years counts for very little. I always had to persuade theatre directors, producers and agents that I knew what I was doing. They did not know. For them the theatre was a job, not their lives. Unfortunately I am passionate about it. And it *is* unfortunate. Fish trust the water and are cooked in it. Sometimes I'm not smart enough to be an idiot. Passion is an emotion you must never show if you want to be effective in England. Play it cool, understate, pretend to be an amateur who has just wandered into the arts by mistake. It is what puts the damp in walls and white hair on old men.

At the start I believed that it was enough to write well, everything would follow. It is not enough and it never has been. Few know what a well-written page is, with all the words looking in the same direction.

So what was I trying to do in these plays? I wanted to write a roller-coaster drama of hairpin bends; a drama of expertise and ecstasy balanced on a tight-rope between the comic and tragic with a multi-faceted fly-like vision where every line was dramatic and every scene a play in itself; a drama with a language so exact it could describe what the flame of a candle looked like after the candle had been blown out and so high-powered it could fuse telephone wires and have a direct impact on reality; a drama that made the surreal real, that went to the limit, then further, with no dead time, but with the speed of a seismograph recording an earthquake; a drama of 'The Garden of Earthly Delights' where a Lion, a Tinman and a Scarecrow are always looking for a girl with ruby slippers; a drama glorifying differences, condemning hierarchies, that would rouse the dead to fight, always in the forefront of the struggle for the happiness of all mankind; an anti-boss drama for the shorn not the shearers.

The theatre is a thermometer of life but our theatre is a theatre without size or daring; a theatre without communion. It contains no miracles. The bread is never changed into flesh or the wine into blood. It is a theatre of carpet-slippers.

'Well, change it then! Nothing's impossible.'

'Have you tried juggling soot?'

There is no creativity only discovery. If I return again and again to the same themes, like a child to the fire, it is because they are essential and I still owe them something. But whatever forms I use, whether it is the drama or the song lyric it is still, above all, *information*.

To strike out, to launch repeated bayonet attacks on naturalism, to write rigorously against the prevailing mode, requires courage. What courage I have I put into my work and I have none left for my life. The word must act for me. Like others I want to help create a people who are sceptical, rational, critical, not impressed or fooled. In a word, free, and in the literal sense, ungovernable. Of course that is not very practical but it is not unthinkable. It says something about our inadequacies and limitations, rather than the bizarreness of the idea itself. However, I who advocate freedom and boldness in my work, cling in my life to routine and habits like the most conforming bourgeoisie, in order to write. But, please, always believe the song not the singer.

At times I feel I could not track an elephant in six feet of snow, but at least I have provided a good home for scores of old jokes who had nowhere else to go. I have laughed a lot when I did not feel a lot like laughing and of course I have made a mess of my life, but then I have made a mess of all my shirts. I write hoping to make the world a little better and perhaps to be remembered. The latter part of that statement is foolish, as I can see, quite plainly, the time when this planet grows cold and the Universe leaks away into another Universe and the Cosmos finally dies and there is nothing but night and nothing. It's the end, but that is never a good enough reason for not going on. A writer who does not write corrupts the soul. Besides, it is absurd to sit around sniffing wild flowers when you can invent them, and new worlds.

Peter Barnes 1981, 1989

Introduction
by Harold Hobson

The most exciting thing that can happen to a dramatic critic
is when he is suddenly and unexpectedly faced with the
explosive blaze of an entirely new talent of a very high order.
This happens very rarely. In twenty years of reviewing plays
it has happened for me, for example, only four times. The first
was the original production at the Arts Theatre in 1955 of
Samuel Beckett's *Waiting for Godot*. The second, John
Osborne's *Look Back in Anger* at the Royal Court a year later.
The third was Harold Pinter's *The Birthday Party* at the Lyric,
Hammersmith, in 1958; and the fourth Peter Barnes's *The
Ruling Class* at the Nottingham Playhouse, directed by Stuart
Burge, in the autumn of 1968.

The peculiar impact of such an experience is that one is
taken completely by surprise. To see John Gielgud in *The
Importance of Being Earnest*, or Laurence Olivier in *Macbeth*, his
finest Shakespeare creation, is a memorable experience. In a
certain sense, too, it holds the unexpected, but not altogether
the unforeseen. Before one sees it one cannot tell what
particular aspect of humanity Olivier will derive from his
performance of Macbeth. Until he had played Macbeth one
did not know that he would heartrendingly present a man
who had so ordered his life that when he came to the end of
it he had no friends, and no man who owed loyalty to him.
But one did know beforehand that in all probability the
performance would be fine and moving, even revelatory. One
knew this for the simple reason that one had seen Olivier on
many other occasions, and had come to recognise in him the
possession of transcendent abilities.

That amazing evening at Nottingham, towards the close of
1968, however, to its other joys and triumphs, added those of
astonishment and discovery. Before the curtain rose on *The
Ruling Class* no one appeared to have heard of its author, Peter
Barnes. Nobody in the theatre appeared to know whether he

had been to university, had written any other plays, was a stripling in his last year at school, or an old gentleman of ninety. It was hazarded to me that Mr Barnes was not a member of the aristocracy, but this was only a deduction from the fact that *The Ruling Class* is hostile to the nobility. As such, the deduction might easily have been wrong. For the production, if not the play, has firm connections with the upper classes that it derides. One of its most charmingly unintelligent characters, Dinsdale, the thirteenth Earl of Gurney's nephew, has been played by two extremely bright young aristocrats, first, by Peter Eyre, whose grandfather was Lord Acton, and later, when Mr Eyre had contractual obligations elsewhere, by Jonathan Cecil, the grandson of the Marquis of Salisbury. Mr Barnes, however, is not himself an offshoot of Debrett, though privately he is very good-humoured about those who are. He has, I later found out, written other plays, and is an assiduous worker in that forcing house of revolution, the Reading Room of the British Museum. Even this information does not amount to very much. But it is more than I could discover on the opening night of *The Ruling Class*.

At that performance the play struck me like a revelation. Prudently I had expected nothing, and overwhelmingly I was given all: wit, pathos, exciting melodrama, brilliant satire, double-edged philosophy, horror, cynicism, and sentiment, all combined in a perfect unity in the theatrical world of Mr Barnes's extraordinary and idiosyncratic creation. Baudelaire, in discussing a nineteenth-century actor, says that the primary condition of a work of art, without which it cannot exist, is energy or life. *The Ruling Class* throbs with life and energy all through. Whatever else it is, it is not dead. From the unfortunate hanging of the thirteenth Earl, through the crucifixion of the fourteenth, the disputable miracle and the battle of rival gods, the episode of Jack the Ripper and the striptease of Marguerite Gautier, it flashes all along with life. Paradoxically, the culminating scene in the House of Lords, with their Lordships cobwebbed, somnolent, and seemingly on the point of dissolution, is almost the most alive of all.

At a time when a great deal of theatrical energy is

concentrated on forcing plays which no one wants to see on the sort of audiences that do not want to see any play at all it came as an immense delight to discover a drama which was not only thoughtful, but also exciting and amusing. For many years now incident and plot have been driven out of our theatre; Mr Barnes brings them back with both gusto and skill. The *coup de théâtre* by which the Lady of the Camellias is brought on to the stage, prompt on cue, is in itself a little marvel of stagecraft. It gives the kind of pleasure we have not had in the theatre for more than a decade. The moment one heard the fourteenth Earl's reply to the question what made him think that he was God, one knew that a new wit had been born in the theatre; and all through the play one has the delightful thrill, which one felt had gone from the theatre for ever, of actually feeling that one wants to know what is going to happen next.

The Ruling Class, then, is immensely entertaining, but it is admirably philosophic, too. It mounts a lively and vigorous attack, not only on the upper echelons of society, but also on all of us who rate cruelty higher than compassion, and consider violence more sane than peace. It brings us into contact with a mind of poise and depth and power; it combines rumbustiousness with delicacy, and in doing so is likely to prove a turning point in the drama of the second half of the twentieth century.

The Ruling Class was first presented at Nottingham Playhouse on 6 November 1968 and was subsequently transferred to the Piccadilly Theatre, London, on 26 February 1969. The play was presented by Gene Persson and Richard Pilbrow with the following cast:

13th Earl of Gurney	Peter Whitbread
Toastmaster	Robert Robertson
Daniel Tucker	Dudley Jones
Bishop Lampton	Ronald Magill
Sir Charles Gurney	David Dodimead
Dinsdale Gurney	Jonathan Cecil
Lady Claire Gurney	Irene Hamilton
Matthew Peake	Brown Derby
14th Earl of Gurney	Derek Godfrey
Dr Paul Herder	David Neal
Mrs Treadwell	Anne Heffernan
Mrs Piggot-Jones	Elizabeth Tyrrell
Grace Shelley	Vivienne Martin
McKyle	Ken Hutchinson
McKyle's Assistant	Terence Ratcliffe
Kelson Truscott, Q.C.	Laurence Harrington
Girl	Vicky Clayton
Detective Inspector Brockett	Peter Whitbread
Detective Sergeant Fraser	Robert Robinson
First Lord	C. Denier Warren
Second Lord	Brown Derby
Third Lord	Timothy Welsh

Directed by Stuart Burge
Designed by John Napier
Lighting by Robert Ornbo

Prologue

Three distinct raps. Curtain rises. Spot Down Stage Centre. The **13th Earl of Gurney** *stands in full evening dress and medals at a banqueting table. On it a silver coffee pot and a half-filled wine glass.*

A **Toastmaster** *in scarlet jacket and sash stands beside him; he has just rapped his gavel for silence.*

13th Earl of Gurney
    The aim of the Society of St George
    Is to keep green the memory of England.
    And what England means to her sons and daughters.
    I say the fabric folds, though families fly apart.
    Once the rulers of the greatest Empire
    The world has ever known,
    Ruled not by superior force or skill
    But by sheer presence. (*Raises glass in a toast.*)
    This teeming womb of privilege, this feudal state,
    Whose shores beat back the turbulent sea of foreign
        anarchy.
    This ancient fortress, still commanded by the noblest
    Of our royal blood; this ancient land of ritual.
    This precious stone set in a silver sea.

Toastmaster   My Lords, Ladies and Gentlemen. The toast is – England. This precious stone set in a silver sea.

13th Earl of Gurney and Voices   England. Set in a silver sea.

He drinks. The National Anthem plays over as his **Lordship** *comes rigidly to attention, whilst behind him, the* **Toastmaster** *exits, and the table is taken off. The Anthem ends.*

Lights up on his Lordship's bedroom. An ornate four-poster bed Stage Centre, and a wardrobe near a door Stage Left. Dressed in a traditional butler's uniform, **Daniel Tucker***, his Lordship's aged manservant, creakingly lays out his master's dressing-gown on the bed; whilst his* **Lordship** *undresses.*

Tucker How was your speech, sir?

13th Earl of Gurney (*dropping jacket absently on floor*) Went well, Tuck. Englishmen like to hear the truth about themselves.

Tucker *painfully picks up the jacket, whilst his **Lordship** sits on the edge of the bed.*

The Guv'nor loved this bed.

Tucker Wouldn't sleep anywhere else, sir.

13th Earl of Gurney Took it all over the world, Delhi, Cairo, Hong Kong. Devilish great man, the Guv'nor. Superb shot.

Tucker (*kneeling to take off his Lordship's shoes*) Did wonderful needlework too, sir. 'Petit-Point'.

13th Earl of Gurney (*undoing his trousers*) Tuck, I'm getting married again.

Tucker Yes, my Lord.

13th Earl of Gurney Miss Grace Shelley. Charles is right. Sake of the family. Gurney name. Been putting it off. Only Jack left.

Tucker This house used to be full of mischief . . . mischief . . .

13th Earl of Gurney Four young devils. Thought I was safe enough.

Tucker Master Paul would have been the 14th Earl.

13th Earl of Gurney District Officer at twenty-one. Dead at twenty-three. Beri-beri. Picked it up off some scruffy fuzzy-wuzzy in a dressing-gown, shouldn't wonder.

Tucker (*getting up slowly*) Young Richard used to play the xylophone.

13th Earl of Gurney   And young Raymond killed in Malaya. Not one of 'em buried in England. Never seen their graves.

Tucker (*crossing to the wardrobe with clothes*)   You could do that on your honeymoon, your Lordship.

13th Earl of Gurney   There's still Jack. (*They look at each other.*) It's all based on land, Tuck. Can't have those knaves from Whitehall moving in. So it's Miss Grace Shelley.

Tucker   Is she anyone, sir?

13th Earl of Gurney   No one. But Charles recommends her as good breeding stock. Family foals well. Sires mostly. There's always room at the top for brains, money or a good pair of titties.

Tucker   Miss Shelley seems well-endowed, sir.

Tucker *comes back with a flat leather case from the wardrobe. He opens it for his* **Lordship**, *who is deep in thought. Inside are four coils of rope, each eight feet long, make of silk, nylon, hemp and cord respectively.*

Your Lordship?

13th Earl of Gurney   What? Eh? (*Looking.*) Yes, I suppose so. Hard day. Need to relax.

Tucker   May I suggest silk tonight, sir?

13th Earl of Gurney   Good idea, Tuck. For St George.

Tucker *takes the silk rope and goes round to a pair of steps. He places them under a cross-beam at the corner of the bed and climbs up with the rope.*

13th Earl of Gurney   Ah, Tuck, there's no end to duty. Every day's like climbing a mountain. How did Tiberius do it at his age?

Tucker   Will-power, sir.

13th Earl of Gurney   The Law's been my life, Tuck. And the reason is the soul of the Law. A judge can't be unreasonable. So how can he be a lover, eh? Ours is a damned dry world, Tuck.

Tucker   A long life, and a grey one, your Lordship.

13th Earl of Gurney   The power of life and death. No need of other vices. If you've once put on the black cap, everything else tastes like wax fruit.

Tucker *ties the rope to a hook on the cross-beam. The rope hangs down in a noose. His* **Lordship** *peers up.*

Noose a bit high, Tuck. Pull the knot down half an inch. That's it.

Tucker *comes down.*

Tucker   Will that be all, your Lordship?

13th Earl of Gurney   Whisky and soda in about five minutes as usual. Oh, Tuck, tell Cook the trial ends tomorrow. She knows I don't like passing sentence on an empty stomach.

Tucker   Very good, my Lord.

Tucker *exits Stage Left. Humming to himself, his* **Lordship** *goes to the wardrobe and brings out a three-cornered cocked hat, a sword in a scabbard and a white tutu ballet skirt.*

13th Earl of Gurney   Nothing like a good English breakfast. Big meal of the day for the Guv'nor. Always sat at the head of the table. All the mail in front of him. He'd pass it out to the rest of us. Same with the newspapers. Always read *The Times* through first, in case there was anything too disturbing in it. Mother didn't know what the word 'Socialist' meant till she was past fifty. Remember standing at the foot of this bed here, telling him I wanted to be a painter. 'The Gurneys have never been slackers,' he said. 'Pulled their weight. Earned their privileges.' Great concession letting me study law. Not the Gurney tradition.

Always the Army. (*He puts the tutu on, delicately flouncing it out.*)
The smell of cordite. The clash of steel. Feet, feet, feet, the
boys are marching! A little more grape-shot Captain Bragg!
Give 'em the cold steel, boys.' (*He straps the sword to his side
and puts on the three-cornered hat.*)

*Now dressed in three-cornered hat, ballet skirt, long underwear and
sword, the* **13th Earl of Gurney** *curtseys and moves towards the
steps, trembling slightly in anticipation.*

Close. I can feel her hot breath. Wonderful. One slip. The
worms have the best of it. They dine off the tenderest joints.
Juicy breasts, white thighs, red hair colour of rust . . . the
worms have the best of it. (*He climbs up the steps, stands under
the noose and comes to attention.*) It is a far, far better thing I do
now, than I have ever done. (*He slips the noose over his head,
trembling.*) No, Sir. No bandage. Die my dear doctor? That's
the last thing I shall do. Is that you, my love? Now, come
darling . . . to me . . . ha!

*Stepping off the top of the steps, he dangles for a few seconds and begins
to twitch and jump. He puts his feet back on the top of the steps.
Gasping, he loosens the noose.*

Touched him, saw her, towers of death and silence, angels
of fire and ice. Saw Alexander covered with honey and
beeswax in his tomb and felt the flowers growing over me. A
man must have his visions. How else could an English judge
and peer of the realm take moonlight trips to Marrakesh
and Ponders End? See six vestal virgins smoking cigars?
Moses in bedroom slippers? Naked bosoms floating past
Formosa? Desperate diseases need desperate remedies.
(*Glancing towards the door.*) Just time for a quick one. (*Places
noose over his head again.*) Be of good cheer, Master Ridley, and
play the man. There's plenty of time to win this game, and
thrash the Spaniards too. (*Draws his sword.*) Form squares
men! Smash the Mahdi, and Binnie Barnes!

*With a lustful gurgle he steps off. But this time he knocks over the steps.
Dangling helpless for a second he drops the sword and tries to tear the
noose free, gesturing frantically. Every muscle begins to tremble. His*

legs jack-knife up to his stomach; they jack-knife again and again with increasing speed and violence. The spasms reach a climax, then stop suddenly. The body goes limp, and sways gently at the end of the rope. A discreet knock on door Stage Left.

Tucker (*voice off*)   Your Lordship? Are you ready?

The door opens slightly. **Tucker** *shuffles in carrying a tray with whisky and soda. He sees his* **Lordship**.

Bleeding bloody hell!

Blackout.

Curtain.

Act One

Scene One

A great church organ thunders out 'The Dead March from Saul'.

The curtain parts enough to reveal the imposing figure of **Bishop Bertram Lampton**, *magnificently dressed in red cope, surplice, embroidered stole and mitre.* **Four Pall Bearers** *in top hats and morning-coats slowly cross Down Stage, bearing a coffin, draped with the Gurney banner.*

Bishop Lampton (*chanting*)   I am the Resurrection and the Life, saith the Lord; he that believeth in me though he were dead, yet shall he live: and whosoever liveth and believeth in me shall never die.

Gilead is mine, and Manasses is mine: Ephraim also is the strength of my head; Judah is my lawgiver.

Moab is my washpot; over Edom will I cast out my shoe: Philistria, triumph thou because of me.

Who will lead me on to the strong city: who will bring me into Edom?

The **Pall Bearers** *exit Right. The curtain opens behind the* **Bishop** *to show his* **Lordship**'s *relatives dressed in black, standing grouped in the drawing-room of the Gurney country house.*

Bishop Lampton *and* **Relatives** (*singing*)   'All things bright and beautiful. All creatures great and small. All things wise and wonderful, the Lord God made them all. The rich man in his castle, the poor man at his gate. God made them high and lowly, and ordered their estate . . .'

As they sing **Bishop Lampton** *disrobes, handing his cope, surplice and mitre to* **Tucker**. *The* **Bishop** *has shrunk to a small, bald-headed, asthmatic old man in dog-collar and gaiters. As the last note of the hymn dies away and* **Tucker** *staggers off Wings Left with the robes, he smooths down his non-existent hair and waddles Up Stage to join the others.*

Scene Two

The large drawing-room of Gurney Manor. It is seventeenth century, except for the high double french-windows, now heavily curtained, Stage Right. Running the length of the back wall Up Stage is a narrow gallery: small stairways, Up Stage Left and Right, lead up to it. On the wall above the gallery are portraits of past Earls. Up Stage Centre, below the gallery, is a wide double-doorway leading to the hall. Just above it the Gurney crest. Door, Down Stage Left, and alongside, a bell-rope. Sofa and chairs Centre Stage. Desk, chair and coffee table adjacent to the windows.

Lady Claire Gurney *is on the sofa: long black cigarette holder, long black velvet gloves.* **Sir Charles Gurney** *stands ramrod stiff, his legs slightly apart, whilst* **Dinsdale Gurney** *lounges on the arm of the sofa, elegantly picking his nose. The asthmatic* **Bishop Lampton** *joins them.*

Sir Charles   Excellent service, Bertie. Created exactly the right impression.

Dinsdale   Damned if I could understand a word of it.

Bishop Lampton   Hardly expected you to, young man. It was a Church service. A service, Charles, I might add, I could not have conducted for someone who may have lain violent hands upon himself. A disturbing rumour has reached my ears. Did Ralph commit suicide?

Sir Charles   Suicide? Tucker found Ralph hanging in the bedroom dressed in a cocked hat, underpants and a ballet skirt. Does that *sound* like suicide?

Dinsdale   I'm sure if Uncle Ralph had wanted to do anything foolish he'd have done it decently. Bullet through the head, always the Gurney way.

Sir Charles   No idea how these malicious rumours get started. The Coroner's verdict is clear enough. Accident brought on by the strain of overwork.

Bishop Lampton (*sitting*)   Had to be sure. He's buried in consecrated ground.

Dinsdale   Still, you know, I must say it's odd, Uncle Ralph found hanging around like that in a ballet skirt.

Claire   Charles didn't you say Ralph always was rather artistic?

Sir Charles   He was wilful, stubborn, and this time he went too far. But he was my brother – well, half-brother. I won't have you calling him *artistic*.

Bishop Lampton   Cocked hat! Why was he wearing a cocked hat?

Sir Charles   Trying it on for size obviously. I told him not to stay a widower. The Guv'nor didn't. Understood his duty to the family. Had to start breeding again. Not pleasant, I grant you, for a man of Ralph's age. But it was something he had to get on top of.

Bishop Lampton   Underpants? Why was he in his underpants?

Sir Charles   Why not? Going to bed wasn't he? Thought our troubles were over when he took a fancy to young Grace Shelley. That would have solved everything.

Claire   Yes, wouldn't it just.

Dinsdale   Frankly, I don't understand all the plother. Uncle Ralph has an heir – Jack, the 14th Earl of Gurney.

Sir Charles   Yes . . . it's going to be awkward. Damned awkward.

Claire   Ralph was aware of the situation. I'm sure he's made proper arrangements. A matter of finding out who he's appointed guardian of the estate.

Bishop Lampton   But what was he doing in a *ballet skirt*? Answer me that!

Tucker *enters Up Stage Centre.*

Tucker   Mr Matthew Peake to see you, Sir Charles.

Sir Charles   Right. Show him in.

Tucker *steps aside, and* **Matthew Peake**, *solicitor, enters and gives him his trilby. He is a dessicated, deferential man with round shoulders, winged collar and a briefcase.*

Sir Charles   I believe you know everyone here, Peake.

Peake   I have had that honour, Sir Charles.

Sir Charles   All right, Tucker, that'll be all. We're not to be disturbed.

Peake   Sir Charles, might I suggest Tucker stays. (*Taps briefcase significantly.*)

Sir Charles   What? Oh quite. Well, Tucker, seems you're going to hear something to your advantage.

Tucker   Yes, sir.

He stands discreetly in the background, holding **Peake**'s *trilby.*

Peake   May I take this opportunity to express my condolences.

Claire   Tucker, *do* sit down.

Tucker   Thank you, madam.

He sits on the edge of a chair, whilst **Peake** *crosses to the desk, and takes out some legal documents.*

Peake   Hmmm, may I say, Sir Charles, how refreshing it is to meet with such restraint. Usually I'm afraid these occasions are so . . . emotional.

Sir Charles   Do get on with it.

Peake   But, Sir Charles, shouldn't we wait? His Lordship's heir . . .

Sir Charles   Jack's been notified. Wasn't able to get away for the funeral. Not likely to come now.

Peake   Very well, Sir Charles. I'll inform him later.

All eyes now on **Peake** *as he puts on horn-rimmed spectacles, and reads in a dry monotone.*

(*Reading.*) 'I, Ralph, Douglas, Christopher, Alexander, Gurney, of Gurney House in the county of Bedfordshire, hereby revoke all former Wills and Codicils and declare this to be my last Will. I appoint Mr Matthew Peake of 17 Brownlow Gardens, Bedfordshire, to be the sole executor of this my Will. I give and bequeath unto my manservant, Daniel Tucker, the sum of twenty thousand pounds free of duty.'

Murmurs of surprise from the listeners. But no reaction from **Tucker** *himself.*

There follow a number of bequests to various charities, which his Lordship was interested in. I'll run through them briefly. 'I bequeath the sum of five thousand pounds to the Tailwavers Registered National Charity. Three thousand pounds to the Bankers Beneficent Society Ltd.' . . .

Tucker   Yippee! (*Shoots off the chair.*) *Twenty thousand! Twenty thousand smackers! Yawee!*

Jumping clumsily into the air, and clicking his heels together, he flicks **Peake**'*s trilby on to his head and gleefully capers forward.* (*Singing in a croak.*) 'I'm Gilbert the Filbert the Knut with a "K". (*Gives gouty high kick.*) The pride of Piccadilly, the blasé roué. Oh Hades! The Ladies (*Ogles* **Claire**.) who leave their wooden huts, For Gilbert the Filbert, the Colonel of the Knuts.' Yah!

Flinging open the door Up Stage he leaps raggedly out, arms held high. There is a crash off as he hits something followed by a cackle of laughter. Silence in the room.

Dinsdale   Tucker seems het up.

Bishop Lampton   'So are the ways of everyone that is greedy of gain.' What about the Zambesi Mission, Peake? And the Overseas Bishoprics Fund?

Sir Charles   Never mind that, Bertie. What about the estate?

Peake (*continues reading*)   'I devise and bequeath all the remainder of my estate both real and personal whatsoever and wheresoever to which I might be entitled or over which I have any disposing at the time of my death, to my beloved son, Jack, Arnold, Alexander, Tancred, Gurney, the 14th Earl of Gurney, for his own use absolutely.'

Sir Charles (*repeating slowly*)   'For his own use absolutely.' But who's been appointed legal guardian?

Peake   No one.

Bishop Lampton   'By the rivers of Babylon there we sat down, yea, we wept when we remembered Zion.'

Sir Charles   You mean Jack is free to run the estate . . . and everything . . . ?

Claire   Think of Jack in the Royal Enclosure.

Bishop Lampton   Jack in the *Athenæum*.

Sir Charles   It's obvious Ralph has let his personal feelings come before his duty to his family. We'll have to fight. Awkward. Scandal an'all. But we've no choice.

Peake (*diffidently reading*)   'If this my Will is contested, the whole of my estate, both real and personal, is bequeathed to the charities named herewith: The Earl Haig Fund, Lord Wharton's . . .

The rest is drowned out as all start shouting angrily. They are too busy yelling to notice **Tucker** *appear in the doorway Up Stage Centre smoking a cigar. He disappears for a second, reappearing immediately carrying a large hall vase. Holding it up, he deliberately drops it on the floor. It smashes with a loud crash. The shouting stops. They all turn in astonishment.* **Tucker** *takes the cigar out of his mouth and makes the announcement in his usual calm, respectful tone.*

Tucker   Ladies and gentlemen. The Queen's Right Trusty and Well Beloved Cousin – Jack, Arnold, Alexander, Tancred, Gurney, the 14th Earl of Gurney.

Surprised gasps. **Tucker** *steps to one side. The sound of approaching footsteps. All eyes on the door.* **Bishop Lampton***'s asthma becomes painfully pronounced as the tension mounts. His breathing turns into a thin, high-pitched screech as the new* **Earl of Gurney** *finally appears in the doorway: A Franciscan monk of the Capuchi Order. His habit is a coarse, brown tunic, cord, girdle, pointed cowl, bare feet in sandals. Tall and ascetic, the* **Earl** *has a sensitive face, fair beard and a magnetic personality.*

Earl of Gurney   Hello . . . (*Hands clasped in his large sleeves, he crosses Down Stage.*) I'm sorry I wasn't here before but I only received the news yesterday. I'm afraid our little community is somewhat cut off. I hope you'll forgive me. I know he would. My sorrow isn't less, or the pain. I've just been to his grave. Thank you, Uncle Charles, for making all the arrangements.

Sir Charles *looks uncomfortable.*

Aunt Claire, it's been so long. You haven't changed.

Claire   Nor you.

Earl of Gurney   You must be Dinsdale?

Dinsdale   Er – yes, I must. How do you do, sir.

Earl of Gurney (*turning to* **Bishop Lampton**)   Are you still angry with me, Bishop?

But speechless with asthma, **Bishop Lampton** *can only wave him away feebly.*

First let me put your minds at rest. The choice has been made. I've come back to take my proper place in the world. The monastic ideal isn't easy. I've had many broken nights. But I've come back refreshed. (*He smiles.*) Though hardly equipped for society. I shall need your help, Uncle Charles.

We're all one family. Let's wash away the old sores. If the Bishop doesn't mind. I think we should pray.

Sir Charles   Pray?

Earl of Gurney   For love and understanding. Surely you pray for love and understanding?

Claire (*looking at* **Sir Charles**)   Every night. Without success.

Peake *moves silently towards the door.*

Earl of Gurney   You too, Mr Peake.

Peake   I'm Methodist.

Earl of Gurney   I'm sure you're still a Christian. (*Gestures gently.*) Come, for me.

Peake   Yes, my lord.

Embarrassed, he begins awkwardly to kneel. **Claire** *smiles slightly and joins* **Peake** *and* **Tucker** *on her knees.* **Sir Charles** *is about to protest but then thinks better of it. Clenching his jaw he follows pulling* **Dinsdale** *down with him.* **Bishop Lampton** *fights off a violent asthma attack with an inhaler whilst the others kneel round the* **Earl**. *The lights start to dim down to a Spot on them as he holds out his hand in blessing.*

Earl of Gurney   A prayer should rise up like incense. For you are acknowledging the power and goodness of God. It's an act of faith and a union. A prayer is not a request, but an appeal. To pray means to ask, to beg, to plead. A prayer is a message to Heaven. You are talking directly to God . . . express your desires freely, don't be afraid, I know them already. (*They all look up at him in horror.*) For I am the Creator and ruler of the Universe, Khoda, the One Supreme Being and Infinite Personal Being, Yaweh, Shangri-Ti and El, the First Immovable Mover, Yea, I am the Absolute Unknowable Righteous Eternal, the Lord of Hosts, the King of Kings, Lord of Lords, the Father, Son and Holy Ghost, the one True God of Love, the Naz!

A strangled cry from **Bishop Lampton** *as he slips off his chair and thuds unconscious on to the floor in the darkness.*

Scene Three

A plain white backing lowered immediately Down Stage Centre into the spot, cutting the **Earl of Gurney** *from view.* **Sir Charles** *and* **Dr Paul Herder**, *a thin man with a cold manner, enter from Wings Left and stand in front of it.*

Dr Herder   His Lordship is a paranoid-schizophrenic.

Sir Charles   But he's a *Gurney*.

Dr Herder   Then he's a paranoid-schizophrenic-Gurney who believes he's God.

Sir Charles   But we've always been Church of England.

Dr Herder   In paranoid-schizophrenia the patient's relationship with reality is disturbed. His idea of the world we live in is determined solely by his feelings. What he feels is – *is*.

Sir Charles   If my nephew's bonkers, why the blazes did you let him out?

Dr Herder   He's a voluntary patient in a private clinic, free to leave when he chooses. His father insisted on no official certification. If you want him permanently detained here, bring him before the Board of Control or get the Master in Lunacy to sign an order.

Sir Charles   Er – later, when we've got a few things settled.

Dr Herder   From the medical point of view a plunge into the waking world won't do the Earl any harm.

Sir Charles   Won't do him any harm. What about the rest of us?

Dr Herder He's not dangerous. Provided he's left relatively secluded it shouldn't be too difficult. It'll be a very interesting experiment. A harsh dose of reality can sometimes help towards a cure.

Sir Charles Cure! You've had him here for seven years already, and look at him. What've you been doing?

Dr Herder Exercising patience and understanding. Something he'll need from his family.

Sir Charles (*testily*) Yes, yes, but why haven't you used the knife?

Dr Herder Because lobotomy is irrelevant and dangerous in this case. He showed classic schizophrenic symptoms by withdrawing from his environment. Then, of course, he never forgot being brutally rejected by his mother and father at the age of eleven. They sent him away, alone, into a primitive community of licensed bullies and pederasts.

Sir Charles You mean he went to Public School.

Dr Herder *nods and they begin to walk slowly to the Wings Left, Spot follows them, whilst another Spot remains on the white backing, which is taken up to show the* **Earl of Gurney** *standing in exactly the same place as before, Centre Stage.*

Dr Herder You must realise the Earl's strange position. It's what makes him such an interesting case. Remember, he's suffering from delusions of *grandeur*. In reality he's an Earl, an English aristocrat, a peer of the realm, a member of the ruling class. Naturally, he's come to believe there's only one person grander than that – the Lord God Almighty Himself.

Sir Charles (*suspiciously*) Are you English?

Dr Herder No.

Sir Charles Ahhh . . .

They exit.

Scene Four

Spot on the **Earl**, *Stage Centre, remains.*

Earl of Gurney (*looking after them*)   Q.E.D. If I saw a man eating grass I'd say he was hungry. They'd have him certified. They claim snow is only percipitation and not candied dew, and the single heart-beat only the contraction and dilation of the central organ of the vascular system. *Whroom.* (*He makes a circular motion with his right hand.*) I'm always thinking so fast. Could a rooster forget he was a rooster and lay an egg? *Whroom.* Space and time only exist within the walls of my brain. What I'm trying to say is, if the words sound queer or funny to your ear, a little bit jumbled and jivy, sing mares eat oats and does eat oats and little lambs eat ivy. Ivy? Who's Ivy? . . . I . . .

Lights come up to show **Claire** *listening attentively on sofa.*

I am that Lord Jesus come again in my body to save the sick, the troubled, the ignorant. I am He that liveth and behold I am alive for everyone. (*Opens his arms mimicking American nightclub entertainer Ted Lewis.*) Is everybody happy? Now hear this, I come to proclaim the new Dispensation. The Gospel Dispensation promised only salvation for the soul, my new Dispensation of Love gives it to the *body* as well. J. Christ Mark I suffered to redeem the spirit and left the body separated from God, so Satan found a place in man, and formed in him a false consciousness, a false love, a love of self. EXPLODE only FEEL, LOVE, and sin no more. Most everything you see, touch and FEEL glorifies my love. (*Mimes putting on a hat.*) The top hat is my mitre and the walking stick my rod. (*Twirls imaginary stick.*) I'm sorry. I really must apologise. Once I get started I find it damnable difficult to stop. They diagnose it as arbitrary discharge from the speech centre. Diarrhoea of the mouth. Nobody else gets much of a look-in.

Claire   It's fascinating.

Earl of Gurney   If there's anything you'd like me to explain, fire away.

Claire   How do you know you're . . . God?

Earl of Gurney   Simple. When I pray to Him I find I'm talking to myself.

Claire   I see. How did it happen? How did you come to be in this state . . . of grace?

Earl of Gurney   Like every prophet I saw visions, heard voices. I ran but the voices of St Francis, Socrates, General Gordon, and Tim O'Leary the Jewish Buddha all told me I was God. Pretty reliable witnesses – agreed? It was Sunday August 25th at 3.32 standard British Summer Time. I heard with my outward ear a terrible thunder clap and I saw a great body of light like the light from the sun, and red as fire, in the form of a drum. I clapped my hands and cried Amen! Hallelujah! Hallelujah! Amen! I cried out, Lord what will you do? But the light vanished . . . a blackness of darkness until a great brush dipped in light swept across the sky. And I saw the distinction, diversity, variety, all clearly rolled up into the unity of Universal Love.

Claire   Where did all this happen?

Earl of Gurney   East Acton. Outside the public urinal.

Claire   What does it feel like to be God?

Earl of Gurney   Like a river flowing over everything. I pick up a newspaper and I'm everywhere, conducting a Summit Conference, dying of hunger in a Peruvian gutter, accepting the Nobel Prize for Literature, raping a nun in Sumatra.

Claire   You don't look any different.

Earl of Gurney (*starts taking off his monk's habit*)   When a parasite called the Sacculina attacks the common shore crab, it bores a tiny hole through the crab's protective outer shell. Once in the body it spreads like a root devouring the tissues and turning the flesh to pulp. It's no longer crab's flesh but Sacculina. The crab is transformed, even its sex changes. The outer shell remains unaltered, but inside is a new creature. (*He is dressed underneath in a loose-fitting white tropical suit and Eton tie: his hair cascades over his shoulder.*) I was devoured by the Divine Sacculina, it hollowed me out. Under this protective shell I'm God-filled.

Tucker *stands in the doorway Up Stage Centre.* **Sir Charles**, *with a briefcase under his arm, comes in behind him.*

Tucker   Your lordship, Sir . . .

As **Sir Charles** *impatiently brushes past,* **Tucker** *grabs the bottom of his jacket and jerks him back.*

Sir Charles   What in . . . ?

Tucker   I *haven't* finished yet, Sir Charles. (*Continuing unruffled.*) Your lordship, Sir Charles Gurney.

Tucker *steps aside, lets the furious* **Sir Charles** *into the room, then exits.*

Sir Charles   Insolent clown!

Tucker (*reappearing*)   I *heard* that, sir.

He disappears again.

Sir Charles   The world's gone mad. He'll have to go.

Claire   Hadn't we better wait till things get sorted out? Someone new might not understand the situation.

Sir Charles (*opening his briefcase on desk*)   How come he's still here anyway, with twenty thousand in the bank? Why's he hanging on?

Earl of Gurney   Out of love. He knows he's needed.

Sir Charles (*taking out a document*)   Love? Tucker? Rot. Now, m'boy, certain matters concerning the estate need clearing up. Nothing important. Just needs your signature. Gives me power to handle odd things.

Earl of Gurney   Of course, Uncle. (*Crosses to him, putting on glasses.*)

Sir Charles (*hastily*)   You don't have to read it. Just take my word.

Earl of Gurney   I take your word. I put on my glasses because I feel cold. Need one of Dr Jaeger's Sanitary Woollens to keep my soul-duft in. Where do I sign?

Sir Charles   Just there.

*The **Earl** signs with a flourish. **Sir Charles** glances triumphantly at **Claire**.*

Excellent. Excellent. Easily done, eh? (*Reads*) 'I the undersigned . . . Mycroft *Holmes*? Who's Mycroft Holmes?

Tucker (*entering carrying robes and coronet*)   Brother of Sherlock Holmes, illiterate oaf!

Sir Charles   But your name's Jack!

Earl of Gurney   Never call me that! (*Strokes forehead.*) Jack's a word I reject absolutely. It's a word I put into my galvanised pressure-cooker, whrr . . .

Claire   Your pressure-cooker?

Earl of Gurney   I don't mince words. I prefer them parboiled fried or scrambled. Jack's dead! It's my old shell-name – a sham name.

Claire   All right, what should we call you then?

Earl of Gurney   Any of the nine billion names of God. My lordship will do, or J.C., Eric, Bert, Barney Entwistle. I don't need to cling to one name. I know exactly who I am.

Tucker (*indicating robes*)   You asked for these, my Lord.

Earl of Gurney   Burn 'em, Mr Tucker. Burn 'em.

Sir Charles   What? Great Scott, man, these are your coronation robes! Marks of our elevation.

Tucker   Lot of tradition here, your lordship.

Earl of Gurney   The axe must be laid to the root. Pomp and riches, pride and property will have to be lopped off. All men are brothers. Love makes all equal. The mighty must bow down before the pricks of the louse-ridden rogues. (*Suddenly warmly embraces* **Sir Charles**.) I love you dearly, Uncle Charles. (*Gestures to robes.*) Keep them if you feel so lost. But soon you will abandon everything to follow me. Come, Mr Tucker, join me in a constitutional before lunch.

Tucker *dumps the robes and they move to french-windows Stage Right.*

Enjoy yourself whilst I'm gone. Relax. Have sex.

He exits with **Tucker**. **Claire** *and* **Sir Charles** *look after him.*

Sir Charles   My God!

Earl of Gurney (*popping his head back*)   Yes?

Claire   No, no. Nothing.

The **Earl** *exits again.*

Well, you heard what he said, Charles.

Sir Charles (*trembling with rage*)   I did . . . bowing before rogues . . . destroying property . . . all men equal . . . (*Pointing after* **Earl**.) My God, Claire, he's not only *mad*, he's *Bolshie!*

Lights down.

Scene Five

Spot up immediately on a metal sun lowered from Flies, Down Stage Centre, Footlights up as **Tucker** *and the* **Earl of Gurney** *enter Wings Right.*

Earl of Gurney   Just smell that soul-duft from the lawns and hedgerows. What a beautiful day I've made. Look –

Soft Thistle and Nigella. (*Crouches down.*) My sweet poetics. (*Ear to imaginary flower.*) What? No water in days? I can't be expected to think of everything. I'll see to it. Remember the Sunday picnics here, Mr Tucker, in my old shell-days? The world was all top hats and white lace.

Tucker (*taking out a hip-flask*)   And the best heavy silverware. A snort, your lordship?

Earl of Gurney   Not during Yom Kippur.

Tucker   You mind if I partake?

Earl of Gurney   Go ahead. I'm God-intoxicated. If only I knew then who I was now. (*Stretching out hand.*) Ah, Mr Grasshopper, of course I bless you, my chirrup, along with General de Gaulle.

Tucker (*drinking*)   First chance I've had of speaking to you alone, your lordship. Be on guard, sir.

Earl of Gurney (*straightening up*)   Mr Tucker, I'm puzzled.

Tucker   The family, sir. I've seen 'em at work afore. They got the power and they made the rules. They're back there plotting against you like mad.

Earl of Gurney   Love cannot doubt nor faith the mustard seed, no more plotting, Mr Tucker, please. It's negativism. Plotting's a word I put into my pressure-cooker, whrr. It's gone. Feeling persecuted's one of the signs of paranoid schizophrenia. Many poor wretches in Dr Herder's Dancing Academy suffered from same. But I am being watched they said. Everybody is against me they cried. (*Shakes himself vigorously.*) You've set up profound negative disturbances with your Kremlin plots, Mr Tucker, I'm going in. (*Turns abruptly and walks Upstage Centre.*) Resist it, Mr Tucker, that way madness lies.

He disappears into the darkness. **Tucker** *looks after him, swaying slightly.*

Tucker   That's the thanks you get. He's the same as all the rest, what he doesn't want to be so just *isn't* so. Tried to help, you stupid old fool. No skin off my nose. My twenty thousand's safe – and I deserve every last penny of it, and more, more, more! Why should I worry – villa in the South of France, and a bit o' golden crumpet every day, breast and buttocks done to a turn. (*He cackles.*) Just pack a tooth-brush and a French letter and you're away Daniel Tucker. What's keeping you then, Dan? You've got the scratch. (*Drinks, gloomily.*) Fear. Be honest now, Daniel. Fear and habit. You get into the habit of serving. Born a servant, see, son of a servant. Family of servants. From a nation of servants. Very first thing an Englishman does, straight from his mother's womb is touch his forelock. That's how they can tell the wrinkled little bastard's English. *Me*, this tired old creeping servant, I'm the real England, not beef-eating Johnny Bullshit. I know my history. Masters and servants, that's the way of it. Didn't think I was like that, eh? A lot yer don't know about Daniel Tucker. Just old faithful Tucker. Give doggy boney. Just 'ere for comic relief. Know who I really am? (*Beckons confidentially.*) Alexei Kronstadt. Number 243. Anarchist – Trotskyist – Communist – Revolutionary. I'm a cell! All these years I've been working for the Revolution, spitting in the hot soup, peeing on the Wedgwood dinner plates. (*Coming to attention and singing.*) 'Then raise the scarlet standard high! Within its shade we'll live or die; Tho' cowards flinch and traitors sneer, We'll keep the red flag flying here.'

Spot out. He exits.

Scene Six

Lights up to show **Earl of Gurney** *crucified on a wooden cross, leaning against the far wall to the right of the centre doorway. The cross-beam is above the gallery.* **Tucker** *is still heard singing faintly off. Lights up to show* **Claire**, *by the sofa, smoking nervously and staring up at the* **Earl** *on the cross.*

Claire   J.C.? . . . Bert? . . . my lord? . . . Barney Entwistle?

Still no response from the **Earl**. **Tucker** *comes in Up Stage, pushing a tea-trolley. He crosses to* **Claire**, *wincing at every sound, obviously suffering from a bad hangover.*

Tucker   Tea, madam?

Claire   Oh, yes. What was that you were singing just now, Tucker?

Tucker   An old German hymn, madam – Tannenbaum. Lemon or milk, madam?

Claire   Lemon.

He pours shakily as a flustered **Dinsdale** *enters Up Stage.*

Dinsdale   I say, where's the Guv'nor? Is that tea? Just the job, Tucker.

Claire   Your father's in town. Another meeting with Sir Humphrey Spens trying to find a way round this mess.

Dinsdale   When's he back?

Claire   Any time now if he doesn't drop in on his mistress first.

Dinsdale *shoots a sidelong glance at* **Tucker**, *who is too busy pouring and shuddering with nausea, to react.*

Dinsdale   Ah, hmm. Hope he gets things settled soon. It's already getting awkward. They're used to us Gurneys being in everything. Mrs Piggot-Jones and Mrs Treadwell and the other old girls thought it'd be a splendid idea for the new Earl to open the Fête, Sunday week.

Claire   Naturally you told them it was impossible.

Tucker   Milk or lemon, sir?

Dinsdale   Lemon, Tucker. But dammit I am prospective Parliamentary candidate for the division. Had to watch my step with 'em. Couldn't say he was 'non-compos'.

Claire   If you're going to be a successful Conservative politician, you'll have to learn to make convincing excuses.

Dinsdale   Where is he now?

Tucker *hands him his tea.*

Claire (*gesturing behind him*)   Up there.

Dinsdale (*turning*)   Oh . . . Ah!

He gives an involuntary cry of fright at his first sight of the **Earl** *on the cross and spills some tea.*

Tucker   Now look what you've done. (*Wipes carpet with foot.*) Never get tea-stains out. Show some consideration.

Dinsdale   Is it Yogi or something?

Tucker *has walked Up Stage to the cross.*

Tucker   Tea, my lord?

Claire   It's no good, Tucker, I've tried. He's asleep; dead to the world.

Earl of Gurney   His Body sleeps but his Divinity is always watching. Yes, Mr Tucker. Milk please. Any toasted muffins?

Tucker   Yes, sir. Shall I bring them up?

Earl of Gurney   No thanks. I'll be right down.

The **Earl** *twists round, and clambers off the cross.*

Dinsdale   It's Yogi, isn't it? A form of Yogi?

Claire   Don't give me another headache, Dinsdale.

Earl of Gurney (*puts his hands together, Indian style*) Welcome, Dinsdale.

Dinsdale   Oh, ah, yes. How are you?

Earl of Gurney   Sometimes my spirit sinks below the high watermark in Palestine, but I'm adjusting gradually.

Tucker *uncovers a dish of muffins and sways slightly.*

Mr Tucker, you look ill. Bed, Mr Tucker. Right now.

Tucker   Thank you, my lord.

Earl of Gurney   Take a cup of Dr Langley's Root and Herb Bitters. It acts directly on the bowels and blood, eradicates all liver disorders, dyspepsia, dizziness, heartburn . . .

Tucker (*exiting*)   Yes, sir.

Earl of Gurney (*calling*)   . . . foul stomach and *piles*.

Tucker *is heard muttering agreement off.*

For what I am about to receive may I make myself truly thankful. (*Eats muffins.*) I must soon be moving on. Sail to Wigan, Wrexham, Port Said and Crewe.

Claire *and* **Dinsdale** *exchange uneasy glances.*

First I shall command the Pope to consecrate a planeload of light-weight contraceptives for the priest-ridden Irish. (*Mimes blessing.*) 'Pax et benedíctio . . . adjutorium nostrum. Dóminus vobíscum.' (*Chanting.*) Arise, shine for my light is come and the glory of the Lord is risen upon thee . . . (*Singing with actions.*) 'Here is the Drag, See how it goes; Down on the heels; Up on the toes. That's the way to the Varsity Drag.' (*He dances round in exuberant ragtime.*) 'Hotter than hot, Newer than new! Meaner than mean, Bluer than blue. Gets as much applause as waving the flag!'

Tucker *appears in doorway Up Stage Centre with two solid, middle-aged* **Women** *in grotesque hats.* **Claire** *glares angrily at a horrified* **Dinsdale**.

Tucker   Mrs Piggot-Jones – Mrs Treadwell.

Earl of Gurney (*singing at newcomers*)   . . . 'You can pass many a class whether you're dumb or wise. If you all answer the call, when your professor cries . . .'

Suddenly, despite themselves, **Mrs Piggot-Jones**, **Mrs Treadwell** *and* **Tucker** *sweep irresistibly Down Stage with the* **Earl**, *in an all-singing, all-dancing chorus line.*

Earl of Gurney, **Two Women** and **Tucker** (*singing*) 'Everybody down on the heels, up on the toes, stay after school, learn how it goes: Everybody do the Varsity . . . Everybody do the Varsity . . . Everybody do the Varsity Drag!'

They finish in line Down Stage, arms outstretched to the audience, puzzled.

Earl of Gurney (*without pause*)   Welcome, ladies. I'm the new Lord.

Mrs Treadwell, *dumpy woman in straw hat decorated with wax fruit, gives a dazed smile, whilst the bony* **Mrs Piggot-Jones**, *in tweeds and trilby, lets out a bewildered grunt. Clutching his head,* **Tucker** *weaves his way out.*

You know Lady Claire and my cousin Dinsdale?

Dinsdale   This is a surprise. Delightful though, delightful.

Mrs Treadwell (*recovering her natural obsequiousness*)   Dear Mr Dinsdale, do forgive us, but we've come to try and persuade his lordship to open our little Church Fête. Do say yes, my lord.

Earl of Gurney   I always say yes, yes, whatever the question.

Mrs Treadwell (*delighted*)   Your lordship.

Mrs Piggot-Jones   Splendid!

Claire   Now ladies, if you'll excuse us, we have a lot to do.

Earl of Gurney   Stay for tea. (*To* **Mrs Treadwell**.) You be mother.

Gurgles of delight from the two women. Whilst **Mrs Treadwell** *pours,* **Dinsdale** *looks uncertain, and* **Claire** *watches with increasing tension.*

Claire (*low*)   Dinsdale, see if your father's come back.

Dinsdale *hurries out.*

Earl of Gurney   Now ladies, tell me my part in this gala opening. Do I charm bracelets, swing lead, break wind, pass water?

Mrs Treadwell   No, you make a speech.

Earl of Gurney   On what text, Mother Superior?

Mrs Piggot-Jones   We leave that to the speaker. It can be any topic of general interest. Hanging. Immigration, the Stranglehold of the Unions. Anything . . .

Mrs Treadwell   So long as it isn't political.

Earl of Gurney   Nat-ur-ally.

Mrs Piggot-Jones   As the fête *is* in aid of the British Legion I've always felt the speeches should be something about Britain and our way of life.

Earl of Gurney (*off-handed*)   Britain is an imaginary island off the continent of Europe, covering 93,982 square miles, with a population of over 52 million, lying in a westerly wind belt. A fly-blown speck in the North Sea, a country of cosmic unimportance in my sight. (*Sadly at them.*) You can't kick the natives in the back streets of Calcutta any more.

Mrs Treadwell (*giggling*)   He's joking again. Aren't you, my lord?

Mrs Piggot-Jones   I am not laughing, Pamela. I'm afraid we can't stay here, Lady Claire.

Claire   Then for Christ's sake, go!

Earl of Gurney   Please don't go for my sake. (*Casually takes a bunch of imitation wax grapes from* **Mrs Treadwell**'*s hat and starts eating them.*) Mmm, delicious. Home-grown?

Mrs Treadwell   No, I bought them, I mean . . .

Earl of Gurney   I've decided to begin my second ministry at your gathering. Last time I preached the Word in Holy Galilee I spoke in parables. MISTAKE. Now I must speak plain. (*Crosses hands on chest.*) God is love.

Mrs Treadwell (*frightened*)   Love?

Earl of Gurney   God is love as water is wet as jade is green as bread is life so God is love.

Mrs Treadwell *and* **Mrs Piggot-Jones** *begin to back towards the door. Up Stage Centre.* **Dinsdale** *is heard calling off beyond the french-windows.*

Earl of Gurney (*advancing after them*)   Mrs Pamela Treadwell, can you love? Can your blood bubble, flesh melt, thighs twitch, heart burst for love?

Mrs Treadwell   Your Lordship, I'm a married woman.

Earl of Gurney   Sexual perversion is no sin.

Dinsdale (*voice off*)   I say, have you seen my father?

Earl of Gurney (*advancing*)   Remember the commandment I gave you, love one another as I loved you.

Mrs Piggot-Jones (*retreating*)   Stay back! My husband is a Master of Hounds!

Earl of Gurney   Fill your hearts, let your eyes sparkle, your soul dance. Be *bird-happy*!

Mrs Piggot-Jones ⎫
                        ⎬ Ahh!
Mrs Treadwell   ⎭

Their nerve breaks. They turn and plunge for the door, but are frozen in mid-flight as they see the cross for the first time.

Mrs Piggot-Jones   What is it?

Earl of Gurney   A Watusi walking-stick! Big people the Watusis. Listen, ladies.

But with cries of fear the two women rush Up Stage Centre. **Sir Charles** *appears in the doorway and is flattened by them as they charge out into the passage, followed by the* **Earl**, *who is heard calling:*

Earl of Gurney (*voice off*)   Don't be frightened. Hear the word of the Lord.

Sir Charles (*picking himself up*)   Treadwell . . . Piggot . . . What the blazes are they doing here? Great Scott, who's the idiot responsible?

Dinsdale (*voice off*)   I say, I say, have you seen my father?

Claire *gestures expressively.*

Sir Charles   Oh. Dinsdale.

Claire   You'll have to do something about that boy.

Sir Charles   He'll soon be off our hands. Old Barrington-Cochran's on his last legs. That means a by-election.

Claire   Dinsdale's such a fool.

Sir Charles   One time thought of bringing him into the business, but it's too risky. Can't have Dinsdale messing about with money. He's proved disappointing.

Dinsdale *re-enters.*

Dinsdale   Oh, there you are.

Claire   What did Sir Humphrey say?

Sir Charles   Gave me a lot o' expensive legal fal-de-roll. As it stands, there's no chance of breaking the Will. Only one possible solution. A male heir.

Claire   A what?

Sir Charles   If Jack had a son, Sir Humphrey says we could have him certified quietly, because everything could then pass to the heir. We'd administer the estate till the boy came of age. That way everything'd remain in the family.

Claire (*sarcastically*)   Oh, brilliant. A small point, but before he can have an heir, our lunatic nephew has to be married.

Sir Charles   Exactly. And the sooner the better!

The **Earl** *enters Up Stage Centre playing a flute.*

Earl of Gurney   Married?

Sir Charles   Yes, J.C., you should take a wife.

Earl of Gurney   Who from?

Claire   I'm sure we'll be able to find you a suitable young goddess.

Sir Charles   Most appropriate, eh-eh?

They chuckle to themselves.

Earl of Gurney   But I can't marry a second time.

They immediately stop chuckling.

Sir Charles   A *second* . . .

Claire (*sceptically*)   Second wife? You believe you're already married?

Earl of Gurney   On August 28th in the year of me, 1961.

Sir Charles *looks across doubtfully at* **Claire** *who shakes her head.*

Somerset House records will confirm. Father wanted it kept secret for some reason.

He walks away to Wings Right playing the 'Drinking Song' from La Traviata *on the flute.*

Sir Charles   This wife of yours? What's her name?

Earl of Gurney   Marguerite Gautier.

Sir Charles   French.

Dinsdale (*slowly*)   Marguerite Gautier? . . . Gautier? . . . I say, isn't that the 'Lady of the Camellias'?

Earl of Gurney   You know her too? Wonderful!

He exits playing the aria. **Dinsdale** *and* **Sir Charles** *exchange looks and rush after him. Blackout.*

Scene Seven

Spot up on white screen lowered Down Stage Left to show **Claire** *and* **Dr Herder** *talking.*

Dr Herder   Of course there's no question of marriage. He has no wife, but he believes he has, which is the same thing.

Claire   Why did he pick on Marguerite Gautier?

Dr Herder   Another martyr for love. His delusions are of a piece. Marguerite is the only person he trusts.

Claire   Why does he keep on about love?

Dr Herder   Because he hasn't had any. Or wasn't shown any, which is just as bad. He wants us all to love goodness. To love goodness is to love God, to love God is to love the 14th Earl of Gurney.

Claire   That's very clever. Is it the truth?

Dr Herder   Lady Claire, don't come to me for the truth, only explanations.

Claire   Does any of his talk mean anything?

Dr Herder   To him, yes. Your nephew suffers from the delusion that the world we live in is based on the fact that God is love.

Claire   Can't he see what the world's really like?

Dr Herder   No. But he will, when he's cured.

Claire   Can I ask one more question?

Dr Herder   If it's as revealing as the others.

Claire   Why does he hate being called Jack?

Dr Herder   Because it's his real name. Naturally he rejects it violently. If he ever answers to the name of Jack, he'll be on the road to sanity.

Claire   How are my questions revealing?

Dr Herder   The first one you asked me was about love.

White screen taken up and lights up as they move into the drawing-room of Gurney Manor where **Tucker** *is pouring drinks.*

Claire   This is our own Tucker, Dr Herder. He's been with the family for over forty years.

Tucker   Man and snivelling boy, sir.

Dr Herder   Really. How do you find the new Earl, Tucker?

Tucker   By sniffing. He's a Gurney, sir. A real Gurney.

Dr Herder   You don't find him odd?

Tucker   Odd? Soda, sir?

Dr Herder   Please. Yes, odd. Peculiar.

Tucker   Oh, you mean *nutty*. Yes, he's a nut-case all right, but then so are most of these titled flea-bags. Rich nobs and privileged arse-holes can afford to be bonkers. Living in a dream world, aren't they, sir? Don't know what time o' day it is. Life's made too easy for 'em. Don't have to earn a living so they can do just what they want to. Most of us'd look pretty cracked if we went round doing just what we wanted to, eh, sir?

Dr Herder   Yes, I suppose . . .

Claire   The late Earl left Tucker twenty thousand pounds. Since then he's been very outspoken.

Tucker *hands a drink to* **Dr Herder** *and another to* **Claire**.

Claire   Not for me, Tucker.

Tucker   Waste not want not. (*He drinks.*) Doctor, you might take a look at my back. The ol' lumbago's acting up again.

Sir Charles *and* **Dinsdale** *enter arguing with the* **Earl of Gurney**.

Dinsdale (*gesturing with the book*)   But I've shown you it's in here. *The Lady of the Camellias* by Alexandre Dumas. *Camille.* The opera by Verdi *La Traviata.* Same woman. A figure of romance.

Earl of Gurney   My dear chap, you prove my point ipso facto, a divine figure of romance. Paul, what a pleasant surprise.

Dr Herder   How are you?

Earl of Gurney   In the middle of a debate on the existence of my wife Marguerite. With passions roused and intellects sharpened, pray continue, Dinsdale Gurney.

Sir Charles   I give up. You did say it'd be impossible to convince him, doctor.

Dr Herder   Impossible. But you can try.

Claire *takes the book from* **Dinsdale**, *opens it and shows it to the* **Earl**.

Claire   Look. It's a play, *The Lady of the Camellias*. Fiction.

Earl of Gurney (*taking book*)   Ah, yes, a biography of my Marguerite – affectionately known as La Dame Aux Camelias. (*Sternly.*) Dinsdale, this book looks tired from over-reading. You should let it out more.

Claire   You aren't married. The woman doesn't exist.

Earl of Gurney   Come, come, you exaggerate unduly. (*Makes circular movement with right hand.*) You'll be saying I'm not God, Jesus, and the Holy Ghost next.

Claire   You're not! God wouldn't be so ridiculous waving his arms like a maniac dressed in a white suit and carnation.

Earl of Gurney   The prophet Ezekiel lay three hundred days on his left side and forty days on his right. He cut his hair and divided it into three parts. The first part he burnt, the second he chopped into pieces, the third he scattered into the wind. Ridiculous, mad, certifiable. It was all merely a sign of something more important. God teaches by signs as well as words.

Dr Herder (*with satisfaction*)   He can defend his beliefs with great skill.

Dinsdale   All right, if you're God, reveal your Godhead.

The **Earl** *immediately starts to unzip his flies.*

No, no. A miracle. Show us a miracle.

Earl of Gurney   A miracle. (*Holds out his hand.*) Here's a miracle.

Dinsdale   Where?

Earl of Gurney   This hand. This city network of tissues, nerves, muscles, ligaments, carpals, metacarpals and phalanges. And what about the hairy-nosed wombat?

Dinsdale   Not that sort. A miracle like the making of loaves and fishes.

Earl of Gurney   Oh, those. You see ten billion million miracles a day, yet you want your conjuring tricks, your pretty flim-flams, from the incense burners. I can't raise Lazarus again, he's decomposed, so bring me that table.

Claire   What are you going to do?

Earl of Gurney   A grade-one Galilee miracle.

Claire *starts to say something but* **Dr Herder** *gestures. He nods to* **Dinsdale**, *who drags the coffee table to Stage Centre, and steps back uncertainly. They are all roughly grouped behind it.*

Earl of Gurney   Instead of raising Laz, I'll raise yon table.

Sir Charles   That table?

Earl of Gurney   Ten feet. Not by mirrors or crippled midgets behind black curtains, but by the power of love.

Claire   Just love?

Earl of Gurney   It moves mountains, and makes the puny weed split the rock. Look.

All eyes now sceptically on the table. The **Earl** *stretches out his hands, palms upwards. As he slowly starts to raise them, lights imperceptibly begin to dim.*

Believe in me, in love, in loving goodness, raise yourself up . . . Rise, up, up. See, see . . . slowly, slowly. One foot, two feet, three, four . . . slowly up . . . five, six, seven . . . rise, rise up . . . Eight, nine, ten. (*His arms are now above his head.*) There! The table floats ten feet in space.

Tucker (*pointing up excitedly*)   Ahhh! Look, I see it! Up there! (*He lurches forward, grasping a half-empty whisky decanter.*) Sh-miracle, sh-miracle, hallelujah, sh-miracle. Praise the Lord and pass t'ammunition.

Sir Charles   Drunken lout!

Tucker *collapses in a stupor in a chair. The spell is broken.*
Claire *crosses angrily to the table.*

Claire   It didn't rise. (*Raps it.*) Here it is.

Earl of Gurney (*making circle with hand*)   Tucker saw, believed, yeees.

Claire   Did you see it, doctor?

Dr Herder   No.

Sir Charles   'Course not. Damned rot.

Earl of Gurney (*shakes his head*)   Into any platinum pressure-cooker, grrh, grrhh, shurhh . . .

Claire   There's no miracle. No wife. She doesn't exist. She's fiction. Part of a play. An opera. She's not flesh and blood. Not real.

Earl of Gurney (*flapping hands, disturbed*)   Gross gree crull craaah . . .

Dr Herder   Shhh. Listen.

From the corridor beyond the darkened room comes the sound of a woman singing. 'Go diam fie—ga-ca-e-ra-pi-do-e il gan dio dell 'a-mo-re . . .' It grows louder. We can hear the rustle of crinoline. They turn towards the doorway. Up Stage Centre: The Lady of the Camellias stands there, in a Spot, carrying a camellia and singing the 'Drinking Song' from La Traviata.

La Dame Aux Camelias (*singing*)   'Eun fior che na—see e muo—re, ne, piu si puv go-der—Go-diam c-In-vi-ta, c'in-vi-taun, fervi do-ac-cen-to-la-sin-gheer . . .'

Earl of Gurney   Marguerite!

Blackout.

Scene Eight

Lights up on the drawing-room of Gurney Manor where **Claire** *and* **Sir Charles** *are arguing with measured ferocity.*

Claire   How *dare* you bring that woman here?

Sir Charles   You should be grateful to Miss Shelley.

Claire   Grace Shelley is your mistress. Hairs on the collar, stains on the sheets, I know you.

Sir Charles   And I know you. Miss Shelley's just a hard-working girl.

Claire   Only on her back. First you try to palm her off on to your own brother.

Sir Charles   Ralph needed a wife. He took a fancy to Miss Shelley.

Claire   That didn't work, so now you try her for the son. It's incestuous.

Sir Charles   Don't talk to me about incest. I remember young Jeremy Gore. You knew his father and I went to school together. But you went ahead and seduced his son. That's incest, madam.

Claire   What's the use? It isn't worth raising one's voice. But why the devil didn't you warn us?

Sir Charles   No time. After what that 'Trick-Cyclist' chappie told me I knew we'd never convince Jack he wasn't married and this Marguerite filly didn't exist. So I 'phoned Grace and explained the position. She got dressed up in some theatrical togs and came down. Put me on a first-rate show, I thought.

Claire   It had impact.

Sir Charles   Anyway, Jack believes she's Marguerite. All she has to do now is convince him he has to marry her again. Shouldn't be difficult.

Claire   Dr Herder'll object.

Sir Charles   Object? He's got no right to object to anything, he's not family.

Claire   He could make things difficult by having Jack declared insane before he's produced an heir for you.

Sir Charles   Damn kraut! You'd better keep an eye on him, my dear. I'll have my hands full getting Grace married and pregnant.

Grace Shelley *comes in Up Stage Centre, a blonde, still dressed in a low-cut ball gown, she gestures with the camellia.*

Grace *What an entrance.* Beautiful, *but* beautiful. The look on your faces. I should have stuck to the classics. I was trained for it y'know – Mrs Phoebe Giavanno, 27A Brixton Hill. She sang with Caruso. Grand old lady. 'From the diaphragm dear, from the diaphragm.' Always said I had the voice. Let's face it, Bert Bacharach is great but he's not in the same class as Giuseppe Verdi. Phew, this dress's tight. How did they breathe? I feel constipated. (*Notices cross by the door for the first time.*) *Christy O'Connor,* what's that? Is the roof falling in or something?

Claire Any minute now. (*Moving Up Stage.*) Your flower's wilting, my dear.

Grace (*waving it cheerfully*) Can't be. It's wax.

Claire Careful your husband-to-be doesn't eat it for breakfast.

She exits.

Grace You're right, Charlie Boy. She's an ice-cold Biddy.

Sir Charles Too clever by half, that woman. But I get things done my way. She doesn't know what she wants.

Grace But I do, Charlie Boy. Lady Grace, Lady Grace Gurney, the Countess of Gurney.

Sir Charles Now look here, Grace, you mustn't call me Charlie Boy. We have to be careful.

Grace If that's what you want.

Sir Charles It's not what I want. It's what has to be. I'm very fond of you, m'dear, you know that.

Grace You've a funny way of showing it. First you push me into the arms of your half-dead half-brother, and then on to his loony son.

Sir Charles I'd make any sacrifice for the sake of the family. You sure you can handle the situation? Tricky an' all, marrying a man who thinks he's God.

Grace   It happens all the time. (*Crossing to french-windows.*) On certain nights. In front of the right audience. When the magic works. I've known what it's like to be a God too. (*Sees someone outside.*) Ah, there he is on the lawn. Let's get the show on the road. Damn, where's my lousy camellia. (**Sir Charles** *hands it to her, she hitches up her dress.*) I'll be glad to get out of this clobber. (*Pats bare bosom.*) No wonder she was dying of consumption. (*Coughs hoarsely.*)

Sir Charles   Careful now.

Grace   Trust me, Charlie B . . . Charles. I've got too much at stake to blow it.

Holding the camellia modestly across her chest, and smiling wanly, she glides out. **Sir Charles** *looks at the audience.*

Sir Charles   Damned plucky filly.

Dinsdale *enters Up Stage Centre.*

Dinsdale   I say, Mother's just told me this lady-of-the-Camellia-woman's a fake. I know J.C.'s as batty as a moorhen, sir, but this isn't playing the game.

Sir Charles   Game? What game? It's no game, sir! This is real.

Blackout.

Scene Nine

Footlights up immediately. A metal sun lowered from Flies. The **Earl** *lying Down Stage Right, rouses himself as* **Grace** *enters Wings Left.*

Earl of Gurney   My dreams made flesh or a reasonable facsimile thereforeto. (*Gets up, bows politely.*) Eh – bien, comment allez-vous, madame?

Grace   Sorry, I don't speak French.

Earl of Gurney   German? Italian? Albanian? Yiddish?

Grace   No. English.

Earl of Gurney   English. Why didn't you say so before?
Nothing to be ashamed of, hard language to master. But we
can't play this love-scene with mere words, be they English,
Japanese or Serbo-Croat.

Grace   Love scene? What now?

Earl of Gurney   Love isn't just for one season. (*Smiles,
flapping arms like a bird.*) Hweet, hweep.

Grace   Hweet?

Earl of Gurney (*arms quivering*)   Tsiff-tsiff-tsiff. (*Hopping.*)
Chiff-chaff-chaff-chaff.

Grace (*laughing*)   Oh, well. (*Flaps arms.*) Chiff-chaff.

They circle round each other with tiny bird movements; **Grace**
bending forward and hopping, the **Earl** *bobbing his head and making
low loping sweeps.*

Earl of Gurney (*long drawn-out, high-pitched*)   Pioo . . . pioo
. . . pioo.

Grace   Cuckoo!

Earl of Gurney (*crescendo*)   Pioo.

Grace (*breathless*)   I'll bet even Ludwig Koch wasn't made
love to with bird cries.

Earl of Gurney   What else would you like? The Grand
Canyon? A musical teacup? A hundred pre-sold holy
wafers? A disused banana factory? Absolution?

Grace   A white wedding.

Earl of Gurney   Will next Tuesday suit you?

Grace   You deserve a big kiss.

Earl of Gurney   Not here in the garden. Last time I was
kissed in a garden – it turned out rather awkward.

Grace   Ah, but Judas was a man.

Earl of Gurney (*nodding*)   Hmm, yes, a strange business. (**Grace** *laughs*.) Who are you?

Grace   A woman.

Earl of Gurney   Descended from Eve.

Grace   No, a doorstep. I'm an orphan.

Earl of Gurney   Then we'll be orphans together, Marguerite.

Grace   Call me Grace, as I don't speak French.

Earl of Gurney   A good name. It means a gift of faith.

Grace   Which is what I have in you. I'm holding you to that wedding.

Earl of Gurney   Hold hard. You'll be my Queen of Queens.

Grace   I'll be satisfied with Lady Gurney.

Earl of Gurney (*takes her hands*)   And I say unto you, thou shall love the Lord thy God with all thy heart and with all thy soul and with all thy mind.

Grace   I do.

Earl of Gurney   I want to show you the bottom drawer of my soul. (*Suddenly joyful*.) Oh, but I'm happy, I'm the sunshine-man, the driver of the gravy-train, chu-chu-chu. (**Grace** *laughs*.) It's all so simple, for me. Paradise is just a smiling face. What's it for you?

Grace   Me? Paradise? Oh, a fireplace. A cosy room.

Earl of Gurney (*nodding*)   A little nest . . .

Hand in hand they go into a dance routine to Wings Right.

Grace (*singing*)   'That nestles where the roses bloom.'

Earl of Gurney (*singing; indicating partner*)   'Sweet Gracey and me . . .'

Grace (*singing: looking at him*)   'And a baby makes three.'

Grace (*singing*)
> 'We're going to our blue heaven.'

Earl of Gurney (*singing*)

Grace *kisses him, exits Wings Right. The* **Earl** *takes out a pocket telescope, opens it out and stares after her as* **Dinsdale** *enters sulkily.*

Dinsdale   What are you looking at?

Earl of Gurney (*handing him telescope*)   Beauty in motion.

Dinsdale (*looking*)   I can't see a thing.

Earl of Gurney   Because you're not looking with the eyes of love.

Dinsdale   Hang it all, whatever else you are, you're still a Gurney. That Camellia woman's really Grace Shelley. Close friend of my father's. He's put her up to it.

The **Earl** *stops humming.*

Got her to dress like that. Absolutely ridiculous.

The **Earl** *shivers with cold.*

He wants you married off.

The **Earl** *puts his hand to his face; when he takes it away his features are covered with white make-up.*

Mother's in it too. Shouldn't be surprised if even old Tuck knew. Everybody but me.

Earl of Gurney (*shrinking miserably*)   Stop! You're making me a crippled dwarf, a deformed midget, a crippled newt!

Dinsdale (*sees the* **Earl** *with bent knees, now half-size*)
What're you doing?

Stage Lights Up.

Earl of Gurney   It's your negative insinuendo.

Dinsdale   Insinuendo?

Earl of Gurney (*making circle with right hand*)   Insinuendo is insinuation towards innuendo, brought on by increased negativism out of a negative reaction to your father's positivism. (*Takes out glasses, breaks them, puts half frame over one eye, peers up at* **Dinsdale**.) Your negativism is fully charged. I see by the Habeas Corpus parchment round your neck.

Dinsdale   I don't know what the devil you're on about, but I resent your attitude. I only told you about Grace Shelley . . .

Earl of Gurney (*tearing off his jacket and shirt*)   She's my Righteous-Ideal-Planned-Wife. Don't forget, besides being God, Christ and the Holy Ghost, I'm also a San D., B.F.C., and D.A.C. – Doctor of Sanitation, Bachelor of Family Life, and Doctor of Air Conditioning. Please remember that you're dealing with the Big One. I've told aged Tucker. Injecting me with his Kremlin-plot negative-microbes. I said verbatim. Feeling persecuted is paranoid schizophrenia-wretches. Dr H. suffered from it. But watched they said against me . . . one of the signs. Many poor 'erder's Dancing Academy. I *am* being EVERYBODY they CRIED . . . whrr! rr! . . . rrr! Krr-krr-krek!

He scuttles absurdly Up Stage and clambers on to the cross. On the back of his vest are painted the words 'God is Love'. **Dinsdale** *exits as the* **Earl** *clings to the cross, his painful metallic cries growing louder and louder. The lights dim down. The cries stop abruptly.*

Scene Ten

Lights Up as **Bishop Lampton** *and* **Sir Charles** *enter Up Stage Centre glancing with distaste at the* **Earl**, *stretched out on the cross.*

Bishop Lampton   I will not solemnise any marriage, even of my own nephew, during the period from Advent Sunday till eight days after Epiphany. So it must be on Tuesday the 12th. Eight a.m. Private Chapel. Ordinary

Licence. But I have grave misgivings, Charles. Grave misgivings.

Sir Charles   Misgivings? About Jack?

Bishop Lampton   No, about the bride, Miss Shelley. Who is she? What is she? I fear she may be using this marriage merely to advance her social position. I hear she's an 'entertainer'.

Sir Charles   I'll vouch for Grace Shelley.

Bishop Lampton   No doubt. I hear she's a most handsome woman. I venture you've been dazzled by her charms. 'A woman whose heart is snares and nets.' I, however, due to my cloth – and age – can take a more dispassionate view of her character and motives.

Sir Charles   Dash it all, Bertie, you know the position. We can't be fussy. Grace – Miss Shelley – is the best we can come up with. This is a crisis.

Bishop Lampton   Even so, we shouldn't be too hasty. God in his infinite wisdom has clouded our nephew's senses. But it can only be temporary. I take it as a sure sign of hope that his delusions are at least of a *religious* nature. Consider the consequences of this mis-mating, Charles. When he recovers, he'll find himself married to a woman who is frankly not suitable. And he *will* recover. God is merciful.

Sir Charles   Can't wait on God's mercy, Bertie, everything's going to pot. Dr Herder agrees.

Bishop Lampton   Dr Herder? 'Herder'? Is he English?

Sir Charles   No.

Bishop Lampton   Ahh . . .

Sir Charles   Mark my words, this'll be the making of Jack.

Bishop Lampton   It's true, there's nothing like marriage to bring a fella to his senses.

They exit Up Stage as Spot Up Down Stage Left on **Dr Herder**
and **Claire** *standing in front of a white backing lowered from the
Flies. A couch to Left.*

Claire   My husband's an idiot.

Dr Herder   I've no idea what he's playing at, and it's not
strictly my concern. The Earl's no longer under my care.
But that charade with Miss Shelley made me feel an
absolute fool, and I don't care to underestimate myself.

Claire   I apologise. Charles has some idea Jack might
accept her if she dressed up as the Lady of the Camellias.

Dr Herder   Sometimes it's very easy to forget that
outside this comedy Sir Charles occupies a position of
responsibility and power. I just learned he's on the Board of
the Guggenheim Research Foundation. Extraordinary.

Claire   Ah, yes, he mentioned you were asking for a
grant. You won't have any trouble.

Dr Herder   It's only a nominal 130,000. For the study of
paranoid schizophrenic rats.

Claire   Sounds fascinating.

Dr Herder   I should have said electrically controlled
paranoid rats.

Claire   Electrically?

Dr Herder   We insert very fine silver wires into the rat's
mid-brain. The rat's behaviour is controlled by the strength
of the current passed through them. By pressing a button
and stimulating one area of its mid-brain, the rat is made to
feel threatened. It attacks any rat in sight. There's really no
threat, but the mid-brain can't tell the difference. Roughly
the same thing happens with a human paranoid. No silver
wires, but an unknown area of his brain is stimulated, and
he feels threatened without cause. Naturally, men aren't
rats.

Claire   Only a man would say so.

Dr Herder (*smiling*)   I'm speaking biologically. Eventually we'll have to conduct similar experiments on the human brain.

Claire   Today rats. Tomorrow the world. Who will you wire for visions?

Dr Herder   First of all myself, naturally.

Claire (*taking off glove*)   I see. Then if I press a button, you'd limp for me, feel fear and love . . .

Dr Herder   Love? No. Desire, yes.

Claire   By pressing a button? (*Raises finger and mimes pressing.*)

Dr Herder (*covers her hand*)   Not too hard. I might get over-stimulated and lose control.

Claire   You, lose control? Think of the risk, doctor.

Dr Herder   There's only one commandment a doctor need ever worry about. 'Thou shalt not advertise.'

Dr Herder *kisses* **Claire**'*s hand. Spot out.*

Scene Eleven

Lights Up. The **Earl** *stops jerking on the cross.*

Earl of Gurney   My heart rises with the sun. I'm purged of doubts and negative innuendoes. Today I want to bless everything! Bless the crawfish that has a scuttling walk, bless the trout, the pilchard and periwinkle. Bless Ted Smoothey of 22 East Hackney Road – with a name like that he needs blessing. Bless the mealy-redpole, the black-gloved wallaby and W. C. Fields, who's dead but lives on. Bless the skunk, bless the red-bellied lemur, bless 'Judo' Al Hayes and Ski-Hi-Lee. Bless the snotty-nosed giraffe, bless the buffalo, bless the Society of Women Engineers, bless the wild yak, bless the Piccadilly Match King, bless the pygmy hippo, bless the

weasel, bless the mighty cockroach, bless me. Today's my
wedding day!

Wedding bells peal out.

Scene Twelve

*Screen lowered immediately Down Stage Centre, cutting out the cross
from view. On it, a photo-collage of Society weddings.* **Bishop
Lampton** *enters imposingly, Wings Right, in full regalia, followed
by* **Claire** *and* **Dinsdale**. **Tucker** *hobbles in from Wings Left.
They cross slowly Down Stage Centre. With* **Claire** *and*
Dinsdale *on his right, and* **Tucker** *on his left,* **Lampton** *turns
and faces the audience.*

The bells stop ringing. An organ plays 'The Wedding March' as
Grace *in a white wedding dress and an apprehensive* **Sir Charles**
enter Wings Right. They all wait for the groom. The **Earl** *scampers
in Wings Right in a cut-away jacket, no shirt and broken glasses and
flute hanging from his chest.* **Bishop Lampton** *shudders.*

Bishop Lampton (*reading from prayer book*)   'Dearly
beloved, we are gathered together here in the sight of
God . . .'

The **Earl** *claps his hands above his head and shakes them
triumphantly.*

'. . . and in the face of this company to join together this
man and this woman in Holy Matrimony, which is an
honourable estate.'

Earl of Gurney   Instituted by me in the time of man's
innocence.

Grace *puts her fingers to his lips.*

Bishop Lampton (*looking up warningly*)   'Therefore if
anyone can show just cause why they may not be lawfully
joined together, let him now speak, or else hereafter forever
hold his peace.'

Claire, **Dinsdale** *and* **Sir Charles** *stare deliberately at the audience. Silence.*

Tucker   Load o' British jelly-meat whiskers! Stand up on your tea-soaked haunches and stop it. Piddling, half-dead helots.

Sir Charles   Quiet, man. Show some respect.

Tucker   I'm always respectful. S'what I'm paid for. No one can say I'm not respectful. (*Removes his false teeth.*) There.

Bishop Lampton   'I require and charge you both that if either of you have any impediment why ye may not be lawfully joined together in matrimony ye do now confess it.'

Earl of Gurney   Yes, I'm afraid I do know an impediment.

His family glance anxiously at each other.

Claire   It's only a rhetorical question, like all the others in the wedding service.

Earl of Gurney   'Tis no good glossing o'er the facts. Certain R.C. knackers think I'm already married to the Virgin Mary.

Sir Charles   We're not concerned with what other people think.

Bishop Lampton   Especially not Roman Catholics. 'Wilt thou have this woman to thy wedded wife, to live together after God's ordinance in the holy state of matrimony? Wilt thou love her . . .'

Earl of Gurney   From the bottom of my soul to the tip of my penis, like the sun in its brightness, the moon in its beauty, the heavens in their emptiness, streams in their gentleness, no breeze stirs that doesn't bear my love.

Bishop Lampton   Blasphemous . . . !

Grace   But will you love *me*?

Earl of Gurney   I will.

Bishop Lampton (*quickly, to* **Grace**)   'Wilt thou have this man to thy wedded husband, to live together after God's ordinance.'

Grace   I will.

Bishop Lampton   Who gives this woman to this man?

Sir Charles   I do.

Bishop Lampton (*to* **Earl**)   Repeat after me. I, J.C., take thee Grace Shelley to my wedded wife . . .

Earl of Gurney   I, J.C., the Holy Flying Roller, the Morning Star, known to his intimates as the Naz, take thee Marguerite, called Grace Shelley because she doesn't speak French.

Bishop Lampton *shudders and plunges on.*

Bishop Lampton (*to* **Grace**)   Repeat after me.

Grace   I know the lines. I, Grace Shelley, take thee J.C. to my wedded husband to have and to hold from this day forward, for better for worse, for richer for poorer, in sickness and in health, to love and to cherish till death do us part, according to God's holy ordinance and thereto I give thee my troth.

Sir Charles *steps forward with the ring and hurriedly puts it on* **Grace**'*s finger.*

Bishop Lampton (*with increasing speed*)   'For as much as these two persons have consented together in holy wedlock, I pronounce that they be man and wife together. In-the-name-of-the-Father-and-of-the-Son-and-of-the-Holy-Ghost-whom-God-hath-joined-together-let-no-man-put-asunder . . .' (*One last effort.*) Lord have mercy upon us!

All   Christ have mercy upon us.

Bishop Lampton   Lord have mercy upon us!

Bishop Lampton *sinks to the floor exhausted, but* **Dinsdale** *and* **Sir Charles** *jerk him up as the bells peal and the organ booms.*

Scene Thirteen

Bells and organ fade down. The screen is taken up to show a small buffet has been laid out – drinks, sandwiches, and a wedding cake. The **Earl** *picks up* **Grace** *and carries her laughing into the drawing-room.*

Dinsdale (*to* **Bishop Lampton**)   Frankly, I thought it was going to be a jolly sight worse.

Bishop Lampton (*being helped out of his vestments by* **Tucker**) Worse? How could it have been worse? When that woman entered in *white* I knew. (*Shudders.*) An actress, married in white, *white.*

Grace   Hildegarde! This is a bit tatty. No reception, no guests, a few curled sandwiches and a deformed wedding cake. William Hickey won't give us a mention.

Tucker   It's not my fault, your ladyship.

Grace   'Your ladyship.' (*Brightening.*) That's better. Now watch 'em creep and crawl at Harrods.

Bishop Lampton *slumps down on a chair whilst the* **Earl** *hands* **Sir Charles** *and* **Dinsdale** *paper hats and coloured balloons. They put on the hats.*

Sir Charles (*to* **Grace**)   We thought you'd prefer a quiet affair.

Grace   It's like a wet Monday in Warrington. What about a toast to the newly-weds or something? Let's try and keep it a bit trad.

Sir Charles   Oh, very well. Ladies and gentlemen – to the long life, prosperity and happiness of the bride and groom.

They drink.

Earl of Gurney (*picking up knife*)   Thank you, ladies and gentlemen, in reply I name this ship 'Loving Kindness'. May I keep her and all who sail in her. (*Cuts wedding cake.*)

Tucker   Ah, your ladyship, you should have seen the late Earl's wedding. Over five hundred guests. The crème de menthe. Wastrels all! Lords of conspicuous consumption.

Sir Charles *has taken* **Grace** *aside.*

Sir Charles (*low*)   Can't say I fancy the idea of you alone with him.

Grace (*low, angry*)   Everything's still yours, even if you've given it away.

Earl of Gurney   Good. Let's have a minute's silence.

Claire   What for?

Earl of Gurney   For all the dead books of World War I. For Mr Moto, the Cisco Kid and Me. Muffle the drums, beat the retreat. Quiet, sshh, silence . . .

The sudden silence is physical. Even after only a few seconds the tension grows. The strain is too much. All burst out at once – 'Why the devil . . .' 'I say. . .' 'Hell . . . !'

(*Sadly.*) Terrible, isn't it? That's why I have to talk, sing, dance.

Grace (*glancing at* **Sir Charles**)   And make love?

Tucker (*singing in hoarse croak*)   'Oh, how we danced on the night we were wed . . .'

While he cavorts around, **Grace** *takes the* **Earl**'s *arm and they slip away Up Stage Centre.*

'We pledged our true love and a word wasn't said.' My mother loved that song. Mammy! Mammy! You weighed twenty stone but you were my little Mammy.

Sir Charles   Tucker!

Tucker   I'm sorry, sir. I thought you might wish me to liven up this wake.

Sir Charles (*noticing bride and groom are missing*)   Where have they gone?

Claire   Upstairs.

Dinsdale   Must say I wouldn't much like to be in her shoes tonight.

Tucker   Not her shoes he'll be in, Master Dinsdale, sir.

Bishop Lampton (*shuddering*)   *White* . . .

Sir Charles   You never stop talking, Bertie. All of you sneering, sniggering. (*Lights dim down.*) We've got to pull together in this. Families like ours set the tone. Doesn't help poking and prying into personal lives. The strength of the English people lies in their inhibitions. What are they doing up there? (*He now stands in Single Spot Down Stage Left, still wearing a paper hat with a tiny bell at the end.*) You go to any foreign country and see the difference. There's always some scruffy chappie on a street corner who wants to tell you all about his love life, and sell you a strip of dirty postcards. What are they doing up there? Sacrifices must be made. Nothing more to be said. (*Looks up.*) *What* . . . *are* . . . *they* . . . *doing* . . . *up* . . . *there?*

Spot out.

Scene Fourteen

Spot up immediately on the four-poster bed and a chair. **Grace** *is stripping to music played softly over. Her movements are provocative, but utterly unselfconscious. Stepping out of her wedding dress,* **Grace** *bends to pick it up. She drapes it over the chair.*

Grace   I always get first-night nerves. Any good performer does. You have to be keyed up to give a good show. I've done it all, from Stanislavski to Strip. Never think I once worked as a stripper, would you? It's true, as God is my witness – no, you weren't there, were you J.C.? Greasy make-up towels, cracked mirrors, rhinestones and beads. What a world. (*Takes off stocking and throws it absently into audience.*) I sang 'This Can't Be Love'. Funny, I did the same act later at the 'Pigalle' for twice the money without removing a stitch. (*Proudly.*) Of course, some women can strip without taking their clothes off. (*She sits on a chair and takes off other stocking.*) Nobody could call me undersexed, but I could never get worked up watching some man strip down to his suspenders and jockstrap. Where's the fun? I suppose some people just enjoy the smell of a steak better than the steak itself. (*Throws stocking into audience.*) If my mother could see me now – it's what she always wanted for me – the Big Time. She never forgave Dad for being born in Clapham. Guess she found it hard to settle down to civilian life after being in a touring company of *Chu Chin Chow*. Nobody need worry about me fitting in. (*Walks momentarily into darkness, left.*) All I have to do is play it cool. (*Reappears into Spot, in black nightdress, miming drinking tea with finger cocked up.*) I can cock my little finger with the best. (*Calls Wings Right.*) What you doing in there, Honey?

She stares as the **Earl** *enters unsteadily from Wings Right, in white pyjamas and riding a one-wheel bicycle.*

It's ridiculous! It's not dignified!

Earl of Gurney (*wobbling*)   Dignity has nothing to do with divinity.

Grace (*sudden panic*)   Not here! Not now! A *bike*? You're mad.

Earl of Gurney   Don't be frightened.

Grace (*recovering*)   I'm not frightened. But I didn't expect to see my husband riding a one-wheel bike on his wedding night.

Earl of Gurney It's the only way to travel. (*Jumps off bike.*) Remember, God loves you, God wants you, God needs you. Let's to bed.

Spot fades out. Music swells up. From out of the darkness the beating of giants wings as a great bird hovers overhead, followed by the sound of rain falling heavily.

Scene Fifteen

Lights up on drawing-room to show **Sir Charles** *standing by the french-windows staring out moodily at the rain.* **Grace** *enters.*

Grace It was a damn long night. I'm starving.

Sir Charles What happened?

Grace Happened?

Sir Charles (*impatiently*) Last night. What did he do?

Grace Rode around on a one-wheel bicycle.

Sir Charles Filthy beast! . . . That must be the Guv'nor's old bike. The attic's full of his junk. So he just rode around all night, then?

Grace First the bike, then me.

Sir Charles Oh.

Grace His mind may be wonky but there's nothing wrong with the rest of his anatomy.

Sir Charles (*gloomily*) We Gurneys have always been damnably virile.

Grace I thought you'd be delighted to find he's not impotent.

Sir Charles (*frowning*) I am. I am. Delighted.

Claire *enters briskly.* **Sir Charles** *quickly lets go of* **Grace**'s *hand.*

Claire   'morning. Well, what happened last night? Was it successful?

Grace   I should have sold tickets.

Sir Charles   Really, Claire, how can you ask a question like that?

Claire   Why not? This is your idea, remember? If your nephew's incapable, then somebody else may have to step into the breach for him.

Grace   Charles, tell her to keep her sharp tongue and low mind to herself.

Claire   She has claws.

Grace   This is my pad now. If you want to keep kibbitzing here, belt up on the snide remarks or you'll find yourself horizontal.

Claire   Horizontal's more your position than mine, dear.

Grace   Listen you Black Witch of the North . . .

There is the sound of a commotion from the corridor. **Tucker** *comes in arguing with* **Dr Herder**.

Tucker   Why can't you look at my back? It's 'cause I'm on the National Health, isn't it? Damn money-grubbers, you and your Hypocrite's Oath . . . Your Ladyship, Dr Paul Herder. Lunch is ready, Madam.

Tucker *shuffles out.* **Dr Herder** *faces* **Claire**, **Grace** *and* **Sir Charles**, *who instinctively unite against him, their internal quarrel forgotten.*

Dr Herder   I've come to offer my congratulations, if that's the right word.

Sir Charles   This is Dr Herder, Lady Gurney.

Grace   How do you do, doctor. So nice to meet you at last. You'll stay for lunch. I want to talk to you about my husband. I'm sorry you weren't told about the wedding, but it was done in such a rush we didn't have time to invite anybody except the close family. Besides, you would have tried to talk me out of it. It wouldn't have done any good . . . you see, I love him!

She exits.

Dr Herder   You should have consulted me before you went ahead. It's madness.

Sir Charles   Come, come, doctor. You said he needed a harsh dose of reality. You can't have a harsher dose of the stuff than marriage.

Dr Herder   It can't even be legal.

Sir Charles   It's legal. My brother-in-law conducted the service. He's a Bishop, and a Bishop would never do anything that wasn't legal.

He exits.

Dr Herder   And what do you say, Lady Claire?

Claire   Congratulations.

Dr Herder   Congratulations?

Claire   On getting your Guggenheim Grant.

Dr Herder   You made love to me to make sure I didn't cause any trouble.

Claire   You seduced me to make sure of that 130,000 for your schizophrenic rats. Don't be tiresome.

Dr Herder   I don't like being made a fool of, Claire.

Claire   You haven't been. Charles would have gone ahead with the marriage anyway. The Gurneys must have an heir. As soon as there is one Charles will have J.C. committed. The only way you would change the plot is by making the 14th Earl of Gurney sane like the rest of us. And you haven't got much time. Lady Grace Shelley isn't the type to survive the rabbit test for long.

Dr Herder   Verdammt. Verdammt. Verdammt. *Blackout.*

Scene Sixteen

A roll of thunder. Spot up on **Grace** *framed in the doorway Up Stage Centre. She is nine months pregnant. Lights full up to show* **Dr Herder**, **Claire** *and* **Sir Charles** *watching her waddle in. The* **Earl** *comes in behind her, with the same heavy tread, leaning on a shepherd's crook, as if he, too, is carrying.*

Grace   Can you beat it, J.C.'s got labour pains too.

Dr Herder   It's called 'couvade'. Sympathetic illness. Psychosomatic. Not at all unusual.

Sir Charles   Hmm. I never felt a thing when Lady Claire here was pregnant.

Claire   I'm sure you didn't.

Earl of Gurney (*helping* **Grace** *into chair, she winces and the* **Earl** *clutches his stomach*)   Oooh-ah, Mighty Mouse is roaring.

Dr Herder   What are you going to call the child?

Sir Charles   Vincent, after the Guv'nor.

Earl of Gurney (*firmly*)   No shell name. We'll call the little beggar Bussay d'Ambois, the UNO Boy-Wonder. And if it's a girl, Capucine.

Sir Charles   Capucine? You can't call anyone Capucine?

Tucker *enters.*

Tucker   Dr Herder. Mr McKyle is here.

Dr Herder   Show them straight in.

Tucker   Certainly, sir, I'll lay down on the doorstep and let 'em walk over me.

He exits.

Claire   Do you need us?

Dr Herder   Yes. But whatever happens, please don't interfere or interrupt, unless I ask.

Claire   What are you going to do?

Dr Herder (*picks up tape-recorder*)   Prove it's impossible for two objects to occupy the same space at the same time. A colleague of mine, Dr Sackstead, has agreed to send me some help as a personal favour.

Sir Charles   All these damned experiments. Look at the last one with the lie-detector. You asked him if he was God, he grinned, said 'No' and the damn fool machine said he was lying.

Dr Herder   You've forced me to risk the unorthodox. (*Takes the* **Earl**'s *arm.*) I'm going to show you the world in the hard light of Truth.

Earl of Gurney   I am the Light of Truth, the Light of the World.

Dr Herder (*into tape-recorder*)   This is experiment fifteen.

Sir Charles   All these damned experiments.

Tucker *enters.*

Tucker   Dr Herder. Mr McKyle . . .

McKyle *enters, brushing past him impatiently, followed by a burly* **Assistant**.

Oh, charming.

He exits.

McKyle (*gesturing*)   Mae assistant, Mr Shape.

McKyle *is a powerful gaunt man, with an iron-grey beard and brusque manner. He is still wearing gloves.*

Assistant   Dr Sackstead was held up. He hopes to be along later.

McKyle   Shall we gie on wi' it?

Dr Herder   Let me introduce you.

McKyle   No need. I'm sure they a' ken me here. (*The others look puzzled; he takes off right-hand glove, extends fingers.*) Ach, who else has electricity streaming fraw his fingers and eyeballs? I'm the High Voltage Messiah.

Claire   The who?

McKyle   The Electric Christ, the AC/DC God. You look fused. Cannae y'see the wall plug in mae forehead? Here, here. The booster converter. Takes everything I eats and drinks and converts it into watts and kilowatts.

All stare except **Assistant** *and* **Dr Herder**. **Sir Charles** *and* **Claire** *are about to protest.* **Dr Herder** *gestures to them to keep quiet and flicks on the tape-recorder.*

Dr Herder   Are you saying you're God too?

McKyle   God 1, 2, 3, 4, 5, 6, 7, 8, 9, 10. AC/DC. Havenae' y' seen God afore?

Earl of Gurney (*quietly*)   They have, Sir. Your remarks are in extreme bad taste. I'm God.

McKyle (*focusing on him for the first time*)   Yer' nae God. Yer' what mae snot-rag's made of. (*Plugs deaf-aid in ear.*) I've obliterated hundreds o' dupe-Messiahs in mae time.

Earl of Gurney (*begins to circle slowly clock-wise*)   You think I'd go around saying I was God if I could help it? Mental hospitals are full of chaps saying they're God.

McKyle (*moving slowly around in opposite direction*)   It's a bit much o' Sackstead sending me twenty million miles through Galactic space and the interplanetary dust piles two feet thick outside the windows, to bandy words wi' a poxy moon-loony who thinks he's me.

Earl of Gurney   I'm here. You're there.

McKyle   Ach, I'm here and I'm there too. (*Opposite each other again.*) Dinnae trifle wi' me. I'm Jehovah o' the Old Testament, the Vengeful God. Awae or you'll be *dropped*.

Dr Herder   You can't both be God.

McKyle   He's only a bleery-eyed blooster, an English pinhead, the hollowed out son o' a Cameronian brothel-keeper.

Earl of Gurney   That's because I'm not myself today. (*To* **Dr Herder**.) You're trying to split my mind with his tongue.

McKyle   Awae home, laddie, afore I burn you to a crispy noodle.

Earl of Gurney   You can't touch me. I'm the Rock. (*Becomes square, massive.*) And the Vine. (*Stretching arms up.*) The goat. (*Springs into chair, fingers as horns.*) The East Wind. (*Blows.*) The Sacred Bug. (*Jumps down, scuttles along.*) The Upright Testicle. (*Jerks upright.*) The Bull.

As they watch him paw and bellow, fascinated, **McKyle** *picks up the empty brandy glass from table and before the* **Assistant** *can stop him takes a bite out of it. Having recaptured their horrified attention, he continues talking with his mouth full of blood.*

McKyle   I saw mae son Jamie dei. He had cancer at the base of his spine and one in his head. They used the black spider treatment on him. It crawled all over, using its feelers, cracking the body vermin and germs wi' its nippers. (*Suddenly to* **Grace**.) I can cure yer bursting. Fire a laser beam doon into yer eye, let a black spider crawl down to clear away the sick puss the sack o' pus, the white puss, the deid . . .

Grace *rises, shaken.*

But first I'll deal wi' yon Irishman. (*Stands on one leg.*) I'm earthed. (*Whipping off glove he suddenly whirls round and stabs forefinger at the* **Earl**'s *stomach.*) Zzzzzzzzz . . .

The **Earl** *tries to protect himself with his hands but slowly doubles up, letting out a long groan which turns into a cry of pain as* **Grace**, *who has staggered to her feet, collapses on the floor clutching her stomach.*

Dr Herder   Damn!

Sir Charles   Grace. Grace.

Claire (*hurrying to the door*)   Tucker!

Sir Charles (*to* **Dr Herder** *bending down to* **Grace**)   Your responsibility, sir. Damn you.

Tucker *appears in doorway.*

Dr Herder   Tucker – Nurse Brice. And tell the midwife to be ready!

McKyle (*taking bulb out of standard lamp*)   I'm *dead*! (*Sticks finger into the socket, shakes violently.*) Re-ch-a-r-ge!

Dr Herder   Get her upstairs.

Sir Charles (*picking* **Grace** *up*)   If we lose this child . . .

They move Up Stage to the door.

McKyle (*shaking*)   B-B-Burn-n-n-n a f-f-f-eath-e-e-e-er o-o-o-n-d-d-er her n-n-nose!

Dinsdale *rushes in excitedly.*

Dinsdale   Super news! Old Barrington-Cochran's dying. It'll mean a by-election.

Claire   Not now, Dinsdale!

Earl of Gurney   Paul, Paul, why persecutest thou me?

All look round and up to the **Earl** *who has, in the confusion, climbed up to the gallery and is now spread out on the cross.* **Sir Charles** *hurries out with* **Grace** *in his arms.* **Claire** *quickly follows as* **Tucker** *reappears in doorway.*

Dr Herder (*to* **Assistant**)   Don't let 'em leave!

He exits.

Tucker   Don't worry, Doctor. I'm a Brown Belt. Fifth Dan. (*Assumes Judo stance, with loud grunts.*) Ho – Ha!

Dinsdale   Will somebody please tell me what's going on?

Tucker (*pouring drink*)   Life, Master Dinsdale, sir. The rich moth-eaten tapestry of life.

Dr Herder *re-enters with* **Claire**.

Dr Herder   Mrs Grant's a fully qualified midwife. She'd resent me interfering professionally. Anyway, I'll be extremely busy down here.

Claire   You're not going on with this?

Dr Herder   It's our last chance. Sackstead will never agree to let McKyle out again.

Dinsdale   Where's father?

Claire   Pacing the corridor upstairs.

Dr Herder   Come, McKyle, get your finger out. (*Up at cross.*) Gentlemen, it's important to know which of you is telling the truth. If one of you is God, the other must be somebody else.

McKyle   Your Worship, Ladies and Gentlemen o' the Jury. I stand accused o' nae being who I am: to wit, the aforesaid, after-mentioned, hereafter-named, uncontested GOD. These are facts. I made the world in mae image. I'm a holy terror. Sae that accoonts fer the bloody mess it's in. Gi' up y' windy wa's McNaughton and plead insanity.

Earl of Gurney   If it's facts you want, the Great Peacock is a Moth which only lives two days. With no mouth to eat or drink it flies miles to love, breed and die. Consider a life o' love without one selfish act, members of the Jury.

McKyle   Ach, and they put me awae for seventeen years. Only the sick wi' spiders webs round their brains clack o'

about lo'e and goodness. I'm a braw God fer bashing bairns'
heads on rocks, a God for strong stomachs.

Earl of Gurney   You're one of the Fu Manchu gang.
(*Gestures at audience.*) They're children of condensed sunlight.

McKyle   The children o' licht you ken, are far awa'. This
is Earth. An early failure o' mine. Earth is where I dump the
excrement o' the Universe, the privy o' the Cosmos.

Earl of Gurney   I'm too full of Grace to listen. People
care for love – love for everything that's necessary for the
continuation of life.

Tucker (*lurching forward*)   We don't want love, we want a
fat slice o' revenge. Kiss me arse!

Dinsdale   Tucker, you're an unmitigated stinker.

Dr Herder   No God of *love* made this world. I've seen a
girl of four's nails had been torn out by her father. I've seen
the mountains of gold teeth and hair and the millions boiled
down for soap.

Earl of Gurney (*he stumbles desperately off the cross, putting
sticking plaster over his eyes*)   S-S-some-times G-G-God turns
his b-b-back on his p-p-people . . .

McKyle   And breaks wind and the stench clouds the
globe! That's settled the verdict 'tween twa' poor Scottish
loons. I'm the High Voltage Man, nearer to God than yon
sentimental clishmac-laverer.

Earl of Gurney   There's a slight truth inside as well as a
light of truth outside.

Dr Herder (*violently*)   Here's the truth! (*Rips sticking plaster
from the **Earl**'s eyes.*) You're *Jack Gurney*, the 14th Earl of
Gurney.

Roll of thunder.

McKyle   I'm Cock o' the North, mae boys. Oh. I'm Cock
o' the North. (*Breaks **Earl**'s staff across knee.*)

Earl of Gurney (*writhing as if in labour*)   ELOI ELOI.

Dr Herder   Your loving family tricked you into marriage because they want an heir.

Earl of Gurney   Pater-Noster-Pater-Noster-Pater-Noster . . .

Dr Herder   If the baby turns out to be a boy they'll have you certified, committed, and in a strait-jacket before you can say another Pater-Noster.

Earl of Gurney (*in great pain*)   I am the Father. Cherish the worm. Errsh . . . I'm splitting. I tear. Torn. (*Writhing.*) Crowned. Coming out crowned. BORN . . . I *AM* THE FATHER.

A clap of thunder. **Claire** *jumps up.*

Claire (*shouting, putting hands to head like horns*)   You're the father of nothing! You're Jack – Jack the *Cuckold*!

McKyle (*firing with both hands at* **Earl**)   Zzzzzzzzzzz . . .

The **Earl** *lets out an extraordinary deep-throated cry, careering backwards, bucking and twisting from the force of the imaginary electrical charge. He crashes against the recorder on the table, starting it playing back at high speed. Simultaneously, there is a clap of thunder, the french-windows fly open and with a rush of cold wind a monstrous eight-feet beast bursts in. It walks upright like a man, covered with thick black hair swept out from each side of its face like a gigantic guinea-pig, and is dressed incongruously in high Victorian fashion: morning coat and top hat. None of the others see the beast, which grabs the* **Earl** *and shakes him violently, to the accompaniment of high-speed jabber from the tape-recorder, thunder-claps and* **McKyle***'s harsh chants 'two million volts zzzzz three million zzzzzzzzzz'.*

The **Earl** *wrestles in an epileptic fit, saliva dribbling from his mouth.* **Claire** *and* **Dinsdale** *watch with well-bred revulsion,* **Dr Herder** *and* **Assistant** *with clinical interest while pushing the heavy furniture out of the way as the beast pummels his victim in a series of vicious wrestling holds. The* **Earl***'s legs and arms are twisted, and his face forced back by a heavy paw. He struggles, but his strength*

*soon leaves him. As the background noise reaches a crescendo, the beast
slams him down across its knee, tosses him on to the floor and then
looking down at the unconscious man, raises its hat, grunts and lurches
out the way it came in.*

The **Earl** *lies still, Stage Centre, one leg twisted under his body.*
McKyle *stops chanting, and* **Claire** *switches off the tape-recorder,
whilst* **Dinsdale** *and* **Tucker** *close the french-windows. Silence.
There is the distinct sound of a single slap and a baby begins to cry
faintly. The* **Assistant** *straightens the* **Earl**'s *leg whilst* **Dr
Herder** *bends down and lifts his head. The* **Earl**'s *eyes open.*

Earl of Gurney (*feebly*)   Jack.

Dr Herder   What?

Earl of Gurney   Jack. My name . . .

Dr Herder (*dawning realisation*)   Yes, Jack. That's right,
your name's Jack. (*Looks up at others.*) It's worked.

McKyle   Cowl the Minnie! Hallelujah! Hallelujah!

Dinsdale   Oh, well done.

Earl of Gurney   Jack. My name's Jack.

Sir Charles *enters Up Stage Centre, a bundle in his arms.*

Sir Charles (*holding up bundle triumphantly*)   It's a boy!

Earl of Gurney   Jack. I'm Jack. I'm Jack. I'm Jack!

The baby starts to cry.

Curtain.

Act Two

Scene One

'Oh for the Wings of a Dove' played over, then out of the darkness
Bishop Lampton's *voice intones:*

Bishop Lampton (*over*)   Vincent, Henry, Edward, Ralph
Gurney, I baptise thee in the name of the Father and of the
Son and of the Holy Ghost.

Baby cries. Photographer's flash momentarily lights a christening group
of **Sir Charles**, **Claire**, **Dinsdale**, **Dr Herder**, **Tucker**
and **Bishop Lampton**, *grouped around* **Grace** *with the child.*

Then lights up on the drawing-room, now containing pieces of
Victorian furniture and bric-a-brac. The cross has gone. **Tucker**
pulls off the **Bishop**'s *robes.*

Grace   What a pair of lungs. The little devil up-staged
everybody. He's a trouper.

Sir Charles (*jovially, at baby*)   Coochy-coochy. He's a
splendid fella, eh, Bertie?

Bishop Lampton   A vessel newly filled with the Holy
Spirit, but I fear regrettably leaky.

Grace   Leaky or not, he's saved you Gurneys from
becoming extinct.

She exits.

Sir Charles   Things are beginning to get back to
normal.

Dr Herder   What are we going to do about his lordship?

Sir Charles   The family came to a decision some time
ago, that after certain matters had been cleared up he'd be
put away. Permanently this time. For his own good.

Claire   That was before, Charles. The situation's
changed.

Bishop Lampton   I gathered he's improved. But we can't be sure he won't sink back into darkness and shadow.

Dinsdale   Sometimes it's worse than when he was completely potty. I mean, we're all just waiting for him to go off again, tick-tick-tick-tick-*boom*. We've been darned lucky up to now but with a possible by-election in the offing, it's too risky.

Sir Charles   Can't say I'm the sensitive type, but the strain of the last few months is beginning to tell. I think it's best all round if Jack were put away. (**Tucker** *staggers off with the vestments.*)

Tucker   I think it's best all round if the whole bloody lot of you were put away.

Sir Charles   And Jack's not the only one we can say goodbye to.

Grace *comes back in.*

Grace   Nothing like a couple of nursemaids to take the curse out of having kids.

Claire   We were talking about Jack.

Grace   He's a helluva problem. What do you say, doctor?

Dr Herder   Thank you for asking. You must realise that the battle between the God of Love and the Electric Messiah was a tremendous breakthrough.

Grace   Is he cured?

Dr Herder   He's on the way to recovery. His behaviour is nearer the acceptable norm. I don't know whether it's permanent. I do know, you mustn't have him committed. I've got a full schedule of research lined up, but I'm taking valuable time out for this therapy. This case could become a classic of psychology – Freud's Anna O., now Herder's Earl of Gurney.

Earl of Gurney   Call me Jack.

*The **Earl** stands in the doorway Up Stage Centre with an ancient shotgun levelled at them. Before they can react he pulls the trigger and says 'click'; nothing happens. He has changed; no beard, his hair is short, and he wears an old-fashioned dark suit with waistcoat and stiff collar. His words and gestures are still slightly out of 'synch'.*

It's a pleasant name. (*Imitating bell.*) J-J-Jack, J-J-Jack, J-J-Jack.

Using his shotgun as a temporary crutch he crosses Stage Centre with a peculiar loping hop.

Sir Charles   And he's recovering? (*To the **Earl**.*) Why are you walking like that?

*The **Earl** pulls off his right show, feels inside, and takes out a large pebble. He shows it to **Sir Charles** by way of reply.*

(*Disappointed.*) Oh. A stone.

Claire   Reasonable.

Earl of Gurney (*gesturing with gun*)   I found it in the attic.

Grace   Why aren't you resting?

Earl of Gurney   I wanted to apologise for not being at my own son's christening.

Grace   The little devil stole the show.

Earl of Gurney   I must be sure before I make my first public appearance. Very important to leave the right impression. When I g-g- huitment, re-return dunt d-d-impression of overall superiority and volatile farts the shadow of it is sludge ghoul of a whore, whoredom's bloddy network. (*Struggles fiercely to regain control.*) Hold sir, hold hold hold hold sir. (*Recovering, to **Dinsdale**.*) A relative who said he was Christ could hardly be a political asset to you, Dinsdale.

Dr Herder   I don't know. A Tory Leader was the son of a carpenter, after all.

Earl of Gurney (*surprised*)   Lord Salisbury's a carpenter's son. Really?

Claire   How are you feeling?

Earl of Gurney   Lazarus felt like I feel. Odour of dung. Duat d' d' d'muss bed sores the executioners arrive for Nijinsky the liquid streets unstable my wooden leg needs morphine. *Back, sir. Back, sir. Back.* Be patient. I'll learn the rules of the game.

Dr Herder   We know you will.

Claire   You've changed already.

Tucker *enters carrying a cape and deerstalker cap.*

Tucker   You wished to take a constitutional at noon, my lord.

Earl of Gurney   Thank you, Tuck. Invaluable man, Tuck.

Tucker   There's some 'ere who don't think so, your lordship. (*To* **Sir Charles**.) No names, no pack-drill. I know they're waiting to give me the boot.

Earl of Gurney   You and me both, Tuck. We must give 'em no cause, no cause.

Grace (*helping him on with the cape*)   Don't stay out too long, Jack.

Earl of Gurney   Just want to get the feel of terra firma. I must learn to keep my mouth shut, bowels open and never volunteer. Come, Tuck.

They exit through french-windows.

Claire   Well? Has he changed or hasn't he? I agreed with you before, Charles, he was hopeless and the sooner we put him away the better. Now it'd be stupid. I know he'll recover.

Grace   And if he does? Where does that leave us? He mightn't understand what we did.

Dinsdale   I say, aren't you all jumping the gun? Look at the way he suddenly goes off. 'Volatile farts a' a' duat.' What's all that then?

Dr Herder   Paralalia – speech disturbance. It would be simpler if a man was paranoid one moment and cured the next. Unfortunately, it takes time.

Dinsdale   There's all this Victorian bric-a-brac stuff he's got everywhere. And what about him thinking the leader of the Conservative Party was the Marquis of Salisbury?

Dr Herder   Sicilian peasants thought Churchill was a kind of tomato. Thousands of Indians have never heard of Gandhi. Political ignorance is not a symptom of psychosis. It might even be considered a sign of mental health.

Claire   Bertie, you haven't seen much of Jack lately. What's your opinion?

Bishop Lampton   The acid test still is, would he pass muster in the Athenæum? Could he be introduced to members without raising eyebrows?

Dr Herder   In the end it's really her ladyship's decision.

Grace   Oh, hell. Thanks a lot. I don't know. There's the baby . . . What if he suddenly . . . ? Have I got to right now? Jeez, I can't make up my mind.

Sir Charles   You don't have to. It's done. I've already asked the Master in Lunacy to come down and certify Jack's insane.

A single shot, off Right, breaks the stunned silence. **Claire**, **Dr Herder** *and* **Grace** *look at each other, then rush out of the french-windows.*

Sir Charles (*hopefully, to* **Dinsdale**)   Do you think Jack's done the decent thing at last?

Bishop Lampton *crosses himself.*

Lights down.

Scene Two

Spot up on metal sun hanging Down Stage Centre: some white feathers float down. Footlights up to show the **Earl** *standing with* **Tucker**, *Down Stage Right, looking blankly at his smoking shotgun, a dead dove at his feet. Voices are heard calling off.*

Tucker (*shakily*)   That's how accidents happen. That could have been me, your lordship. You've been waving that gun all over the place. (*Takes out hip-flask.*) Not that anyone'd have cared much. No one to weep for poor creeping Tucker. (*Drinks.*) But I'm not ready for stoking the fiery furnace yet. I've got an awful lot of living to do. Girls by the hundreds to name only a few . . .

Grace, **Claire** *and* **Dr Herder** *rush anxiously on Wings Right.*

Grace   What happened? You all right?

Tucker   As rain, your ladyship. Just a little accident. The gun went off. But Ironside never flinched.

Claire   You're not hurt, Jack?

Earl of Gurney (*indicating dove, takes off hat*)   R.I.P.

Grace   Where the devil were you, Jeeves?

Claire   Guzzling! Your job's to look after his lordship, Tucker.

Tucker   I know my job, Lady Claire, and my place. And that's indoors. It's f-f-freezing.

With the exception of the **Earl** *the others are already feeling cold. They shift from one foot to the other to keep warm during the rest of the scene.* **Sir Charles** *hurries on, Wings Right.*

Sir Charles (*sees* **Earl**)   Oh. Still in one piece?

Claire   Disappointed?

Earl of Gurney   I was trying to do what's expected. I recall it's a sign of normalcy in our circle to slaughter anything that moves. All I did was . . .

He aims the shotgun up at the Flies off Left, and pulls the trigger. To everyone's horror, the second barrel fires. There is a bellow of pain from the Flies, a cry 'Ahhhhh . . .' followed by a crash as someone hits the ground.

Sir Charles   Poachers! Damn poachers! (*Grabs the* **Earl***'s gun.*) Come on, Tucker. After him!

Sir Charles *rushes off with a reluctant* **Tucker**. **Dinsdale** *can be heard calling 'I say, where is everybody? H-e-ll-ooo', as* **Claire**, **Dr Herder** *and* **Grace** *look suspiciously at the* **Earl**.

Earl of Gurney   I had a stone in my shoe and an accident with an old gun, so you still think I'm insane. I know a man who hated the sight of his wrinkled socks, so he wore his girl friend's girdle to keep 'em up. Now she's his wife. I've got to stop talking. (*Takes* **Grace***'s hand.*) Just give me time.

Dr Herder   Sir Charles has asked the Master in Lunacy to come here to commit you to an institution.

Earl *lets go of* **Grace***'s hand; he becomes rigid and sways.*

Naturally I'll oppose any commitment. But in the end it depends on how you act.

Earl of Gurney (*stops swaying*)   Perhaps it's for the best. If I satisfy the Lunatic Master, I'll be officially sane, and I'll have a certificate to prove it. But Charles has been unwise. (*All shiver.*) You'll catch your deaths out here. Odd expression.

Dr Herder   L-L-Let's get in then. We've got work to do.

Earl of Gurney   I'll stay a moment and compose myself.

Dr Herder *nods and exits briskly Wings Right, with* **Claire**.

Grace   What a family. Enough to drive anyone round the bend. Will you be all right, Jack?

Earl of Gurney (*arm around her*)   The only sensible thing I've done in the last seven years was to marry you.

Grace   There now. There now. Don't stay out too long, Honey. (*Moves off, shivering.*) Charles is a bloody moron. I'll have his guts for garters.

As she exits Wings Left, the metal sun is taken up.

Earl of Gurney   Soft. Softly. Down, down, down, oh, let me keep it down, pianissimo, damp down, damp down. Down. I'm a soft grub ununduuulating. They'll rip me open. Nail my brain to my skull. Strom, strom, grunk, grok. *Crunk*. Fug. That means you. *Fug. Fug. Fug.* Silence when you speak S-i-l-e-n-c-e. Steady the Buffs, waiter, I say, waiter, there's a moustache in my soup. Kerr-un-crrrr. KORKSHIST – KORKSHIST – KUK-KUK-KUK-KUK-KUK-KUK . . .

Unable to stop he takes out two strips of sticky-tape and sticks them across his mouth. Now he can't speak and his savage struggle to control himself can only be expressed in abrupt body movements. He starts leaping, spreading out his cape; higher and higher, till a last climactic leap, and he lands, crouching in a ball, Down Stage Centre. Dim Lights Up Stage Centre, to show a dark shadowy figure waiting in the drawing-room behind him: it is the **Master in Lunacy**.

Scene Three

Lights up on the **Master**, **Kelso Truscott, Q.C.**, *in the drawing-room, which now contains more Victorian bric-a-brac: stuffed pheasants, wax fruit under glass, and a red-plush sofa. The* **Earl** *straightens up resolutely and is joined by* **Tucker**. *The* **Earl** *hands him his hat and cape and* **Tucker** *gives him* The Times *newspaper in return. The* **Earl** *puts it under his arm and sticks a briar pipe firmly in his mouth. Turning sharply on his heels, he squares his* *shoulders and marches purposefully Up Stage to join* **Truscott**, *a big hard-faced man who is looking through some documents.*

Truscott   Where did you spring from?

Earl of Gurney   You must be Truscott, the Lunatic fella.

Truscott (*frowning*)   I'm the Master of the Court of Protection. The title 'Master in Lunacy' isn't used nowadays.

It is obvious **Truscott** *is scrutinising the* **Earl** *closely.*

Earl of Gurney   How about a snifter? No? All right then, Tuck.

Tucker   Very good, sir. Watch yourself now. He looks a fishy-eyed, light-fingered gent to me. (*Glaring at* **Truscott**.) I know the price of everything in this room. So if there's anything missing we shall know where to look.

He exits Up Stage Centre. **Truscott** *stares after him.*

Earl of Gurney   Splendid fella. Very loyal.

Truscott   Hmmm. You know why I'm here?

Earl of Gurney   I'd better introduce myself first. Jack Gurney. (*With slightest emphasis.*) The Earl of Gurney. I believe Charles considers me incapable and you're here to commit me officially.

Truscott   Not exactly, my lord. I make a recommendation to a Nominated Judge and he does the actual committing. My main concern is property and its proper administration. This investigation, however, is rather informal. A favour to Charles. (*Takes out silver snuff box.*) Yours is a confusing case. (*Taps the snuff box three times and takes snuff.*) Two doctors recommend you to be put under care, but Dr Herder says you're nearly back to normal. Of course, he *is* a foreigner and his idea of normal may not be mine.

Despite himself the **Earl**'s *hand trembles, as he fills his pipe.*
Truscott *watches closely.*

Earl of Gurney   How do you find out?

Truscott   You talk. I listen.

Earl of Gurney (*sits on sofa*)   Ah, yes, talk. Judas talk t-t-t-t-talk . . .

Truscott (*glances at file*)   Do you still believe you're Christ, my lord? (*No reply.*) Are you God? (*No reply.*) Come, sir, are you the God of Love?

The **Earl** *stares into space, deep in thought, then slowly rises and points at him.*

Earl of Gurney   Harrow may be more clever.

Truscott   What!

Earl of Gurney (*singing*)   'Rugby may make more row. But we'll row, row for ever. Steady from stroke to bow. And nothing in life shall sever the chain that is round us now . . .'

Truscott *crosses grimly to the* **Earl**, *stares at him, and then, without warning joins in, in a barber-shop duet.*

Truscott *and* **Earl of Gurney**   'Others will fill our places, dressed in the old light blue. We'll recollect our races. We'll to the flag be true.' (*They mime rowing.*) 'But we'll still swing together. And swear by the best of schools. But we'll still swing together and swear by the best of schools!'

Earl of Gurney   I didn't realise – you're *Kelso* Truscott. *The* Kelso Truscott who scored that double century at Lords.

Truscott   A long time ago.

Earl of Gurney   Of course, I was pretty low down the school when you were in your glory, Truscott. They said when you got back after the Lords match dressed in a kilt, you debagged the Chaplain and hit the local constable over the head with an ebony shelalee.

Truscott (*chuckling*)   Ah, schooldays, schooldays. It's all ahead of you then . . . You realise, your lordship, the fact that we're both Old Etonians can have no possible influence on my recommendation. (*Taps snuff box.*) Of course, I find it even harder to believe now. Etonians aren't exactly noted for their grey matter, but I've always found them perfectly adjusted to society. (*Sniffs.*) Now, are you the God of Love?

Earl of Gurney   He no longer exists. I was wild with too much jubilating. I've been raving for seven years, Truscott. But everyone's entitled to one mistake.

Truscott   Seven years. That accounts for your not being at any of the Old Boys' Reunion Dinners.

Earl of Gurney   I went around saying the Lord looooooves you LOOOOOVES. Tch. Grrk. (*Bites hard on pipe.*) Sorry there, Truscott. It's embarrassing for a fella to remember what a spectacle he made of himself. Naturally I get tongue-tied. Bit shame-faced, don't y'know.

Truscott   You seem right enough to me, but these things are deceptive. Is there anything you feel strongly about, your lordship?

Earl of Gurney   My w-w-wasted years. I woke up the other day and I had grey hairs. Grey hairs and duty neglected. Our country's being destroyed before our e-e-eyes. You're MOCKED in the Strand if you speak of patriotism and the old Queen. Discipline's gone. They're sapping the foundations of our society with their adultery and fornication!

Truscott *crosses Down Stage Left and pulls bell-rope.*

The barbarians are waiting outside with their chaos, anarchy, homosexuality and worse!

Sir Charles, **Claire**, **Grace** *and* **Dr Herder** *hurry in Up Stage Centre.*

Grace   Well?

Truscott (*putting papers into the briefcase*)   Dr Herder you said you thought his lordship was on the road to recovery. I can't agree.

Sir Charles   *There.*

Truscott   You're too cautious. For my money he's recovered.

Grace *kisses the* **Earl** *impulsively.*

Grace   We're grateful to you, Mr Truscott.

Truscott   Thank you, your ladyship. (*To the* **Earl**.) We'll expect you at the next Reunion Dinner, my lord. Lady Claire, a pleasure. Dr Herder, congratulations. Splendid achievement. (*To* **Sir Charles**.) You're lucky this was only a friendly investigation, old boy. We take a dim view of frivolous complaints.

He exits.

Sir Charles   Truscott's a damn ass. Can't he see I'm right?

Grace   Right? I've had enough of your right. You've stuck your aristocratic schnozzle into my affairs for the last time. Right? Jack's changed. Right? Everything's changed – you, me, us, them. It's a new deal all round. Right? You know what I mean. Right? *Right!*

She exits.

Sir Charles   Did what I thought best.

Dr Herder   The best you can do now is to leave Jack alone. He's made a spectacular breakthrough. We're in the process of making a new man.

Claire   I'm always on the lookout for new men.

Sir Charles *exits.*

You did it, Jack. Wonderful.

Dr Herder   Leave him, he's been under a great strain. I didn't think he was ready for that blockhead Truscott.

Claire   Blockhead or not, he brought in the right verdict.

Dr Herder   I suspect the Earl's behaviour just happened to coincide with his idea of sanity. Your nephew needs very delicate handling at this stage. And if possible, a little love.

Claire   That shouldn't be too difficult.

Dr Herder   You helped Sir Charles crucify him.

Claire   Jack's changed. He's strong now.

Dr Herder   What about us?

Claire   We're too much alike. Ice on ice. I wanna' feel *alive*.

Dr Herder   And you think Jack'll perform that miracle?

Claire   Oh, rats to you.

Lights dim to a Spot on the **Earl** *as they exit.*

Scene Four

The **Earl** *hunches his right shoulder and drags his left leg.*

Earl of Gurney   Deformed, unfinished, sent before me time, those eminent doctors of Divinity, Professors McKyle and Herder cured me of paranoid delusions fantasy obsessions of love, that's where it ended, a solvental of inner and outer tensions. No more inter-stage friction. See how I marshal words. That's the secret of being normal. (*He pulls the words out of his mouth.*) 'I' – straighten up there. 'AM' – close up, close up with 'I' you 'orrible little word. 'GOD' . . . I AM GOD. Not the God of Love but God Almighty. God the Law-Giver, Chastiser and Judge. For I massacred the Amalekites and the Seven Nations of Canaan, I hacked Agag to pieces and blasted the barren fig-tree. I will tread them in mine anger and trample them in my fury, and their

blood shall be sprinkled upon my garments. For the day of
vengeance is in my heart! Hats off for the God of Justice, the
God of Love is dead. Oh, you lunar jackass. *She betrayed you.*
Lust muscles tighten over plexus. Guilty, guilty, guilty. The
punishment is death. I've finally been processed into right-
thinking power. They made me adjust to modern times.
This is 1888 isn't it? I knew I was Jack. Hats off. I said Jack.
I'm Jack, cunning Jack, quiet Jack, Jack's my name. (*Produces
knife, flicks it open.*) Jack whose sword never sleeps. Hats off
I'm Jack, not the Good Shepherd, not the Prince of Peace.
I'm Red Jack, Springheeled Jack, Saucy Jack, Jack from
Hell, trade-name Jack the Ripper! . . . Mary, Annie,
Elizabeth, Catherine, Marie Kelly. (*Sings.*) 'Six little whores
glad to be alive, one sidles up to Jack, then there were five.'

He exits Wings Left, slashing the air with his knife.

Scene Five

Lights up to show **Grace** *and* **Dinsdale** *talking in the drawing-
room, now completely furnished in authentic Victorian style.*

Dinsdale   How could you have asked 'em? What about
my career?

Grace   Politics is no career for a healthy young chap. You
should go out to work like the rest of us.

Dinsdale   But look what happened the last time.

Grace   That's why I got 'em to come again. When they
see how Jack's changed they'll spread the word.
Everybody'll know he's back to normal.

Dinsdale   I don't think he is.

Grace   You're just siding with your father. He won't
admit Jack's cured because it doesn't suit him.

Dinsdale   I don't know how you persuaded 'em to come.

Grace   I'm her ladyship. Sixty miles outside London an awful lot of cap tugging and forelock touching still goes on. You couldn't keep 'em away.

Tucker *enters.*

Tucker   Mrs Treadwell and Mrs Piggot-Jones, your ladyship.

Two heads, topped with absurd hats, peer round the door.

Mrs Treadwell *and* **Mrs Piggot-Jones** *edge their way apprehensively into the room. Though relieved to see the cross has gone they keep close together for protection.*

Grace   Welcome, ladies. You can serve tea now, Jeeves.

Tucker *crosses to the tea-trolley.*

Mrs Treadwell *(nervously)*   Everything's changed.

Grace   Yes his Nibs – Jack's just crazy about this Victorian stuff.

Mrs Piggot-Jones   It's very hard-wearing.

Grace   I hear the atmosphere was a trifle strained on your last visit.

Mrs Treadwell   Well, it was our first meeting with his lordship. Neither Mrs Piggot-Jones nor myself knew him personally. Though of course we knew his father.

Grace   I never knew mine. But my mother knew Lloyd George.

Dinsdale   He wasn't himself, don't y'know. Bit unsettled. Didn't have a wife and family then.

Mrs Treadwell   How is the Right Honourable Lord Vincent, your ladyship?

Grace *(laughing)*   'The Honourable Lord Vince.' Oh, he's fine, just like his dad.

The two women look startled.

(*Quickly.*) I know Jack wants to explain about last time.

Tucker *serves tea.*

Mrs Treadwell (*tentatively*)   He asked me if I loved. Your manservant heard him.

Tucker (*cupping right ear*)   What's that? Speak up, missus.

Mrs Treadwell   Why did he say God is love?

Earl of Gurney   Because he was mad. Mad with grief. His father had just died.

A sombrely dressed **Earl of Gurney** *enters smiling, with* **Claire**. *He is quiet, self-possessed.* **Claire** *sits on the sofa, fascinated.*

Grace   Talk of the devil. Darling, you remember Mrs Piggot-Jones and Mrs Treadwell?

Earl of Gurney   Tucker, why are those table legs uncovered? Stark naked wooden legs in mixed company – it's not decent. Curved and fluted, too. Don't you agree, Mrs Treadwell?

Mrs Treadwell   Well, I do think young girls nowadays show too much. After all, the main purpose of legs isn't seduction.

Earl of Gurney   Cover 'em with calico or cotton, Tucker.

Tucker   Yes, sir, no, sir, three bags full, sir. I'm a 104-year-old Creep and I 'ave to do everything.

He exits, mumbling.

Earl of Gurney   Now ladies, when did we meet?

Mrs Treadwell   Remember you asked me if I loved?

Earl of Gurney   *Please*, not in front of women and children.

Mrs Piggot-Jones   I've told Pamela not to brood about it.

Earl of Gurney   Let's have no talk of bestial orgasms, erotic tonguings. It burns small high-voltage holes in the brain. It's been proved in oscillographs.

Grace   My husband hates anything suggestive.

Mrs Piggot-Jones   So do I. I find the whole subject distressing. I can't understand why the Good Lord chose such a disgusting way of reproducing human-beings.

Earl of Gurney   Anything more refined would be too good for producing such two-legged, front-facing Hairies.

Claire   Who did you finally get as Guest Speaker for your Church Fête?

Mrs Treadwell   Sir Barrington-Cochran. That was just before he became ill.

Mrs Piggot-Jones   Made a splendid speech, didn't he, Pamela, about the rise of crime and socialism.

Dinsdale   I intend to campaign actively, for the reintroduction of the death penalty.

Earl of Gurney (*trembling*)   You mean there's no death penalty in England's green and pleasant?

Mrs Treadwell   Surely you knew, your lordship?

Grace   We're a bit out of touch. My husband only reads *Punch*.

Earl of Gurney   Is nothing sacred? Why, the Hangman holds society together. He is the symbol of the Great Chastiser. He built this world on punishment and fear.

Mrs Treadwell *and* **Mrs Piggot-Jones** *nod vigorously.*

Snuff out fear and see what discords follow. Sons strike their doddering dads, young girls show their bosoms and ankles and say rude things about the Queen. Anything goes and they do it openly in the streets and frighten the horses.

Mrs Piggot-Jones   It's the times we live in. But what can one do?

Earl of Gurney   Bring back fear. In the old days the Executioner kept the forelock-touching ranks in order. When he stood on the gallows, stripped to the waist, tight breeches, black hood, you knew God was in his heaven, all's right with the world. The punishment for blaspheming was to be broken on the wheel. First the fibula. (*Mimes bringing down an iron bar.*) Cr-a-a-ck. Then the tibia, patella and femur. *Crack, crack, crack.* The corpus, ulna and radius, *crack.* 'Disconnect dem bones, dem dry bones. Disconnect dem bones dem dry bones. Now hear the word of the Lord.'

Irresistibly the two women join in.

Earl of Gurney, **Mrs Piggot-Jones** *and* **Mrs Treadwell** (*singing*)   'When your head bone's connected from your neck bone, your neck bone's connected from your shoulder bone, your shoulder bone's connected from your backbone. Now hear the word of the Lord. Dem bones dem bones dem dry bones. Now hear the word of the Lord . . .'

Earl of Gurney   We understand each other perfectly. But that's only to be expected. Breeding speaks to breeding.

Mrs Piggot-Jones   How splendid, your lordship.

Mrs Treadwell   I've always believed I'm descended from the Kings of Munster, even though my family originally came from Wimbledon.

Mrs Piggot-Jones   Forgive me for saying so, my lord, but this is so different from our last visit. Such an unfortunate misunderstanding.

Earl of Gurney   Don't give it another thought, madam. I don't hold it against you. I'm sure I forgot it the moment you left. (*Crosses to desk.*) Now forgive me, I have so much to do. (*To* **Grace**.) My dear, why don't you show our guests round the estate?

Grace   Fine. Give us a hand, Dinsdale.

Earl of Gurney   Don't forget to show these good ladies
my coronation robes, the mantle of crimson velvet lined
with white taffeta, edged with miniver. Good day, ladies.
You may withdraw.

He dismisses them with a regal wave of his hand. **Mrs Piggot-
Jones** *and* **Mrs Treadwell** *find themselves curtseying. The* **Earl**
turns away and picks up some letters from his desk.

Mrs Piggot-Jones (*low*)   He's so impressive, your
ladyship, such natural dignity.

Grace   He's still a bit eccentric.

Mrs Piggot-Jones   Runs in the family. But it's only on
the surface. Deep down one knows he's sound.

They stop in the doorway and look back at the **Earl** *calmly slitting
open a letter with a paper-knife.*

Mrs Treadwell   He's so like his father. He gets more like
him every day, it's frightening.

As they exit **Dinsdale** *turns, gives a delighted thumbs-up sign and
hurries after them.*

Grace   Claire . . .

Claire   I'll stay and keep Jack company.

Grace   You seem to be doing a lot of company keeping
lately. Don't put yourself to so much trouble.

Claire   No trouble. It's a pleasure.

Grace   We're going to miss you when you leave.

She exits. **Claire** *watches the* **Earl** *deftly slitting open envelopes one
after the other.*

Scene Six

*The **Earl** puts down the paper-knife and smiles. Throughout the scene the lights imperceptibly fade down as dusk falls.*

Claire Good. That leaves the two of us.

Earl of Gurney I'm still not word perfect. That talk of bestial orgasms, erotic tonguings – was very unfortunate.

Claire They didn't mind much what you said. Your manner won 'em over. Just the right blend of God-given arrogance and condescension.

Earl of Gurney I stand outside myself watching myself watching myself. (*Pulls up the corners of his mouth.*) I smile, I smile, I smile.

Claire I like your smile. Before I was only sorry for you.

Earl of Gurney Ah, before, madam. Before I was a mass of light. Mad, you see. Nothing was fast enough to match my inner speed. Now I'm sane. The world sweats into my brain, madam.

Claire Don't keep calling me madam.

Earl of Gurney It's hard to look at people from down-wind. They smell, they stink, they stench of stale greens, wet nappies. It's terrible but it's the real thing.

Claire I've always wanted to find the real thing. Do you remember our first talk together after you came back?

Earl of Gurney I remember nothing.

Claire Explode, only feel, you said. Poor Jack. You didn't know how impossible it was for our sort to feel.

Earl of Gurney Why do you remember now what I said then, when I can't remember myself?

Claire Because you're so different. I keep thinking abut something that happened in my last term at Roedean. There'd been reports of a prowler in the grounds, probably

a Peeping Tom. Something woke me about 2 a.m. and I
went to the window and looked out. There was a shadow in
the shadows. Somebody was watching me. It was a hot
night but I started shivering and shaking. It was *marvellous*.

Earl of Gurney   Yea, I say unto you, fear Him. I'm no
shadow. I'm flesh and blood. Touch.

Claire (*touching his cheek*)   Perhaps I'm not really dead, only
sleeping. Wake me with a kiss.

Earl of Gurney (*takes her hand away*)   Remember our
common consanguinity.

Claire   Don't be ridiculous. I'm married to your father's
half-brother for my sins. That makes us practically
strangers, bloodwise.

He attempts to move away. She steps in front of him.

Earl of Gurney (*smiling*)   Are you accosting me?

Claire (*playing up*)   That's right, ducks. 'Ow's about it?

*They come close in the half-light. She kisses him on the mouth. The Set
begins to change to a nineteenth-century slum street in Whitechapel. A
gauze lowered Up Stage, shows a dark huddle of filthy houses, broken
doors, windows stuffed with paper. Beyond, an impression of dark
alleys, low arches, row upon row of lodging houses. It is dank and
foggy. Stage Left, a single flickering street lamp. Stage Right a filthy
brick wall with the name of the street: 'Buck's Row'. Drunken singing
and street cries can be heard off: 'Apple-a-pound-pears, whelks, they're
lovely' and the clip-clop of a horse-drawn van over cobbles.*

*The overall effect is of a furnished room in the middle of a London
street.*

Moonlight shines through the french-windows as the **Earl** *and*
Claire *cross the street to the sofa.*

We'll be alone here. They're all out except Tucker and he's
drunk. Listen . . .

They listen to a drunk singing in the distance.

You don't seem surprised this has happened to us, Jack?

Earl of Gurney   We were destined to meet.

Claire   That sounds romantic. More please.

Earl of Gurney (*low, passionate*)   Suuuuuck. GRAHHH. Spinnkk. The flesh lusteth against the spirit, against God. Labia, foreskin, testicles, scrotum.

Claire   *That's* romantic?

Earl of Gurney   Orgasm, coitus, copulation, fornication. Gangrened shoulder of sex. If it offends. Tear. Tear. Spill the seed, gut-slime.

Claire   I know some women like being stimulated with dirty words, filthy talk. I don't.

She starts taking off his jacket, waistcoat and shirt.

Earl of Gurney   You want maggots crawling through black grass.

Claire   I want to hear you say you love me, even if it isn't true.

Earl of Gurney   I've seen three thousand houses collapse exposing their privees to the naked eye. *Oh, run, Mary. RUN.*

Claire   You're talking nonsense again, Jack.

Earl of Gurney   If thy eye offends thee pluck it out. You'll be nicked down to your bloody membrane, Mary.

Claire   I want to hear how beautiful you think I am.

Earl of Gurney   You want two seconds of DRIPPING SIN to fertilise sodomised idiots.

Claire   Say something soft and tender.

Earl of Gurney   You want gullet and rack. Gugged SHAARK.

Claire   Tell me I'm fairer than the evening star. Clad in the beauty of a thousand nights.

Earl of Gurney (*now stripped to the waist, she caresses him*)
Cut-price lumps of flesh: three and six an hour. Calves
paunches, tender tongue, ear-lobes, e-e-ar-lobe-sss, hearts,
bladders, teats, nippllezzz.

Claire (*shivering*)   Lover.

Earl of Gurney   The word of the Lord is filled with
blood.

Claire (*trembling violently*)   Stop talking Jack, and make me
immortal with a kiss.

*Putting his left arm around her waist he pulls her close, forcing her
head back with a kiss. Taking out his knife, he flicks it open, and
plunges it into her stomach. Bucking and writhing with the great knife
thrust,* **Claire** *can only let out a muffled cry as the* **Earl***'s mouth is
still clamped over hers in a kiss. She writhes, twists and moans under
two more powerful stabs. He lets her go.*

AHHHRREEEE. I'M ALIVE. ALIVE.

She falls and dies. The **Earl** *stands listening for a second, puts his
knife away, picks up his clothes crosses Stage Right and leaves silently
by the french-windows. Even as he does so, the Set begins to change
back to the drawing-room interior, the gauze and street lamp are taken
up as the noises off grow louder. Someone is heard yelling: 'Help!
Police!' Sounds of men running. A police whistle blows shrilly, followed
by a jumble of panic-stricken cries. These merge into a Newsboy
shouting 'Read all about it 'Orrible Murder. Murder and Mutilation
in White-Chapel. Maniac claims another victim. Mary Ann Nichols
found murdered in Buck's Row. Read all about it!' The drawing-room
set is now completely restored. The hysterical hubbub dies down to a
solitary drunk singing incoherently: 'Come Into the Garden Maud'. It
grows louder as he comes closer.* **Tucker** *enters swaying and singing.*

Tucker   'Come into the sh' garden Maudy.' Did you s'
ring? (*Blinks, sees* **Claire** *on the floor.*) S'Lady Claire . . . are
you comfortable? Stoned, eh? (*Stumbles over.*) Can I be of . . .
aeeeehh.

He gives a great rasping intake of breath at the sight and stands mumbling in shock. Then he shakes all over. But not from fear.

(*Gleefully.*) One less! One less! Praise the Lord. *Hallelujah.*

Convulsed with glee he capers creakingly round the corpse in a weird dance. He freezes in mid-gesture as voices are heard off. **Sir Charles**, **Dinsdale** *and* **Dr Herder** *and* **Grace** *come in.*

Sir Charles   No lights, Tucker?

Dinsdale *switches on the lights.*

Dr Herder   My God!

They rush over. **Grace** *puts her hand to her mouth in horror. Appalled,* **Dr Herder** *bends to examine the corpse while* **Sir Charles** *stares in disbelief, unable to find words to express himself. Finally he turns and explodes indignantly at the audience:*

Sir Charles   All right, who's the impudent clown responsible for this?

Blackout.

Scene Seven

A great church organ plays, and a choir sings the 'Dies Irae'. As the last note of the terrifying hymn dies away, lights up on the drawing-room to show **Detective Inspector Brockett***, a middle-aged man with tired face, feeling his stomach, whilst his assistant,* **Detective Sergeant Fraser***, checks through some notes. The carpet by the sofa has been pulled back and there is a cardboard outline of* **Claire***'s body on the floor.*

Fraser (*reads quickly*)   'Five-inch gash under right ear to centre of throat severing windpipe. Three stab wounds in lower abdomen. Two knife wounds, one veering to right slitting the groin and passing over the lower left hip, and the other straight up along the centre of the body to the breast-bone. Severe bruising round the mouth. The pathologist thinks the murderer must have had some medical knowledge.' Reminds me of the Drayhurst killing, sir.

Brockett   Not really. Martha Drayhurst was found all over the place. Arms and legs in Woolwich, trunk in Euston Station, and the rest of her turned up in Penge. Old Sam Drayhurst had a quirky sense of humour for a butcher. At least Lady Claire was all in one piece.

Footsteps outside.

They're back. Bishop Lampton'll be with 'em. How do you address a bishop?

Fraser   Bishop, sir.

Brockett   Bishop, Bishop.

Bishop Lampton *enters supported by* **Sir Charles** *and* **Dinsdale**. *They have just come from the funeral.*

Bishop Lampton   This house is doomed, Charles. I should never have allowed my poor sister to marry into this accursed family. It's another House of Usher.

Carefully avoiding the outline on the floor they half-carry him Down Stage Left and drop him into a chair, gasping.

Sir Charles   Don't talk rubbish, Bertie. Terrible business, but we mustn't lose our heads.

Dinsdale   How could anything like this happen to us? What was mother thinking of?

Sir Charles *(urgently)*   Not in front of strangers, Dinsdale. Brockett, why aren't you running this animal to earth?

Brockett   Don't you worry, sir, we'll get him. But there's still a few points I'd like to clear up. We know the butler found the body just after the killer left by the french-windows. When you came in a moment later, whereabouts was he standing?

Sir Charles   Who? Tucker?

Grace *enters.*

Grace   The baby's asleep. What are you lot doing?

Sir Charles   Brockett, this is her ladyship. He wants to know how we found Tucker beside Claire's body.

Grace   Oh, here.

She stands beside the outline, puts her left foot out and raises both her arms.

Like the Hokey-Cokey.

Brockett   Why would he be doing anything like the Hokey-Cokey?

Dinsdale   He was drunk and he had his teeth out.

Brockett   I'd better have another word with Tucker. Run a double check on him, Sergeant.

Sir Charles   Senile old fool should have been booted out years ago. Not the only one you should re-check. What about my nephew?

Grace (*deliberately*)   You've been through a lot, Charles, but I warn you.

Dinsdale   That's rather disgraceful, Father.

Bishop Lampton   Uncalled for, Jack's behaved splendidly.

Sir Charles   I'm not saying he's involved but . . .

Grace   *But.* I'll give you *but.*

Brockett   We have the medical reports on his lordship. But if you have something to add.

Grace   Charles isn't doing this 'cause of what happened to Claire. He's jealous 'cause I love my husband. Charles and me were lovers! I was this randy old goat's mistress!

Bishop Lampton (*wailing*)   Accch. Cleanse your hands, you sinner.

Sir Charles   Madam, you'll *never* be a Gurney.

Grace   I'd rather be dead.

Dinsdale (*stricken*)   Mother knew, she knew before she died. Father, I have to say this. You've proved a big disappointment to me.

Sir Charles   It's *mutual, sir.*

Brockett   Does his lordship know about the relationship, Lady Grace?

Grace   No, and he's not going to unless somebody blabs. (*Looks round at* **Brockett**.) Anyway, it's none of your business, Copper!

Bishop Lampton   Private matters, sir. A gentleman would have left!

As the family are suddenly conscious again of the two policemen and start yelling at them, the **Earl** *enters, a commanding figure in black carrying a black silver-top cane.*

Earl of Gurney   Is this the way to act in the presence of death? (*They stop shouting.*) Remember where you are and what happened here.

He pauses by the outline on the floor. Embarrassed, the others clear their throats.

Bishop Lampton   Forgive them, they know not what they do.

Earl of Gurney   Oh, Dinsdale, you should answer those messages of condolence. Even if you don't feel like it.

Sir Charles   Nonsense. Let 'em wait.

Dinsdale   You're right, Jack. Create a good impression. It'll take my mind off things. Been a bad day for me what with one thing and another.

He exits Up Stage Centre. **Grace** *moves round beside the* **Earl**.

Brockett   My lord, there are still a few details I'd like to clear up. On the night of the murder you talked with Lady Claire till 11.30. How was she when you left her?

Earl of Gurney   Unhappy.

Brockett   Why's that?

Grace   What with one thing and another, she had plenty of reasons, don't you think.

Sir Charles   Dammit, Brockett, what the devil does it matter how my wife was feeling.

Brockett   You went straight up to bed and heard nothing.

Earl of Gurney   I thought I heard Tucker singing.

Brockett   Hmm, but he said he didn't leave the kitchen till 12. Odd. Important question, my lord. Think hard now. Has anything unusual happened here recently; anything out of the ordinary?

The **Earl** *thinks, shakes his head.*

Bishop? Your ladyship?

They shake their heads.

Sir Charles?

Tucker *is heard singing off.* **Brockett** *turns swiftly.*

Get him, Fraser!

Fraser *rushes out Up Stage Centre and reappears dragging* **Tucker** *who is dressed in a striped jacket, bow-tie and straw hat; he carries a battered suitcase festooned with foreign labels.*

Tucker   What's the idea? I got a plane to catch.

Brockett   You going somewhere, Tucker?

Tucker   *Mr* Tucker, *Flatfoot.* Looks like it don't it. It's cockles and champagne for yours truly, gay Paree where all the girls say oui oui.

Grace   Bit sudden, isn't it?

Tucker   I'm a creature o' impulse, your ladyship. (*Singing melodiously as he shuffles to exit with suitcase.*) 'Goodbye, I wish you all a last . . . g-o-o-d-b-y-e.'

As he gestures farewell **Fraser** *pulls him back into the room.*

Brockett   You're not going anywhere, Tucker, me lad. I've got questions I want answering.

Tucker   I told you all I know.

Brockett   Have you? . . . Daniel Tucker alias Alexei Kronstadt Communist Party Member Number 243!

Sir Charles   Murdering swine!

Tucker *gives a frightened cry and rushes for the exit Up Stage Centre, but the* **Earl of Gurney** *bars the way.*

Tucker   Let me pass, let me pass!

As **Fraser** *pulls* **Tucker** *back amid excited shouts,* **Dinsdale** *hurries in.*

Dinsdale   What's going on?

Grace   They say old Jeeves is a Bolshie.

Earl of Gurney   T-U-C-K-E-R. Are you a low-life leveller? An East End agitator?

Tucker   How can I be an agitator? I've got a weak chest. (*Suddenly defiant.*) What if I am? You don't know what it's like being a servant, picking up the droppings of these Titled Turds. Everybody has to have secrets. What's it to you how I spend my leisure time, Flatfoot?

Brockett   You're a suspect in a murder case. You concealed certain facts about yourself. What else are you hiding, Tucker?

Tucker   Suspect? Suspect? I don't *do* anything. I just pays me dues to the Party and they send me pamphlets, under

plain covers. And every year I get a Christmas card from
Mr Palme Dutt.

Brockett (*sticks out leg and raises arms*)   Why were you
standing like this beside the body? EH? EH? You told me
you discovered her dead just before the others came back.
But his lordship swears he heard you down here in this
room a *half-hour* earlier.

Tucker (*frightened*)   You got it wrong, my lord. I wasn't
here. This is ol' Tuck, your lordship. (*Jigs up and down.*) All
talk, no action. (*Sobbing.*) I couldn't do a crime even if I
wanted. Not the type.

*As he takes out a handkerchief to wipe his eyes, a half-dozen silver
spoons fall out of his pocket with a clatter.*

Grace   Jeeves!

Sir Charles   You brainwashed thug!

Brockett *puts the silverware on to a chair and gestures impatiently
for* **Tucker** *to disgorge.*

Tucker   Hope there's no misunderstanding. Just a few
little keepsakes. (*Brings out a handful of knives and forks from a
bulging pocket.*) Mementoes of my 107 happy years with the
Gurney family. (*Produces complete silver cruet set.*) I took 'em for
their sentimental value. They call me Mr Softee. (*Produces
jewel-encrusted snuff box.*) A few worthless trinkets to help keep
the memory green when I'm swanning on the Cote de Jour.
(*Finally adds gold bowl from the back of his trousers.*)

Brockett   You forgotten something?

Tucker   No, that's the lot. Oh, goodness me . . . (*Removes
hat with feigned surprise and takes out a small silver dinner-plate
hidden in the crown.*) Tell you what, your lordship. I'll keep
these instead of the two weeks money you owe me in lieu of
notice.

Dinsdale   I say, look here, Inspector.

He and **Fraser** *have opened* **Tucker**'*s suitcase. All the others move over except the* **Earl**.

Brockett (*bringing out books*)   Lenin's *Complete Revolutionary*. Mao Tse-Tung's *Selected Writings*.

Fraser (*discovering pile of photographs*)   Look at these, sir.

Brockett (*looks at them slowly*)   Dis-gus-ting . . .

Shocked gasp from **Sir Charles** *and* **Dinsdale** *as they glance over his shoulder.* **Grace** *takes a photograph and turns it round and round.*

Grace   How the devil did she get into that position.

Brockett   We'll keep this as evidence.

Tucker *staggers over to the* **Earl** *who stands dark, implacable.*

Tucker   Your lordship, say something fer me. You're the only one who can help. You always was my favourite, Master Jack. You always was my favourite. (*Sobbing.*) Before he died the old Earl, s'bless him, said look after that feeble-minded idiot Master Jack fer me, Tuck. I could have gone but I stayed.

Earl of Gurney   If thy hand offends thee, cut it off. Tuck, Tuck, you rot the air with your sexual filth. And there's an innocent baby upstairs. It was you, spawned out of envy, hate, revenge. *You* killed her. *Oh, Dan, Dan, you dirty old man.* (*Lifts* **Tucker** *up bodily by his armpits and drops him in front of* **Brockett**.*)* Take him away, Inspector.

Brockett   Daniel Tucker, I must ask you . . .

Tucker (*at the* **Earl**)   Judas Jack Iscariot! You've sold me down the sewer, hard-hearted, stony-hearted, like the rest. And I knows s'why. You did it. You and Sir Charles, standing there like a pickled walrus. You Gurneys don't draw the line at murder. (*Suddenly exploding with rage and fear.*) Upper-class excrement, you wanna' do me dirt 'cause I know too much. I know one per cent of the population owns half the property in England. That vomity 'one per cent' needs kosher killing, hung up so the blue blood drains out slow and easy. Aristocratic carcasses hung up like kosher beef *drip-drip-drip.*

Fraser *grabs him as he lurches forward. The* **Earl** *whispers to* **Dinsdale** *who helps* **Fraser** *pick* **Tucker** *up. As they carry him off, stiff and horizontal Up Stage he starts bawling:*

Tucker   'Then comrades come rally. And the last fight let us face. The International Army, Unites the human race.' (*Passing* **Grace** *he tips his hat.*) 'I'm only a strolling vagabond, so good night, pretty maiden, *good night.*'

Grace   What an exit.

Brockett   Sorry you heard all that, your ladyship, but I had to let him rave on. The more they talk, the more they convict themselves.

Grace   At least, Inspector, this destroys any doubt anyone might have had about Jack.

Brockett   Of course, my lady.

Sir Charles   Good work, Inspector. Let me show you out.

Brockett (*to the* **Earl**)   My lord, I'd just like to say what a pleasure it's been meeting you. It couldn't 'ave been easy. But you realised I was only doing my job. You've shown me what 'noblesse oblige' really means.

He gives a slight bow and exits, with **Sir Charles**.

Bishop Lampton (*looking down at the outline*)   She was beautiful as Tirzah, comely as Jerusalem, the darling of her mother, flawless to her that loved her. Dead now. Gone, down, down, down, down.

Earl of Gurney   Up, up, up, up, she flies. Her soul flies up. Surely you believe she's gone to another place to enjoy even greater privileges than she had on earth?

Bishop Lampton   I have to. I'm a bishop. Forgive an old man's wavering. I remember her fondly, such a terrible death.

Earl of Gurney   Lean on me. Trust in God's judgement.

Bishop Lampton   You make an old man ashamed. You've become a great source of strength to me, Jack. (*Grasps his arm.*) I won't forget what you've done, Jack. You were the instrument that restored my faith. I feel reborn. I've found the way. Now let me walk humbly with my God.

The **Earl** *walks with him Up Stage, then hands him to* **Grace** *and the two exit.*

Scene Eight

The **Earl** *takes out a pair of binoculars from the desk as cries are heard off.*

Tucker's Voice (*hysterical*)   I done nothing! I want justice!

Brockett's Voice   Justice is what you're going to get, Tucker. If he gives you any trouble, Fraser, break his arm. Now. MARCH!

Tucker's Voice   I'm another Dreyfus case!

The **Earl** *leans on his cane and looks out of the french-windows through the binoculars.*

Earl of Gurney   Left-right, left-right, left-right, left-right, left-right.

Dr Herder, *tired and sick, enters with the aid of a walking-stick. He stares at the* **Earl**, *crosses, and stops beside* **Claire**'s *outline on the floor.*

Dr Herder   Mir ist es winterlich im Leibe. She was cut up like meat.

Earl of Gurney   Left-right, left-right, left-right.

Dr Herder (*looks across at* **Earl**)   It's not possible. I cured you. You could never turn violent. It's not in your illness. If I'd failed I'd know it. You'd retreat back into delusion. You haven't. You've accepted the world on its own terms. You believe more or less what other people believe.

Earl of Gurney (*turns, raising cane in salute*)   En garde. Your job's done, Herr Doktor. I'm adjusted to my environment. I brush my teeth twice daily. And smile. You trepanned me, opened my brain, telephoned the truth direct into my skull, as it were.

Dr Herder   Let me be the judge of that.

Earl of Gurney   There's only one Judge here. (*Looks at him through the wrong end of the binoculars.*) You've shrunk to a teutonic midget.

Dr Herder   You call that being adjusted?

Earl of Gurney   Behaviour which would be considered insanity in a tradesman is looked on as mild eccentricity in a lord. I'm allowed a certain lat-i-tude. (*He lunges at* **Dr Herder**.)

Dr Herder (*involuntarily parrying stroke with his stick*)   I want to know about Claire.

Earl of Gurney   An irreversible rearrangement of her structural molecules has taken place, doctor. She's dead. One of the facts of life.

Dr Herder   I know that.

Earl of Gurney   She lies stinking. Algo mortis, rigor mortis, livor mortis. She's turning to slime, doctor. She's puss, doctor, stinking puss, doctor!

Dr Herder   I don't wish to know that!

Earl of Gurney   Then kindly leave the stage. (*Lunges.*) These are scientific facts.

Dr Herder (*parrying*)   You killed her.

Earl of Gurney   A touch.

Dr Herder   You killed heeeeeeeeer.

He leaps at the **Earl**, *flailing wildly with his stick.*

Earl of Gurney (*parrying the stroke*)   Ha, a swordsman worthy of me steel. Didn't we meet at Heidelberg?

Dr Herder   You killed her!

Earl of Gurney (*driving him back*)   You were fornicating lovers. Sperm dancers.

Dr Herder   It's a lie. Lady Claire meant nothing to me.

Earl of Gurney   Cock-a-doodle-do!

Dr Herder (*lashes out*)   *You* killed her.

Earl of Gurney (*beating off the attack*)   I'm cured, Herr Doktor, M.D., Ph.D. You cured me. I was a pale lovesick straw-in-the-air moon-loony. You changed me into a murderer, is that what you're saying?

Dr Herder (*attacking wildly*)   Yes. No. Yes. May God forgive me.

Earl of Gurney   *Never.* What proof have you?

Dr Herder   I don't need proof, I *know.*

Earl of Gurney (*parrying with contemptuous ease*)   Physician heal thyself. Don't you recognise the symptoms? You suddenly *know* against all the evidence. You don't need proof from anybody or anything. This monstrous belief of yours that I'm guilty is a clear case of paranoia. I've heard of 'transference', doctor, but this is ridiculous! . . . If they ask about me at the trial, tell them the truth.

Dr Herder   What truth?

Earl of Gurney   That I'm a hundred per cent normal. (*He lunges and hits* **Dr Herder**, *who sits with a bump.*) Touché, Herr Doktor.

Clicking his heels, he salutes with his cane and crosses Up Stage Right.
Dr Herder *remains on the floor. The lights dim slightly as he punches the ground in frustration.*

Dr Herder   He's right. He is normal. It's only a feeling. (*Shudders.*) I can't rely on feelings. Everything he's done conforms to a classic recovery pattern. His occasional paralalia is normal. Even his trying to blackmail me into saying he's completely normal, is normal. Natural I should have doubts. This is pioneer work. Claire's death, one of those terrible ironies – nothing to do with the case. Unpleasant as he is, the good lord's himself again . . . My head's splitting. I've had an abdomen full of the upper classes. Claire, Claire, I should have specialised in heart diseases. (*Suddenly trembling with rage.*) Cock-a-doodle-do. Scheisshund! He made me deny you. (*He picks up and clasps cardboard outline tenderly.*) Cock-a-doodle-do. Cock-a-doodle-do. Cock-a-doodle-do.

He exits crowing with the cardboard outline.

Scene Nine

Sir Charles *and* **Grace** *enter Up Stage Centre.*

Sir Charles *There.* It's what I've always said. You simply can't give the working-class money.

Grace (*to the* **Earl**)   It must have been a terrible shock for you, Sweet. Someone like Jeeves – someone you've known all your life turning out to be a killer. I was proud of you.

Sir Charles   Yes, Jack, this time you behaved like a Gurney should.

Grace   You might apologise for all the stinking things you've said about him.

Sir Charles   Jack understands. I did what I had to.

Earl of Gurney   I won't forget what you did, Charles. (*Arm round* **Grace***'s shoulder.*) Or you, my dear.

Grace   Jack, let's take off. It's been hell here. We need a holiday.

Earl of Gurney   No. Here I stand. Now our little local difficulty has been solved I must show myself. It'll be the perfect story-book ending.

Dinsdale *enters carrying the* **Earl***'s Parliamentary robes.*

I'm taking my seat in the House of Lords.

Sir Charles   What . . . ?

Grace   What, now? So soon after your illness? I mean, are you ready for them?

Earl of Gurney   Are *they* ready for me, madam?

Dinsdale   We're going to work as a team once I get elected. Jack in the Lords, me in the 'other place'. We think alike on lots of things.

Dinsdale *helps the* **Earl** *on with his Parliamentary robes.*

Sir Charles   It's asking for trouble. What happens if you have a relapse? Fine spectacle you'd make, gibbering in the Upper House.

Grace   You're so bloody tactful, Charles. (*Helps* **Dinsdale***.*) If Jack thinks he's ready, then he's ready and I'm with him all the way.

Sir Charles   It's out of the question.

Earl of Gurney   Who asked you a question, pray? Did anybody here ask him a question?

They shake their heads.

Nobody asked a question so I'll ask a question. Who's the legit head of the family Gurney-cum-Gurney?

Sir Charles   You are, Jack, but . . .

Earl of Gurney   Don't let me hear you answering unasked questions again.

Dinsdale   Don't make a complete ass of yourself, Father.

Grace   From now on just keep quiet, Charles.

Earl of Gurney   Your days of hard manipulating are over. Your brain's silting, Charles!

Sir Charles (*starts to grow old, his limbs shake slightly*)   Don't talk to me like that! After all I've done. (*Voice quavers.*) Where'd you be without me? No wife, no Gurney heir without me – answer me, sir! (*Passes hands over hair and moustache: they turn white.*) I'm giving you the benefit of my experience, years of . . .

Dinsdale *sniggers.*

Sir Charles   What are you sniggering at, you young pup?

Dinsdale   I wasn't sniggering.

Sir Charles   You were sniggering too. I know sniggering when I hear it, I'm not deaf. You've got nothing to snigger about. It'll happen to you one day. You'll be standing there and then suddenly nobody's taking any notice. You start coughing and coughing. Skin goes dry and the veins show through. Everything turns watery. It dribbles away, bowels, eyes, ears, nose . . . hmm. The hard thing is you're still twenty-one inside, but outside your feet go *flop, flop, flop, flop,* nothing you can do, *flop, flop, flop . . .*

The **Earl** *points to* **Sir Charles.** **Dinsdale** *nods and leads him firmly Up Stage.*

Dinsdale   That's enough, Father. You've had a long innings. It's beddy-byes and milk-rusks for you now.

Grace (*carefully adjusting the* **Earl***'s robe*)   He's getting tiresome, but I feel obligated. He did introduce us, Honey. Luckily Dinsdale can handle him. That boy's come on. He worships you, you know.

Earl of Gurney   Splendid fella, Dinsdale.

Grace   Guess we've all changed. You're more than just cured, Jack. People look up to you now. You've got something extra. What we used to call star quality!

Earl of Gurney   Ek, ek, ek, ek. It's going to be a triumphant climax.

Grace   Talking about climaxes, we must get together again. We were more loving when you were batty. (*Closer to him.*) Now it should be even better. Do you love me, Jack?

Earl of Gurney   Y'know, in Roman times it was always the women who turned down their thumbs when defeated gladiators asked for mercy, Annie.

Grace (*laughing*)   Annie? Why Annie?

Earl of Gurney   Mary, Annie, Elizabeth, Catherine, Marie Kelly – a name by any other name would smell as sweet.

Grace   Jack, you're not going off again?

Earl of Gurney   It's nothing m'dear. Don't forget I've a big day ahead of me. I'm speaking in the House of Lords.

Grace   Oh, you've got first-night nerves. Don't worry, you'll kill 'em.

Earl of Gurney   In time. Perhaps.

Grace   I know it. Then you'll get around to me, I hope. Promise?

*The **Earl** nods, smiling.*

Jack, Jack, you're so attractive when you smile like that. (*Kisses him.*) Jack, Jack . . .

Earl of Gurney   Must get my grunch thoughts in order, marshal my facts, prepare my argument, pro and contra.

Grace   You don't have to worry. After all, you're one of 'em, only more so. Be your own sweet self and they'll adore you as I adore you, Jack. (*Kissing him again and moving Up Stage.*) I just love happy endings.

The lights dim. The 'Pomp and Circumstance March' is played softly over.

Scene Ten

The image of the **Earl** *in his Parliamentary robes Down Stage Centre is menacing as he hunches his shoulder and drags his leg.*

Earl of Gurney   Tash t'ur tshh t'aigh, s'ssssh kkk? Freee 'eee u Me Me Me epeeeeee . . . tita a-a-a- grahhh scrk Khraht! (*Sounds now coming from back of throat, rising intensely.*) Grak GRACK. Graaa gruuuuuuaaKK ka-ka-ka-ka-ka. YU. OOOO. YU. (*Arm jerks out convulsively at audience, his leg twists under him.*) YU. Screee. Fuuuuuth, CRUUUKK-aa-K. (*Grinds heel into ground, face contorted with rage.*) HRRRUUUR TRUGHUUUK. (*As if bringing up phlegm, the cries now come from the pit of the stomach.*) Ha-CH-U-UR-UR. URRR. GoooooaRCH. TROKK! EK-K-Y. Arri-Bra-K-Yi-Skiiii, Arrk-ar-rk ARR ARR K-K-K-K, YIT YIT TRUGHUUGH ARK KKKK A-A-A-A-A-A-KRUTK! aaaaaaaaaaaaAAAARRRRRR!

Scene Eleven

Even as the scream dies away a backcloth with a blow-up photograph of Westminster captioned 'House of Lords' is lowered, Stage Centre. On either side of it massive purple drapes. The 'Pomp and Circumstance March' is loud now as two tiers of mouldering dummies dressed as Lords and covered with cobwebs are pushed on either side, Stage Right and Left. Smothered in age-old dust, three goitred **Lords** *with bloated stomachs and skull-like faces crawl on stage groaning, to take their places beside the dummies and the* **Earl of Gurney**. *One of them drags a skeleton behind him. The music stops as the* **First Lord** *hauls himself as upright as his twisted body allows.*

1st Lord (*croaking*)   My Lords, I wish to draw attention to the grave disquiet felt throughout the country at the increase in immorality.

2nd Lord (*wheezing*)   I must support the noble Lord. For thirteen years there has been no flogging, and there has been a steadily rising volume of crime, lawlessness and thuggery. I believe the cissy treatment of young thugs and hooligans is utterly wrong.

3rd Lord   My Lord, we must step up the penalties by making hanging and flogging the punishments for certain State crimes. In order to protect the public the criminal must be treated as an animal.

The **Earl of Gurney** *jerks up. All eyes on him.* **Dinsdale** *and* **Sir Charles** *hobbling on two walking sticks, enter Wings Left.*

Earl of Gurney   My Lords, I had doubts about speaking here but after what I've heard, I realise this is where I belong. My Lords, these are grave times, killing times. Stars collapse, universes shrink daily, but the natural order is still crime – guilt – punishment. Without pause. There is no love without fear. By His hand, sword, pike and grappling-hook, God, the Crowbar of the World, flays, stabs, bludgeons, mutilates. Just as I was – is – have been – flayed, bludgeoned . . . (*Recovering.*) You've forgotten how to punish, my noble Lords. The strong MUST manipulate the weak. That's the first law of the Universe – was and ever shall be world without end. The weak would hand this planet back to the crabs and primeval slime. The Hard survive, the Soft quickly turn to corruption. (*Shuddering.*) *God the Son* wants nothing only to give freely in love and gentleness. It's loathsome, a foul perversion of life! And must be rooted out. *God the Father* demands, orders, controls, crushes. We must follow Him, my noble Lords. This is a call to greatness . . .

On, on you noblest English.
I see you stand like greyhounds in the slips
Straining upon the start. The game's afoot

Follow your spirit; and upon this charge
Cry, God for Jack, England and Saint George.

A pause, then all burst into spontaneous shouts of 'hear-hear', 'bravo', as the excited **Peers**, *waving order-papers, stumble over to congratulate the* **Earl**.

Dinsdale   Bravo! Bravo! You see, Father, you see. He's capable of anything.

Sir Charles (*waving stick excitedly*)   *He's one of us at last!*

They all exit except the **Earl**, *singing exultantly.*

All (*singing*)   'Let us now praise famous men
And our fathers that begat us.
Such as did there rule in their kingdoms
Men renowned for their power.'

Epilogue

The **Earl** *is alone amongst the dummies. The chorus fades down with the lights.* **Grace** *enters Up Stage Centre singing, in a black night-dress.*

Grace (*singing*)   'Along came Jack, not my type at all . . .
You'd meet him on the street and never notice him . . .
But his form and face, his manly grace. Makes me – *thrill* . . .
I love him . . .'

He stands smiling as she circles him sensually.

'I love him, because he's . . . wond-er-ful . . .'

She yields as he pulls her close.

'Because he's just my Jack.'

Faint street-cries are heard over and they kiss passionately. As the **Earl** *envelops her in his Parliamentary robes, his hand reaches for his pocket. The lights fade down slowly, then, out of the darkness, a single scream of fear and agony.*

Curtain.